Aquatic Facility Management

Paul Fawcett

Human Kinetics

Library of Congress Cataloging-in-Publication Data

Fawcett, Paul, 1968-
    Aquatic facility management / Paul Fawcett.
        p. cm.
    Includes bibliographical references and index.
    ISBN 0-7360-4500-7 (hardcover)
    1. Aquatic sports facilities--Management.   I. Title.
    GV770.7.F39 2005
    797--dc22
                                        2004020664

ISBN: 0-7360-4500-7

The Web addresses cited in this text were current as of October 2004, unless otherwise noted.

Acquisitions Editor: Amy N. Clocksin
Developmental Editor: Ray Vallese
Assistant Editor: Derek Campbell
Copyeditor: Pat Connolly
Proofreader: Julie Marx Goodreau
Indexer: Marie Rizzo
Permission Manager: Dalene Reeder
Graphic Designer: Fred Starbird
Graphic Artists: Tara Welsch and Denise Lowry
Photo Manager: Kelly J. Huff
Cover Designer: Keith Blomberg
Photographer (cover): P. Degginger/Robertstock.com
Photographer (interior): Kelly J. Huff, except where otherwise noted.
Art Manager: Kelly Hendren
Illustrator: Accurate Art
Printer: Edwards Brothers

We thank Decatur Park District in Decatur, Illinois, for assistance in providing the location for some of the photos in this book.

Printed in the United States of America   10 9 8 7 6 5 4 3 2 1

Human Kinetics
Web site: www.HumanKinetics.com

United States: Human Kinetics
P.O. Box 5076
Champaign, IL 61825-5076
800-747-4457
e-mail: humank@hkusa.com

Canada: Human Kinetics
475 Devonshire Road Unit 100
Windsor, ON N8Y 2L5
800-465-7301 (in Canada only)
e-mail: orders@hkcanada.com

Europe: Human Kinetics
107 Bradford Road
Stanningley
Leeds LS28 6AT, United Kingdom
+44 (0) 113 255 5665
e-mail: hk@hkeurope.com

Australia: Human Kinetics
57A Price Avenue
Lower Mitcham, South Australia 5062
08 8277 1555
e-mail: liaw@hkaustralia.com

New Zealand: Human Kinetics
Division of Sports Distributors NZ Ltd.
P.O. Box 300 226 Albany
North Shore City
Auckland
0064 9 448 1207
e-mail: blairc@hknewz.com

I'd like to take this opportunity to dedicate this book to my family. To my parents, Gordon and Judy Fawcett, for all their encouragement and for taking me to various and sundry pools for swim lessons over many years. To my brother, Bruce, for setting a sterling example of how to write and for being an all-around great brother. To my girls, Lilly and Grace, who are the light of my life and the inspiration for most things I do. Last, but certainly not least, to my beloved wife, Holly, who listens to my ideas and offers much encouragement. Thank you all.

Contents

CHAPTER 3 Promoting Programs and Public Relations . . 47

CHAPTER 4 Budgeting 65

CHAPTER 5 Developing Staff 81

6 Lifeguarding 107

CHAPTER

7 Managing Risks and Planning for Emergencies 139

CHAPTER

CHAPTER 8 Managing Water Chemistry and Filtration 167

CHAPTER 9 Managing Facility Operations 185

Introduction

Aquatics is a popular, ever dynamic field encompassing activities that take place in, on, under, and around the water. Aquatic activities include, but are not limited to, swimming, diving, scuba, boating, instructional activities, and family activities. The popularity of aquatics has created a wealth of employment opportunities for aquatic professionals. Opportunities exist at universities, public and private schools, parks (federal, state, and local) and park districts, YMCAs, YWCAs, community centers, military bases, health clubs, hospitals, and community service organizations.

The operation of aquatic facilities has become increasingly complex in recent years. Due to advances in technology and the proliferation of aquatic certifications and regulations, aquatic professionals are now required to be better trained and educated than in the past. The days when certification as a water safety instructor and a good understanding of how to test water for chlorine and pH were sufficient for employment as an aquatic professional are over. Aquatic facility management is now a profession, with increased training requirements, recognition, and career opportunities to match.

This text is designed to assist you, as an aquatic student or professional, with operating your aquatic facility. This text isn't designed to replace formal aquatic training but is intended to supplement and expand on that training. At numerous points in this text, certifications appropriate for aquatic professionals are listed. You should take every opportunity to advance your knowledge and skills by obtaining these and other certifications. You can obtain these certifications from regular classes at aquatic facilities, through university courses, or from periodic intensive aquatic seminars or camps. Once you've obtained these certifications, you'll become more valuable and employable because of what you know and what you're certified to do.

Responsibilities and duties that are required of aquatic directors may include program development, program promotion, budgeting, staff development, lifeguarding management, risk management and emergency planning, pool operations and maintenance, and facility operations. This text explores each of these responsibilities in detail and provides you with current industry standards, expert guidance and information, and helpful reference materials. Each chapter also contains a list of resources including recommended Web sites and books that provide more in-depth material to amplify the topics covered in that chapter. The appendixes offer detailed information on agencies that provide aquatic services, agencies responsible for state bathing codes, and suppliers of aquatic equipment, along with dozens of reproducible forms you can use at your facility.

CHAPTER 1: CHOOSING AND DEVELOPING AQUATIC PROGRAMS

There are a wide variety of aquatic programming options that you can implement to serve all of the prospective user groups at your aquatic facility. You need to understand who your clients are and select the programs most likely to interest them. You must also ensure that you have the appropriate staff and supplies to operate the programs that you select.

Chapter 1 provides you with a list and full description of programs that you can implement, along with a list of equipment, supplies, and staff qualifications required to operate each program. There's a wide range of programming possibilities available. This chapter helps you choose which ones are best for your facility by describing what it takes to implement each program.

CHAPTER 2: MANAGING PROGRAMS

Chapters 1 and 2 are closely related. While chapter 1 provides ideas about what programs may be right for your facility, chapter 2 helps you manage those programs effectively. Well-managed programs will make it easier for your patrons to access your facilities and services and will help them to have a better experience when they do. Logical management strategies also provide your staff with guidance on how to properly operate your facilities and programs.

Chapter 2 provides suggestions for organizing program registration (forms and procedures), organizing classes, implementing class orientation procedures, evaluating students' progress, and collecting program statistics.

CHAPTER 3: PROMOTING PROGRAMS AND PUBLIC RELATIONS

Marketing and promotions are essential for the successful operation of your aquatic facility. You can have the cleanest, most up-to-date, best-operated facility in your state, but if no one knows about it, patrons will not come, and your facility will fail. Whether you're marketing new programs or trying to jump-start existing programs, this chapter is designed to help you.

For your marketing to succeed, you have to carefully select the correct marketing method for the programs you offer. You must also make sure that you relay the most important information about the program to your patrons.

Chapter 3 provides you with information regarding how to select the most effective marketing strategy for your programs. It also provides you with information regarding what details must be communicated and the timing of your marketing in relation to your program.

CHAPTER 4: BUDGETING

Budgeting for your aquatic facility involves managing where your money comes from, where it goes, and how to keep track of it properly. If you can't budget your money properly, you will habitually mismanage your finances.

Chapter 4 provides an explanation of the various budget types as well as an explanation of purchasing procedures and spending controls. It also includes a description of income and expenditures. By reading through this chapter, you can decide which budgeting type is best for your facility based on your needs. You can also explore ideas to help you better track and manage your money. Ideas presented in this chapter include budget reviews and computerized budgeting programs.

CHAPTER 5: DEVELOPING STAFF

Staff is the most important element in the operation of your facility. Managing your staff properly involves recruiting, interviewing, hiring, retaining, and training them. Supervising aquatic staff consumes much of the aquatic director's time and is one of the more crucial aspects of facility operations. You rely on your staff to operate your programs and services and to keep your patrons safe as they swim at your pools or beaches.

Chapter 5 provides useful information regarding how to organize screening and training programs for lifeguards and aquatic instructors. Sample position descriptions for common aquatics jobs (such as director and pool operator) are included as well as recommended and required certifications for each position.

CHAPTER 6: LIFEGUARDING

Although lifeguarding is part of risk management, its importance to your facility and its increasing complexity make it worthy of its own chapter. Lifeguards are the backbone of the safety program at any aquatic facility. For your lifeguards to be effective, they must be properly stationed and trained, and proper procedures must be in place. As the aquatic professional, it is your responsibility to organize and train your lifeguarding staff to maximize their effectiveness. If you place lifeguarding staff at your aquatic facility but provide them with no direction or organization, you will fail to make the best use of their abilities.

Chapter 6 focuses on the topic of lifeguards. Valuable information you will find in this chapter includes how to station lifeguards and how to set up lifeguarding systems such as rotations, safety zones, and communication procedures. Additional helpful tips such as how to operate buddy boards and guarding procedures for persons with disabilities are also included.

CHAPTER 7: MANAGING RISKS AND PLANNING FOR EMERGENCIES

Chapter 7 goes hand in hand with the chapters on facility operations and lifeguarding. Risk management has to be a total package of staff policies and operations. Aquatic activities by their very nature have hazard associated with them. Although the risk of injuries, drowning, and illnesses can be managed, it requires careful planning and preparation on the part of the aquatic management.

Chapter 7 provides the aquatic manager with comprehensive sample emergency plans, hazard identification assistance, and information regarding state and local codes. This chapter also includes helpful sections about emergency protocols and legal issues related to aquatics. The section on emergency and safety equipment can help you determine the items your facility needs to be well prepared for injuries and accidents.

CHAPTER 8: MANAGING WATER CHEMISTRY AND FILTRATION

Clean and sanitary pool water is essential to the safe and successful operation of any aquatic facility. Aquatic professionals must have expert knowledge of the correct chemical and mechanical operation of the facilities they manage, including knowledge of water testing, implementation of the state bathing code, and chemical safety.

Chapter 8 guides you through what can be the most confusing topics of pool operations. This chapter explains the elements of water chemistry, including disinfection, filtration, alkalinity, total hardness, and temperature. Details about the operation and selection of filtration systems are provided to help the operator decide which system would be best in replacing aging filters or installing new ones.

CHAPTER 9: MANAGING FACILITY OPERATIONS

Aquatic facility operations encompasses maintenance and cleaning tasks needed to keep the facility within acceptable standards. Care and maintenance of equipment and facility inspections are also a large part of the aquatic director's duties in this area. This chapter goes hand in hand with chapter 8 on water chemistry. Water chemistry specific to spas and hot tubs is also covered in this chapter.

Pool operators and aquatic managers will find chapter 9 to be a useful and informative chapter.

This chapter suggests daily, weekly, and annual cleaning and maintenance schedules. Helpful information on energy conservation and cost-saving procedures associated with heating, cooling, and water are also included in this chapter. Procedures for inventory control, equipment maintenance, and storage will be of assistance to those who are responsible for the care and operation of the facility's equipment.

APPENDIX A

A dizzying array of agencies provide services related to the field of aquatics. These agencies can be government organizations, nonprofit agencies, industry membership organizations, and professional associations. Knowing who these agencies are and what they do is essential to your professional development and helps you offer a safe facility and enjoyable programs to your patrons. Appendix A provides a comprehensive list of aquatic agencies subdivided into categories such as aquatic certification agencies, professional membership agencies, regulatory agencies, sport-specific regulatory or membership agencies, and boating agencies. Information provided for each agency includes services provided, address, telephone number, and Web site.

APPENDIX B

The state bathing code identifies the regulations established by the state government to set standards for various aspects of swimming pools and bathing beaches. Topics that you may find covered in your state code include the following:

- ▶ Requirements for lifeguards
- ▶ Requirements for lifeguard certification
- ▶ Required pH range for pool water
- ▶ Minimum standard for residual disinfectant (chlorine or bromine) in pool water
- ▶ Requirements for rescue equipment such as rescue tubes, first aid kits, and backboards

The state code is a document that you should know well and that every aquatic professional should have a copy of. Appendix B contains a list of state agencies that are responsible for the bathing code along with information on how to contact them. For those states that have posted their bathing code on the Internet, a Web site address is included.

APPENDIX C

Managing your aquatic facility will require you to regularly purchase equipment and supplies. Your needs will range from everyday supplies such as adhesive bandages and buckets to large and expensive equipment such as diving boards and filters. Some of the everyday items can be purchased at local department stores and hardware outlets, but there are many specialized aquatic items (such as rescue equipment, chemicals, and deck fixtures) that you'll have to buy from commercial suppliers. Appendix C contains a handy list of aquatic suppliers, their phone numbers, and Web sites.

APPENDIX D

Record keeping is of major importance to the safe and efficient operation of your facility. Keeping complete and accurate records will verify what maintenance, cleaning, and safety procedures you've taken at your facility. If you haven't recorded these actions, then you can't prove that you've done them if you need to do so in a legal situation. Appendix D helps simplify the record-keeping process by providing a wide range of forms for organizing and recording important aquatic tasks at your facility. The appendix includes maintenance checklists, incident and accident reports, staff evaluations, and program evaluation forms.

GLOSSARY OF AQUATIC TERMS

For newcomers to aquatics, it often seems as if everyone is talking in code, whether discussing zone coverage, RWIs, or oxidation-reduction potential. The glossary provides an easy-to-read alphabetized list of aquatic terms and their definitions, taking much of the mystery and guesswork out of understanding what can be confusing new terms. Throughout this book, terms that are included in the glossary appear in bold text so that you know help is available.

Choosing and Developing Aquatic Programs

Chapter Objectives

After reading this chapter, you should be able to

1. list and describe a variety of aquatic programs,
2. understand which programs are best for your facility,
3. describe methods that can be used to enhance existing aquatic programs,
4. develop an effective aquatic program evaluation, and
5. understand when a program should be dropped.

Aquatic programs give patrons the opportunity to expand their experience at your facility beyond lap swimming. Well-designed and well-administered aquatic programs can provide participants with improved aquatic skills, increased fitness, and increased enjoyment.

Programs are the reason many patrons come to your facility and are also one of your major sources of revenue. But what programs should you offer? There's a wide variety of choices. This chapter describes various types of aquatic programs that can be offered at aquatic facilities. For each program, the information provided includes a description of the program, facility requirements, staff qualifications, and equipment needs. These details will help you decide which programs are right for your facility.

This chapter also reviews safety considerations for each program, including required safety equipment, required staff, and facility safety considerations. Safety has to be the primary consideration

in every program. No matter how popular a program is or how much revenue it generates for your facility, if it poses an unacceptable risk to your patrons, you can't offer it.

Quality control of your programs is another crucial element to ensuring their success and profitability. You'll need to regularly assess your instructors as well as your customers' feelings about your programs. If you don't conduct regular quality checks, program performance and profitability could decline, and patrons may take their business elsewhere. This chapter includes an explanation of how to perform these and other assessments and provides you with forms to make the job easier.

Not every program is right for every facility; you should carefully research a program in relation to your facility before offering it. This chapter concludes with information regarding enhancing existing programs, adding new programs, and deciding which programs to drop.

AQUATIC PROGRAMS

Not all aquatic programs are appropriate for every facility. You should carefully select programs based primarily on the interests and abilities of your customers and on whether the programs meet the main purpose of your pool. However, you will also need to determine if your facility has the staff, space, and equipment to offer the programs you're considering. (See "Deciding Which Programs to Offer" later in this chapter.) There are many different types of programs that you can offer at your facility, including lap swimming, swimming lessons, water exercise, competitive swimming, synchronized swimming, **scuba,** certification courses, diving, water polo, and special events.

Lap Swimming

Lap swimming permits swimmers to utilize the pool to complete personal lap routines. It differs from an open or "free" swim in that lane ropes are normally in the water and non-lap-swimming activities are discouraged. For the comfort and convenience of the patrons, lanes can be marked according to the swimmers' speed: slow, medium, or fast. You can place a cone or sign indicating lane speed at the shallow end of each lane. This convenience reduces the frustration of faster swimmers needing to pass slower swimmers. You can also post signs instructing swimmers on the courtesy of "circle swimming," a method of swimming up the right-hand side of the lane and down the left-hand side. This method permits more swimmers to use an individual lane.

Keeping a chart that allows swimmers to record their distance swum, such as a "Swim Across America" or "Swim the English Channel" chart, can provide incentive and generate interest in lap swimming. When creating the chart, you should provide a block for swimmers to record their name and a horizontal bar graph for them to record distances swum. These distances are compared against a goal—for example, swimming 1,000 yards (914.4 meters) might represent swimming from Maine to New York, with the eventual goal of swimming across the United States. This program requires little or no supervision. Set the chart up in the pool area and allow swimmers to record their own distances. If you want, you can require swimmers to get their distances verified by having a staff member initial each entry that is made. You can also offer cards or certificates for those swimmers who complete the goal; this provides a low-cost incentive to participate in the program. For those patrons who don't want to post their progress publicly, you can provide a binder with a page specifically for them to track their yardage.

Minimal staff is required for a lap-swimming program. Qualified **lifeguards** should be allocated based on the size of the pool and the number of swimmers present. An instructional assistant is a helpful added service to the fitness swimming program. This assistant can help swimmers with stroke corrections and help them create workouts. Your staff member filling this role should be **certified** as a swimming instructor by a national agency and should be currently certified in lifeguard training, first aid, and **CPR.** Previous experience in competitive swimming is also helpful.

Equipment

- **Kickboards**
- Pull buoys
- Hand paddles
- Pace clock
- Chart or pages for recording distance swum

Swimming Lessons

An instructional swimming lessons program focuses on the development and improvement of swimming skills. Preferably, instructors will group students together based on their skill and ability. This method permits the instructor to focus on skills common to all students. You can offer swimming lessons for many different groups, including adults, children, and persons with disabilities. Normally, adult and child lessons are offered at different times.

For swimming lessons, keep your pool water temperature at a constant 81 to 82 degrees. This is particularly important for younger children, because they can become chilled rapidly in cooler water. Air temperature should be maintained at 3 to 5 degrees warmer than the water temperature to ensure the comfort of swimmers when exiting the pool.

Because the clientele for swimming lessons is predominantly children, the availability of shallow water for instruction is very important for the safety and comfort of the students. Preferably, your pool will have a shallow area with a maximum depth of 2.5 to 3 feet (76.2 to 91.4 centimeters) that will enable preschoolers to stand comfortably while receiving instruction. Because most pools are multipurpose in nature and do not have shallow ends of this depth, the use of a **tot dock** may provide a safe, relatively inexpensive alternative (see figure 1.1).

A tot dock is a raised platform with railings that is designed to be placed in the pool, reducing the water depth for smaller children. Several manufacturers produce platforms of this type, which may be constructed of stainless steel or sand-filled plastic. Tot docks may be obtained from aquatic supply companies such as Recreonics and Suspended Aquatic Mentor (see appendix C).

Qualified swimming instructors are the most important element in any swim lesson program. Swimming instructors must be currently certified in lifeguard training, CPR for the professional rescuer, and first aid. Lifeguard training agencies such as the American Red Cross and YMCA of the USA (see appendix A) are beginning to incorporate training for **automatic external defibrillation (AED)** and oxygen administration in their basic level lifeguard training courses. If your staff members do not have this training, arrange for updated training from one of these national agencies. You should also look for instructors who are certified as swimming instructors by a national agency such as the American Red Cross or YMCA of the USA.

© Arnold Kaplan/Photri

Swimming lessons are especially popular with children.

The number of students an instructor can teach varies based on the age and skill level of the students. Beginning swimming classes, which are normally populated by young children, should have a

Figure 1.1 A tot dock lets young children stand more safely in water.

ratio of one instructor for every five participants. This low ratio allows for safe supervision and the close attention that these young swimmers need. This ratio may grow larger as the children become older and more skilled.

Provide lifeguards to supervise swim lessons in order to ensure the safety of the participants. The lifeguards' duty is to supervise the pool at large, safeguarding all classes, activities, and any other swimmers who may enter the pool. Assign lifeguards no other duties (e.g., cleaning pool decks) aside from supervision of the pool while they are on duty (American Red Cross, 1996). Lifeguards should be clearly identified by a distinctive uniform such as a shirt or jacket. This enables the lifeguard to be readily located in an emergency. Use of a rescue device, such as a **rescue tube,** while on duty permits the lifeguard to more easily execute a rescue if needed. In cases where several swimming classes are in session at one time, with large numbers of children present, more than one lifeguard may be required to ensure that the swimmers are being properly supervised. Since children are the most common participants in swimming lessons, and small children can accidentally drown in seconds, never compromise their supervision.

> **KEY POINT** Lifeguards are an important part of ensuring the safety of participants. Don't assign lifeguards any other duties besides supervising the swimmers.

Required qualifications for lifeguards include current certification (from a national agency) in lifeguard training, CPR for the professional rescuer, and first aid. Certification in the use of automatic external defibrillators, oxygen administration, and preventing disease transmission is also desirable.

Swim lesson supervisors are staff members who supervise the overall operation of the program. These staff members are present on deck during lessons, ensuring that enough lifeguards and instructors are in place and that classes begin on time. They also deal with parent questions and concerns, direct students to the correct class, and perform record-keeping duties. Your swim lesson supervisors should be experienced instructors who possess certification in lifeguard training, CPR, first aid, and swimming instruction.

Equipment

- Kickboards
- Life jackets
- Pull buoys
- Hand paddles
- Diving rings
- Water polo balls
- Rescue tubes and reaching poles
- Ring buoys
- Pool toys such as toy boats, plastic buckets, balls, and sponges
- Course completion certificates for each child in the program

Water Exercise

The types and styles of water exercise offered by an aquatic facility are limited only by the imagination of the aquatic staff. Water exercise provides patrons with the opportunity to experience cardiovascular exercise without the potential damage to joints associated with land-based exercise. Shallow water exercise permits nonswimmers to take part without the need to acquire new skills. People with arthritis, injured athletes, and surgery patients may improve their range of motion, flexibility, and strength through warm, shallow water exercise. Deep water running permits those wanting a more challenging workout to enjoy the pool. By setting water exercise to appropriate music, you can control the tempo and the intensity of the workout (U.S. Water Fitness Association, 2002).

The instructor may be on deck or in the water with the students, depending on whether the students need to see the activity demonstrated by the instructor. If the instructor is standing on deck, the students can more easily see the required footwork and can clearly see how the whole exercise is performed. However, this makes it more difficult to hear and interact with the instructor. An instructor teaching from the deck should stand on a mat to prevent slipping and should use a microphone so that he can be heard more easily.

If you offer deep water running, you must provide an area of at least 6 feet (182.9 centimeters) in depth, and your pool must have sufficient width to allow ample jogging distance. The width of a six-lane pool is considered the minimum space.

Equipment

- Kickboards
- Pull buoys
- Ankle weights
- Aqua jogging belts or vests
- Stereo sound system
- Styrofoam dumbbells
- Styrofoam barbells
- Hand paddles
- Aqua paddles
- Resistance boots
- Foam mat for instructor demonstrations on deck
- Lift for elderly or arthritic clients' ease of water entry
- Storage racks for supplies

Shallow water exercise normally requires a depth of 3 to 5 feet (91.4 to 152.4 centimeters). Your water must be shallow enough to permit an adult to stand at hip depth (minimum) and chest depth (maximum). The varying depths allow for varying levels of resistance while your patrons are performing their exercises.

For **aquatics** classes for people with arthritis, rehabilitation classes, and senior aquatics classes, you should maintain water temperature between 83 and 88 degrees as specified by the Arthritis Foundation (cooler water causes muscle stiffness and cramping, which defeats the purpose of the exercise). Water temperature for aerobic fitness aquatic exercise classes in either deep or shallow water can be as cool as 80 degrees. The cooler water is more tolerable to this group because they are more vigorously active and generate more body heat.

KEY POINT *The temperature of your pool water is crucial to the program and to the satisfaction of the participants.*

Normally, only one water exercise instructor is required per class. A qualified instructor will possess certification in lifeguard training, CPR, and first aid. Specialty certification in the area of water exercise is available from the Aquatic Exercise Association, YMCA of the USA, and U.S. Water Fitness Association (see appendix A). The YMCA of the USA in conjunction with the Arthritis Foundation offers training in the specialty area of arthritis aquatic exercise through the Arthritis Foundation YMCA Aquatic Program (AFYAP). Your aquatic exercise instructors should hold certification from one of these agencies. Having a certified lifeguard on duty during water exercise classes ensures that patrons will be well cared for in the event an injury or illness occurs. This is particularly important considering the fact that your clients in this program may be older adults and may be in poor health.

Competitive Swimming

Competitive swimming is one of the most popular aquatic activities available today. All age groups, from children through senior citizens, enjoy competitive swimming. Competitive swimming provides your patrons with the opportunity to improve their fitness while setting and achieving goals.

The swim team program that you offer is dependent on the age group or groups that you want to serve. Youth competitive swim leagues are usually called "age group" and are offered through a variety of agencies, including USA Swimming, the YMCA, and schools and community programs. Adult programs are offered through U.S. Masters Swimming (see appendix A). Participants normally must be at least 18 years old to participate (U.S. Masters Swimming, n.d.). There is no maximum age limit. Leagues sanction meets, certify and train coaches and officials, and publish rules.

Running an effective swim team program requires a commitment of your facility resources. The main requirement is pool space; the larger and more active your team, the more space required. Many teams practice both morning and evening for several hours and may run several sessions at those times to accommodate several age groups or skill levels. It is normally not possible for other activities to take place in an area where competitive swimming is taking place.

Swim meets, however, require the largest commitment of time. Dual meets can require several hours of uninterrupted pool time, while larger meets can extend for several days and last from early in the morning to late at night, precluding other activities in your pool. Be sure to inform your customers that their routine will be altered by the meet. Post signs in advance of the meet stating the pool closure dates and times. Be sure to reflect this information in your aquatic program brochures as well.

Any swimming pool can be used for swim team practice, but regulations dictate certain parameters for officially sanctioned meets. Requirements are usually stated in league rule books and pertain to required pool length, depth, and width.

The key to the success of your swim team will be your coaching staff. Preferably, your coaches will have experience as competitive swimmers themselves so that they have firsthand knowledge of stroke mechanics as well as competitive swimming skills. Additional qualifications should include lifeguard training and completion of a nationally recognized coaching clinic.

Safety must be a primary concern for your swim team. Regardless of age and skill level of the participants, a lifeguard must always be on duty during swim team meets and practices. This lifeguard should have no duties assigned other than watching the swimmers; therefore, the lifeguard is usually not a member of the coaching staff. Some people feel that lifeguards are unnecessary, particularly when dealing with more experienced swimmers. This is a false and dangerous assumption. Illness, horseplay, and mistakes can all cause injuries or fatalities, which can be prevented by a well-trained lifeguard responsible for direct supervision of the swimmers.

Correctly positioning starting blocks is crucial to ensuring the safety of your swimmers. Starting blocks must never be placed over a depth less than 5 feet (152.4 centimeters). You should not allow starting blocks to be used by anyone other than trained competitive swimmers and only then under the supervision of a trained coach. Instruction in starts should begin from the side, not the blocks, and preferably in the deep end. When the starting blocks are not in use, you should consider placing cones or specially made obstructions over them to prevent their use by unauthorized persons.

Meets can draw large numbers of participants and spectators to your facility, which opens up a wealth of opportunities. You can showcase your facility to the public and media as the meet results are reported. The large number of visitors to your facility provides you with revenue opportunities through sales of facility merchandise and food. If your facility has a snack bar, make sure it is well stocked before a meet. If you don't normally have a concession service, consider organizing a temporary one for large swim meets. Sodas, bottled water, pizza by the slice, popcorn, and prepackaged snacks are easy to stock, require little preparation, and can reap large profit margins. You should also ensure that your vending machines are fully stocked to provide an alternative source of snacks for your patrons.

Equipment

- Kickboards
- Pull buoys
- Hand paddles
- Touch pads
- Timing system
- Lane ropes
- False start stanchions and ropes
- Starter's horn
- Starter's pistol
- Pace clock
- Lap counter boards
- Starting blocks

Synchronized Swimming

Synchronized swimming (commonly called **synchro**) is an aquatic sport that is made up of two components: figures and routines. During the figures performance, athletes perform designated ballet-like skills that are judged against a standard. In this event, competitors are required to wear black one-piece swimsuits and white swim caps. The purpose in doing so is to reduce the possibility that judges will recognize athletes and show favoritism. Competitors can perform routines as individuals (solo), pairs (duet), or teams as large as eight. Routines are set to music and combine a series of gymnastics and dancelike skills that highlight athletes' strength, agility, and grace. The athletes perform a significant portion of the routine below the surface, which requires them to have good lung capacity.

Swimmers can begin synchronized swimming as young as 5 or 6 years old (assuming that they can swim) and may continue with the sport well into advanced age. Women make up the largest participant group in synchronized swimming; however, men's synchronized swimming programs are available.

Synchronized swimming coaches should possess sport-specific training from an agency such as United States Synchronized Swimming (see appendix A) as well as coaching certification from the American Sport Education Program (ASEP). Coaches should have additional certifications in first aid, CPR, and lifeguard training.

Water depth required for synchronized swimming will vary depending on the age of the participants. Beginning participants will require standing depth shallow water of 3 to 5 feet (91.4 to 152.4 centimeters) to enable them to practice basic skills safely. Older, more advanced participants will require water at a depth of 10 feet (about 3 meters) or greater. This will provide sufficient depth to enable them to safely practice routines that may require them to develop enough lift force to raise one another out of the water.

Equipment

- Costume swimsuits (individually selected by teams)
- Black swimsuits (for figures)
- Nose clips
- White swim caps (for figures)
- A good sound system for practice sessions

Scuba

Scuba instruction involves teaching students the safe performance of recreational diving activities and the use of associated equipment. As a recreational activity, scuba diving encompasses a wide range of specialty activities, such as underwater photography, ice diving, wreck diving, cave diving, night diving, and many others. Many students who are interested in scuba also want to pursue related leadership training, which includes certification options as a scuba teaching assistant, assistant instructor, instructor, and dive master.

Scuba is a very equipment-intensive sport, requiring an air tank, buoyancy compensator, weight belt, mask, fins, and snorkel for each student enrolled in the course. Open water dives (which are required for certification) require additional equipment and supplies. Refilling air tanks and the repair and maintenance of equipment require a considerable investment of money and facility space.

© Mary E. Messenger

Scuba divers practice in a pool.

Due to the considerable expense associated with the operation of a scuba program, many facilities opt to rent facility space to a local scuba shop or subcontract to an instructor for the operation of this program. If your scuba program is subcontracted to an outside source, your facility must retain control over safety, liability, and quality of instruction. You must ensure that the instructors teaching your program are currently certified as instructors by a nationally recognized scuba agency. You should keep copies of the instructional staff members' certification on file. You must provide the subcontracted instructors with a list of facility policies that they and their students must obey; this includes the minimum age at which students may enter the class and required instructor-to-student ratios. You must also provide a copy of your emergency procedures to the instructional staff before classes begin. Conducting an orientation that includes information such as the location of the telephone, first aid kit, and emergency evacuation routes also helps to eliminate confusion in an emergency. Although the provision of lifeguards may not be desired by the renting agency, they should be included as part of the rental agreement. You should not allow scuba instructors to take the place of facility lifeguards, because the instructors are not oriented to the emergency procedures of the facility and their training is not pool rescue specific.

Scuba instruction requires the use of classroom as well as pool space. The number of classroom and pool hours required for certification of students is mandated by the certifying agency.

Most scuba agencies require that the instructor carry personal liability insurance in the minimum amount of one million dollars in case legal action should arise as a result of a mishap during instruction. Additional insurance is not required on the part of the renting facility, because the liability insurance carried by the instructor will cover the renting facility as well as any associated employees.

You and the scuba instructors must agree on fundamental principles; the purpose of the program is to provide safe, enjoyable, and well-managed instruction. This agreement must include such basics as students' rights, instructor conduct, management responsibilities, and instructor responsibilities. If either party does not adhere to this understanding, the rental agreement should be terminated.

Nonprofit agencies (such as the YMCA) that provide rental facilities to "for-profit" entities (such as scuba shops) do place their tax-exempt status at risk if the operational agreement is not handled properly. To safely stay within tax law, you must control the scuba program, including advertising, fee collection, and program supervision. The instructor should be paid an agreed upon wage, either an hourly or per student fee. This arrangement permits the nonprofit entity to maintain tax-exempt status by controlling the program.

Numerous agencies offer certification in the sport of scuba diving. Some of the better-known agencies include the YMCA of the USA, the Professional Association of Diving Instructors (PADI), and the National Association of Underwater Instructors (NAUI; see appendix A). The certification that your students will receive on successful completion of their course will depend on the agency that your instructor is certified by. To instruct and certify students in scuba, an individual must hold current certification as an instructor from a recognized national agency. Teaching assistants, assistant instructors, and dive masters cannot teach without the direct supervision of an instructor. Instructor-to-student ratio for basic scuba is dependent on certifying agency requirements and can range from 1:10 to 1:20; during open water dives, one

instructor or assistant instructor is required for each student buddy pair (YMCA of the USA, 1991). Scuba instructors should also be currently certified in CPR and first aid. A certified lifeguard should also be on duty any time students are in the water.

Equipment

- Mask, fins, and snorkel (purchased by students as personal gear)
- Air tanks (Facilities that purchase their own tanks must also purchase an air compressor and cascade system for refilling tanks.)
- Buoyancy compensation devices
- Regulators
- Lead weights for weight belts
- Gear for open water dives, such as wet suits, boots, and hoods (owned or rented by students)
- Slates
- Underwater flashlights
- Grease pencils
- Glow sticks
- Instructional materials, including texts, log books, videotapes, and tests
- VCR and TV
- Chalkboard or dry erase board

Certification Courses

There is a wide range of aquatic certification courses, including lifeguard training, lifeguard instructor, water safety instructor, small craft instruction, and small craft safety. These courses usually follow a national agency curriculum that stipulates content and instructional time requirements.

Lifeguard training will probably be the most popular course that you offer, because it allows the students to get a job after they complete it. Common certifying agencies for lifeguard training include the YMCA of the USA, the American Red Cross, and Ellis and Associates (see appendix A). A good lifeguard training course will include (or require the student to receive) certification in CPR and first aid as well as lifeguard training. The minimum age for students in most courses is 15 years old. Instructional time for these classes can range anywhere from 16 to 32 hours, depending on certifying agency requirements.

If you offer lifeguard training, your facility must have both deep and shallow water areas. Shallow water areas should be 4 to 5 feet (121.9 to 152.4 centimeters) deep to permit the practice of shallow water spinal injury rescues. Deep water areas must be a minimum of 9 feet (274.3 centimeters) deep to permit students to perform the prerequisite skill of retrieving an object from deep water, which is required by both the YMCA and the American Red Cross programs (American Red Cross, 2004; YMCA of the USA, 1998).

Lifeguard training courses are an excellent opportunity for you to develop your own staff. Regularly check these classes as a source of prospective staff. You'll be sure the people are well trained—you trained them!

The YMCA of the USA and the American Red Cross most commonly offer swimming instructor courses; the time requirement for these courses is normally more than 35 hours of combined pool and classroom sessions. The minimum age required for students to be eligible for swimming instructor courses is 18 years old. You may want to consider offering your swimming instructor course in conjunction with children's swim lessons. This will allow your new swimming instructors to get some real-life experience with children. Schedule practical teaching experiences so that they coincide with swim lessons of the same skill level as the lessons to be taught. Prearrange with the instructors of the children's swim lessons to allow your student instructors to participate. The children's regular instructors should remain with the class to assist with any problems, because the children know them and will be more comfortable with them there. Instructor trainers should be in the background to evaluate student instructors and to manage the transition between student instructors and regular instructors. Teaching evaluations or feedback for student instructors should be conducted away from the children's classes to avoid disruption to both the class and the evaluation. Do not overload classes with student instructors—no more than one student instructor should be assigned to every five children, unless one-on-one skill teaching is desired.

You can offer small craft safety courses and introductory boating sessions for canoeing and kayaking in your pools. Small craft safety courses focus on skills such as putting on life jackets in the water, using clothing for flotation, and other

survival skills. This class is an excellent preseason safety refresher for people who fish and recreational boaters if you market it that way. Groups such as Boy Scout and Girl Scout troops may want to participate in these types of programs to meet merit badge requirements or for adventure trip preparation.

You should select an agency-recognized program for your small craft instruction. Groups that offer these programs include the American Red Cross and the U.S. Power Squadron. Small boats such as canoes and kayaks can cause damage to the pool tiles or coping by striking it. Try to avoid this by reminding your students to be careful when near the pool edge. Dragging boats across the deck can also cause damage to both the deck and the boat. During your first class, instruct your students on the proper method of moving the boats.

Equipment

- Rescue tubes
- Ring buoys
- Throw bags
- Shepherd's crook
- Reaching poles
- Kickboards
- Pull buoys
- **Backboards** and straps
- Head immobilization device
- CPR mannequins
- Rubbing alcohol
- First aid training supplies, including gauze pads, triangle bandages, and splints
- Rubber-coated diving bricks
- Life jackets
- Paddles
- VCR and television
- Chalkboard and chalk
- Instructional materials mandated by the certifying agency, including textbooks and videos
- Clipboards
- Instructional checklists
- Certification rosters
- Certification tests and answer keys

A pair of students should take each boat, one by the bow (front) and one by the stern (back). The boat should be lifted clear of the deck, moved to its new location, and then set down gently.

Life jackets are a must during boating drills or trips, even in the pool. Have students hang their life jackets up to dry after each use to ensure that the jackets do not begin to rot or mildew.

The critical element in the offering of a certification course is a properly qualified instructor. Certifying agencies require that their courses be taught by an instructor in possession of the agency's certification. Your program instructors for certification courses should also be trained in CPR for the professional rescuer, lifeguard training, and first aid. The training regulations published by the certifying agencies set the instructor-to-student ratio, and you must follow their guidelines if you want to offer their program. A currently certified lifeguard must be on duty at all times when courses are in session.

Diving

The sport of diving involves the execution of standardized dives judged against established criteria. Elements of acrobatics, gymnastics, and dance are combined in this challenging sport. Diving instruction requires an aquatic facility with one or more 1-meter and 3-meter diving boards. If you want to offer advanced training, your pool will require 5-meter and 7-meter platforms. You must have adequate water depth beneath your diving boards to ensure that your divers are safe (see table 1.1).

Select qualified diving coaches who have attended a safety seminar and dive coach training offered by USA Diving (see appendix A) (USA Diving, n.d.). Diving coaches should have experience as competitive divers. A qualified lifeguard should always be present during diving activities.

Equipment

- Trampoline and pulley system (used by coaches to enable divers to practice new dives on land)
- Mats for stretching
- Scorecards
- Score sheets
- Rule books

Water Polo

Water polo is a competitive aquatic sport played by opposing teams of seven players per side, the objective being to shoot a 12-inch (30.5-centimeter) ball through the opposing team's goal. Water polo is a physically challenging sport that requires good swimming skills, the ability to tread water for long periods, and good ballhandling skills. USA Water Polo (see appendix A) stipulates that the required pool dimensions for a sanctioned match include a length of 66 to 98 feet (20 to 30 meters), a width of 33 to 66 feet (10 to 20 meters), and a minimum depth of 6 feet (1.8 meters) (USA Water Polo, n.d.).

Water polo players are required to wear regulation headgear with chin straps and plastic ear guards designed to protect the player. Caps must be "quartered" (i.e., segmented in four parts) with team colors, and the goalkeeper's cap must be a solid color. Each cap must bear the player's number.

Coaches are the main staff members needed for water polo. Coaches should have prior experience as water polo players and formalized coaching training from a nationally recognized agency such as ASEP. Sport-specific coaches' training should also be required. Having certification in lifeguard

Table 1.1   Recommended Minimum Safe Diving Depths

Diving board	Recommended minimum safe depth
1-meter spring board	12 feet (3.7 meters)
3-meter spring board	13 feet (4 meters)
5-meter platform	14 feet (4.3 meters)
7-meter platform	15 feet (4.6 meters)
10-meter platform	17 feet (5.2 meters)

© Empics

Water polo players wear regulation headgear.

training and CPR will assist them in safeguarding athletes.

Water polo officials are required whenever a match is played. Normally, two officials are required for each contest. Officials must be certified or accredited by the agency sanctioning the event. Scorekeepers and timers will also be required for sanctioned matches. You can contact your sanctioning agency for a list of officials in your area. An officials' club or association may also be available locally; if so, you can also use that resource to meet your needs.

Equipment

- Officiating flags
- Whistles
- Regulation size goals
- Balls
- Time clock
- Scorecards
- Rule books
- Team caps with ear protection

Special Events

Special events by their nature exist in a class by themselves within aquatic programming. The number and type of special events are limited only by your imagination. Some sample special events include dive-in movies, family swim parties, lifeguard competitions, water carnivals, after prom or after graduation parties, midnight swims, and birthday swims.

In deciding which special events to offer, think about your pool's customers to determine which programs may fit their needs.

Dive-In Movies

A dive-in movie event involves showing a movie at your swimming pool. Swimmers can float on inner tubes or rafts while watching the movie. Choose the movie based on the type of customers your pool has. Families may enjoy *The Little Mermaid* or *Free Willy*. Young adult audiences may enjoy traditional aquatic films such as *Jaws* or *Orca*. You should provide bleachers or seats on deck for those who do not want to get wet, or you can even permit patrons to bring their own lawn chairs to make themselves more comfortable.

Darkness is a key element in successfully offering this program. Because of this, you should run this program at indoor facilities (and at night if you have windows in your pool area). The best way to ensure that your customers can hear and see the movie is to show it using a video projector and projection screen. This prevents the screen from shaking and provides good sound quality and a clear picture. If you don't have this technology, you can use a large bedsheet and a 16-millimeter reel-to-reel projector (be sure to tie down the sheet at all four corners to prevent it from shaking).

Showing a video or movie to a public audience requires you to purchase one-time rights to the movie. Cost for the purchase of this permission varies with the popularity of the movie and can range from one hundred to several hundred dollars.

Because this program will take place in darkness, you should take some extra safety precautions. Ensure that your emergency pool lighting is turned on so that you will still have some lighting even though your main lighting is off. Turn your underwater lights on in the pool. This will add to the atmosphere during the movie and will also assist your staff in seeing the bottom of the pool. Place extra lifeguards around the perimeter of the pool to help eliminate blind spots that may be caused by the flotation devices in the pool. Also consider placing a staff member who is certified in scuba on the bottom of the pool. This person can eliminate the worry that anyone has slipped off a flotation device and was unseen by lifeguards at the surface. Be sure to provide your staff with waterproof flashlights for use in an emergency.

Equipment

- Video projector or 16-millimeter reel-to-reel projector
- Projection screen
- Video or 16-millimeter movie
- Inner tubes
- Bleachers
- Benches
- Flotation rafts
- Flashlights

Family Swim Parties

Family swim parties involve a "host family" providing activities at the aquatic center for other families. Your host family should be one that enjoys the water as a group, and they should be good swimmers. You should also look for a family that is friendly, outgoing, and mixes easily with new people. This family should be regular users of your facility and well known to your staff. Before they begin their host duties, be sure to meet with them to explain what it is you want them to do. Offer activity suggestions, show them pool items they can use, and review safety procedures and pool

rules. Lifeguard supervision during this activity is also an important safety factor.

Your hosts should greet other families as they arrive and invite them to join in activities in progress or to start new ones. Races, games, songs, and family fun activities are the order of the day. The activities that you choose should be family friendly with opportunities for young children to participate. Activities should be mainly noncompetitive and should focus on inclusion. Try to select games that don't eliminate anyone; patrons are there to play and have fun.

Providing pool toys for preschoolers to use with their parents (e.g., balls, buckets, toy boats, sponges, and rubber ducks) is also a nice option for those families that do not want to play games or for children who are too young to participate.

This activity is best offered on Friday or Saturday nights early in the evening to accommodate young children. Due to the potential for large numbers of parents and small children, you should provide a large shallow area for this activity. Other events and activities should not be scheduled at the same time or should be kept at a distance (in large pools) due to the noise this activity will generate.

Equipment

- Hula hoops
- Bathtub toys
- Toy boats
- Balls
- Diving rings

Lifeguard Competitions

Lifeguard competitions provide an opportunity for staff from several different aquatic facilities to test their skills against one another. These events are best offered during the summer months because there is a larger number of eligible teams when summer pools are in operation. Popular events include towing rescue relays, CPR skills events, first aid scenarios, rescue skills scenarios, run-swim-run races, and spinal injury management scenarios. No standardized set of events exists for these competitions, leaving you free to select whatever events you'd like to offer. However, you must specify the standards on which competitors will be judged. The easiest way to do this is to

Equipment

- Rescue tubes
- Backboards and straps
- Head immobilization device
- First aid supplies (gauze, triangle bandages, splints)
- CPR mannequins (adult, infant, and child)
- First aid makeup kit for simulating injuries
- Stopwatches
- Whistles
- Premade judging sheets
- Calculators
- Pencils
- Paper
- Clipboards

use the lifeguard training standards of a national lifeguard training agency. In this case, you would state in your event materials that all technical skills (such as spinal injury management) will be judged according to American Red Cross or Ellis and Associates standards (Rennie, 1987).

A large number of judges, staff, and people to play the part of victims are required to successfully run this type of event. Competition judges should be selected from senior lifeguard instructors and CPR instructors. You may be able to recruit "victims" from among age group swim teams, lifeguard classes, and older swim lesson groups. Any volunteer who has an interest can fill the role of other officials such as marshals and runners; these volunteers may include parents, other nonaquatic staff members, and former lifeguards. It is customary that competitors be currently certified in lifeguard training and CPR before being permitted to compete (Fawcett, 1998).

Lifeguard competitions can be offered as beach or pool events and typically take a full day. National and international competitions can take several days. (See chapter 6 for staff descriptions and sample events for lifeguard competitions.)

Water Carnivals

Carnival events are an excellent opportunity for an aquatic facility to showcase the talent of its staff and students. Typically, aquatic sports teams, clubs, and classes from the facility put on a demonstration of their skill or event. Popular events include synchronized swimming demonstrations, diving shows, scuba demonstrations, children's swim lessons showcase, and lifeguard skills demonstrations (staff). Much coordination and planning are required for this event. Parents, grandparents, and family members of the participants are often the main spectators. This event can provide a great deal of enjoyment for students and spectators. (See chapter 3 for information about this event as a promotional idea.)

© Sport The Library

Young swimmers prepare to demonstrate their skills.

Equipment

- Carnival banners
- Carnival programs (optional)
- Loudspeaker or sound system
- Spotlight
- Flashlights
- Tickets
- Table for ticket sales
- Cash box
- Change fund
- Trash cans

After Prom or After Graduation Parties

Parties at swimming pools are becoming popular as part of a package of using a recreation center as a whole for activities after a prom or graduation. High school students are locked into the facility for the night, precluding the opportunity for alcohol consumption. Aggressive marketing for this event can result in a number of reservations from area high schools. Staffing these events is challenging because schools normally want to hold this event during the late night and early morning hours. Providing lifeguards at 2:00 A.M. may be a challenge. You may want to consider paying time and a half or more for these extreme late night events (and passing the cost along to the renter). Some groups will want to bring their own lifeguards to alleviate the need and expense of hiring your staff. You should not permit this, because these lifeguards are not familiar with your facilities and procedures.

Be sure to properly prepare your facility for this event. Control access to the facility through a single point to prevent unauthorized access.

Equipment

- Trash cans
- Barriers to block access to restricted areas
- Sound system
- Inner tubes
- Rafts
- Trash cans

Provide many large trash cans and arrange for frequent trash removal. Well in advance of the event, you should discuss with the renting party your facility policy regarding chaperones, including their presence in the pool. For large groups staying all night, you may want to require the renting group to hire a police officer for the event to prevent any problems from arising.

Midnight Swims

Midnight swims can be used for several purposes: They can give adults an opportunity to swim at a community pool without the presence of young children, or they can be used as a special event to draw teenage swimmers to the pool. They can also be used as an event for teens to provide an alternative to activities that may cause mischief. Mature, responsible lifeguards are required to supervise this activity. Adequate lighting should be provided by floodlights if a midnight swim is held at an outdoor facility. Lifeguards should be equipped with flashlights in case of a power failure or simply to provide extra lighting for dark corners of the pool area.

Equipment

- Flashlights
- Floodlights
- Lane ropes (for adult swims)
- Pull buoys (for adult swims)
- Kickboards (for adult swims)
- Sound system (for teen events)

Birthday Swims

Birthday swims provide an opportunity for children to congregate at the pool for fun and enjoyment to celebrate a child's birthday. Package arrangements regarding entrance fees to the pool are helpful in simplifying the administration of this program. To make this program more enjoyable, provide a room for the cake and presents, as well as a refrigerator for storage of ice cream and drinks. Assign a facility staff member to meet the group on arrival, escort them to the pool, and assist them with storage of the cake and gifts. Prior to the event, mail the host family a list of facility rules, including chaperone requirements while in the pool. A ratio of one chaperone in the pool for every five children is recommended, excluding lifeguards. You can require fewer chaperones if the children are older and good swimmers. Before allowing the group to enter the pool, give them a safety briefing—this should be short, to the point, and heavy on humor. When your staff meets the group at the door, the staff should direct them to an area where the safety talk can be given. This also gives your staff an opportunity to make sure an adequate number of chaperones are present before the group enters the pool. If not enough chaperones are present, keep the group out of the pool until they arrive. Your staff can also use this opportunity to introduce themselves to the group leader or party sponsor. This establishes a good relationship and lets the leader know who to go to with a question or problem.

Equipment

- Balls
- Toys
- Tables and chairs in adjacent area for cake and presents
- Refrigerator for cake and ice cream
- Trash cans in "party room"

Water Safety Education

You can offer water safety education even at times when you don't have access to a pool, or you can include it as a separate unit in an existing program. Although it's best if the instructors in your water safety education program have previous training or experience in water safety education, there are many land-based programs (designed for school-teachers and activity leaders) that do not require any prior experience at all. These packages are often available from the government or nonprofit agencies for little or no cost. Common elements in these programs include video presentations, lecture and discussion ideas, and activity pages for children. The American Red Cross, the U.S. Army Corps of Engineers, and the U.S. Coast Guard Auxiliary are examples of agencies that offer water safety education programs (see appendix A).

If you are a schoolteacher, you can include water safety units during the warm months before the students break for the summer; this is when they often need refresher training in water safety. Aquatic facilities can use water safety programs at health fairs, in lobby displays, at schools, and at any other location where they can spread the word about the importance of water safety.

Equipment

- TV and VCR
- Chalkboard or white board
- Copies of activity pages
- Classroom

DECIDING WHICH PROGRAMS TO OFFER

When choosing programs to offer at an aquatic facility, it's best to first consider what the pool's primary purpose is. For example, a school pool's main purpose is providing activities for the school's students (e.g., academic classes and sports such as swimming and diving), while a YMCA pool's purpose may be to offer many different types of programs to service all the different interests of a diverse group of patrons.

Every facility has a mission. This mission is set out by the owner, city council, recreation board, board of directors, or whatever governing body directs the facility. Keep this mission in mind when making programming decisions. For example, if a children's swim lesson program is not making money, but your facility is city owned and safe recreation opportunities for children are a high priority, the cost may be underwritten and you may continue to offer the program anyway.

Be sure to take into account who your customers are, including their ages and interests, when considering what programs to offer. For example, in an area with a large population of stay-at-home mothers or fathers, a weekday parent-tot swimming class may be very popular, while this same program might draw no registrations in a retirement community. College campuses, with their high population of young and adventurous students, are often good places to offer scuba and lifeguard training classes. You should consider the wants and needs of your primary customers when you're planning programs. If a new program displaces current patrons from their normal activity or time at the facility, the new program may fail due to lack of enrollment. It may also cause patrons to be angry because their favorite activity was moved or taken away.

> **KEY POINT**   *Your facility's primary purpose should determine what programs you offer.*

One of the best ways to determine if a program will be popular with your customers is to ask them. Your survey should focus on determining those programs that patrons would like to see offered and the popularity of the programs you offer now. Surveys should be no longer than a single page (typed) and should be formatted for multiple-choice responses. This makes it easy for your patrons to complete the survey; if it's too long or too difficult, they won't complete it and you won't get any information. Survey forms may be placed at the reception desk of the facility and returned in a receptacle provided there. Another way to get the information you need is to have a staff member ask the patrons the questions on the survey as they leave the facility and fill in the form for them. If you do this, you may be more likely to get some information because you directly ask the patrons, and you can also be more certain that the survey will be filled out correctly. Be sure to ask the patrons if they have time for your questions prior to beginning the survey. If a patron appears to be in a hurry, don't ask that patron the survey questions. (See appendix D for a sample patron survey.)

Your primary considerations when choosing aquatic programs should include the availability of instructors, equipment, and supplies, and the availability of the facility itself. Offering a scuba class may seem like a good idea, but if no local instructors are available, it may not be feasible. You should review the qualifications of your staff to see if you have anyone that meets the qualifications needed to teach your new program. If not, you must consider alternatives. It may be possible to send one of your staff members who has an interest in the new program to receive instructor training. Agencies such as the YMCA and the Red Cross regularly offer instructor training needed to teach their courses. You should contact your local Red Cross chapter or the national YMCA of the USA for information on instructor courses in your area. You may also be able to hire a new instructor to teach your new program.

When considering programs in which certification is granted by an agency, such as lifeguard training or scuba, review the instructor manual first. The instructor manual will identify requirements such as how deep or shallow the pool has to be and what equipment you need to conduct the course. You may find after reading the manual that your facility doesn't meet the requirements to offer this course, or that you need to purchase additional equipment. This may change your decision on whether or not to offer this course. (See appendix D for a new aquatic program worksheet.)

You must also determine if facility space is available for your new program. Use the space evaluation method described in the "Evaluating Program Quality" section of this chapter to determine when pool time is available and to determine if other programs can share the facility during the new activity. Some programs are not compatible with each other in the pool at the same time.

Consider what level of noise each program will create. For example, water exercise programs often create a high noise level due to the instructor calling out directions and the use of a stereo system. A program that requires detailed instructor-to-student direction and interaction, such as scuba, may not be appropriate in the pool at the same time as water exercise.

Also consider the types of clients that may be sharing the pool. Programs for people with arthritis often have participants who are unsteady on their feet and require assistance for balance. Scheduling a children's swim program in the pool at the same time may create risks—for example, the risk of a running child accidentally colliding with an arthritis program participant and knocking the participant down. Never hold small craft programs in the pool with other activities because a boat could strike and injure a swimmer.

> **KEY POINT**   *Noise level and safety should be the primary factors in determining which programs should share facility space.*

You must also determine if the time you have available will be suitable for the program you want to offer. Pool space available at 9:00 P.M. will be useless if you want to offer children's swimming lessons.

Each program that you offer will require a different set of equipment and supplies. (See the "Aquatic Programs" section of this chapter for specific lists.) Determine whether or not your facility owns the correct equipment to offer a program before you make a final decision to offer it. If your facility does not have the correct equipment for a program, you must include the cost of purchasing equipment when considering the expenses of the program. (See appendix D for a program revenue evaluation worksheet.) For programs that you offer only occasionally, you may be able to rent the needed equipment, saving the expense of purchasing and maintaining it. For example, if you only offer lifeguard training once a year, you may be able to rent videotapes and mannequins from the local Red Cross unit.

In many cases, you will have staff members who are certified as instructors by many different agencies, such as the Red Cross, YMCA, or Ellis and Associates. If this is the situation at your facility, you should conduct an in-service session for instructors where you explain the standards and policies at your facility. This will help ensure that all of your staff use the same basic instructional techniques. For example, you do not want to have two instructors side-by-side teaching beginning swimming lessons when one uses flotation devices and one does not.

If you have a programming idea, but you're just not sure if it will draw enough registration, you can "pilot test" it. Often called "I tried" courses (I tried scuba, I tried water exercise, and so on), pilot tests give patrons a chance to try a new activity for one class period to see if they'd like to register for the program. For example, if you're considering a country line dancing water exercise program for your facility but aren't sure if there's any interest, you would offer a 1-hour session of that program, letting patrons try it out. You can use the "I tried" format to gauge interest in the program or as part of a marketing strategy to draw interest to a newly established activity. The advantage of using an "I tried" format is that the patrons don't have to invest a large amount of time or money in a program that they may not enjoy. The facility gets similar benefits in that you haven't committed advertising or pool space to a program that may not be offered. In fact, the "I tried" program becomes advertising for the full program, because patrons who enjoyed the program on a one-time basis will often register for the whole course. If you have decided to offer the full course, you should make sure that registration materials are available on the day of your "I tried" activity so that you can take advantage of your customers' interest and register them right away. If possible, offer the "I tried" program free of charge to draw more participants.

Once you've determined what programs to offer, you need to decide when to offer them.

Again, you need to consider who your customers will be for each program. For example, offering children's swim lessons from 4:00 to 5:00 P.M. may seem like a good idea, but not if many of the children in your area are in after-school day care at that time.

ENHANCING EXISTING PROGRAMS

Revitalizing existing aquatic programs can draw patrons to a program they might not have previously considered. When you're considering revamping aquatic programs, you have to determine if changes need to be made. Changing a familiar and successful program may create confusion and dissatisfaction among previously happy patrons. Changing a program is not a bad thing to do, but it must be carried out for a legitimate reason. If you're not sure whether or not to change a program, ask your regular patrons for their opinion. If your patrons are enjoying the current program, that doesn't mean it can't be altered, but you should take extra care to keep those aspects of the program that the patrons feel are most important.

Once you've determined that you need to change an existing program, the question becomes how to do so. You first need to identify the shortcomings of the program. You should consult with your program instructor and with the participants to determine this. In consulting with the program participants, you may take a survey or may simply meet with them for a few moments before their program to get feedback. Be sure to record their feedback. If you think that the instructor may be the problem, you may want to take a survey, because the students may not want to voice complaints about the instructor while the instructor is present. Meet with your program instructors one-on-one and ask for their feedback regarding the program. Attend the program sessions yourself so that you can identify where the weaknesses are. Possible problems with programs may include old or outdated equipment; facility problems such as lighting, air temperature, or water temperature; bad time of the day for this particular program; participant dislike of the program format; or poor instructor quality.

After you've determined what the problem is, you can determine what you are going to do about it. Take into account all feedback from the students and instructors and your own observations.

Changes may be minor and could include such modifications as purchasing new equipment or changing the class time. For more serious overhauls, such as changing course formats, be sure to stay in touch with your students and staff to inform them in a positive way about the changes. Once you've done what you feel you need to do to make the program successful, market it in a way that emphasizes the new aspects. Work closely with your staff to ensure that they take ownership of the new program and assist in positively marketing it.

Equipment

One method of renewing an existing program is to purchase new equipment. New equipment can allow an activity to be carried out more safely, efficiently, and comfortably. Types of equipment that may be helpful in revitalizing aquatic programs include safety equipment (for all programs), instructional equipment (for certification classes and swimming lessons), toys (for children's swim lessons), exercise equipment (for water exercise classes), rescue equipment (for certification classes), and competitive swimming equipment (for Masters programs and competitive swimming classes).

First, you should do an inventory of your equipment to see what you have and what shape it's in. Consult with your staff to determine if you have enough equipment and if what you have is suitable for the programs you are offering. If you identify a need, you should include your instructors in the purchasing process to ensure that the equipment you purchase is what they need. If you are considering a piece of equipment and you are unsure if it will fit your needs, contact the supplier and ask a customer service representative to describe it for you. Before buying, be sure to obtain pricing from at least three suppliers to get an idea of a fair price. Ask the sales representative what discounts are available for bulk orders and if setting up an account will reduce the cost. Purchasing the majority of your supplies from one vendor may reduce your overall costs. You should also ask what the payment terms are and if shipping is included in the purchase price.

New equipment creates excitement by its brighter colors, fresher smell, and better function. If possible, you should store old and new equipment separately, because the contrast with the newer equipment can make the old equipment appear shabby by comparison.

Program Format

Altering aspects of an existing program to create a new feeling is another revitalization method. For example, offering new music choices during water exercise (such as big band, swing, or jazz) can create a new tempo and generate interest from a different clientele. Offering a new style of an activity in an existing course, such as country line dancing water exercise or family style swim lessons, may accomplish similar results.

Changing the time of day or the days of the week that you offer a program can give your customers a fresh perspective. For example, your weekday parent-tot class may be tried in the morning, before the children's nap time rather than after.

You may also want to consider changing the number of days per week that you offer a particular program. A water exercise program that is successful 3 days a week may provide better service 5 days a week. You may want to give your customers a choice of the number of days per week that they want to participate. You can do this by having them pay a flat fee for a set number of class sessions. When the customers sign up for the class, they receive a punch card for the number of classes they paid for. Each time they attend class, a hole is punched in their card. When all their classes are "punched," they purchase a new card. Using this method allows the customers to choose the number of classes they attend per week, and it allows them to vary the number of times per week and the days they attend based on their changing schedule. This method works best for exercise-based courses such as water exercise or Masters swimming. It would not work for certification classes where attendance is mandatory.

A guest instructor can provide an exciting change of pace for both customers and staff. Inviting a college swim coach to visit with and provide training tips to your age group swim team will benefit not only your swimmers but can also provide new ideas for your coaching staff. On a simpler level, you may have instructors rotate classes for one session so that everyone gets a fresh perspective.

Be constantly aware of new instructional aids such as videotapes and books. Purchase them when you feel they would benefit your staff. These new materials often plant new ideas in the minds of your staff and can greatly assist with revitalizing your classes.

Instructor Development

Staff development is one of the most important things that you can do to keep your programs fresh. You may consider offering regular **in-service training** for instructors as well as lifeguards. The instructors can share their teaching tips, teach each other games and songs, and observe each other teach. By doing this, your instructors can reap the benefits of each other's experience and can then apply what they've learned to their classes. You can also offer instructor courses in specialty training (such as water exercise, adapted aquatics, and water polo) at your facility. Encourage your staff to participate; it makes them more well rounded and benefits your program as a whole.

Periodically rotating instructors out of a program they traditionally teach can provide a renewing experience for both customers and staff. The patrons might enjoy seeing a new face and hearing a different voice. The staff may enjoy teaching new people and trying a different activity. Discuss this change with instructors before it happens so that it becomes a mutual choice and not something they will resent.

EVALUATING PROGRAM QUALITY

Establishing and maintaining aquatic program quality are key components of success. Well-managed programs draw repeat customers; word of mouth of these satisfied customers also attracts new clients. In well-managed aquatic programs, the safety of patrons is a priority above all else. Some ways you can help ensure safe programs include making sure qualified lifeguards are present during all class sessions and checking the certifications of your program instructors. The quality of instruction you provide to your students is also a very important factor in the patrons' impression of the program.

National agencies such as the American Red Cross and the YMCA of the USA set program standards for the courses they sponsor. These standards are often found in program manuals or can be obtained through an organization's national office. The standards include guidelines such as the instructor-to-student ratio, required instructor qualifications, safety standards, and curriculum guidelines. Review these standards for the programs you offer and consider them to be guidelines for maintaining quality. If the YMCA recommends that a lifeguard be present during children's swim lessons, and you do not provide one for your YMCA swim lessons program, you are not maintaining safety and quality standards.

You should also set your own standards for program quality. These standards should include items such as employee dress and conduct standards, safety and supervision standards, methods for handling complaints, and instructional quality standards. Your standards should be a logical extension of the national standards and should never conflict with the standards set by the national agency for the programs you teach.

You must communicate your standards clearly to your staff. Be sure to include this information in the staff manual that you distribute to them. You should also inform staff of dress and grooming standards when they are hired. You must enforce whatever quality controls you set or they will be worthless. Regularly evaluate your programs to see that the standards are being met and take action to correct problems if you find that they are not.

You or an assistant should regularly attend aquatic program sessions at your facility. During the visit, you can evaluate facility cleanliness, water quality, staff alertness, and performance of duty. Walk through and spot-check to ensure that the decks are clean and clear of obstructions, water clarity is good, and that your lavatories and locker rooms are clean. Also check to ensure that trash cans are emptied and that paper products and soap are stocked in the lavatories. During your walk-through, stop to talk with your on-deck instructors or program supervisors. Inquire about whether all staff are present and if they need anything. This spot check allows you to correct small problems before they become larger and to avert customer complaints by eliminating problems. If possible, take this opportunity to visit informally with your customers. Introduce yourself and ask them how they are enjoying the program. Try to learn their names so that you can greet them in the future. By doing this, you make your customers feel more at home in your facility. You also find out informally what they like and dislike about your program. You can use this as a method of identifying problems you need to solve and identifying the programs that customers are enjoying.

Periodically, you should observe and evaluate each staff member's performance of duties while teaching or lifeguarding. Tell your staff that they will be evaluated during a session, but not the exact date. Evaluation of staff members should be different for instructional staff versus lifeguards. Lifeguards may be evaluated on criteria such as **scanning** technique, proper uniform, use of rescue equipment, and interaction with patrons. Instructor evaluation focuses on competencies such as lesson preparation, interaction with students, and use of instructional time. (See appendix D for an example of a swimming instructor evaluation form.) After the evaluation, give the staff member a written report of the results and explain it to her during a one-on-one meeting.

Participant Evaluations

At the conclusion of a program, provide participants with a standardized evaluation form that allows them to rate the program, instructor, and facilities. If the participants are children or they are mentally incapable of completing the form, give it to the participants' parents or guardians.

Provide several methods for the customers to obtain the evaluations. A stack of forms can be placed at the reception desk for patrons to fill out as they enter or exit. For certification classes that offer classroom sessions (such as scuba or lifeguard training), students can complete their evaluations during that time period. For children's swim lessons, you may want to have a supervisor circulate through the parents' waiting area to distribute the forms, collect them, and answer any questions regarding them. Be sure to provide pencils to make filling out the forms as easy as possible. For adult classes in the pool, such as water exercise or Masters swimming, the instructor should explain that forms are available at the front desk or on deck and should ask patrons to complete one at their convenience.

Do not require customers to include their names, but provide a space for their names on the form in case they want a reply to their comments. Results of participants' evaluations should be typed, formulated into a log, and reviewed. This information provides a basis for making positive changes to a given program based on the desires of those participating in it. (See appendix D for a sample participant aquatic program evaluation form.)

Staff Evaluations

Also grant your program staff an opportunity to periodically evaluate their programs. The best way to ensure that your staff completes the evaluations is to distribute them during a staff meeting or in-service training session. Some staff members may be uncomfortable completing this survey while their supervisor is present, particularly if they think their supervisor won't like their comments. To avoid this, you may want to have a staff member who is not directly associated with aquatics, such as a facility manager or front desk clerk, distribute and collect the surveys. These evaluations should focus on gathering suggestions for improving programming. Feedback regarding items such as teacher-to-student ratios, instructional materials and equipment, and class times can be solicited from your program staff. Your staff will have a perspective on your program that is different from any other group. They will be able to tell you how well your program really runs and what it would take to make it better (Clayton, 1989). After you collect their comments, you should read them and log them. If a suggestion or comment comes up repeatedly from several different staff members, you should consider it carefully and determine if you can fix the problem they've identified. The best solution to a problem your staff identifies may be to take the problem back to them for a discussion and their suggestions. (See appendix D for a sample staff aquatic program evaluation form.)

External Reviews

You should have an external review of your entire aquatic programming system conducted on a recurring basis. Respected colleagues from other aquatic facilities can be invited to evaluate your aquatic programs based on quality, safety, profitability, space utilization, and staffing issues.

Give a copy of your standards (as discussed earlier in this section) to the people who will review your programs. This will give them a yardstick for measuring your programming system based on facts, rather than opinions.

You must give the reviewers access to records and class sessions. You must also give them permission to talk to staff, patrons, and parents of minor patrons. At the conclusion of the review, a report from the reviewers should be presented to the aquatic facility manager. You should carefully read the report, paying close attention to their comments and suggestions. This report is particularly valuable because the reviewers have no stake in your facility or any of its programs. You can trust that their comments are true and unbiased. Because of this, you should make every effort to act on their suggestions.

Internal Reviews

Each quarter, you should conduct a revenue and space evaluation of each program. The purpose of a revenue evaluation is to determine if a program is supporting itself financially and if it is producing a profit. In performing a revenue evaluation, you must identify the expenses related to the program. These expenses include wages, utilities (e.g., heat and light), and equipment and supplies (e.g., pool toys, safety equipment, and office supplies). Computing wages for a program requires knowing the wages for each staff member in the program, adding the hourly wage of all employees together, and multiplying it by the number of hours the program is in operation. Utilities may be more difficult to compute if the pool is part of a larger facility such as a recreation center. You may be able to estimate lighting and heating costs by zone because some regulatory computers produce data that way. If not, the utility bill for a month would have to be divided by the approximate percentage of the building the pool occupies; this produces the approximate utility cost for the pool per month. This figure is then divided by the number of hours per month a given program runs. You now have the utility cost for operating that program. Add all costs together and you have a rough estimate of what it costs to operate the program.

Revenue is much easier to compute. Add together all fees taken in from registration and include any donations or other sources of funds. Subtract revenues from expenses to determine if that program is at a profit or loss. (See appendix D for a sample program revenue evaluation worksheet.)

The above method of calculating profit and loss assumes that the pool has to cover all of its expenses from its own revenue. Not all facilities operate this way; different institutions have different sources of funding. Some college and university pools are funded from student fees and may need to produce only a part of their operating expenses from revenue. Some municipal facilities are wholly funded by the city council as a service to the community and are required to produce no profit at all. If this is the case, it may change your priorities when considering canceling or reducing services that would be seen as "unprofitable" in a business setting. You should always be aware of the amount of money your individual programs are producing and what could be done to increase that amount, but you should also consider the funding source at your aquatic facility.

Evaluate the use of aquatic facility space to determine if the pool is being fully used at all hours of the day. To perform this evaluation, observe the pool during each hour of programming, count the number of patrons registered and present, and evaluate the amount of space the program is utilizing. In some cases, the available space may be reallocated to another program, thereby generating more revenue per hour. Before reallocating what appears to be extra space, first discuss the situation with the instructor whose program would be affected. Some programs, such as arthritis classes or those for persons with disabilities, are best not combined with other groups; the instructor may provide valuable guidance in this area.

DECIDING WHEN TO DROP A PROGRAM

Before you cancel an aquatic program, you should carefully consider what the effects would be. When a program has been offered for a period of time, the customers can become attached to it and may not want it to be canceled. Customers may become attached to a program because they enjoy the activity or because they like visiting with friends while doing the activity. They may even become attached to your staff members. Canceling a program that is well liked by patrons may cause unhappiness. Patrons who are unhappy may take their business elsewhere and may also tell other potential customers about their unhappiness. The public relations aspect of canceling a program should be very carefully considered in the process.

A major factor that you should think about when making your decision is the financial impact of the program. Determine early in the process if this program is making money, losing money, or breaking even. If the program is making a profit, consider very carefully whether canceling it would be wise.

> **KEY POINT**   *Program profitability and patron satisfaction should be primary considerations when deciding to drop a program.*

However, just because a program is losing money does not mean it must be canceled. Explore your organization's policy regarding profit. If this program is losing money yet providing a valuable service, the organization may consider supporting it from revenues of other programs. Also, if you cancel an unprofitable program but do not replace it with a profitable one, you have lost all revenue from the pool at that time. However, you have not eliminated all expenses because the pool must still be heated and water must still be kept clean and disinfected. It may be better to gather some revenue from this program to offset these costs, rather than no revenue at all from canceling it.

You must also consider what role this course plays in your overall aquatic program. For instance, if you offer a progression of diving classes, and you are considering canceling your introduction to diving course, you must consider what impact this will have on the rest of your diving program. Introductory courses and advanced courses often have a mutual relationship in that each needs the other to exist. Beginning classes prepare students for advanced classes; students need advanced classes so that they can logically progress once they master the skills in the basic class. If you cancel one of these, you disrupt the natural flow of students through your program.

Also think about what changes you could make to the program that might improve its appeal to patrons or increase its profitability. By revitalizing the program, you may be able to eliminate the need to cancel it. See the "Enhancing Existing Programs" section earlier in this chapter.

Once you've decided not to offer a particular program, the method in which you handle it is very important. First, make sure your organization, supervisor, and staff are on board with this change. Be sure you've thought it through carefully, know how it will affect everyone in the program, and can justify the change. Then let program participants know that the change is coming and why the change is being made. If you have alternative programs that could serve their needs, tell them.

Canceled Courses

When you publish your registration material, be sure to include a cancellation policy that clearly states that classes may be canceled for low registration or for any other reasons that you want to specify. Explain in your policy what you will do for customers who are inconvenienced by the cancellation of a course (for example, refund their money, register them for a similar class, or let them choose either of these options).

When you've determined that the class isn't going to be offered, have your staff contact the registrants by phone as soon as possible to inform them of the cancellation and the reason for it. The staff must be prepared to offer the customers options such as a full refund or registration in a similar program. Your staff members should try to register the customers in a similar program if possible to retain their business. After the initial call, mail a cancellation letter to the customers explaining the program change, apologizing for the inconvenience, and outlining the options available to them. This will help ensure that no customers are left out of the notification process. If you are still unsure if all registrants have been notified, have a supervisor go to the pool at the scheduled class time to meet with any customers who may show up.

If the reason for the cancellation is a mistake on the part of the facility management, such as double booking the pool with two programs, you must be prepared to compensate your customers. In this case, you should fully refund their fees and offer free registration for a similarly priced program of their choice. Although this may cost money in the short run, you will have succeeded in maintaining customer satisfaction and increased your chances of retaining their business in the future.

Customer satisfaction must be a major focus. If you fail to keep your patrons happy, they will not use your facility, and all programs, services, and staff will be pointless.

SUMMARY

Programming is a big part of operations at your facility. Well-run and carefully selected programs can increase your patrons' enjoyment of your facility, which can in turn result in increased revenue. After reading this chapter, you should have a better understanding of what programs would be appropriate for your facility, and you should be familiar with a wide variety of programs that you can choose from to meet your facility needs. Evaluation of your programs is the key to determining what is working and what your patrons are enjoying. This chapter also provided you with information to assist you in finding out the best aspects of your programs as well as those that may need some improvement. The section related to dropping programs should help you decide when it's best not to offer a program and why that may be so.

REVIEW QUESTIONS

1. Describe three aquatic programs you could offer at an indoor aquatic facility.
2. Describe a lifeguard's primary purpose.
3. What items can an aquatic supervisor evaluate during a regular visit to an aquatic program?
4. When deciding which programs to offer, what is the primary factor to consider?
5. What factors are most important when evaluating an instructor?
6. What is the purpose of conducting a revenue evaluation?

BIBLIOGRAPHY

American Red Cross. (1991). *Water safety instructor manual.* St. Louis: Mosby Lifeline.

American Red Cross. (1996). *Swimming and diving.* St. Louis: Mosby Lifeline.

American Red Cross. (2004). *American Red Cross lifeguarding instructor's manual.* Boston: Staywell.

American Red Cross. (2004). *Lifeguard training.* Teterboro, NJ: Staywell.

Clayton, R. (1989). *Professional aquatic management.* Champaign, IL: Human Kinetics.

Ellis and Associates. (n.d.). Ellis and Associates lifeguarding agency home page. Retrieved September 2003, from Web site: www.jellis.com/default_reg.htm.

Fawcett, P. (1998, March/April). Everyone's a winner at lifeguard competitions. *Aquatics International,* 10, 25-29.

Fawcett, P. (Ed.). (2001). *Aquatic director's handbook.* Corvallis, OR: National Intramural Recreational Sports Association.

Gabrielsen, M.A. (1987). *Swimming pools: A guide to their planning, design, and operation* (4th ed.). Champaign, IL: Human Kinetics.

Katz, J. (1993). *Swimming for total fitness, updated edition.* New York: Doubleday.

Lifesaving Society Canada. (n.d.). Lifesaving Society Canada home page. Retrieved September 9, 2003, from Web site: www.sauvetage.ca.

Rennie, W. (1987, May). *Lifeguards and the role of competition.* Rescue '86 Symposium, Vancouver, BC.

USA Diving. (n.d.). U.S. Diving home page. Retrieved October 25, 2003, from Web site: www.usadiving.org.

USA Swimming. (n.d.). USA Swimming home page. Retrieved October 25, 2003, from Web site: www.usswim.org.

USA Synchro. (n.d.). USA Synchro home page. Retrieved October 25, 2003, from Web site: www.usasynchro.org.

USA Water Polo. (n.d.). USA Water Polo home page. Retrieved October 25, 2003, from Web site: www.usawaterpolo.com.

U.S. Masters Swimming. (n.d.). U.S. Masters Swimming home page. Retrieved October 25, 2003, from Web site: www.usms.org.

U.S. Water Fitness Association. (2002). U.S. Water Fitness Association home page. Retrieved July 6, 2004 from Web site: www.uswfa.com/info_regarding_water_ex.htm.

YMCA of the USA. (1991). *YMCA national scuba leadership instructional manual.* Atlanta: YMCA of the USA.

YMCA of the USA. (1998). *Instructor manual for on the guard II.* Champaign, IL: Human Kinetics.

YMCA of the USA. (1999). *Teaching swimming fundamentals.* Champaign, IL: Human Kinetics.

RESOURCES

Resources for Lap Swimming Programs

Colwin, C. (2002). *Breakthrough swimming.* Champaign, IL: Human Kinetics.

Dean, P. (1998). *Open water swimming.* Champaign, IL: Human Kinetics.

Guzman, R. (1998). *Swimming drills for every stroke.* Champaign, IL: Human Kinetics.

Hines, E. (1999). *Fitness swimming.* Champaign, IL: Human Kinetics.

Thomas, D. (1990). *Advanced swimming: Steps to success.* Champaign, IL: Human Kinetics.

Swimmers World online magazine Web page: www.swimmersworld.com.

Swimming interest Web page: www.swimnews.com.

Resources for Swim Lessons

American Red Cross. (1996). *Swimming and diving.* St. Louis: Mosby Lifeline.

American Red Cross. (1996). *Water safety instructor manual.* St. Louis: Mosby Lifeline.

YMCA of the USA. (1999). *The parent/child and preschool aquatic program manual.* Champaign, IL: Human Kinetics.

YMCA of the USA. (1999). *Teaching swimming fundamentals.* Champaign, IL: Human Kinetics.

YMCA of the USA. (1999). *The youth and adult aquatics program manual.* Champaign, IL: Human Kinetics.

American Red Cross Web site: www.redcross.org/services/hss/aquatics

Recreonics, Inc. Web site: www.recreonics.com

Suspended Aquatic Mentor: www.aquamentor.com

YMCA Web site: www.ymca.net

Resources for Water Exercise

Case, L. (1997). *Fitness aquatics.* Champaign, IL: Human Kinetics.

Katz, J. (1995). *Water fitness during your pregnancy.* Champaign, IL: Human Kinetics.

Lee, T. (1995). *Water fun and fitness.* Champaign, IL: Human Kinetics.

Pappas Gaines, M. (1993). *Fantastic water workouts.* Champaign, IL: Human Kinetics.

Sova, R. (1995). *Water fitness after 40.* Champaign, IL: Human Kinetics.

White, M. (1995). *Water exercise.* Champaign, IL: Human Kinetics.

Arthritis Foundation Web site: www.arthritis.org.

The following resources are available from the United States Water Fitness Association. Contact them at 561-732-9908 or on the Web at www.uswfa.com for more information.

Lee, T. (1990). *Aquacises: Terri Lee's water workout book.* Lee Publishers.

McHale, G.A. (n.d.). *Deep water training and aerobics.*

Tarpinian, S., & Awbrey, B.J. (1997). *Water workouts.* New York: Lyons and Buford.

Resources for Competitive Swimming

American Sport Education Program. (1995). *Rookie coaches swimming guide.* Champaign, IL: Human Kinetics.

Guzman, R. (1998). *Swimming drills for every stroke.* Champaign, IL: Human Kinetics.

Hannula, D. (2003). *Coaching swimming successfully* (2nd ed.). Champaign, IL: Human Kinetics.

Troy, M. (2001). *The workout exchange book.* American Swim Coaches Association.

Resources for Scuba

Graver, D. (2003). *Scuba diving* (3rd ed.). Champaign, IL: Human Kinetics.

Pierce, A. (1985). *Scuba life saving.* Champaign, IL: Human Kinetics.

Divers Alert Network (DAN) Web site: www.diversalertnetwork.org.

National Association of Underwater Instructors Web site: www.naui.org.

YMCA of the USA Scuba Web site: www.ymcascuba.org.

Resources for Certification Courses

American Red Cross. (2001). *Guide for training American Red Cross lifeguarding instructors.* Boston: Staywell.

American Red Cross. (2001). *Lifeguard training.* Boston: Staywell.

YMCA of the USA. (2001). *On the guard II: The YMCA lifeguard manual* (4th ed.). Champaign, IL: Human Kinetics.

American Red Cross Web site: www.redcross.org/services/hss/aquatics

Ellis and Associates Lifeguard Training Web site: www.jellis.com.

United States Lifesaving Association Web site: www.usla.org/index.shtml.

YMCA Web site: www.ymca.net.

Resources for Diving

O'Brien, R. (1992). *Diving my way.* Champaign, IL: Human Kinetics.

O'Brien, R. (2003). *Spring board and platform diving* (2nd ed.). Champaign, IL: Human Kinetics.

Many publications and materials are available from USA Diving, including the USA Diving Rules and Regulations. Contact them at 317-237-5252 or on the Web at www.usdiving.org for more information.

Resources for Water Polo

USA Water Polo Association. (n.d.). *USWP level I coaching manual.*

USA Water Polo Association. (n.d.). *USWP rules of the United States Water Polo Association.*

USA Water Polo Association. (n.d.). *USWP U.S. Water Polo wet ball manual.*

USA Water Polo Association Web site: www.usawaterpolo.com.

Water polo interest Web page: www.h2opolo.com.

Resources for Lifeguard Competition

Competition planning manuals are available from Lifesaving Resources Inc. Contact them at 603-827-4139 or on the Web at www.lifesaving.com for more information.

A list of current lifeguard competitions is provided on the aquatic Web site www.aquaweb.org.

Resources for Synchronized Swimming

The following resources are available from United States Synchronized Swimming (USSS). For more information, contact them on the Web at www.usasynchro.org or write to them at this address: 201 S. Capitol Avenue, Suite 901, Indianapolis, IN 46225.

U.S. Synchronized Swimming. (n.d.). *Sport training manual for synchronized swimming.*

U.S. Synchronized Swimming. (n.d.). *USSS meet management guide.*

U.S. Synchronized Swimming. (n.d.). *USSS official rulebook.*

U.S. Synchronized Swimming. (1988). *Coaching synchronized swimming effectively.*

U.S. Synchronized Swimming. (1990). *Adapted programs handbook.*

U.S. Synchronized Swimming. (1993). *USSS risk management and loss prevention guide.*

Resources for Aquatic Safety

American Academy of Pediatrics water safety tips Web page: www.aap.org/family/tipwater.htm.

American Red Cross water safety tips Web page: www.redcross.org/services/hss/tips/healthtips/safetywater.html.

National Children's Center drowning prevention Web site: http://research.marshfieldclinic.org/children/Resources/Drowning/Strategies.html.

U.S. Army Corps of Engineers water safety Web site: http://watersafety.usace.army.mil.

Virginia Water Safety Coalition Web site: www.watersafety.org.

Managing Programs

Chapter Objectives

After reading this chapter, you should be able to

❶ develop program policies and explain the reasons for them,

❷ develop a program registration system,

❸ develop a plan to organize classes for optimal facility usage,

❹ develop a method to evaluate student progress, and

❺ create ideas for collaborative relationships with community groups.

Programs are the mainstay of many aquatic facilities. Your customers come to you to learn new and exciting skills, to become more fit, or to learn how to be safer around the water. As an instructor or aquatic programmer, few things are more exciting than seeing students learn a new skill. However, to make this happen, you must have policies and plans in place to effectively manage your aquatic programs. Your policies should cover circumstances and situations that are specific to your facility. They should be both reasonable and enforceable, and they should take into account the best interests of the facility and the patrons.

This chapter covers program policies, registration procedures and policies, and working with outside groups. You must develop effective policies for the sake of your staff and your patrons. If you don't, everyone is confused and no one is happy. This chapter helps you decide which policies may work at your facility and explains how to implement them.

The **Americans With Disabilities Act (ADA)** is also discussed in this chapter. This law may require you to make adjustments to your facilities and programs in order to accommodate persons with disabilities. Physical adjustments that you can make to your facility may include changes to locker rooms, entryways, and the aquatic facility itself. You can accommodate your patrons with disabilities by providing a range of options, from separate programs to program aides who provide individual assistance to these patrons. This chapter provides a list of potential accommodations that you can make as well as facility compliance methods you should review to ensure that you meet ADA standards.

DEVELOPING PROGRAM POLICIES

Your program policies serve as guidance for your staff on how to operate. It's best to compile all your program policies into a manual and give it to new employees when they are hired. You can then review the policies with the employees after they've had a chance to study them. Post your most commonly used policies, such as refund policies and policies on making up classes that are canceled due to weather, at the registration desk area so that your customers see them when they register. It is also a good idea to include a brief description of your most important policies in your registration materials. (See figure 2.1 for sample policies.)

KEY POINT *Clear, organized program policies are an important element in allowing your staff to effectively administer your programs.*

This section describes some of the policies you should develop for your facility, including policies regarding length of classes, number of classes per session, late registration, canceled classes, missed classes, and weather cancellations.

Length of Classes

The length of classes should depend on two main factors: the age of the participants and the type of activity. Here are some things to consider when setting the length of your classes:

- Preschool and beginning swimming classes should not be scheduled for longer than 30 minutes. Small children often have difficulty paying attention for any longer than 30 minutes. Also, young children often get cold if classes last any longer than this.

- Older children in swim lessons can participate for 45 minutes up to 1 hour if they are preteens.
- Older swimmers tend to have longer attention spans, and they can better adjust to the water temperature because their higher skill levels cause them to be more active.
- Water exercise classes should range from 45 minutes to 1 hour in length. Lesser time periods do not permit an adequate warm-up, main exercise period, and cool-down.

Schedule sport programs such as Masters swimming, synchronized swimming, and water polo for at least an hour of uninterrupted swim time in order to allow for physical conditioning and skill practice.

You may schedule upper-level certification classes, such as lifeguard training and swimming instructor classes, for several hours consecutively. It is not uncommon for these classes to be formatted for an entire weekend, although two or more long weekends may be required to meet the time requirements set forth by certifying agencies. If you schedule long instructional periods, remember that students will become tired. Be sure to include adequate rest breaks and meal times in your schedule, as well as at least 15 to 20 minutes for students to transition from pool to classroom (in classes such as lifeguard training and swimming instructor). If possible, schedule your classroom sessions first so that you will lose less instructional time during transition—transition time to the pool will be shorter than coming

The following includes a sample of policies you may want to include in your brochure:

Late registration: If space permits, registration is permitted in classes up to the second week of 10-week classes and up to the second day of 1-week classes. Late registrations must pay the full registration fee. Late registrations are not permitted for lifeguard training, scuba, CPR/first aid, or instructor courses due to certification requirements.

Refund policy: Full refunds are granted for cancellations made before the start of the first class. Refunds are prorated for withdrawals after the class start date.

Children in the locker room: Children aged 5 and over may not enter the locker room of the opposite sex.

Spectators during classes: Parents and spectators are not permitted on the pool deck during classes. You are welcome to view classes from the gallery or viewing rooms.

Returned checks: There is a $25 surcharge on all returned checks.

Early registration: Registration may only be made during the designated registration period.

Figure 2.1 Sample program policies.

from it because the students will not need to dry off or shower.

When selecting a time to offer a particular type of course, you should consider who the potential customers are and select a time most convenient for them. Table 2.1 shows a list of commonly offered programs and their recommended times.

It is also helpful to know what other activities are being offered in your community, such as youth sports, school activities, and church group activities. Knowing this information will enable you to take these activities into account and avoid potential time conflicts that may eliminate some of your customers.

Number of Classes per Session

The number of classes you schedule per session is often a function of the desire of the patrons. Some patrons want to have fewer classes in shorter sessions, such as a 5-week period. This is particularly popular for children's swim lessons during summer months when family vacations may interrupt longer sessions. You can condense summer classes into sessions as short as a week, offering programs such as water exercise and swim lessons daily during this period. This format permits visiting vacationers to participate and also allows for flexibility in the schedules of local customers.

Patrons tend to register for and attend programs more regularly in the winter months (as opposed to summer when vacations and outdoor activities often take their attention). During these winter periods, longer sessions with more infrequent classes may be more suitable for your customers. Seven- to 10-week sessions with swim lessons meeting only one or two times per week and water exercise classes meeting two or three times per week are commonly used formats.

The length of lifeguard training sessions is dependent on the time of year. Fall and winter lifeguarding sessions are traditionally longer, with classes meeting only once or twice a week. Spring and summer sessions tend to be compressed into weekend or weeklong formats, because students often need to complete their certification rapidly in order to secure summer jobs as lifeguards. Lifeguard training courses offered by the YMCA and the American Red Cross require approximately 30 clock hours, so consider these requirements when choosing a session format (American Red Cross, 2004; YMCA of the USA, 1998).

Late Registration

Ensure that your registration dates are included in all program materials, including posters, flyers, registration forms, and advertisements. Even if you do this, some patrons will undoubtedly want to register after the cutoff date. Although late registration is a service that patrons appreciate, it must be weighed against the administrative problems it can create.

Table 2.1 Commonly Offered Programs

Program	Recommended time
Competitive swimming (Masters, age group)	Early morning, evening, noon for Masters programs
Seniors program	Morning
Parent-tot program	Midmorning, midafternoon, Saturday mornings
Swim lessons	Afternoon, Saturday mornings, weekdays in the summer
Lifeguard training	Weekends, weekday evenings
Water polo/synchro	Later evenings
Water exercise	Noon hour, early evenings
Scuba	Later evenings
Lap swim	All day if possible, but definitely early morning, noon hour, and early evening
Diving	Afternoon/evening

Permitting late registration exposes you to a host of problems, such as when to stop taking registrations and whether patrons are permitted to register for classes already in session (if so, fees are prorated based on the number of classes actually attended). The number of instructors you will require for a given program is often based on student enrollment; late registrations may require adding instructors, which can create staffing problems. Decisions regarding whether to cancel classes or offer them may be based on class registration; late registrations may change this decision as well. When late registration is permitted, you may often find yourself asking the question, "Is this registration tally the one I can accurately base my decisions on?"

Late registration also disrupts the flow of a class. The instructor must incorporate the new students by providing them with an orientation, evaluating their skill level, and attempting to catch them up on missed work. The teacher's lesson plan is affected, and the other students lose the instructor's attention while a new student is assimilated. In any course, a dynamic is established between the teacher and the class, and each time a student is added, the dynamic changes, disrupting learning.

The simple solution regarding the problems associated with late registration is not to permit it. If you do allow late registration, you must allow it uniformly in all similar situations. You should assess a late registration fee to discourage patrons from repeatedly registering late. You must announce late registration fees in registration materials to eliminate misunderstandings.

For courses such as lifeguard training, scuba, and swimming instructor classes, do not permit registration after the classes have begun because the students may miss essential information. Having students join a class after it has begun also does not allow them to meet the required number of hours for certification as outlined by the certification agency.

Canceled Classes

Before canceling a class, you must first consider what effect such a decision might have. The decision to cancel a class is often based on insufficient revenue to meet program costs or failure to generate an acceptable profit. If this is the reason for canceling a class, then an alternative class projected to draw more registrants may be planned to take its place.

Other reasons for canceling a class include the inability to find a qualified instructor and insufficient facility availability. You should seek all possible solutions to these problems before canceling the course. (See "Deciding When to Drop a Program" in chapter 1 for further discussion on this topic.)

Missed Classes

Missed classes may occur for any number of reasons: illness on the part of the student or instructor, inclement weather, power outages, and many other reasons. Have a plan in place to deal with these cases. Any missed classes caused by the facility, such as one missed due to instructor illness, should either be made up or discounted from the customers' future registrations. A separate policy may be needed for cases such as student illness. You may want to set aside time in your pool's schedule for makeup classes to occur; any classes needing to do so could meet at that time and cover any remaining lessons to be made up.

Weather Cancellations

In the event of bad or threatening weather (such as snowstorms, flooding, hurricanes, or tornadoes), you should cancel classes for the safety of customers and staff. A good rule of thumb is to check with area schools, and if they cancel classes, you may also want to cancel sessions at your facility. Always close your facility when the National Weather Service issues warnings for severe weather that may threaten the safety of your customers.

Outdoor pools present a special challenge regarding weather cancellations. Swimmers should never be in the pool during severe weather. Lightning, thunder, fog, and even high winds may necessitate closing the facility or canceling classes. In general, if you can't see the bottom of the pool or you can't see one end of the pool while standing at the other end (due to fog, rain, or hail), swimmers should not be in the water. Also, swimmers should never be in the water during an electrical storm due to the risk of electrocution from a lightning strike. In the event of thunder, evacuate the pool until 15 minutes have passed since the last thunderclap, because thunder indicates the possibility of lightning.

Outdoor pool managers should constantly monitor the National Weather Service for severe weather warnings. Be sure to have an emergency evacuation and shelter plan in place for the sudden onset of severe weather.

When you do decide to cancel classes or close the facility due to weather, contact area radio stations so that your information can be added to the list of canceled activities. You should also have your staff contact the students in the canceled classes to inform them. Don't forget to contact any staff members who may be affected and tell them not to report for work. If the weather is too dangerous for the staff on duty to leave, you may want to recommend that they stay until conditions improve.

ACCOMMODATING CHILDREN IN LOCKER ROOMS

Children's swim lessons present the challenge of providing proper dressing areas for young children. Often, an opposite sex parent brings a child to class, so he or she must dress the child in a locker room with other children of the opposite sex. At what point is this not acceptable? At age five, most children have begun to understand sex differences, so they should not be permitted in the opposite sex locker room after that age. Allowing the child in the locker room may make other adult patrons uncomfortable and is inappropriate for the child. However, you must still provide an acceptable alternative area for children who are too old to be in the opposite sex locker room but too young to dress themselves on their own.

One way you can accommodate these families is to provide family or assist locker rooms. A well-designed family or assist locker area consists of a series of large stalls in a common enclosed hallway with floor to ceiling partitions (see figure 2.2). The hallway leads to activity areas. If you can provide lavatories in these stalls, it will eliminate the need for parents to enter opposite sex lavatories as well. The stalls contain benches and a few lockers for storage of personal belongings.

If a family or assist locker area is unavailable, consider providing a rest room or other suitable room. Carefully consider how to balance the needs of the children against the needs of your other patrons.

PROGRAMS FOR PEOPLE WITH DISABILITIES

The Americans With Disabilities Act of 1990 requires that reasonable accommodations be made to allow accessibility to all facilities and programs for those with disabilities. This includes making modifications to registration areas to permit ease of use for patrons in wheelchairs, providing TTY phones for people who are hearing impaired, and making allowances for people who are visually impaired, such as providing large-print forms and braille materials.

> **KEY POINT** *The Americans With Disabilities Act requires that you make modifications to your facilities and programs to accommodate persons with disabilities.*

Facility Accommodations

The facility itself must be accessible from the main entrance through to the pool deck. You should equip the main entrance with an automatic door that is triggered by a large button or sensor from both inside and outside the building. Your patrons with mobility impairments must be able to easily open interior doors; replacing doorknobs with handles makes this much easier for them to do. Your changing areas should offer reduced size lockers with hasps and hooks set lower to the ground so that patrons in wheelchairs can access them. Equip lavatories with stall doors that swing out, grab rails, and sufficient space (depth) to accommodate a wheelchair. Situate drinking fountains at a lower level and choose fountains that have trigger mechanisms, such as bars instead of buttons, for those with motor impairments. Several of the suppliers listed in appendix C, including Lincoln Commercial Pool Equipment and WMS Aquatic Specialists, can provide this equipment. You may want to install a family or assist locker room (as described previously) to provide privacy for people with disabilities as they change, especially if they need assistance from someone of the opposite sex.

Water temperature for people with disabilities, particularly those with poor mobility, may need to be several degrees warmer than the temperature for lap swimming. Air temperature should also be several degrees warmer, because your clients with disabilities may not be as active as others (depending on impairment) and therefore may not be able to generate as much body heat.

Equip the pool with either a ramp or a lift to permit access by patrons in wheelchairs (see figures 2.3 and 2.4). Preferably, the lift will be removable to permit swim meets and lap swimming without the risk of swimmers striking the lift. You must ensure that your staff is properly trained in how to install and operate any lifts that your facility owns. You should also train your staff in safe manual lifting techniques in case your lifts become inoperable or if your facility does not own a lift or ramp.

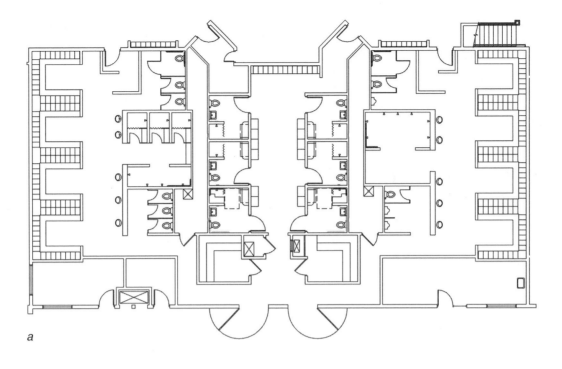

a

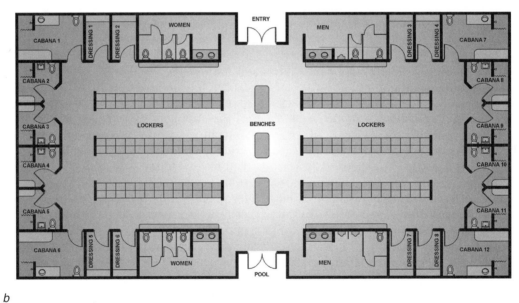

b

Figure 2.2   Locker room design: *(a)* The floor plan of an existing family locker room at a recreation center; *(b)* a sample conceptual design using the same space and entry points but with more changing rooms and a co-ed locker area.

Reprinted, by permission, from Athletic Business.

Instructional Modifications

You'll also need to consider the unique program needs of your patrons with disabilities. Some individuals may require extensive assistance with dressing and showering to the point that one-on-one care may be needed. In some instances, your patrons may have a spouse, parent, or caregiver that can provide this assistance. In other cases where your swimmers come from a group home or institution, they may not have someone to assist them. You should carefully consider how to handle this sensitive situation. If you elect to provide one-on-one assistance, it will significantly add to your

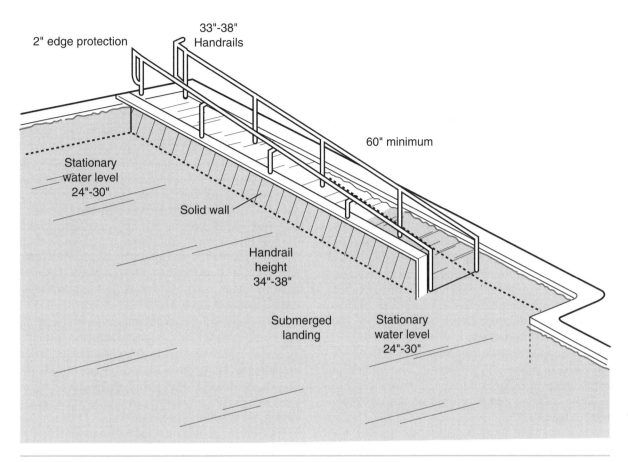

2" edge protection

33"-38" Handrails

60" minimum

Stationary water level 24"-30"

Solid wall

Handrail height 34"-38"

Submerged landing

Stationary water level 24"-30"

Figure 2.3 A diagram of a pool ramp.

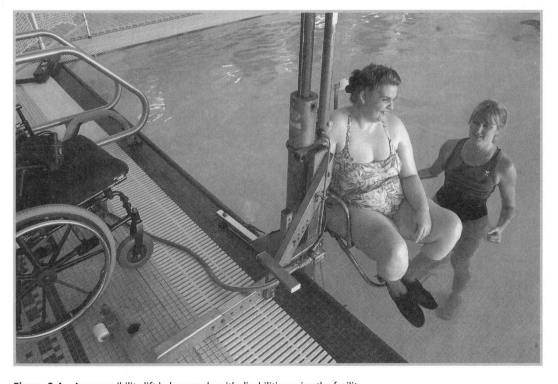

Figure 2.4 An accessibility lift helps people with disabilities enjoy the facility.

personnel needs. You must also carefully screen those who perform this task. The patrons they assist may be adults physically but may not have an adult mental capacity. You must also consider what to do if you have an unequal gender balance—it's not common to let adult males assist in dressing adult females, but will you allow adult females to help dress adult males? If you permit this, you may need to make special accommodations in your locker areas to allow females in the male locker room. Be sure to provide instruction and preparation for staff members who undertake this duty. Topics you should cover include preserving patron dignity, adjusting water temperature for showers, applying body braces, and isolating body substances during toilet procedures. Although college level adapted aquatics courses are often the best place for you or your staff to gain this in-depth knowledge, the YMCA of the USA **Special Populations** Instructor course and the American Red Cross Adapted Aquatics course also provide training in this area. (The American Red Cross program is no longer administered at the national level and is offered on a chapter by chapter basis.)

When making programming decisions for people with disabilities, you must determine (much as you do for other groups) the goal of the program. Some groups may need swimming instruction; other groups may already know how to swim and may want fitness training. Other patrons with severe mobility impairments may be unable to swim but may want a therapeutic program to improve range of motion at the joints. Gather information from the patrons themselves or their caregivers to help you determine the best programs to suit their needs.

Staffing for Special Programs

The two main staffing issues that you may face regarding people with disabilities are the need for additional staff and the need for specialized training. Due to the particular needs of people with disabilities, you often must add additional instructors. For safety reasons, students with mobility impairments may need individual attention from an instructor. Students who have full mobility but cognitive impairments may be able to receive group instruction. Some people with disabilities require no changes to your traditional staffing plan. You must assess each group based on its particular needs.

Preferably, the instructors who teach in your programs for people with disabilities will be certified to teach such patrons, in addition to having lifeguard training, CPR for the professional rescuer, and first aid certification. The YMCA of the USA offers certification in this area.

The labor intensiveness of one-on-one instruction can be offset by the use of volunteers. While your lifeguards, program directors, and some instructors are likely to be paid and certified staff, volunteers can fill the gaps. Volunteers can assist with tasks such as changing and showering patrons, lifting patrons into the pool, and providing shallow water assistance to patrons while the program director is with another student. You should never allow untrained volunteers to assume primary duties such as lifeguarding or program supervisor.

One source of potential volunteers is area universities. Contact the special education, physical education, and recreation departments and try to establish working relationships. Some instructors may be willing to offer course credits or bonus points to students who provide verification of having worked in your program.

It's best to provide an orientation session for new volunteers before allowing them to work in your program. During this orientation, you can explain the purpose of your program and what roles you expect volunteers to fill. Be sure to include basic information such as the days and times of the program, appropriate clothing for volunteers to wear, and when to show up. Provide a tour of the facility and demonstrate equipment that the volunteers may work around or operate (such as lifts or ramps). Ask volunteers to fill out a brief questionnaire that provides basic information about them. Retain these forms for your files. (See appendix D for a sample volunteer questionnaire.) Giving your volunteers a certificate of recognition at the conclusion of the program is appropriate and fitting.

Modifying individual programs to meet ADA specifications requires forethought and ingenuity on the part of both the instructor and programmer. In some cases, modifications can be as simple as providing additional flotation devices for students with mobility impairment. In other cases, students with multiple impairments may require an individual aide. You must speak with the participants or their guardians to determine where on the spectrum of needs they are. Most individuals want to be in the least restrictive environment possible; do your best to accommodate their wishes.

ORGANIZING PROGRAM REGISTRATION

Your registration process is a key component to ensuring that your programs go well. Take time to prepare your staff, develop functional registration forms, and organize your registration area. By organizing and controlling registration, you help ensure that the right students and the right number of students are registered for the correct classes. You also make the process more efficient and less confusing for your customers, which makes their repeat business more likely. Topics discussed in this section include when to do program registration, where to hold registration, how to prepare your staff for registration, how to develop registration forms, online registration, and how to determine participants' skill level.

> **KEY POINT** *Preparing a well-organized and smoothly operating registration process makes it easier to administer your programs and also ensures a better experience for your customers.*

When to Register

Schedule program registration to allow enough time for customers to register. Registration periods of 1 to 2 weeks are usually appropriate; however, you may make this period as long as you feel is necessary. Your registration time should begin 2 to 3 weeks in advance of the program start date and should end at least 2 days before the program begins. This 2-day cushion allows you to evaluate your final numbers and determine if you need to add more instructors or classes or if you should consider canceling any classes.

Some program managers like to offer "open registration" for classes, meaning patrons can register and join a class any time it is in session, often with fees prorated appropriately. This is very convenient for customers because there is no disappointment at missing a registration deadline. However, this registration method makes it difficult to plan for enough instructors and to get a firm number of students registered for a given class. You should not use this method for certification classes such as lifeguard training, but it may be appropriate for classes such as water exercise where missing introductory classes may not be

as crucial (particularly if the customer has been in the class before). This repeat customer will not require the initial instructions regarding class organization and how to perform the exercises.

Where to Register

Hold registration in a large open area with access to writing surfaces, tables, chairs, a cash register or cash box, and a computer if one is used for registration (see figure 2.5). Although many facilities have a front desk where customers are usually received, you may want to consider moving registration to a multipurpose room that provides additional space. You can organize tables, chairs, registration forms, and pens to accommodate the large numbers of people you may see during a registration "rush." By using tables and chairs, you provide a comfortable area for your customers to sit and complete the forms, rather than expecting them to stand at the front desk. Posting signs at the entrance to the registration area also assists the customers in understanding the process. This can help streamline the process, taking less time out of your customers' day for registration.

Be sure to provide greeters to assist your patrons through the process. The greeters can help customers complete forms, answer their questions about classes, and direct them to the next step in the process. Station cashiers at a front table to take payments and verify enrollment. If your registration generates a large amount of cash, you may want to arrange for a regular drop into your facility safe to eliminate the possibility of theft or other loss. Scheduling multiple cashiers will also eliminate a bottleneck for your customers when they are ready to complete the registration process.

Preparing Your Staff

At many aquatic facilities, customer service staff (rather than instructional staff) take registrations. Many of these customer service staff members know only a few details about the programs they sign the customers up for. Take time to familiarize your customer service staff with your programs so that they can answer questions fully and in an informed manner. You may even want to schedule times for them to observe your most popular programs so that they have a better idea of how these programs work. Ensure that your customer service staff members have read all your promotional materials and that they have at least a basic understanding of all your programs. They

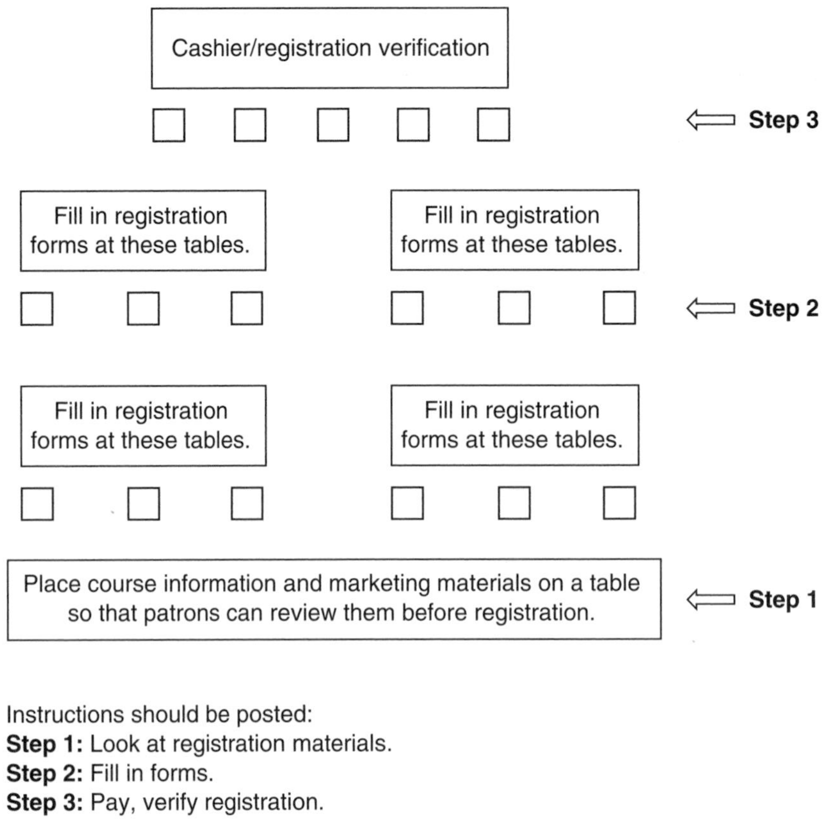

Instructions should be posted:
Step 1: Look at registration materials.
Step 2: Fill in forms.
Step 3: Pay, verify registration.

Figure 2.5   A sample layout for a program registration area.

must also understand all of your registration policies, such as refunds, class cancellations, and discounts.

One way to ensure that all staff members are well versed in registration procedures—including cash handling and the use of computer registration procedures—is to provide them with a "break-in" period when they begin working as customer service staff. During this time, they work with an experienced staff member, gradually learning policies and procedures and assuming greater responsibilities as they learn until they are qualified to work on their own. This process will result in an employee who is fully trained and indoctrinated in your method of doing business.

To help your staff retain this knowledge, meet with them prior to registration periods to review policies and explain new ones. During this staff meeting, review registration procedures, including the proper way to complete forms or to register using the computer. Be sure to provide your staff with samples of all your promotional materials to review. Also give your staff a contact list of employees they can call if a patron has a specific question about a program. This will eliminate the possibility of any false information mistakenly being given out.

A method that you can use to assist customer service staff during very busy registration periods is to ask instructors to be present to help customers with forms and course selection and to answer any questions about specific programs. If you use this method, be sure to provide guidance to your instructors regarding registration procedures.

Registration Forms

Ideally, you will be able to create one registration form that can be used to register patrons for any of the classes your facility offers. This form should contain space for the patron to specify her name, address, day and evening telephone number, and the name and age of the person taking the course (if not the patron). This information is important if you need to contact the customer in the event a class is canceled or the location or time must be changed.

The next section of the form should allow the customer to specify the class, including days and times, that she wants to register for. If your facility offers multiple sessions of one class on different days and at different times, ensure that all this information is captured on the registration form so that the patron is registered for the correct class.

You should consider including a tear-away section at the bottom of the registration form. Patrons can take this part of the form with them to remind them what classes they signed up for, including the start dates, times, and locations. This helps eliminate confusion regarding where and when your customers' classes begin. (See appendix D for a sample registration form.)

Many facilities use computer-based registration procedures, which eliminate the need for paper forms. However, computers can slow down the process because usually only one or two registrants can be serviced at a time, depending on the number of terminals available. Registration for new customers can also be time consuming because all their information must be added to the database while they wait. To eliminate this waiting period, you may want to use paper forms in addition to the computer. This would allow you to complete the registration process for the patron and then add her information to the database later, so the customer is not forced to wait. This also creates a hard copy backup in case the registration system crashes.

Online Registration

Internet-based or online registration enables the customers to easily and conveniently register from their home or office without ever having to come to your facility. It eliminates standing in line and enables customers to see what classes are available before attempting registration. You can design the Web site to accept payment by credit card. You should begin your Internet-based registration and paper sign-ups on the same day to be fair to all parties. Be sure to record all registrations in the same database to avoid overbooking any classes.

When initially instituting your Web-based registration system, it is helpful to produce brief announcements and easy-to-follow directions to distribute to your patrons. This serves two purposes: It alerts your customers to this new service that you are offering, and it explains how to utilize it. After this initial period, you should include information about online registration in all the registration brochures, flyers, and booklets that you distribute. Your registration program should be easily accessible from your main Web page.

Your Web-based registration program should be easy to navigate and should contain class dates, times, locations, descriptions of classes, and links to any policies that you want patrons to see. The information that you collect from patrons in your Web-based registrations should mirror that collected in your paper ones. Your Web site should prompt the patrons to print a copy of the registration confirmation for their records.

Determining Participants' Skill Level

Aquatics classes require the instructor to determine the students' skill level in order to make sure they are in the correct class. In most cases, it's not possible to skill test everyone prior to the start of class to determine if they are registering for the correct class. However, to simplify this process, you can create a basic scale for adult classes that is applied to each class. This scale would include the designations of beginning, intermediate, and advanced skill. Each adult class you offer would be rated according to this scale (e.g., this class requires advanced swimming skill). In your registration materials, you would specify what skills a person with beginning, intermediate, or advanced skills should have (see figure 2.6). The customers can compare their skills to the description and determine if they are suited for the class. The description for beginning swimming classes should include the phrase, "no swimming ability required."

One way to simplify the skill level determination process for swim lesson programs is to ask students to identify previous classes they have taken and to indicate if the classes were successfully completed. This enables registration personnel to more easily determine the next class a student should be in. You should also include information in your printed materials regarding what prerequisite skills or classes are required to register for a particular program.

Children's classes create more of a challenge because the parents register them and are often not quite sure of their children's abilities. In this case, your registration materials should provide a brief description of the skills covered in each course and allow the parents to guesstimate where their children should be placed.

The first event in any children's swimming class should be a skills evaluation. Any children not in the correct class should be moved to the correct one. In many cases, multiple levels of lessons are

Skill Levels

No skill level required: Used for beginning swimming classes where the aim is to learn to swim.

Basic swimming skills: Must be comfortable standing in shallow water, must be able to hold breath and submerge, must be able to regain footing from a floating position. Used for shallow water exercise classes where no deep end skills are conducted.

Intermediate swimming skills: Must be able to swim on front and back, must be able to complete a minimum of 100 yards swimming without stopping. This level of skill is usually used for deep water exercise, diving classes, boating classes, and some swimming classes.

Advanced swimming skills: Must be able to swim 500 yards without stopping. Must be able to demonstrate freestyle, backstroke, breaststroke, and sidestroke. Must be able to tread water for 2 minutes and dive to a 9-foot depth to retrieve an object. This level of skill is usually required for lifeguard training and scuba.

Figure 2.6   Sample categories for assessing swimmer skill levels.

in the pool at the same time, and this process is simply a matter of walking the child to a new class. Be sure to let the parent know the reason for the move and the correct level for the child.

ORGANIZING CLASSES

Organizing classes requires some behind-the-scenes preparation to ensure that the correct number of students and instructors have the correct amount of pool space available at the correct time. This section deals with the topics of monitoring class registrations, instructor-to-student ratios, using pool space efficiently, maximizing pool space, and maximizing use of time.

> **KEY POINT**   *Organizing classes effectively is an important factor in ensuring that your classes are the correct size and have sufficient space to operate and the correct number of instructors.*

Monitoring Class Registrations

Monitor class registrations as they come in so that you can make adjustments in response to enrollment. Some classes may have a maximum enrollment limit. These numbers are often set by national agencies. For instance, scuba instructors are often limited to 20 students or less per class, unless they have an assistant instructor. Beginning swimming lessons for children may have a recommended ratio of only 5 students to every instructor. By monitoring your registration, you can determine when you are approaching maxi-

mum enrollment, and you can take action before any patrons are turned away. You may want to add additional sections of your most popular classes or add additional instructors to enable expansion of the classes you do have.

Likewise, if you determine that registration is low for a particular course, you may be able to take early steps to remedy this. You may want to contact patrons who have previously been in the class to inform them it is being offered again. A short-term publicity campaign may also boost enrollment in a course. If you continually monitor registration, you can react early.

Instructor-to-Student Ratios

Many national aquatic agencies specify instructor-to-student ratios for their courses. A good rule of thumb to consider is this: The younger your students are, the lower your ratios should be. However, you must also take into account the maturity and swimming ability of your students.

Prevent overregistration for a class by setting a maximum number of students for every class. When the maximum number is reached, create a second section of the class and roll any additional registrants into that section. If you cannot create a second section because you do not have enough staff or facility space, place any interested customers on a waiting list. If any customers from the class drop out or cancel their registration, you can fill their spot with someone from the waiting list.

Ratios of instructors to students can be increased through the use of instructional aides. Aides do not take the place of trained instructors and cannot teach classes of their own. They assist a certified instructor with demonstrations, clerical tasks, supervision, and organization. Aides can be used in any type of program, including scuba, swimming lessons, lifeguard training, and water exercise. Some types of programs, such as water safety and scuba, have formalized training programs for aides; other types, such as water exercise, do not.

Do not allow the instructor-to-student ratio to exceed that recommended by national agencies. To do so jeopardizes the safety of the student and places the facility on a legally dangerous footing.

Using Pool Space Efficiently

An empty pool generates no revenue for your facility, and an underutilized pool generates only a part of the profits it is capable of generating. Maximizing the use of pool space and time available helps you maximize your profits and the services you provide for your customers.

Maximizing Space

Whenever possible, try to combine activities in the pool to avoid any unused space. Carefully consider which activities to schedule together. Combine activities that will not conflict with each other in terms of noise interference or competition for equipment or supplies. Examples of programs that can share pool space well include the following:

- ▶ Children's swim lessons at the shallow end and deep water running at the deep end
- ▶ Lap swim and Masters swimming, using lanes on opposite sides of the pool
- ▶ Diving practice at the deep end and water exercise at the shallow end
- ▶ Swimming instructor class and children's swim lessons

When scheduling children's swim lessons, include a variety of skill levels during each hour of class. Beginning classes can use the shallow end, intermediate classes can use the middle area of the pool, and advanced classes can use the deep end or diving well. You may be able to schedule several sections of a class in the pool at one time, depending on the size of your pool. Diagram your pool and place classes on the diagram where they would actually be in the pool (see figure 2.7). This will help you determine how many classes you can schedule per hour. Be sure to take into account the amount and type of space each class will need.

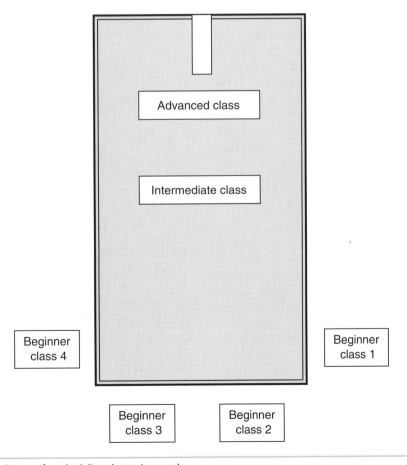

Figure 2.7 A sample diagram for scheduling classes in a pool.

Maximizing Time

You should avoid having "dead time" in your facility. Dead time refers to periods when the pool is not in use. When the pool is not in use, your patrons are not receiving services and your facility is losing money because you are heating and lighting an empty pool. Schedule classes reasonably close together. A brief period between classes is normally needed to allow time for one class to exit the pool before another begins. Usually 10 to 15 minutes is sufficient for this to occur. Classes for students with physical impairments may require additional time for the students to exit and enter the pool, requiring a longer period between classes.

During periods when you are not offering programs in your facility, you can schedule recreational swims or lap swims in your facility. You may still generate revenue from daily use passes as well as satisfy your members' need and desire for free recreational time.

ORIENTATION

Orientation sessions usually take place before the actual class starts. These sessions give participants an indication of what types of activities the class will include. Children's swim programs often offer orientations for parents in order to explain policies regarding locker rooms, pickup and drop-off of children, safety rules, and diapers for infants. Additional information that may be included in an orientation session includes what the program will teach, what the child should bring to class, and registration policies. A facility tour that includes the locker rooms is helpful. Be sure to introduce your staff, including the aquatic director; parents want to know who is teaching their children.

Scuba courses and lifeguard training courses are the other programs most likely to offer orientation sessions. Both of these programs include a precourse swim test to ensure that the students possess the proper skill level to be in the class. Other information covered in these orientations may include required textbooks and supplies, attendance policies, and required test scores for completion of the certification.

FIRST DAY ORGANIZATION

The first day of any aquatics class is an exciting time for both students and instructors. Both are often excited and anxious to meet each other. The first day can also be a confusing time for students who may be new to the facility and the activity.

Be sure to tell your instructional and customer service staff to be on the alert for new participants and to guide them to the locker and changing areas. Also make sure that the routes to the changing areas and pool are clearly marked with appropriate signs.

When your students arrive on the pool deck, a supervisor or instructor should greet them, and one or more lifeguards should be on duty. Students will often want to verify that they are in the correct location for their class; the supervisor can answer any questions they may have. Never leave students unattended on the deck because they may enter the pool and become injured or drown.

Once the supervisor or instructor greets the students, he should direct the students to be seated on bleachers or benches in the pool area to wait for their instructor. The instructors should always have the most up-to-date class roster possible when their class begins. The class instructor should call the roll and redirect any students in the wrong location or class. Once each instructor has confirmed his class, he should review swimming pool rules and, if needed, give students a brief tour of the pool, pointing out deep and shallow areas, rest rooms, emergency exits, ladders, and other features.

During the first day of a program, particularly a children's program, students are often evaluated to determine their skill level. It's not uncommon to discover that students are not registered for the correct class and need to be shifted to a higher or lower skill level. Try to be as flexible as possible in accommodating your students. Whenever possible, you should move the student to the correct skill level as rapidly as you can. This is easiest in children's programs where several skill levels are often in the pool together.

Children's swimming lessons add the dimension of parents' involvement. On the first day, your supervisor should address the parents regarding pickup of their children and should tell the parents where they may wait for and watch their children. Many facilities ask parents not to remain on deck during swimming lessons because they think the children will give more attention to the instructor if the parents are not present. If this is the case at your facility, you must explain this to the parents and provide a reasonable alternative such as a viewing room or bleacher area where they can wait.

One method of organizing sessions where a large number of children will be on deck for classes is to place symbols or shapes made from laminated colored poster board at the sites on the deck where instructors will meet their students. Using this method allows students to remember where their class will be by remembering the shape or symbol. To find their instructor on the first day, they need only go to the shape or symbol.

During very busy first days, such as the first day of children's swim lessons when multiple classes and instructors are present, the staff and supervisor should meet 15 minutes before lessons begin. This allows the supervisor to distribute class rosters, check that enough instructors are present, and answer any last minute questions from staff.

SUPERVISING INSTRUCTION

Supervising your staff during classes serves several purposes, including

- helping to ensure the safety of the students in the class,
- providing a form of quality control over instruction, and
- giving the aquatic manager a true picture of what is happening in the program.

When the pool is particularly busy with multiple classes going on at one time, a supervisor should be on deck to coordinate activities. This supervisor should be a senior instructor who has no direct teaching responsibilities. The supervisor's job is to ensure that lifeguards are on duty and are supervising classes, to answer questions from patrons and parents, to handle complaints, to direct latecomers to the correct class, and to deal with personnel issues such as staff members who are late or who fail to show up. The supervisor can also distribute customer evaluations of the program and program-related information, as well as evaluate the instructors' quality of teaching.

In situations where a small number of students in one program use the pool by themselves, it is not cost efficient to provide a supervisor in addition to the instructor and the lifeguard. In this case, you or another supervisor may make periodic visits to the pool. During these visits, you can observe the instructor's teaching and assist with any problems that may arise. Try to make instructors feel as if you are there to help them, not "check up" on them. If you catch your staff doing a good job, tell them so. Praise your staff in public, and discipline them in private. After the class, if circumstances and time permit, talk to the instructor briefly about the things that you liked or

suggestions you may have. If you have a concern, take your discussion to a private location.

Be sure to inform your staff that you will randomly visit while they teach. You should also provide them with a method of contacting a supervisor immediately if a problem arises. Problems may not be limited to emergencies and may also include complaints and personnel issues. Your staff should be able to get assistance from a supervisor in any of these situations.

EVALUATING STUDENTS' PROGRESS

Programs that are skill based and not recreational or exercise oriented may require you to evaluate each student's performance. The evaluation may be needed to determine if a student will receive a certification or to determine what class the student should register for in the future. Usually, evaluations are given out at the end of the program. For older students in classes such as lifeguard training or scuba, you may want to have the instructor talk one-on-one with each student when giving the evaluation. This allows the students to ask any questions and helps ensure that they have been evaluated fairly. For children's classes, evaluations are often in the form of "report cards" that are given to parents. (See appendix D for a sample student progress report form.) Individual meetings are usually not held for children's classes.

The instructors should always try to be positive when evaluating students. If a one-on-one meeting is held, they should begin and end by telling the student what she did well. Between the positive things, instructors should explain what areas need improvement and provide specific suggestions for how to improve. Instructors should be sure to perform verbal evaluations in private because students may not want others to overhear. Instructors should always be sensitive to the students' feelings when performing evaluations and should try to leave them feeling positive about their experience, even if much improvement is needed.

Written evaluations should include positive comments only. Focus on those things the students did well and provide specific feedback about areas they need improvement in. Written evaluations are often given out at the same time as course completion certificates. Children love to receive these certificates. To avoid disappointing any children in your program, you may want to consider giving "has participated" certificates to children who are not advanced to the next level.

Instructors should evaluate students throughout their program by observing student skills and comparing them against standards established for the completion of that course level. Conducting evaluations on a single day can produce test anxiety and place a lot of stress on both the student and the instructor. Single-day evaluations also fail to account for the fact that students may not be feeling well when they are evaluated or may simply be having a bad day.

In certification courses such as lifeguard training and scuba, instructors should tell students at the beginning of the class what is required to earn certification. This information should include attendance policies, required test scores, and the skills that must be completed by the end of the course. If you determine that students have not completed all the requirements to receive their certification, be sure to tell them what options are available to them. These options may include retaking written tests, attending study sessions, retaking practical skills tests, or taking the entire course again.

COLLECTING PROGRAM STATISTICS

You should collect several types of statistics related to your programs, including the number of students participating in a particular type of class or program each session, the amount of revenue generated during a given session, the amount of staff during a session, and the amount of money spent on advertising during a session. Compile your statistics by using data from class lists, registration databases, and revenue and expense reports from your business offices. It's often helpful to create a spreadsheet to assist in recording your data. Record data for each program session you offer. Once you've collected data for several sessions, you can create a chart to compare the sessions (see figure 2.8).

Viewing the chart will tell you whether a program is gaining or losing enrollment and revenue over time. By comparing your advertising expenses to your revenue, you can determine whether your advertising is effective—that is, whether you see an increase in enrollment related to an increase in advertising.

Statistics can assist you in planning when classes should be offered during the year by showing when enrollment has been highest in the past. Statistics can also help you recognize a problem with a program by indicating a steady

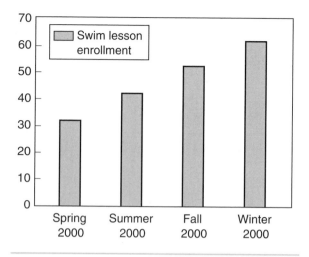

Figure 2.8 A sample statistical comparison chart.

decline in registration. An increase in revenue shown by statistics may indicate that you should offer additional sections of that class. However, statistics are only indicators; they never tell the full facts of any program. If you believe you see a trend (either positive or negative) that may affect a programming decision, be sure to talk with program staff and patrons before making a decision. Statistics may not be providing a clear indication of all the facts.

WORKING WITH OUTSIDE GROUPS

Providing facility space or services to outside groups can be a tremendous source of added income for your facility. You may rent your facility on a one-time basis for activities such as birthday parties, parties after proms or graduations, and youth group parties. Renting on a recurring basis for Boy and Girl Scout merit badge testing and training, or for school physical education swimming classes, also provides an alternative source of revenue.

Rental Agreements

When an outside group wants to rent an aquatic facility, they should first be given a standard rental agreement form. The rental agreement form should include a fee schedule and information about the group renting the pool. Information you will need includes the following:

▸ Group name

▸ Name of the group leader and contact information

- Number of swimmers attending
- Number of chaperones or leaders attending
- Age range of the group
- The purpose for which the group wants to use the pool

The rental agreement should also contain a full list of policies and pool rules that may affect your rental groups. This list may include such things as rules regarding acceptable swimwear, leader-to-swimmer ratios, and pool safety rules. You may want to have a section on the rental form that the group leader must sign to indicate that he has read and agrees to abide by the pool rules. See appendix D for a sample facility rental form and agreement.

Safety for Outside Groups

Ensuring the safety of outside groups visiting your facility is a greater concern than for groups of regular patrons. The outside groups may not have visited your facility before and may not be familiar with your pool, policies, and staff. To alleviate some of the risks associated with visiting groups, one of your staff members should meet them as they enter the building and confirm that they are at the correct place and time for their reservation. Your staff member can then escort the group to an area where she can give the group an explanation of facility policies and features and tell them where to leave their possessions. When the group enters the pool area, they should be met at the doors by a lifeguard supervisor who directs them to be seated on benches or bleachers. When the entire group is present, the supervisor can deliver a safety briefing, explaining pool rules and pointing out features of the pool such as deep end and shallow end areas. This briefing should be short and age appropriate. Aquatic staff should also take this opportunity to ensure that the group has the appropriate number of leaders or chaperones present (as specified in their rental agreement). If they do not, the group should remain on deck until the required number of leaders is present.

Always provide lifeguards in your facility. Do not allow the rental group to bring their own guards in place of facility staff. There are several reasons for this. First, you may be unable to verify the qualifications of the guards they bring and will be unsure if they are properly trained. Additionally, the guards that outside groups supply are not trained in your facility emergency procedures, and they will be unaware of such details as the location of your telephone and first aid kit or how to activate your emergency action plan. In your rental agreement, factor in the cost of a minimum of two lifeguards, and specify at what number of swimmers extra staff will be added and what the cost per hour will be. If the rental group will be using the facility after hours, you should also factor in costs for a facility supervisor and a swimming pool custodian. The supervisor will provide support in supervising the group when they are not in the pool area. The custodian will be needed to clean the pool and locker areas after the group leaves to ensure that these areas are ready for use the next day.

OUTSIDE AGENCY COLLABORATIONS

Your swimming pool can be a focal point for community organizations and activities if you think creatively. Organizations such as schools, churches, child care centers, senior citizens centers, youth groups, police and fire departments, and businesses may be interested in partnering with your facility. The range of partnership options includes swimming instruction, water rescue training, pool parties, fitness instruction, and as many other options as you can imagine. This section discusses suggestions and program ideas for cooperative agreements with outside agencies, as well as the need for written agreements with partnering agencies.

Why Collaborate?

You want your facility to appeal to the widest range of people possible. Partnering with outside groups draws new people and activities to your pool and helps achieve that goal. In some cases, such as partnering with school groups, you may be providing an important service (e.g., swimming instruction) while generating revenue for your facility. You may also be helping to create a new generation of swimmers, which can benefit you in the future.

You may sometimes collaborate with an outside group for no profit. For example, you may provide pool space and staff support free of charge for a swim-a-thon to raise money for a charitable cause. You should do these things because it's a public service but also because it reflects positively on your facility.

Generation of revenue through the rental fees associated with outside group collaboration is also an important consideration. These external group participants may also enjoy the facility so much that they decide to purchase a membership or register for other programs that you offer.

> **KEY POINT** *Collaboration with a number of community groups strengthens your facility's community ties, diversifies your programs, and provides new sources of potential customers.*

Examples of Possible Collaborations

The possibilities for partnering arrangements are limitless. When considering what groups you may develop agreements with, think of active groups in your community and create activities that you may cooperate on. You may want to begin with your telephone book for some ideas. The following list provides some possibilities.

Schools

Many schools, from elementary through high school, provide end-of-the-year activities for their students. These activities may be rewards for perfect attendance or high grade point averages, or they may simply be end-of-the-year farewells. Consider offering a package deal for schools to bring their groups to your facility. You may provide free swim options, supervision, and space for lunch or other activities. These programs are most popular during April through June.

In a similar vein, many high schools provide after prom or after graduation activities for their senior classes to reduce the risk of alcohol-related accidents. You can provide an opportunity for these groups to use your facility during off-peak hours, because after prom or graduation activities normally take place through the late night hours. Much logistical coordination is required for this to work; be sure to coordinate closely with the school sponsors regarding details such as number of participants, security requirements, food, chaperones, and types of activities desired. (See "After Prom or After Graduation Parties" in chapter 1.)

Churches

Youth groups associated with churches are often looking for a place to have some fun where the participants can be easily supervised. These groups may want to rent the entire pool for several hours or may want to have access during your open swim time. Be prepared for requests for a change in your swimming attire regulations. Many religious groups do not consider current swimsuits modest enough and may want their youth to be permitted to swim with T-shirts over their swimsuits.

Boy Scout and Girl Scout Troops

Merit badges are the major concern of most scout troops seeking your cooperation. Merit badges that troops may need assistance with include swimming, lifesaving, lifeguard training, first aid, and boating. In this case, the troops may not only need the use of your facility but also the expertise of your staff. You may want to contact the local Boy Scout and Girl Scout councils and explore having your key aquatic staff members designated as merit badge instructors for aquatics. You may then be able to provide a regional service for an entire council as a specialist in aquatics. This is an area of expertise that scouting troops often lack. The regional council may direct troops seeking instruction in this area to your facility.

Police and Fire Departments

Some police and fire departments require their officers to have basic water rescue training so that they are able to perform nonswimming reaching and throwing rescues from land or in shallow water. Many public safety agencies prefer basic aquatic training that does not require swimming skills due to the inability of some officers to swim, the shortage of time available for aquatic training, and the desire to leave major aquatic rescues to more well-trained professionals (such as lifeguards and coast guard or marine patrols). You should determine if this is the case for your area. You can offer a prepackaged course for the officers, such as the American Red Cross Community Water Safety or Basic Water Rescue class. Some departments have their own curriculum and only need the use of your staff expertise to make it work.

Other collaboration ideas for these departments include providing a regularly scheduled officer swim time to improve their health, fitness, and swimming skills. You may also be able to provide support in terms of training facilities for dive or water rescue teams.

The Armed Forces

Similar to the police and fire departments, the armed forces have specific swimming and water rescue skills that they must master. Contact the commanding officers of National Guard reserve and active duty units to determine what skills they need to master. You can then approach the units about providing facility space and the expertise of your staff to assist them in completing their skills training.

Charitable Organizations

Many charitable organizations (such as the American Cancer Society, the Epilepsy Foundation, and many others) are always seeking opportunities to raise awareness and funds for their causes. Your pool may be able to sponsor an activity to raise money for your favorite cause. You may sponsor a water carnival, swim-a-thon, triathlon, or some other event, with the proceeds going to charity. This partnership will provide a public service to the charity, make your staff feel good about helping a cause, and provide positive publicity for your facility.

Senior Citizens Centers

Senior centers are often searching for new, exciting, and enriching activities for their members. These groups can provide a wealth of assistance to your facility. You may want to offer them the opportunity to help as swim volunteers in children's swim lessons or beginning swim teams. Some of the more vigorous seniors may want training as instructor aides or even lifeguards.

Activities that you can offer for this group include water exercise, a social/swim time, and senior swim lessons. Be sure to tailor the programs to the participants' activity level and interests; work closely with the senior center coordinator while developing your plans.

Hospitals and Medical Professionals

Many people who are recovering from illness or injury can benefit greatly from aquatic therapy. The buoyant properties of water allow the patrons to begin exercising without undue stress on muscles or joints. Your partnership agreement with hospitals and medical professionals should focus on referrals. Invite these professionals to visit your rehabilitation, water exercise, and arthritis classes to see the potential benefits for themselves. You can then provide them with brochures to distribute to their patients when prescribing rehab or exercise. If necessary, you can work with medical professionals to develop a class or service that meets the needs of their clients.

Businesses

Businesses have begun to realize that maintaining their employees' health and fitness benefits them through fewer lost workdays due to illness and injury. Tap into this by becoming the "corporate fitness center" for area companies. Offer package deals to area businesses where a set number of passes are purchased by the company that can be used by all employees on a checkout basis. Provide lap swimming times in the early morning (before work), noon hour, and after work hours to accommodate these customers. Towel and locker service for a separate fee at the employees' personal expense is often an attractive option as well.

Collaboration Agreement

When approaching an organization about partnering, carefully outline each party's role. Important points to consider include what each partner will provide, how any profits will be divided, who has the authority to terminate the agreement, who will own any equipment or supplies purchased to operate the program, who is responsible for safety during the activities occurring under the partnership, and what company names or logos will be used in advertising associated with the activity.

Have a written agreement drawn up to avoid any confusion regarding the responsibilities and legalities of the agreement. Employ attorneys to draft the agreement, and have the agreement signed by authorized officers of the participating agencies.

SUMMARY

Managing your aquatic programs effectively allows you to take your ideas (developed and selected from the previous chapter) and bring them to fulfillment. By developing reasonable program policies, implementing an effective registration system, and organizing your classes for optimal facility usage, you can better implement the programs you've developed. Developing a mechanism for evaluating student progress helps your students understand where their skill level is and where it's going, and hence allows them to get more out of your program. Establishing collaborative relationships with outside groups helps add possibilities to the program options that you offer and the groups that you offer them to. Instituting these and other options can assist you in better organizing and developing your aquatic programs.

REVIEW QUESTIONS

1. Describe three program policies that you should set to ensure the smooth administration of aquatic programs.

2. Explain three accommodations that an aquatic facility can make to ensure that persons with disabilities have equal access to facilities and programs.

3. What factors should you consider when setting instructor-to-student ratios for aquatic programs at your facility?

4. What is "dead time," and what can you do to reduce it?

5. What aquatic program statistics should you collect?

6. Give five examples of community agencies that you can partner with to develop aquatic programs.

BIBLIOGRAPHY

American Red Cross. (2004). *American Red Cross lifeguarding instructor's manual*. Boston: Staywell.

Brown, S. (Ed.). (1999). *Managing the collegiate recreational facility*. Corvallis, OR: NIRSA.

Giles, R. (1984, February). *The aquatic programmer: Obstacles and solutions*. Aquatic Programming Symposium, Ottawa, ON.

Rossman, R. (2000). *Recreation programming: Designing leisure experiences* (3rd ed.). Champaign, IL: Sagamore.

Tourney, J., & Clayton, R. (1981). *Aquatic organization and management*. Minneapolis: Burgess.

YMCA of the USA. (1998). *Instructor manual for on the guard II*. Champaign, IL: Human Kinetics.

RESOURCES

The National Weather Service Web site includes information on national severe weather watches and warnings: www.noaa.gov.

The U.S. Department of Justice Web site contains the Americans With Disabilities Act text: www.usdoj.gov/crt/ada/pubs/ada.txt.

Online registration software programs are available from several commercial vendors. Two such programs are Peak Software's Sportsman program and the Recware Recnet systems. For more information, see the following Web sites:

www.peakinfo.com/sports/index.html

www.recware.com/recnethome.html

U.S. Access Board Web site: www.access-board.gov.

Resources for Programs for People With Disabilities

American Red Cross. (1992). *Swimming and diving*. St. Louis: Mosby-Year Book.

American Red Cross. (2004). *Water safety instructor's manual*. St. Louis: Mosby-Year Book.

Lepore, M., Gayle, G., & Stevens, S. (1998). *Adapted aquatics programming*. Champaign, IL: Human Kinetics.

Promoting Programs and Public Relations

Chapter Objectives

After reading this chapter, you should be able to

1. determine an audience for advertising materials,
2. list and describe key promotional points,
3. list and describe promotional outlets,
4. understand the elements that affect a facility's image,
5. institute crisis communications in an emergency, and
6. understand the benefits of hiring a marketing agency or specialist.

You can have the best program idea in the state and the most fantastic staff to teach it, but if no one knows about it, it won't be a success. Marketing a program to potential customers is an essential step in its success. The wider the variety of marketing tools that you use, the more potential customers you're likely to reach. Your options include radio, news releases, media advisories, television, newspapers, bulletin boards, marquees, pixel boards, and the Internet. But since you probably have a limited budget for promotions, you have to decide what medium is most likely to reach your target audience. This chapter helps you identify how to do that.

Of course, promotion involves more than just advertising your programs. A crisis can happen at your facility at any time. When it does, you can bet that the media will be close behind looking for information. This chapter also helps you prepare for these situations. The skill and poise with which you deal with the media will affect the image your facility projects during the crisis, which in turn will influence the public's perception of you.

Finally, an aquatic facility manager must be a master of many things, including water chemistry, teaching, safety procedures, public speaking, and personnel management. If you're the boss, your responsibilities may also include public relations and marketing. But do you have the time, imagination, and skills to do the job properly? If not, it may be time to think about alternatives for developing your image and organizing your public relations campaign. Options may include hiring a marketing professional of your own or subcontracting the work to an agency. Whatever option you choose, this chapter will help you get the most value for your dollar.

YOUR AUDIENCE

When considering what form of promotion to use, you must determine who your audience is. You can identify your audience by reviewing your program or event and figuring out who your most likely clients will be. Your selection of media will be based on this information. For example, if your program is an aquatics class for people with arthritis, you may send information to retirement communities or to local reporters and editors who cover senior issues. You may also want to think about advertising with those media organizations that cater to senior audiences. Likewise, children's swim programs may be promoted by forwarding the information to reporters who cover children's issues for the local newspaper or local parenting magazines. Again, advertising is also an option to explore.

There are two main methods of marketing and promotion. The "rifle" method (so named because of its specific aim) is used to target specific populations when the program has narrow appeal. The "shotgun" method (so named because of its more widespread targeting) gets information to a large and diverse audience because of the potentially wide interest in the program. You need to decide which type of strategy to use based on your program.

KEY PROMOTIONAL POINTS

Once you determine who your audience is and have a basic idea of how you're going to communicate with them, you need to decide what information to communicate. Providing too much information or the wrong information can be worse than not providing enough information. Selecting the correct amount and type of information is important. Here are some key points to include in your information:

▶ **The name of the program.** The name should describe what the program is, as well as generate initial interest. Be sure to use the same program name on all marketing and registration materials. Also, make sure that your staff members call the program by its correct title (i.e., no nicknames) to eliminate any confusion. Try to select program names that are descriptive and eye catching. For example, you might call your parent-infant aquatics class "Diaper Dip" or your high-level aquatic exercise program "Aqua-Power Workout."

▶ **Dates and times of the program.** Specify the dates and times the program will run. Include the year to avoid confusion with previous years' marketing materials.

▶ **Registration dates.** This includes start and end periods for registration. Also mention if late registrations are accepted and if a late fee will be assessed at that time.

▶ **Registration procedures.** How do I sign up? Mention if on-site registration is necessary or if Internet registration is available. If Internet registration is available, be sure to provide the URL.

▶ **Cost.** What are the registration fees? Include information about any discounts available.

▶ **Contact information.** State your facility name, location, telephone number, and the name of a specific contact person (if applicable).

Always double-check your materials for the presence and accuracy of these facts before you publish and distribute them. Failure to include any of these facts, or publishing inaccurate ones, can lead to a great deal of problems. See appendix D for a sample program marketing planning and cost estimation sheet that can assist you in developing a marketing strategy for your programs.

PROMOTIONAL OUTLETS

There are many different methods that you can use to market your facility and its programs. You should choose a method based on your promotions budget and the audience you want to reach. In most cases, you will want to use more than one method of marketing or promotion to maximize exposure. Some of the marketing methods available include radio and television advertisements, news releases, media advisories, newspaper ads, bulletin boards, brochures, posters, flyers, magazine articles, video presentations, and direct mail. Later in the chapter, information is provided about the use of marketing professionals who can create many of the products you need in-house, freeing you from that responsibility and creating a more professional image for your facility.

Radio Advertisements

Radio spots are normally purchased based on the length of the ad and the number of times the ad is played. Radio advertisements are typically 20 to 30 seconds or 60 seconds in length. Usually, the best time to play radio advertisements is during **drive time,** which is that period of the day when a large portion of the population is in their vehicles commuting to and from work and school. Drive time normally encompasses the period from 6:00 to 9:00 A.M. and from 3:00 to 6:00 P.M., but these time slots may differ depending on local traffic patterns. Radio stations may charge a premium for advertisements that are played during this period due to the popularity of the time. For pricing information, contact an account manager in the sales department of the radio station you want to purchase time from. Be sure to select a radio station that services the population demographic that you want to reach with your advertisements. If your advertising budget permits, you may want to consider advertising with multiple stations.

Selecting the proper radio station to reach your intended market is just as important as what you say in your advertising spots. Consider the demographics of the audience that you want to reach—its age, background, interests, and so forth. Next match that demographic with a station that serves that group. For example, if the market you're trying to reach is senior citizens, you may want to select a station whose format includes oldies music (e.g., big bands, jazz, or swing). If your market is teens, select a more contemporary rock station. Talk to the stations' advertising staff to help you determine if the market they serve is right for your ads.

When preparing copy for radio advertisements, be sure to include all pertinent information, including the name of the program, location, dates and times, cost of the program, prerequisites, and contact information. All information should be presented in a clear and logical manner so that the listener can understand it. You may want to have the most important pieces of information, such as the contact information for your facility, repeated more than once. Be sure to seek assistance from the station's production or sales staff when preparing your radio advertisements.

News Releases

The most universal tool for soliciting any kind of nonpaid media coverage is the news release, whether sent by mail, fax, or electronic mail. A news release notifies the media that something has occurred or is about to occur. News releases containing information that naturally fits into special departments, such as seniors' or children's issues,

should be sent directly to that department's editor or beat reporter.

News releases differ from standard advertising in that you don't normally pay for news pieces, whereas you do for advertising. News sources will not normally print straight ads in their news sections. However, special interest pieces may make it. For example, if you're planning a CPR Saturday and want to certify 100 people in CPR at one time, or if you're presenting a synchronized swimming class for people with disabilities, these are unique events that newspapers, television, and radio may report on. Also, results of events such as swim meets, synchronized swimming meets, or other competitive events might be of interest to news sources.

A news release should lead with the most important information first (see figure 3.1). The reader should know the purpose of the release before reading the second paragraph. Be sure to include the "five W's" in the first two paragraphs of your release: WHO, WHAT, WHEN, WHERE, and WHY. Submit the release on your organization's letterhead and make sure you include a name and contact number. Also indicate when the item should be released. Finally, know the deadlines of the media sources to which you are sending the release. Each form of the media has different deadlines. It's helpful to contact media sources and record their news release deadlines so that you can refer to them when preparing your release. You should make sure your information arrives at least a week to a week and a half in advance of your key event date or program start date. If you are reporting the results of a competitive event, they must be submitted to the news source immediately after the conclusion of the event. Ask the news source if this information should go to the sports department or some other department. Many agencies have a fax machine set up to receive sporting event results at any hour. Here's a rule of thumb: News releases should be no longer than a page to a page and a half in length. See appendix D for a sample news release worksheet.

Media Advisories

A media advisory is a shorter version of a news release. It usually contains one lead paragraph with the rest of the "five W's" presented in bullet-point format. Like the news release, the advisory should be submitted on your organization's letterhead with key contact information included.

Sandra King
Public Information Officer

Phone: 954-786-4527
Date of Press Release: 3/18/2003

PRESS RELEASE

City of Pompano Beach
100 West Atlantic Boulevard
Pompano Beach, Florida 33061

Press Release 03-07

City of Pompano Beach Lifeguards Chosen Beach Patrol of the Year

The Florida Beach Patrol Chief's Association, who represents Florida's community of lifesaving agencies located throughout the State of Florida, has named the lifeguards of the Pompano Beach Patrol "Beach Patrol of the Year for 2002." The prestigious award will be presented at the annual Lifesaving Awards Banquet held on March 29, 2003, in Delray Beach.

Pompano Beach has a guarded public beach area that consists of approximately 1,000 yards. There are 27 beach lifeguards, most of whom are trained as emergency medical technicians (EMTs) and paramedics. There are eight elevated and fully enclosed, state-of-the-art fiberglass towers equipped with the most up-to-date safety and rescue equipment, including a radio, soft top rescue boards, buoys, and all required first aid supplies. Pompano Beach Ocean Rescue also utilizes two four-wheel drive vehicles and two ATVs on the beach. A personal watercraft, inflatable rescue boat, and automatic external defibrillators (AEDs) are available for water and medical emergencies.

The Pompano Beach Patrol is United States Lifesaving Association (USLA) certified. They provide numerous water safety lectures and aquatic presentations at local schools and work in conjunction with the annual Seafood Festival regarding aquatic safety and public education. Beach Patrol members assist Pompano Beach Fire-Rescue with basic water safety as part of their new hire orientation. Pompano Beach also hosts an annual sprint series lifeguard tournament and boasts one of the state's largest junior lifeguard programs. Beach members continue to provide water safety instruction at the advanced level as well as teach neighborhood children how to swim. They also provide rescue personnel at the annual holiday boat parade and continue to promote public relations within the community of Pompano Beach.

The City of Pompano Beach is proud to have such an elite group of men and women acknowledged by the Florida Beach Patrol Chief's Association as the best lifeguard agency in the State of Florida.

Figure 3.1   A sample press release.
Reprinted, by permission, from City of Pompano Beach, 2003.

Advisories are an effective "reminder" tool as a follow-up to a news release. Media advisories are never longer than one page in length.

Television Advertisements

Television advertisements are the most expensive form of advertisement due to the high cost of production and placement. Because of the cost associated with television spots, you may want to use this form of media only for those programs that have extremely wide appeal and are likely to generate a revenue return sufficient to justify the expense of the advertisements.

An alternative to broadcast television is local cable television. Local cable television tends to offer less expensive advertising rates.

Newspaper Advertisements

Newspapers are one of the most cost-effective forms of advertising due to the comparatively low advertising rates and the relatively large audience that they reach. If your budget does not allow for paid advertising, you may want to contact the newspaper's newsroom to suggest the possibility of a story related to your facility. To make this a more attractive option for the newspaper, you should present them with a story idea of interest to their readership. Stories related to children's swim lessons, youth swim teams, and programs for people with disabilities are often good story ideas.

If you want to purchase advertising space in addition to or instead of a feature story, you should contact the newspaper's sales department for advertising rates and policies. Newspaper advertisements are often sold in two types: display ads, which contain graphics and different styles of text, and classified ads. Display ads are recommended for aquatic programming advertisements. Newspapers normally sell advertisements by the "column inch," meaning that the larger your advertisement is, the more it will cost you. The number of times your advertisement will be run also affects the cost. Some newspapers also charge a higher rate for Sunday advertisements due to the popularity of that day's paper.

When arranging for a newspaper advertisement, you must provide the sales representative with all pertinent information to accompany the ad. It may be cheaper to prepare a preprinted ad including camera-ready artwork rather than having the newspaper's art department create the ad for you. Another option is to produce inserts that can be placed inside newspapers. Although this method is more expensive than purchasing an ad, inserts may be more cost effective because they are more likely to be seen, and one insert can advertise multiple programs.

Bulletin Boards

Bulletin boards are most often maintained at the facility where programs are conducted. Bulletin boards provide the public with easy access to information regarding your facility and its programs. You can use bulletin boards to highlight a specific program in your facility, such as your learn to swim program, or you can create a collage effect that features many of your programs. Including pool hours on your bulletin board is very helpful to your patrons. You may want to create a flyer that lists lap swim, family swim, and open swim hours and place a number of these in a pocket on your bulletin board so that patrons may take them. This is a convenience they will appreciate. Place bulletin boards in high traffic areas (e.g., lobbies and waiting rooms) where patrons can easily stop and view the information without disrupting the flow of traffic.

Bulletin boards should be designed to be eye catching. The use of colorful background paper and borders is often a good first step. Items to place on the bulletin board may include facility hours, upcoming program information, and facility policies. Use flyers with large text, bright colors, and graphics to attract the reader's attention. The bulletin board should be updated regularly. Assign one staff member to be responsible for maintenance of your board, including removing out-of-date information, updating program announcements, and removing unauthorized announcements. Bulletin boards in pool areas should be encased in glass to prevent the rapid deterioration of paper due to the high humidity.

Although bulletin boards are an excellent way to inform your current customers of upcoming activities, they are not effective for marketing to the public at large and should not be relied on as the sole form of marketing.

Marquees

Marquees are signs posted outside of buildings to convey information or advertising. Usually, marquees have a series of plastic letters that can be hooked or slid into place to create a message. A marquee is an excellent way for you to advertise your programs because anyone passing by can see it. You can use the marquee to announce upcoming special events, such as swimming or synchronized swimming meets, or to announce program registration. Consider lighting your sign so that it can be seen at night as well. Placing the marquee on the front lawn close to the street will enable you to place messages on both sides of the sign and allow these messages to be easily seen by passersby. The sign should have an overlay of Plexiglas that covers the message and locks into place. This will help protect the sign from damage and help prevent theft of the letters.

Marquees often become very popular due to their high visibility. Many staff members will want information for their programs posted. You will need to develop policies to fairly distribute this opportunity. To make it easier for everyone involved, you should develop a request form that is filled out with the desired message and posting dates. (See appendix D for a sample marquee request form.) Provide a central point where the forms are submitted and assign the task of selecting the messages to one staff member.

Pixel Boards

Pixel boards use a series of small, colored lightbulbs to create a scrolling message. They can be placed on the interior or exterior of buildings. Pixel boards are very attractive and eye catching. They are best placed in prominent locations inside buildings, such as lobbies or information booths. You can use them to announce upcoming events such as registration dates or swim meets. Although they are effective at conveying information, pixel boards may be cost prohibitive for some facilities.

Brochures

Brochures are a very cost-effective form of mass marketing. Brochures can be as simple as a single trifolded sheet printed on both sides with a single color, or as elaborate as several pages with multiple colors. Your promotional budget will determine the type you choose. A reasonable-quality computer and a good graphics program, along with a high-quality printer, can enable you to produce your own brochures in-house, saving money on design and printing.

Clip art is an excellent cost-effective and easy-to-use tool for sprucing up brochures and flyers. Clip art provides artwork that can be purchased in a book and CD combination (look it up in the book, download it from the CD), or there are sites on the Internet that you can download directly from. There are many excellent pieces of aquatic-specific clip art available, such as lifeguards, swimmers, pools, divers, water polo players, and so forth. Clip art can be used in color or black and white and can be used with many computer applications, such as Microsoft® Word® or PowerPoint®. If you are downloading clip art from the Web, be sure that you are not infringing on copyrights and that you follow usage agreements.

Brochures can be used as a multipurpose marketing tool. You can provide a supply of brochures at your guest services area for your current customers. You can also mass mail brochures to potential customers (often as bulk mail to save postage costs). Additionally, the brochure can be distributed to walk-in potential clients at your facility. A rack should be placed in your registration desk/lobby area and should be stocked with brochures for easy access by walk-in patrons.

Information contained in your facility brochures should include the following:

- Upcoming program information, including program names, dates, registration dates, cost, location, and eligibility requirements
- A tear-off registration form
- Registration procedure instructions
- Facility hours, facility address, and telephone numbers
- Facility name and logo
- Directions to your facility
- Recreational swim hours

When creating your brochure, also consider drawing the readers' attention by sprucing it up with different sizes and styles of type and different color inks. Anything that you can do to set your brochure apart and make it more interesting will help your marketing campaign. Figure 3.2 shows a sample brochure.

Posters

Posters announcing programs and events at your facility can be elaborate, multicolored, glossy creations, or simple one-color, in-house creations. You can decide which option is appropriate based on your available funding and the importance of the event. Posters should always be neat and attractive. Be sure to include the essential information: name of the event, date, time, location, cost, registration procedures, and contact information for the event. The event name should normally be at the top of the poster in large type. An eye-catching graphic is also helpful in drawing attention. You should be careful not to overload the reader with too much information or use too many fonts or graphics; otherwise, your message may be lost in the clutter.

The unit cost of your poster production will depend on the number that you print. The more you print, the lower the unit cost. However, the total cost will rise with more units printed. You should therefore carefully consider how many posters you will need and plan where you will place them. Possible locations to put up promotional posters include the following:

- Your own facility
- Schools
- Colleges and universities
- Shopping malls
- Community centers
- Supermarkets
- Hotels and motels
- Child care centers
- Retirement communities

Always ask permission of the owners before placing any posters at their facility. Many require that the item be inspected for content and initialed so that staff will not remove it. Some public facilities have community announcement bulletin boards that you may be able to utilize. Look into these factors when deciding how many posters to order.

Flyers

Flyers are similar to posters in that they contain the same information and are designed to be hung in many of the same public places. The difference

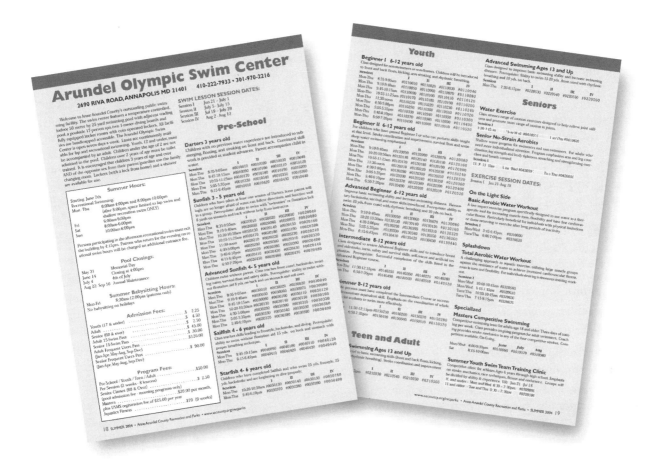

Figure 3.2 Excerpts from an Arundel Olympic Swim Center brochure.

Reprinted, by permission, from Anne Arundel County Recreation and Parks, 2004.

is that flyers are smaller, usually a standard 8 1/2-by-11-inch page. Because of this, flyers are less expensive to produce and easier to fit on bulletin boards. If cost and ease of production are a major consideration, flyers may be the best option. Your flyers can also be handed out during open house events, placed in racks for patrons to take, or included with direct mailings. The versatility and low cost of using flyers make them an excellent no-frills marketing tool. Be sure to include your facility Web site address and contact phone number on your flyers, much as you would in brochures or other forms of marketing.

Calendars

Program calendars are a fun, innovative, and handy way to distribute your program information. To create a program calendar, you should gather all information about the aquatic programs taking place, including facility hours, special events, swimming and diving meets, and planned clos-

ings. Then group the information by month. Use a calendar computer program to create a month block calendar, and insert your information into the calendar. You can use photos of your facilities and activities to fill the opposite page from the calendar pages (digital photography makes this task much easier).

If you want a high-quality, glossy color product, you will probably have to work with a professional printer to produce it. This will significantly increase the total and per unit cost. If you're willing to settle for a lesser quality, you may be able to create it in-house using color printers and digital photography. By investing in the initial cost of the calendar, you may be able to forgo some flyers or other direct mailings because the calendar covers a variety of topics and issues.

Distribute your calendars to patrons either at information and registration booths or through direct mail. The hope is that they will post the calendar and be continually reminded of your facility each time they see it.

Magazine Articles

Magazine articles are a particularly attractive form of promotion because they cost you nothing and provide in-depth exposure for your facility and programs. For a magazine to be interested in featuring your facility or a specific event, there must be some item of interest to the readership of the magazine. You should be familiar with the magazine and its content and try to match your facility with its needs. In some cases, you can write the article yourself and submit it; in other cases, a writer from the publication may contact you.

Types of magazines that may be interested in articles about aquatic facilities and programs include the following:

- Senior citizens magazines
- Children's magazines
- Parenting magazines
- Community living publications
- Recreation magazines
- Professional trade journals (such as *Athletic Business* or *Aquatics International*)

Magazines of all types are written on the local, regional, and national level. Consider which type is most likely to be interested in your story before contacting them. A query letter, phone call, or e-mail to the editor is often a required first step. Although national publications usually have the largest audience, they often have the most restrictive submission guidelines. Also consider the reason for publishing the article and who you want to see it. If your purpose is to draw new business, a local or regional magazine may be more suited to your needs. Check local supermarkets and newsstands to see what publications are available in your area and which ones are best suited to your needs.

Video Presentations

A video presentation is an exciting, visual, and dynamic method to get your facility message out. When planning a video presentation, think about what you want to use the video for. Possible uses include showing it to groups of prospective customers, continually showing it at promotional fairs or in your lobby, or sending it to possible donors. These factors will determine the length of your production as well as its content. Most videos should not exceed 10 to 12 minutes in length; otherwise, the viewers can become bored and saturated with information. In addition, the cost of production rises with the length of the project.

Your video must be of high production quality or it will show your facility in an unfavorable light. For high-profile projects, you may want to hire a professional videographer or production firm on a contract basis. Although the cost for a project of this scope can run into the thousands of dollars, you are assured a high-quality product that you may use for years. The alternative is to utilize a home video camera and your own staff. Common problems with this option include poor sound quality, interference from background noise, lack of effects or graphics, and overall poor production.

The highest cost of the project is often in creation and postproduction. Actual duplication of the video is relatively cheap. Be sure to create multiple copies of the video once complete. Retain the master copy in a secure location so that it can be duplicated as needed. Finally, label all copies so the tapes can be identified. Here are some things to keep in mind when planning the content of your video:

- The actual content of the video can focus on the facility as a whole—highlighting features such as the pools, locker areas, guest services, and ancillary facilities—or on programs.
- It's often best to show the facility in use. This gives viewers a better idea of its function. The introduction to the video should include a text graphic indicating what the video is about and where the facility is located.
- A voice-over narrative throughout is helpful in explaining what is being seen. Consider adding the narrative in the studio, not during taping, to eliminate noise interference.
- You may also want to include interviews with staff, explaining aspects of the facility and programs. If you do this, add a caption at the bottom of the screen indicating the staff member's name and title. Rehearse the interview before you tape it. It's best if the staff member wears a facility shirt or uniform because it appears more professional to the viewer.
- You must receive consent from anyone who is included in the video.

Direct Mail

Direct mail involves sending a letter, brochure, or flyer to current or potential customers of your facility. It is a highly effective form of promotion because you are ensured that the intended recipient directly receives your materials (and, you hope, reads it). Sending direct mail to current and former customers can reap returns in repeat business and is worth the cost. The first step in doing this is to create a mailing list from program registration and member lists.

You should note, however, that direct mail can be expensive because you must now add the cost of mailing to the cost of the production and duplication of your promotional materials. The cost of mailing is directly related to the weight of the object mailed. Because of this, try to keep the size of the mailer small and the weight of it as low as possible. Most direct mail projects fall under bulk mail regulations, which is the most inexpensive form of delivery. Check with your local post office regarding direct mail regulations and procedures. Be sure to follow any directions given by the postal service or your mail will not be delivered.

A final comment about direct mail: Unsolicited direct mail runs the risk of being perceived as "junk mail," which in turn could create a negative image of your facility. This is why careful attention should be given to the development of your mailing list.

Web Sites

Web sites more and more are becoming the public's preferred method for gathering consumer information. A well-designed and user-friendly site is becoming a must-have for any aquatic facility. Your site should include information regarding your programs, facilities, and staff. Photos of your facility and of people participating in your programs can make your site more interesting and helpful. To ensure that your Web site is found by prospective consumers, arrange for links to your site to be placed on local and regional sites of interest, such as your state tourism site or city visitors site.

Appoint a staff member to be the "Web master" who is responsible for maintaining and updating your facility's site. Updated and correct information is essential if the public is to trust your site and use it to access information about your programs.

Your Web site should be one-stop shopping for your facility. In today's "wired" society, Internet research is often the first step for many potential customers. Therefore, you need to ensure that your site contains as much information related to your facility as possible. Here are some suggestions for information that you might want to include on your Web site:

- An overview of your facilities and services, including photos of main activity areas
- Facility schedules
- Course descriptions and schedules
- Facility location information, including address, local map, and directions
- Facility phone number
- Program staff list and e-mail addresses
- Major facility and program registration rules and policies
- Online program registration
- Listing of employment opportunities at the facility

The University of Virginia department of intramural recreational sports has an excellent aquatics Web page, complete with downloadable job application, class descriptions, facility hours, and management contact information. The Web address is www.virginia.edu/ims/aquatics/index.html.

Water Shows

Water shows are a fun way for you to showcase your programs to the community. In a water show, each of your program areas presents a brief demonstration of what they do in their classes. Some ideas for elements you can demonstrate include synchronized swimming, springboard diving, scuba, lifeguard rescue skills, water polo skills, and children's swimming skills.

Make the event open to the public and free of charge. The goal is to get as many people to visit your facility as possible. Here are some ways to make your show more interesting and to help it run more smoothly:

- Have a well-prepared announcer or commentator.
- Use a good sound system.
- Control lighting for effect.
- Use music that matches the events.

- Create an inexpensive printed program listing the events (printed in-house).
- Ask older swimmers to act as "ushers" for guests.
- Invite a VIP to be a special guest (e.g., a member of the city council or the mayor).
- Invite members of the press (you can issue a news release).
- Have a greeter at the main entrance to the facility to provide directions to the pool.

Although a large number of your attendees will be family of the show participants, you will undoubtedly draw other visitors to your show. A well-produced show can generate excitement about your facility. It can generate good will from families, positive media attention, and a feeling of accomplishment among the participants. Be sure that you have lots of promotional materials available for your guests. Also ensure that you have adequate customer service staff on hand to deal with the extra questions and extra business.

Contests

Another way that you can increase the visibility of your facility is through the use of contests. One popular contest is a water safety coloring event.

© Empics

Audience members enjoy a demonstration of water ballet.

Children are provided with a water safety picture and are asked to color it and submit it for judging. A panel consisting of facility staff and local dignitaries judges the entries. You can cooperate with a local merchant, such as a grocery or department store, to distribute the entry forms and pictures and to post the children's work. This helps to spread the water safety message and allows your facility to receive some publicity (be sure to include your facility name on the posters announcing the contest). The prize announcement and award presentation can be made at the partner merchant location, again providing publicity for both parties. You may have the aquatic director and a local dignitary present the award, providing a good photo opportunity for all involved. You may also want to provide stickers for all children who participate so that all the children feel like winners.

When organizing a contest such as this, be sure to clearly state all entry requirements to avoid any disappointment caused by improper entries. Specify age requirements, residency rules, what can be used to color the picture (e.g., crayons, colored pencils, or markers), and whether or not parents can assist in any way.

Displays and Demonstrations

Displays and demonstrations follow the principle of taking your programs to the public. Displays are more static in nature, normally featuring a display board with photographs to draw visitors in and paper promotional materials for them to take. The display board should feature your facility name and bright, colorful photos of your facility and its programs in action. The display board should be stood on a table with handouts available in front of the display. Displays can be used at activity fairs (common at colleges), open house nights, shopping malls, and any other place potentially interested persons may congregate.

Demonstrations focus on showing a skill that could be learned by enrolling in a program at your aquatic facility. Because many aquatic skills do not lend themselves well to demonstrations outside the pool, CPR and first aid demonstrations are most often used. You can set up displays where passersby can observe lifeguards or other responders performing CPR on mannequins. A display of promotional materials related to upcoming classes can be stationed nearby for interested potential customers. Be sure to have a knowledgeable staff member available to answer technical questions and provide registration information. Possible locations to set up demonstrations include your facility lobby, shopping malls, parks, and beaches.

Sponsorships

Sponsorships of community events such as charity 5K or 10K runs, swim-a-thons for charity, or similar types of events help show your facility in a positive light. Publicity is gained for the facility by listing the facility name on T-shirts, banners, and programs and by mentioning it in advertising spots. Sponsorship of charity events is a public good in and of itself, but it has the added benefit of helping your facility's public image. The service or monetary donation that you make will be far outweighed by the positive public exposure. If your facility has the resources, you may want to approach a public charity about hosting a charity swim-a-thon or triathlon to raise money for their cause. Hosting the event yourself allows you to draw spectators and participants to your facility who otherwise might never come. Additionally, any media photos or footage taken of the event will take place in your facility, providing additional exposure. Of course, while the guests are in your facility, you can have promotional materials available for them regarding your aquatic facilities and programs.

Aside from sponsoring charity events, your facility may also sponsor a sport team (e.g., a swim team, diving club, synchronized swimming team, or water polo club). In this instance, you provide the team with services such as reduced fees for pool usage or with contributions toward uniforms. In return, your facility name is attached to the club or team. This means that your facility logo and name will be placed on team uniforms and that your facility name will be referred to when the team is mentioned in press releases and other media. The fact that your name is attached to the team may be a potential risk as well because all the team members' actions (good and bad) will be attributed to your facility. Because of this, you should require signatures on a carefully prepared agreement before becoming a sponsor. Your agreement should include a conduct clause stating that consistently poor or illegal behavior by the club, its officers, or its members will result in immediate termination of the sponsorship and all its benefits. The agreement should also specify an agreed upon team or club name (featuring your facility name) and should specify restrictions on when, where, and how your corporate logo is to be displayed.

> **KEY POINT**   *There is a wide variety of marketing opportunities available for promoting your aquatic facility. Using a variety of these helps ensure that your message is exposed to a large audience. Carefully consider who you want to reach; this will help you decide how you want to expend your marketing dollars.*

CRISIS COMMUNICATIONS

Crisis communications refers to the ability to portray your facility's image appropriately during times of emergency or turmoil, such as after a death at the facility, a fire, or a natural disaster. Crisis communications procedures are used during those times when it is important that correct information is relayed and that misinformation is corrected.

Public Relations Officer

A public relations officer is a member of your senior facility staff who has the authority to respond to inquiries from the press regarding incidents and official policy. The public relations officer must be available to your staff at all times in the event of an emergency. Because of this, it is helpful for your public relations officer to carry a cell phone or pager that your aquatic supervisors have the number for. You should ensure that your public relations officer is fully trained in all facility policies and has a full understanding of aquatic safety. Your public relations officer must project a confident, polished image to the press and public during times of stress and conflict. For this reason, you may want to ensure that your public relations officer has some formal training in public affairs or crisis communications. Except for very large organizations (such as municipalities), the public relations duty is usually a collateral assignment for a senior staff member.

Public Relations for the Non-PR Professional

In most cases of crisis or emergency, it's best if your junior staff members (such as lifeguards) leave interaction with members of the press to senior staff, preferably your public relations officer. However, there may be cases when the public relations officer is unavailable or other cases when it may be better or necessary for a lifeguard to give a statement to the media. Here are some basic guidelines to assist your staff members when giving an on-camera interview or making a statement:

▶ Never speculate or conjecture; give only the facts that you know.

▶ Look at the interviewer unless directed otherwise.

▶ Stand straight and keep your hands clasped comfortably behind your back (for stand-up interviews).

▶ Appear as neat and clean as possible.

▶ Speak plainly and clearly and never use profanity.

▶ Remember that there are no such things as comments made "off the record."

▶ Always assume that any cameras and microphones are on and that what you say and do are being recorded.

▶ Never allow members of the press to witness the actual scene of a disaster, particularly while in progress. The scene of an accident or its aftermath can create a very unfavorable impression, regardless of the actual facts, when taken out of context.

▶ Never make statements regarding the identity of injured persons or their potential for recovery.

▶ Always remove sunglasses; it presents a more professional image.

You can include public relations training in your staff in-service training program. You should also include some basic public affairs guidance in your aquatic staff handbook. Constantly remind your staff of the phrase "stay in your lane"—meaning they should never make comments about topics that they do not have firsthand knowledge of. Make sure your staff members know that if they feel they cannot give an interview due to the stress of a situation or because they feel unprepared, they may simply refer all inquiries to the public relations officer.

> **KEY POINT** *When it all goes bad at your facility, and when you'd least like to have publicity, you're likely to get it. The skill with which you deal with the press will in large part determine how your facility's image will survive the crisis. Be sure to spend time with your staff planning and preparing for media relations.*

A lifeguard responds to questions from a television news crew.

FACILITY IMAGE

You can have excellent facilities and programs, but if the public is given a poor impression of your staff or your facility, they will not patronize your business. They're also likely to tell others about their impressions. Image is important. It is essential that you project friendly, courteous service and a clean, safe, well-run facility.

Staff

Your staff is absolutely essential in developing the impression that customers have of your facility. They are your "frontline ambassadors"—the public's first contact with your facility and your programs. You must train your staff regarding how you want them to interact with your patrons. You must also provide them with the tools necessary to do their job well. If you don't do these things, you can expect your customer service to suffer and your business to drop accordingly.

Initial and regular training for all staff members, whether they are lifeguards or the front desk receptionist, is important in establishing your expectations of them. Provide a basic indoctrination that includes your facility's background and its mission. This gives your employees a frame of reference and helps them feel like part of the team. Next, provide job-specific training that covers policies, procedures, and essential skills for their job. Try to allow new employees to shadow experienced good performers to help them learn their job. Instill in all employees that customer service is important, and explain what that means. Provide examples of correct methods for answering phones and in-person greetings. Explain to your employees that they should do whatever is reasonable to resolve a customer complaint at the lowest staff level possible, but if the customer is unsatisfied, a supervisor is always available.

Your staff must be familiar with all policies, including refunds, late registration, chaperoning of children, and required swimwear. All policies must be enforced fairly and uniformly; otherwise, complaints will arise. Any time policies are amended or repealed, you must inform all staff or there will be confusion over which policy to use.

Image Ideas

You can take some inexpensive and simple steps to improve your facility image. Often it's the little things that create an impression of your facility in the minds of your customers. Strive to make those little things positive. Periodically, you may want to have a trusted colleague from another facility visit and give you her impression of how your corporate image is presented. She can do a walk-through of your facility and give you a brief report of how things went. You can arrange a return visit if necessary. Some ideas to help maintain your corporate image include cleanliness, proper lighting, uniforms, and a corporate logo. See appendix D for a daily checklist that identifies items you should check each day to help improve or maintain the polished image of your facility.

Cleanliness

Nothing turns away customers faster than a dirty facility, particularly dirty rest rooms. Ensure that your lavatories are checked on an hourly basis and cleaned as needed (they should be cleaned a minimum of twice per day). Paper products and soap should also be replaced as needed. The pool deck should be kept clear of litter and debris and should be washed daily. Trash cans on decks and in locker rooms should be emptied at least once daily, more often if needed. Dirty trash cans attract insects and breed disease. Walk through the entire facility every day and note cleanliness issues and maintenance concerns. Check for gum on decks and floors, black marks on floors, trash, and so on. Immediately resolve any issues. Facility cleanliness is a task for all staff regardless of duties. Try to foster a sense of ownership of the facility among your staff. They are much more likely to help keep "their" facility clean. You should also provide an easy way for your customers to report any repair and cleaning issues they encounter. Place customer comment cards at your member services desk for this purpose. See appendix D for a sample customer comment card.

Lighting

Lighting is a powerful "impression" tool and an important safety issue. Dark, poorly lit spaces give the impression that your facility is dingy, dirty, and unsafe. Use a light meter to assess the level of lighting in your aquatic facility, including locker areas, lobbies, and activity spaces. Compare your readings against codes published by the national regulatory agencies. Attempt to make your facility brightly lit and pleasing to the eye. Bright-colored paint schemes are often used to enhance current lighting. A quick touch-up with the brush and roller is also more cost-effective than replacing lights and can often produce the same end result—a more appealing facility.

A staff member at your facility, normally a maintenance employee, should conduct a weekly walk-through of the facility to check for burned-out bulbs. At that time, bulbs are replaced so that poor lighting does not develop due to unreplaced bulbs. Ensure that your staff maintains an adequate supply of all types of bulbs used at the facility to enable rapid response to lighting problems.

Staff Uniforms

If you want your staff to feel and act professional, then helping them look professional is an important first step. All staff should be issued uniforms and should be required to wear them while on duty (figure 3.3). Lifeguards should be provided with a uniform shirt and swimsuit at minimum. Administrative staff should wear collared polo-style shirts bearing the facility logo. Maintenance personnel should be issued a uniform appropriate to their duties as well. Provide each staff member with at least two shirts to ensure that the uniform remains clean and in good shape. You should check each day to make sure that all staff members are wearing the proper uniform before beginning their shift. Providing each staff member with a name tag bearing his or her first name is also helpful for the patrons.

Corporate Logo

A corporate logo is your facility's calling card—the way the public identifies your facility and your products quickly. Your logo should be represen-

tative of your facility. Although you can pay a marketing firm to create one for you, a logo can often be made inexpensively on a desktop publishing program. Once you develop a logo and have it approved by the appropriate supervisors, you should use it on all marketing materials and correspondence. A distinctive logo allows the public to instantly associate anything bearing that logo with your facility. In other words, you've created "brand-name recognition," such as that enjoyed by the well-known symbols for the YMCA or the Red Cross.

Signage

Try to make your facility as user friendly as possible. Place easy-to-read signs identifying rest rooms, locker rooms, routes to the swimming pool, and other important areas of your facility. Universal picture signs are helpful for those who cannot read or for those who speak a language other than English. The pool area should have easy-to-read signs indicating facility rules and the location of locker room entrances and exits. This seemingly small step helps prevent patrons from becoming lost and confused in your facility (and helps prevent the accompanying frustration that goes with it).

If your aquatic facility is very large, or if your aquatics area is only one part of a larger recreation or physical education complex, you may want to post maps of the facility. Maps can be color coded

Figure 3.3   Lifeguards should have professional attire and rescue equipment.

by activity area and should clearly identify rest rooms, locker areas, telephones, the swimming pools, other activity areas, and exits. Maps should also identify the different floors within the facility. Your facility maps should be large and permanently painted on wood or Plexiglas. Post your maps in your main lobby, in waiting areas, and in main hallways.

You can also use small maps printed on paper to distribute to new or potential patrons. The reverse side of the map can contain descriptions of areas located on the map as well as facility hours and contact information. Be sure to have copies of your facility map available at information areas along with promotional materials. Figure 3.4 is a sample map of the Student Recreation Center at Southern Illinois University at Carbondale.

Tours and Guest Hosts

Potential new users and members of your facility can often be deterred because they are unfamiliar with how your facility "works." You can help these customers overcome their fear of being new by providing tours and guest hosts.

Tours show potential or new patrons the facility and what services are offered. Tours should focus on facility areas such as the swimming pool and locker rooms. Train your staff to point out amenities such as swimsuit dryers, saunas, mirrors, pace clocks, aqua jogger belts, and towel service. Tours also provide an enticement for purchasing a membership. You should provide tours on request for anyone interested.

Train as many staff members as possible to conduct tours. New staff members should receive a brief written description of what items to mention when giving a tour as well as what areas of the facility they can and cannot visit. Trainees should accompany experienced staff on several tours, taking part as they feel able, until they can comfortably give a tour on their own. The value in doing this is that it keeps your staff aware and up-to-date about issues and changes affecting your facility.

Guest hosts are members who agree to meet new members on their first day and accompany them on an activity. This hosting program eliminates the feeling of being an outsider early in a new member's experience. You can develop a list of current members who want to participate in this program, and then make it available to new members and customers as they register for classes. The participants are provided with each other's name, and they meet at an agreed upon location and time. Do not provide telephone numbers or addresses to participants in this program to protect the privacy of the members.

> **KEY POINT** *Perception is everything. The image that your patrons have of your facility determines what they will tell other potential customers about your facility and if they will come back themselves. If you always present a clean facility and a friendly, helpful staff, you will be well on your way to a good impression with your customers.*

PROFESSIONAL MARKETING AND PUBLIC RELATIONS

If you're searching for some assistance with marketing and public relations, there are two options you may want to consider: hiring a professional marketing agency or hiring your own in-house marketing specialist. Each carries its own possibilities for furthering your marketing potential.

Marketing and Public Relations Agencies

For large aquatic facilities, it may be beneficial to hire a marketing and public relations firm to handle all needs in this regard. A good public relations firm will design all brochures, posters, flyers, and other printed materials produced for the facility. As the facility representative, you will meet with the agency to provide them with the information you want to convey. The agency will design the material and produce a sample for you to approve. After your approval, they will print it and ensure delivery of the product. Professional agencies can also assist with press releases, direct mail letters, television and radio spots, and a myriad of other marketing details. The major benefit of hiring a professional agency is that they take much of the work and stress of marketing away from aquatic managers, enabling them to do what they do best—manage aquatics.

Some agencies require a retainer before signing a contract to begin work. The retainer is a fee paid to the agency before work is begun; the retainer is then applied to project fees. No project fees are paid until the equivalent value of the retainer has been met. After that point, you pay for each

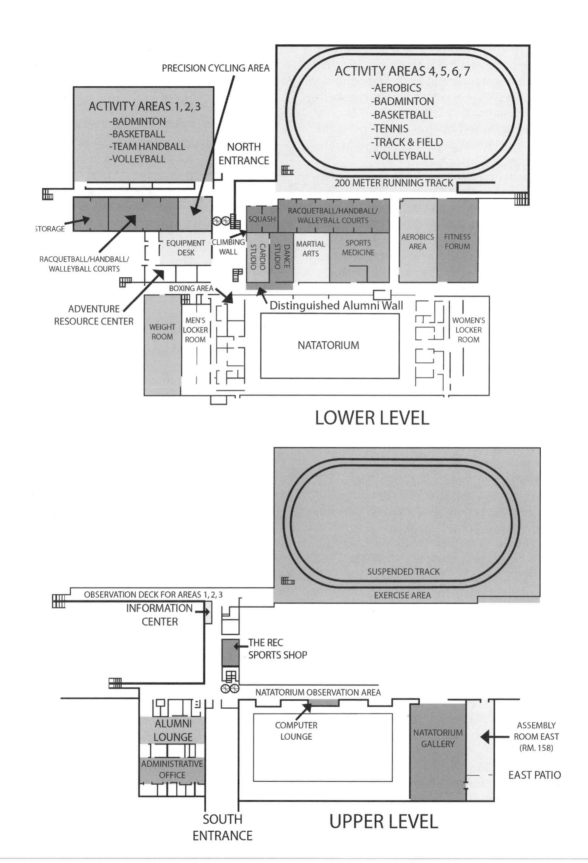

Figure 3.4 A map of the Student Recreation Center at Southern Illinois University at Carbondale.

Map courtesy of Elizabeth Copher, University of Southern Illinois.

project as you go. The retainer is normally paid each year. Other agencies work on a pay-as-you-go basis, charging only for each project.

When thinking about hiring a public relations firm, you should weigh the potential savings in time and effort against the cost of the product. Before signing a contract, you should view the agency's previous products to see if you like their materials. It may also be helpful to talk with other clients of a firm to determine if the agency is responsive to customer needs, meets deadlines, and is easy to work with.

In-House Marketing Specialist

Another option is hiring a full- or part-time marketing or graphic design specialist for your facility. This person would create all posters, flyers, bulletin boards, and other marketing materials in-house. There are several advantages to having an in-house marketing specialist (versus contracting with an agency or doing the work yourself):

- An in-house specialist is a member of your staff and should know your programs well. This will enable him to create materials that more accurately represent your programs.

- An in-house specialist is on-site, so you can more easily communicate with him regarding your deadlines and your specific needs.

- An in-house specialist (being a member of your staff) can become an integral part of the planning process, attending your meetings and responding quickly to unanticipated needs.

- An in-house specialist can visit your programs regularly and create a file of images and notes (using a notebook, sketch pad, camera, or other medium). This file will be on hand for all your marketing needs.

- An in-house specialist frees you, the aquatic manager, for other tasks.

When creating a job description and requirements, you should carefully consider what tasks you want your marketing specialist to perform. Due to the visual and creative nature of the job, be sure to ask candidates to bring portfolios of their work to job interviews. Qualifications that you may want to require include the following:

- A degree in graphic design, public relations, or marketing

- The ability to write engaging and accurate copy

- Working knowledge of design, imaging, and layout software

- Basic photography skills

- The ability to create bulletin boards, posters, and flyers

- Experience in copywriting, graphic arts, marketing, and promotions

Although having an on-site marketing and promotions professional is ideal, cost and support are major factors in your decision. In addition to the salary needed to fund this position, you'll also need to provide this staff member with office space, computer support, and special tools needed for the job (such as a camera, film, cutting boards, paper, and graphic arts tools). You must weigh the costs of hiring your own staff member versus the costs expended by hiring an agency to do the work or the time expended by performing these tasks yourself.

> **KEY POINT** *Marketing and public relations involve a complex set of tasks. As an aquatic manager, you'll need to determine whether you want to attempt these tasks yourself, contract out the duties, or hire an in-house marketing professional. Whatever route you take, be sure that your facility will receive the most positive exposure for your investment of time and money.*

SUMMARY

Marketing and promotion are key elements to ensuring the success of your programs. Failure to have and carry out an effective marketing plan could result in the public not knowing about your programs and therefore not registering. Understanding who your audience is and deciding what information you need to convey are key first steps in your plan. Next, you'll need to determine what methods to use to reach your audience. You may also want to consider using a marketing service or specialist to create a more polished image and to relieve your staff of this task. Finally, you must develop a facility image that conveys who and what you are and makes patrons want to come back.

REVIEW QUESTIONS

1. If you want to run an ad on a radio station, what factors should you consider when choosing one station over another?

2. List three cost-effective forms of marketing and describe the benefits and drawbacks of each.

3. What does your facility have to gain from sponsoring a community event?

4. What advice would you give to a member of your staff who was about to be interviewed by a local television station?

5. Describe three inexpensive and simple ways to improve the image of your facility.

6. What are the advantages to hiring a marketing specialist for your facility?

BIBLIOGRAPHY

Bayley, R. (1986, May). *Marketing for money: An aquatic illustration.* Rescue '86 Symposium, Vancouver, BC.

Forrester, P., & Rubin, A. (1998). A marketing panacea: Connecting to the four year client. *NIRSA Journal,* 22(3), 11-17.

Wilkinson, D. (1986, May). *Marketing for money: Principles.* Rescue '86 Symposium, Vancouver, BC.

RESOURCES

Michaels, N., & Karpowicz, D. (2000). *Off the wall marketing ideas.* Holbrook, MA: Adams Media.

The Web address for Microsoft's clip gallery is http://office.microsoft.com/clipart.

Budgeting

Chapter Objectives

After reading this chapter, you should be able to

❶ understand the budgeting process and the types of budgets,

❷ list and describe sources of revenue at an aquatic facility,

❸ list and describe expenses at an aquatic facility,

❹ describe how to effectively manage a budget, and

❺ describe the factors involved in making a major purchase for an aquatic facility.

Creating an aquatics budget involves determining all your possible sources of income and expense and trying to make sure the income is more than the expense. In your budget, you should also try to allocate the income judiciously to meet all your needs, including wages, rent or mortgage, utilities, supplies, and other expenses. Your budget must be realistic so that you can use it once it's created.

Where does all the money go? If you've worked on a budget before, you know that the answer is that it goes to a lot of different places. If you don't know exactly where it goes, how much goes to each place, and for what purpose, you can't control cash flow or budget properly. To help you manage your facility's expenses, this chapter explores different types of expenses and also suggests some methods for reducing expenses.

It's just as important for you to understand where your income comes from as it is for you to know where it goes. Therefore, this chapter includes information regarding potential sources of income at an aquatic facility, including some possibilities for revenue generation that you may

not have considered. It also discusses how to calculate the break-even point for a program, identifies a number of methods for managing a budget, and describes end-of-year fiscal reports.

Decisions regarding major purchases need to be made with a lot of care and consideration. Let's face it, when a big chunk of money is being allocated to one item, you need to be sure that the item you purchase will do what you want it to do and that you can use it at your facility. This chapter helps you with this by describing how to research major purchases and how to decide if the item you want is right for your needs.

THE BUDGETING PROCESS

Budgeting is an essential process to ensure that you are accounting for all sources of income and expense. If you fail to create a budget, you can place your facility in serious financial difficulties.

If your aquatics budget is only one part of a larger budget created for a whole agency, such as in the case of a YMCA or university recreation department, the format of your aquatics budget must conform to that of the agency budget. It must cover the same period and must be submitted on the same schedule.

Once your budget is created, and before it can be implemented, it must be approved. The budget approval process will vary depending on the management structure for a facility. Here are some examples:

▸ **City council approval.** This method is utilized by municipal aquatic agencies. The aquatics budget may be a part of a larger recreation budget. The budgets of several aquatic facilities may be combined into one operating budget. In this instance, once the aquatic budget is approved, it may become a part of the municipality's budget and may be available for view by the general public. Full disclosure of budgeted and actual revenue and expenses is required due to taxpayer involvement.

▸ **Board approval.** An organizational board often governs agencies such as YMCAs and summer camps. In this case, a budget may need to be prepared for submission to the board for approval. Often, many different units of an organization are competing for limited budget dollars, and units may need to defend and justify their expenses.

▸ **Director approval.** For entities such as university recreation departments, a budget may need to be submitted to the recreation director, who may make the approval based on a set number of budget dollars provided to the department.

▸ **Preapproval (budget designation).** This option is used in cases where the aquatic facility has no control over its own budget. A fixed budget may be handed down from higher authority with no input permitted. It may come in the form of a fixed dollar amount to be spent however needed to operate the facility for the year or may be broken out by line item.

▸ **No approval (independent budget).** This option is used by independent aquatic facilities not affiliated with other agencies. In this case, the facility's budget is developed based on the projections of income and expenditures for the facility.

Aquatics budget officers must know whether any profits derived from membership fees and registration fees can be spent at the facility level or if profits must be turned over to the larger organization. If revenues generated cannot be spent, this must be accounted for in the budgeting process.

Once you've established a draft budget, you may be required to submit it up the chain of command and eventually hold a meeting with your superior to discuss it before it's finalized. During this meeting, you may explain those projects that you want to undertake for the coming year, outline major purchases you want to make, and make a revenue projection. At this time, the approving authority may ask for clarification or justification for projects and purchases. Only after your approving authority has accepted the budget can you implement it.

A budget must be set up to coincide with a "fiscal year." This is a 12-month budgetary period that businesses operate under. Fiscal years can begin and end in any month that is convenient for your organization. They may or may not coincide with the calendar year. At the end of the fiscal year, profit or loss is calculated, and a new budget is implemented on the first day of the first month of the new fiscal year. Many facilities suspend purchasing, except for emergencies, a month before the end of the fiscal year so that deliveries can be made and bills paid before the closeout of the fiscal year and before balancing the books.

You may want to divide your budget into smaller intervals (e.g., monthly and quarterly intervals) over the 12-month period, because it's easier to compare your actual expenses and revenues to the amounts projected in the budget based on these shorter time frames. Also, if you determine that you are exceeding your projected expenses or falling short on income at one of these intervals, you have time to take corrective action before it becomes too serious.

Have an emergency plan in place in case your budget gets cut or you fail to make the expected revenue you've projected. Many managers delay large purchases and expensive projects until well into their fiscal year. That way, if the budget is cut or income is down, they can reallocate the money earmarked for those purchases and projects to cover expenses. Your plan may include reallocating money from different accounts or reducing operating hours. However, never compromise safety by reducing staff below recommended ratios to overcome financial difficulties.

INCOME

For an aquatic director and programmer, income is the bottom line; it's the money you make from the programs and services you offer. Income can come from many sources—the more sources the better. Diversified income means that if one of your programs or services becomes less profitable, you should still be able to survive financially off the remaining income sources. Organize your budget on a spreadsheet or computer budgeting program to make it easier to access and understand. (See appendix D for a sample budget spreadsheet.)

The following is a listing of types of income sources:

▶ **Registration fees.** These are the fees charged for classes taught at your facility, such as swimming lessons, water exercise, swim team, and lifeguard training. Registration fees are normally charged at the beginning of a program to cover the length of that session. To determine the amount of income from registration fees for a program, multiply the number of students by the amount charged in registration fees. Subtract out any students who were given free registration for any reason, and take into account any discounts given. Repeat this procedure for each program you offer and you will have the total amount of program revenue. (See appendix D for a sample program revenue evaluation worksheet.)

▶ **Membership fees.** Membership fees are charged for entrance into the facility for a set period of time, usually a year, half year, or quarter. Membership fees entitle the users to use the facility (pool) but may not give them access to programs without payment of additional fees. Many facilities offer various membership packages, including packages for individuals, couples, or families (number of persons in a family is usually defined by the facility). Of course, the fees increase with the number of persons included in the membership package and the length of time the package covers. Some enterprising facilities offer "plus memberships," which may include additional amenities that are not available to other members, such as locker and towel service or access to a sauna or whirlpool.

▶ **Merchandise sales.** A full-service aquatic facility will offer items for sale that customers may want to purchase for personal use during workouts or water play. Examples of popular sales items include swim goggles, latex and nylon swim caps, nose clips, earplugs, sunscreen (outdoor pools), and personal care items such as combs, lotion, and shampoo. Larger aquatic facilities may sell these items in a "pro shop" and may include additional items such as swimsuits, aqua shoes, kickboards, and athletic bags. Pro shops require a commitment of space and staff, but the profits can be substan-

Many facilities sell goggles, fins, and other aquatic items.

tial in a high-volume facility. However, even smaller income facilities can offer a few items for sale at the front desk area. Patrons who lose a seemingly minor item, such as swim goggles, may be unable to complete a workout or class. Having these items readily available for sale at your facility enables these patrons to complete their workout or class with minimum disruption.

▶ **Concessions.** Concession sales provide the convenience of on-site food and beverage service to your customers. This can be a particularly welcome amenity during events such as age group and synchronized swimming meets when families are often at the pool for long periods and are unable to leave to eat. Concessions can serve a variety of foods depending on the customers' needs and the level to which the facility wants to be involved. Full-service menus with salads and hot foods (e.g., pizza) are provided at some large multipurpose facilities. Facilities with less space to commit may serve only prepackaged items that require no preparation, such as candy bars, canned or bottled drinks, or packaged snack foods. Concessions are normally regulated by the state and must be licensed and inspected. It can be expensive to maintain the level of cleanliness, sanitation, and service necessary to operate a full-service concession area; consider this carefully when choosing the level of service you want to offer. Concession stands also require the commitment of space for customer seating (Hodgkinson, 1998).

▶ **Vending machines.** Where pro shops or concessions are not possible or are impractical, vending machines offer a viable alternative. Vending machines can be configured to sell beverages (such as water, soft drinks, and fruit juices) or food items (such as candy, crackers, muffins, and even microwave foods). Vending machines can also be stocked with smaller merchandise items such as swim caps, swim goggles, and combs. Often, the vending machines are owned by a third party that stocks and services the machines and collects the income. A percentage of profits is paid to the facility for the privilege of placing the machines on the property. This is a no-cost, low-maintenance service that a facility can provide to its patrons.

▶ **Fund-raising.** Facilities such as YMCAs and schools often seek additional funds from the community to cover their operating expenses. Fund-raising can involve the sale of items such as T-shirts, candy, candles, or any other item you can think of. In this type of fund-raising, before any money is made, an outlay of cash is required to purchase the items to be sold. With this in mind, be sure that the items you select will be popular. Popular sales items include chocolate bars, sub-

marine sandwiches, and frozen cookie dough. Ask yourself the question, "Would I want to buy this item?" Scented candles may sound like a good idea, but your market for these will be limited. Fund-raising can also be accomplished through other means, such as car washes and sales of advertising space in printed programs.

▶ **Donations.** Individuals, estates, public service agencies (e.g., the Rotary, Lions, or Kiwanis club), alumni associations, or any other groups can give donations. Donations are sometimes made for general operating expenses, or they may be tied to a specific project or event, such as a pool renovation or swim meet. You may solicit donations if your facility charter permits it, or interested parties may simply give donations on their own. Whenever a donation is given, seek the appropriate way to thank your donor. For smaller donations, a thank-you letter may suffice; for large donations, you may consider naming the pool after your benefactor or placing a plaque in her honor in your facility. If the donation is tied to a specific purchase or purpose, you must honor the donor's wishes; you cannot reallocate the money according to your own desires. If you do so, you may jeopardize future donations and lose the good will of your donor.

▶ **Grants.** Grant money is given by both government and nongovernment agencies to further specific goals. You must find a grant and apply for it in order to receive money. You must also ensure that your facility is eligible to receive a grant and that the project you are planning matches the criteria set out by the granting agency. At colleges and universities, your best resource for grant assistance is the sponsored projects office. This entity will help you search databases that contain grant opportunities tailored to your needs. If you don't have access to a sponsored projects office, you can join the Community of Science Internet database (www.cos.com), which will search databases for grants on your behalf and send you e-mail alerts about grants that match

Swimmers visit the concession stand for treats.

> **KEY POINT** *Diversifying your facility's sources of income is important to your financial stability. If you are too dependent on one source of income (such as program fees), and the source experiences a weak point or lull, you could be in grave financial difficulties.*

your criteria. The following Web site provides access to government funding opportunities: www.fundsnetservices.com/gov01.htm (Tourney and Clayton, 1981).

EXPENSES

Expenses include all those items that you spend money on. Some expenses are relatively fixed, such as the price of your building mortgage or rent, and some are extremely variable, such as your staff wages. The following is a list of the types of expenses you may have at your facility.

▶ **Mortgage or rent.** This category refers to the money that is paid monthly for the use of the facility. Of course, if you have raised enough money to pay for the facility in advance, if the facility is donated by an agency (e.g., the Kiwanis or Rotary), or if the mortgage is paid off, you will no longer incur this expense.

▶ **Wages.** Wages include all of the money expended on staff, which may include an aquatic director, aquatic supervisors, lifeguards, instructors, pool custodians, customer service staff, identification checkers, security personnel, and concessions staff. Any benefits that the employees receive and the employer pays for or contributes to should also be accounted for in this category. These benefits may include retirement plan contributions, health care coverage, dental plans, and vision plans.

▶ **Utilities.** This category includes power, heating, lighting, and water bills. You can find your monthly expenditure information in your utility bills. The power company can often provide a surprising amount of useful information to help you pinpoint your energy expenditures. Information such as your hours and days of highest use, months of highest use, and even zones of most energy use can sometimes be obtained simply by calling the power company.

▶ **Equipment.** Equipment refers to large, costly, relatively permanent items. Examples might include diving boards, starting blocks, lifeguard chairs, desks, and other furniture. Equipment and supplies (see next item) are often different line items in a budget. Facilities define the specific differences between the two according to their needs. Often, the difference between the two is a set dollar amount. If the price of an item is over a certain amount, the item is considered to be equipment; if the price is under the set amount, the item is considered to be supplies.

▶ **Supplies.** Supplies are usually expendable in nature. This category includes items that you may use up or that have a short usage life. Examples include paper, pens and pencils, cleaning solutions, mops, brooms, buckets, and hoses.

▶ **Swimming pool chemicals.** Although you could consider this a subcategory of supplies, it represents such an important part of your operations and such a significant part of your expenses that you can give it its own category. This expense includes chlorine or bromine, soda ash, **muriatic acid,** water test kits, and reagents.

▶ **Uniforms.** If the facility provides uniforms for staff members—such as shirts, swimsuits, sweat suits, or hats—these should be accounted for as an expense. Personal items provided for staff members can also be included in this category (e.g., sunscreen, towels, athletic bags, and waist packs).

▶ **Insurance.** This may refer to corporate liability insurance, fire insurance, flood insurance, insurance covering the contents of your facility, or any other type of coverage you have. You should also include any insurance paid on vehicles owned by the aquatic facility in this budget line. Personal liability insurance is often purchased by staff members and is not paid for by the facility (and thus is not included in this category).

▶ **Promotional expenses.** This category includes the costs for the production of brochures, newsletters, course catalogs, posters, and flyers. Other expenses related to promotions are newspaper advertisements, radio spots, and television commercials. Postage costs for direct mailings may be accounted for here as well.

▶ **Repairs, improvements, and alterations.** Maintaining a safe, clean, and pleasing aquatic facility requires regular maintenance, improvements, and repairs. You must budget for and account for these expenses. Although the actual repair projects that must be undertaken may be unforeseen, the fact that something will need to be repaired is a given. You may divide this budget line into commodities and services.

  ▶ Commodities are items such as paint, swimming pool tiles, lumber, and other materials that are used in the actual construction and repair. You can purchase some commodities in advance (for smaller, everyday projects) and reduce the cost by purchasing in bulk. For emergency repairs, you may not be able to do this.

  ▶ Services refer to contractual arrangements that you may make for the repair or upgrade of your facilities. Examples of services include carpentry, iron working, plumbing, and electrical work. Although you can plan for some projects, you should assume that emergencies will arise, and your budget should include funds for the immediate use of services. If your facility has in-house tradespeople, you may not need to include this expense in your budget.

KEY POINT *You must understand where your money goes. Track all your expenses so that you know where it goes. You can then begin to make changes to reduce the outflow of your money.*

BREAK-EVEN POINT

Every program has a "break-even" point. This is the point at which the income from registrations has covered all expenses associated with the class—the point at which the class can begin to turn a profit. When figuring out the break-even point for each program, you'll need to compute all expenses, including wages for instructors, lifeguards, and supervisors; equipment and supplies; and this program's share of the facility utilities. Registration income must reach this total expense amount before any profits can be made. Take this figure (total expenses) and divide it by the reg-

istration fee for the class. The number that you get will tell you how many registrants you need in a given class to cover costs (see figure 4.1). Many facilities set this number as the minimum enrollment required for a class to be offered to ensure that a loss is not taken by teaching a class (Rossman, 1989).

MANAGING A BUDGET

After you've estimated your yearly and quarterly expenses and income (and allotted what you hope are the correct amounts for all of your line items), you should do your best to manage your budget. Managing a budget involves a variety of activities, including appointing a fiscal officer, tracking your budget, increasing your enrollment, allocating costs properly, reallocating money, paying bills, controlling purchasing, preventing loss, and completing payroll procedures.

Appointing a Fiscal Officer

One way to improve the management of your budget is to appoint one person at your facility to oversee the total budget. This fiscal officer can be your business manager, bookkeeper, accountant, chief executive officer, or any other appropriate employee. The important qualifications are that this person must understand the budgeting process, must be incorruptibly honest, and must not be afraid to tell other employees "You can't spend that" when he has to. The position of fiscal

Note: This calculation is based on a 30-hour class taught by one instructor and supervised by one lifeguard. The lifeguard receives pay only for those hours the class is in the pool. Wage rate and utility costs shown are for demonstration purposes only. Textbook and pocket mask are purchased separately by students.

Instructor:	30 hrs × $5.50/hr	$165.00
Lifeguard:	15 hrs × $5.50/hr	$82.50
Mannequin rental:	4 × $10/day × 1 day	$40.00
Video tape rental:	4 × $4/day × 4 days	$64.00
Facility usage costs:	Light/heat/water	$200.00
Advertising costs:	Brochures/flyers	$150.00
Total costs for this course:		**$701.50**

Registration fee for this course is $100/student (exclusive of books).
The break-even point for this course is roughly seven students.

Figure 4.1   A sample break-even calculation for a lifeguard training class.

officer isn't always the most popular job, but it is a position that is vitally important to the financial survival of any facility. Your fiscal officer should also have a good understanding of your services and programs in order to better understand those areas where you can cut corners financially and those where you can't (such as safety).

Tracking Your Budget

Track your expenses on at least a monthly basis, and compare them against your budgeted amounts to determine if you are within your budgeted allowance. You can track your expenses by investigating payroll reports to determine wages, utility bills to determine utility expenses, and purchase orders to calculate equipment and supply costs. The key is to determine early if you are over budget. If you notice early that you are over budget, you can take steps to correct the problem. If you don't find out until late in your fiscal year, it is too late to reduce expenses or take any other action to correct the deficit.

Your budget should include some projections regarding the amount of revenue you will bring in from registration fees, rental fees, membership fees, and sales of merchandise. Assess your revenue reports to determine if you are below, meeting, or exceeding your revenue projections. The revenue projections you make should be realistic and based on previous years. This is particularly important if the payment of your bills is dependent on the money you make from fees. In this case, if you are not meeting your revenue projections, you may be unable to pay some of your expenses. If you determine that you are not making the revenue you thought you would, try to find out why and what you can do to correct it. Begin by talking with customers and staff. If you determine that your revenue is falling short, there are several things you can do to try to correct the problem:

▸ **Offer a promotion plan for programs or services.** One such plan is a frequent user swim card: Daily pass customers buy a card for 5 or 10 swims in advance. Each time they swim, a hole is punched in the card. When the card is full, they turn the card in for one free swim. Swimmers like this plan because it represents a value for them. It benefits the facility because you get your swim fees up front.

▸ **Add additional sections for programs with a waiting list.** This generates more revenue and makes patrons happy.

▸ **Offer a bonus for membership referrals.** Members receive a discount on their own membership fee for referring a new member who subsequently signs up and pays dues.

Increasing Enrollment

Increasing enrollment in your programs generates more income, which assists in paying your bills and generating profits for your facility. Take whatever steps you can to ensure that your program registration is as high as possible. Advertising is usually a prerequisite to full enrollment, so your selection of an advertising method is crucial. Review the advertising options available to you (see chapter 3) and select the most cost-effective way to get your program message out.

You can increase enrollment by providing a flyer to customers at the end of a session indicating the dates and times for the next session. This helps in maintaining repeat business. You can also offer small discounts for early enrollment or repeat customers; this encourages customers to sign up early and keeps cash flow up for your facility.

Allocating Costs Properly

Many organizations use budgeting systems that have multiple accounts that they draw from to cover costs (e.g., separate accounts for wages, commodities, and services). Make sure you are allocating charges to the correct account. This allows proper tracking of expenses and proper accounting of funds. Failure to do so may also exhaust one account while leaving another untouched.

Reallocating Funds

If your facility has a flexible budgeting system, you may be able to reallocate funds from an account where they are not needed to an account where they are. For example, if your account for supplies has a large amount of money that has not been expended, and you are experiencing trouble with the wages budget, you may be able to reallocate money from supplies to wages. You should not do this until it becomes necessary to do so; if you determine a need for supplies later, but you have already reallocated the money and spent it, you can't make the needed purchase. Your fiscal officer should be the only person authorized to make reallocations of money from different accounts. This helps ensure that it will only be done when necessary and that it will be done correctly. If you've had to reallocate funds, you should investigate your budget to determine why. Sometimes the reason is beyond your control—for example, if a flood in your locker room requires emergency renovations that you didn't budget for. If you could have foreseen the circumstance that necessitated the fund reallocation, try to take it into consideration in next year's budget so that you will not have to reallocate again.

Paying Bills at the Proper Time

Always pay accounts payable when they are due; failure to do so is bad business and can ruin a corporate credit history. However, the specific timing with which bills are paid is important. The longer cash remains in the bank, the more interest it accrues. Therefore, paying bills before they are due is not beneficial to the bill payer. Structuring your bill payments to take maximum advantage of this arrangement is in the best interest of your facility. Of course, overdue bills incur late charges and must be avoided.

Controlling Purchasing

Only a limited number of staff members should have access to the corporate funds used for the purchase of supplies or equipment. This limits the possibility of misappropriation, overspending, and unneeded purchases. A good policy is to require that the facility manager approve all large dollar purchases. The definition of "large dollar" is relative to the facility. For some facilities, it would be anything over $500; for other facilities, it may be $5,000. The purpose in instituting this control is to ensure that large purchases are truly needed and can be covered by corporate funds. A justification should also be required for all expensive purchases. Any time that a purchase is made, it should be reported to the fiscal officer and entered into the budget ledger. This enables you to track expenditures and to know (in real time) what funds are available.

Purchasing Wisely

Your facility should keep records of those products it has purchased in the past and at what quantities they were purchased. Reviewing this information will assist you in estimating the quantities you will need in the future. This is particularly important because many of the chemicals that are used

at swimming pools have a short shelf life. For example, you would not want to purchase a large quantity of **phenol red,** which is used in water tests as a **pH** indicator, because it has a shelf life of only 6 months. Similarly, you do not want to underorder because you may run out of a crucial product. Rush ordering a product can increase the cost of an item significantly.

You should purchase expendable supplies (such as pool chemicals, paper products, and cleaning supplies) in quantities to last for a period of no more than a few months; these quantities can be estimated based on purchases from the same period of previous years. Ordering for longer periods may result in unusable goods due to exceeded expiration dates, and it also increases the risk of theft or pilferage. If you're not sure whether a given product has a shelf life, read the label; if you're still unsure, contact the manufacturer. To help you determine if a product is still within its useful lifetime, write the date it was purchased on the container. If you're purchasing items by the box or crate, date the box.

When a chemical has reached the end of its life span and is still not used up, dispose of it in the manner directed by the manufacturer. Using products after their expiration date can be dangerous and does not save money, because the active ingredient in the chemical is no longer useful.

At aquatic facilities, some commonly used items that have expiration dates include the following:

- Pool test kit reagents
- Chlorine (particularly liquid)
- Cleaning chemicals
- First aid equipment

Ordering products such as soap, paper towels, office supplies, and pool chemicals in bulk can reduce the unit cost per item. If an organization has multiple pools or multiple facilities, site managers should attempt to coordinate and combine orders to save money. This may require standardization of certain equipment—such as chlorinators, office machines (e.g., photocopiers and computer printers), and facility fixtures (e.g., soap dispensers)—so that bulk purchase of items such as chlorine, toner cartridges, and soap can take place. Contact your suppliers to determine the discount for bulk ordering. If none exists, attempt to negotiate one.

Never purchase from the first sales source you find; always comparison shop. This is now easier than ever with the widespread use of the Internet.

Shop online to compare prices of products you need from various vendors. For those without access to the Internet, catalogs are normally available free of charge simply by calling the supplier's toll-free number. Also compare prices of national chains with local suppliers; the local stores may be willing to make a better deal because they want your repeat business. A good rule of thumb is to have a minimum of three price quotes for any large purchase. (See appendix C for a list of pool supply companies.)

Preventing Loss

Often it's the small losses that can contribute to cost overruns. Use of a business phone for personal calls, misuse of photocopiers, vandalism, pilferage of supplies, and outright theft all contribute to lost profits and unneeded expenses. Take steps to counteract these problems, such as using telephone or copier codes and keeping supplies in a secure area.

Telephone Codes

Issue telephone codes to those employees who are authorized to make long-distance calls. Calls made with each code can be listed on a separate telephone report, and each code holder can be asked to verify his calls monthly. This mechanism assists in reducing unauthorized long-distance calls, which can result in considerable expenses for your facility. The same control can also be placed on fax machines.

Photocopier Control

Much like the telephone codes, copier codes are issued to those authorized to make copies. The copier is programmed to require the code prior to copies being made, and copies made are attributed to that code. This control reduces the use of the copier for unauthorized purposes.

Other mechanisms that you can use to maintain security over photocopiers include removing paper supplies to a locked area after business hours, requiring clerical staff to make all copies, and locking the copier in a storage area.

Supply Security

Supplies are likely to be stolen or pilfered unless they are secured. Store office supplies in a locked cabinet or storeroom, with the key in the possession of the office manager. Other supplies such as paper products and bulk first aid supplies should be accessible only to the appropriate staff mem-

bers. First aid kits should be available throughout the facility and easily accessible in the event they are needed. Storing supplies in a locked area discourages misappropriation of these items. Be sure to permanently label supplies and equipment such as backboards, rescue tubes, and first aid kits with your facility name so that they are more difficult to steal.

> **KEY POINT**   Loss prevention is a key factor in cash management. Although you need to have a certain level of trust with all of your staff, if you don't take some protective measures to guard your assets, you'll lose a lot of money through overuse, misuse, and pilferage.

Applying Wage Control and Payroll Procedures

Wages are a large expense at most aquatic facilities. You must invest an appropriate amount in the individual salaries and hourly wages of your staff to ensure quality employees. However, it is important that you impose rules regarding overtime, hours claimed, and other issues related to compensation.

If your facility uses a time clock to track employee hours, you should monitor when employees are clocking in and out. If the clock is unmonitored, it is easy for unscrupulous employees to claim extra time by clocking in well before their shift and staying clocked in well after it even if not assigned duties. You may want to require staff members to come to a central location to clock in so that the clock can be easily monitored.

If your facility does not use a time clock, you should consider using time sheets to record hours for hourly wage staff. The time sheets should have space for employees to record the date worked, their time in and out, and to initial the entry to verify it. A space should also be provided for the employees' supervisor to sign after reviewing the time sheet. Supervisors should collect all time sheets, review them for truthfulness and accuracy, sign them, and then turn them over to the payroll department.

Set a policy for your staff regarding the number of hours per week that they may work. You should specifically address the issue of overtime. If working additional hours will require the payment of overtime, you may want to require employees to get approval by supervisory staff before doing so. Assess the reason for the overtime and decide if the assignment could be completed without the need for the expenditure of overtime funds. Sometimes the need for additional lifeguards may require you to approve overtime. In this situation, you should determine if the cost can be passed on to a rental group or other fee-paying group. However, be aware of high-volume dates for aquatic facilities, such as Memorial Day and the Fourth of July. Do not compromise safety for the sake of a few dollars of overtime. Similarly, if a maintenance emergency arises, keep in mind that repairing the problem immediately may result in savings that far outweigh the cost of overtime for maintenance personnel.

You should always distribute pay via check or direct deposit, never by cash. Checks and direct deposit enable easier accounting procedures and increased security. Inform all your employees about where and when checks will be distributed (if they are not mailed to their home). You should keep the checks in a secure location, such as a safe, until they are distributed. If you don't know all your employees on sight, require them to display photo identification before receiving their check. Place checks in envelopes to maintain security. Never distribute checks to anyone other than the recipient. If you leave direct deposit statements in employee mailboxes, ensure that the area is monitored so that unauthorized persons do not access them. See appendix D for a sample payroll sheet.

METHODS OF PAYMENT

Once you've decided to make a purchase of any type, you'll need to decide what method of payment to use. The method of payment that you select will depend on several factors, including your facility policies and procedures, cost of the purchase, vendor policies, and how quickly you need the item. There are several methods you can use to make the purchase:

▶ **Purchase order number.** Purchase order numbers are tracking numbers generated by a fiscal officer, business manager, or purchasing department. The purchase order number allocates funds from a given account for a specific purchase. A specific product, dollar amount, and supplier must be identified before a purchase order number

can be issued. It is also common to require a supervisor's signature before the purchase order number is issued. The supplier is given the number when the order is placed. Once the facility receives the item and invoice, the business manager uses the invoice and purchase order number to generate a check drawn against the account from which money was allocated. Before you attempt to order anything, you'll need to determine if the supplier that you want to purchase from will accept a purchase order number. Some stores and suppliers will not accept a purchase order number because it requires no money in advance of the purchase, which many suppliers do not like.

▶ **Purchase order.** A purchase order is very similar to a purchase order number; all the same steps are required, including specification of goods and costs, and allocation of funds. The difference between the two is that when a purchase order is used, a document is generated describing the product specifications, source of supply, costs, and delivery time frame. The document is provided to the supplier when placing an order to ensure that all details and required information are clearly relayed. The determining factor between using a purchase order or purchase order number is often the cost of the item. More expensive items often require a purchase order because it is more detailed and provides a written set of specifications for the supplier.

▶ **Corporate credit card.** Many aquatic facilities have a corporate credit card available for the purchase of items needed for the facility. There are several advantages to using a credit card. The primary benefit is ease of use; you just call the supplier and give the credit card number or visit the store and display your card. This method of payment does not require advance preparation by a fiscal officer and therefore can be used for emergency purchases after hours and on weekends and holidays. Additionally, major credit cards are almost universally accepted by all stores and supply houses, further easing your purchasing process.

However, there are some disadvantages in using corporate credit cards for purchases. One of the major risks with credit cards is that they will be used by someone to make unauthorized purchases. To prevent this, you should secure the card in a locked drawer or cabinet when it is not in use. You should also carefully limit the personnel that are allowed to use it. After statements are received each month, you should reconcile the statement against purchases made and investigate any discrepancies. Another disadvantage is the interest fee charged for carrying a balance on the credit card. To avoid this potentially expensive cost, you should pay off the balance as soon as possible after charges are made. Be careful when using credit cards to make purchases over the Internet. Be certain that the site is reputable and secure; otherwise, you risk having your card number stolen and misappropriated for other uses.

▶ **Cash.** Some facilities maintain a petty cash fund for emergency purchases. The major advantages of cash are that it's simple to use and that it's universally accepted. However, you must be present at a store to use it, which means that Internet and catalog orders are out, and it's very easily stolen or misappropriated. If you do have a petty cash fund, lock it up when it's not in use. You should also have very strict guidelines regarding who is authorized to use it and what it may be used for. Additionally, you should require that receipts be retained for all purchases made against petty cash funds and that they be turned in to the fiscal officer. Petty cash should only be used when no other means of purchase is available.

▶ **Confirming purchase order.** In this instance, the staff member orders or purchases the item and then requests a purchase order or purchase order number from the business office. This practice is not recommended because the funds may not be available to allocate to this item or the fiscal officer may not approve the purchase. Many organizations prohibit the use of confirming purchase orders.

▶ **Check.** Sometimes called a "pro forma," a check may be sent with an order via mail, taken to the store, or sent in advance of the purchase. In many ways, a check is the cleanest method of payment. The suppliers normally like this method because they're getting payment at the time of purchase. Checks are also easy to track, and they make it difficult to cheat or steal because the check is made out to a specific company. As with other forms of purchasing, you should limit who has authority to write and request checks. Checks should be computer printed with your facility information and logo on them. Blank checks should be stored in a secure area.

▶ **Bid process.** In the bid process, you specify the object that you want to purchase, but not the supplier. You must create a detailed description of what you want to purchase, including color, size, amount, composition, and any other significant details. Your specifications are sent to prospective suppliers along with a request for them to submit a cost estimate for your object and a determination of whether they can meet your deadline. After you receive the bids, select the one that meets your cost and time line requirements. It's important that you write your specifications clearly so that you receive the item you want. Bids are normally sought for very costly purchases. The definition of "very costly" depends on your facility budget.

See appendix D for a sample purchase tracking sheet.

> **KEY POINT** There are many methods of payment for goods and services. Not every method is right for every situation. Develop a policy at your facility regarding how you pay for things.

FISCAL REPORTS

You should create and issue a fiscal report after the books are closed each fiscal year. The report should contain what expenses were projected and what they actually were, along with what revenues were projected and what they actually were. The report should break down each line item in your budget and should be very precise in identifying what actually happened financially in your organization that year.

In determining your revenue for the report, research all money brought in from all programs, rentals, sales, donations, and fund-raising. Create spreadsheets for each source if necessary. Determine expenses by researching wage reports, utility bills, and purchase orders to create a whole picture of the money spent.

The report is normally in the form of spreadsheets but can also contain explanations and a summary from the fiscal officer. The purpose of the report is to let your board of directors, shareholders, city council, managers, or anyone else in authority know the state of your financial affairs. On a daily working level, the report helps you determine how to realistically project the figures you will put in next year's budget. Keep fiscal reports on file for reference purposes when recording financial progress.

BASIC PRINCIPLES OF CASH FLOW MANAGEMENT

Managing the facility's money can be a difficult task if you're not properly prepared. You'll need to take steps to control the intake and outflow of money at your facility to ensure accountability at all points. The following are some basic principles of cash flow management and security:

▶ **Always issue a receipt to customers for goods and services purchased.** This allows you to balance cash in the register against transactions and reduces the likelihood of theft. An added benefit is that it makes refunds easier because the customer has a transaction record proving payment.

▶ **Have a safe for securing cash during the day.** If your facility handles large amounts of cash, consider making bank deposits throughout the day. You must provide locking deposit bags for this purpose. Never send employees to make deposits alone. You may want to have security personnel escort employees with large amounts of cash.

▶ **Never leave cash in an unoccupied facility, particularly overnight.** This invites break-ins and theft.

▶ **Have a cash register at points of sale.** This helps organize cash, provides a receipt for all transactions, and allows for some security because the registers can be locked.

▶ **Whenever possible, have more than one cashier at a point of sale.** This increases accountability and honesty, and it reduces the possibility of pilfering, theft, and just plain mistakes.

▶ **Establish and post a policy related to returned checks.** If you are going to assess a surcharge on returned checks, state that and be able to identify a good reason for doing so. If you have returned checks for the same customer on more than one occasion, you may want to decline further checks from that person and insist on cash for your own protection.

▶ **Never make purchases for the facility with your own money and ask for reimbursement.** In many cases, this is expressly against policy; you may be faced with refusal of reimbursement on a number of grounds and be forced to pay the bill yourself.

▶ **Conduct random audits.** Institute a procedure of random audits of cash deposits. The purpose is to ensure that record keeping is being done properly and that theft is not occurring.

FINANCIAL CRISIS PLANNING

As much as aquatic managers don't like to think about it, accidents and disasters can occur at aquatic facilities. Fires, earthquakes, tornadoes, hurricanes, and vandalism may cause significant physical damage or total destruction of your aquatic facility. Your first concern is certainly for the safety of your patrons and staff; however, once you've determined that everyone is safe, your attention must turn to your facility and business operations. There are several steps that you can take to prepare for a crisis.

Have Duplicates of Financial Records

Every facility has an essential set of financial documents, including bank statements, insurance papers, fiscal plans, payroll sheets, and budget ledgers. These documents are crucial to providing a picture of where your facility is financially (i.e., what your current resources are and where you're going). If you lose these documents, continued fiscal operation would be possible, but difficult.

To avoid this added stress in an emergency, create backup copies of fiscal records and store them in a safe location away from your main facility. This alternate location might be a bank safe deposit box or a different branch of your facility. If possible, update these records regularly so that the information is current. Include hard copies as well as electronic copies so that you will be able to access the information even if you do not have access to a computer.

Have a Plan

You need to consider in advance what a closure of your facility might mean. Items to plan for may include the following:

▶ Salvaging equipment and supplies
▶ Protecting undamaged portions of your facility
▶ Notifying patrons of the closure of your facility
▶ Relocating programs during the closure of your facility, if possible
▶ Contacting your insurance provider

Closure of your facility for any reason has an immediate adverse effect on your income. You can't make money if you're not open. For this reason, you'll need a plan to relocate as many of your programs and services as possible to alternate locations until you can reopen your facility. Land-based classes (e.g., first aid and CPR) and the lecture portions of courses such as lifeguard training and instructor courses can be taught in school classrooms, gymnasiums, community centers, or senior citizens centers. Explore the possibility of renting or borrowing space in one of these facilities in an emergency. If your organization has multiple locations, such as with metro YMCAs or large municipalities, you may be able to shift aquatics classes such as swim lessons and water aerobics to another location. If your organization has access to only one pool, explore the possibility of renting space on an emergency basis from another organization.

Make sure your insurance provider's phone number is stored with your policy in your backup files. Contact your provider as soon as you determine that you have damage to the facility. The faster you make contact, the sooner you can expect reimbursement.

You need to return to revenue generation as soon as possible. If you do not, you may be unable to reopen at all due to lack of funds.

Assign Duties to Staff

In an emergency, the assignment of crucial duties to your staff will lend order to the chaos and will speed you on your way to recovery. Provide training for your staff in advance so that they will know how to accomplish these tasks under the stress of an emergency. Although you can assign these duties in advance, remember that some staff members may not be available to you in an emergency for any number of reasons (e.g., they may be personally affected by the disaster and may be unable to report for duty). Tasks that you can allocate to your staff members include the following:

▸ Accounting for all staff and notifying staff of operational status

▸ Conducting preliminary damage assessments

▸ Contacting your insurance provider

▸ Serving as media liaison regarding operation of your facility (See "Crisis Communications" in chapter 3.)

▸ Retrieving your financial files from your alternate location

▸ Communicating with members and patrons regarding rescheduled or moved programs

The duties that you assign to your staff should be spelled out clearly in your disaster plan. Duties should be assigned to staff based on their skills and positions. Include a staff phone list with your emergency plan and store the entire plan with your financial documents at your alternate site (Perry, 2001).

MAKING MAJOR PURCHASES

Major purchases of permanent fixtures such as diving boards, large inflatable toys, slides, or other high-cost items should be carefully planned. When contemplating such a purchase, you should ask yourself, "What are the benefits of buying this item?" Ultimately, to justify the purchase, it must provide a service that your customers want, assist in drawing new clients to your facility, or enable you to offer a program that you believe your customers want. If a high-cost item doesn't meet at least one of these criteria, you should rethink making the purchase.

© Mary E. Messenger

A diving board is an example of a major purchase item.

When making your decision, you should visit other facilities that currently have the item that you want to purchase. Discuss the item with the staff at the facility you visit and ask them the following questions:

- Has the purchase made the impact that they wanted at the facility or on a specific program? Why or why not?
- What maintenance procedures are required to maintain this item?
- Were additional after-purchase items required that were not included in the initial cost?
- Was any special instruction or training required to learn how to operate and maintain this item? Did the manufacturer or supplier provide this training?
- Are any special considerations necessary when installing this item in the facility? How long does installation take?
- Were safety instructions included with the item when it was purchased?
- Did the new item require the development of any new safety rules?
- Are there any particular hazards associated with this device to be aware of?

While making the facility visit, try to make a point of seeing the equipment you want to purchase being used, or ask if you can try it yourself. Also ask for copies of any rules or procedures that the facility has developed for this product. Don't forget to send a thank-you letter after your visit and to offer to host a visit in exchange.

When you've decided that you do want to purchase the item, you should begin researching sources of supply. Be sure to comparison shop at several companies. You should contact customer service representatives from a minimum of three different suppliers and ask the following questions:

- What is the current price for this item?
- Does the company provide customer support after the purchase?
- Does this product come with a guarantee or warranty?
- Does the sales company install this item or can it recommend a local installer?
- Will the supplier service this product?

- What is the expected life of this product?
- How long does it take for this product to be shipped and installed?
- What are the payment terms associated with this item (e.g., prepaid only, purchase orders, credit card required)?

You may want to create a comparison chart of all the companies you've researched and compare their costs and services to determine which one will provide the best package of low cost and good service. Try to work with a well-known supplier if possible, one that has a reputation for standing by its product and providing good customer service.

You may also want to make more in-depth inquiries regarding the safety record of the product. Contacting other facilities that have had this product for several years may provide insight by revealing injury trends associated with the product. You can also research this product on the Web to see if product reviews are available there. For definitive information regarding a product's injury-related track record, contact the Consumer Product Safety Commission (CPSC) and request data related to the product (see appendix A).

KEY POINT *The advice "buyer beware" fits for large purchases. Be sure to thoroughly research any major purchase before you buy it; it represents a major investment of your facility capital.*

SUMMARY

Maintaining a well-organized and balanced budget is essential to the efficient operation of your facility. You must understand what expenses and revenue your facility generates so that you can explore opportunities to boost revenue and cut expenses. You should carefully monitor and control your facility budget so that you can maintain fiscal accountability. Large purchases can be a major expenditure of facility funds. Carefully plan for these purchases by comparison shopping, by performing research on the product, and by visiting other facilities that have similar items to ask questions before your own purchase.

REVIEW QUESTIONS

1. List and describe sources of revenue for an aquatic facility.
2. Describe how to determine the "break-even" point for a program.
3. Describe the fiscal officer's duties.
4. List the basic principles of cash flow management and security.
5. List and describe methods of payment an aquatic facility can use to buy items.
6. What is a pro forma?

BIBLIOGRAPHY

Gordon, D., & Gamble, D. (1983). *The balance sheet. Aquatic programming: Reaching today's market.* Ottawa, ON: Royal Life Saving Society Canada.

Hodgkinson, N. (1998). Cashing in on food concessions. *Aquatics International,* 10(2), 30-32.

Kent, J. (1986, May). *Volunteer management.* Rescue '86 Symposium, Vancouver, BC.

Perry, P. (2001, April). All the way back: A recovery plan must be in place before disaster strikes. *Athletic Business,* 25, 36-37.

Rossman, R. (1989). *Recreation programming: Designing leisure experiences.* Champaign, IL: Sagamore.

Tourney, J., & Clayton, R. (1981). *Aquatic organization and management.* Minneapolis: Burgess.

RESOURCES

Dove, K. (1999). *Conducting a successful capital campaign* (2nd ed.). San Francisco: Jossey-Bass.

Grace, K.S. (1997). *Beyond fundraising.* New York: John Wiley and Sons.

Schaff, T., & Schaff, D. (1999). *The fundraising planner.* San Francisco: Jossey-Bass.

Developing Staff

Chapter Objectives

After reading this chapter, you should be able to

1. develop a job description for an aquatics position,

2. list and describe methods for recruiting staff,

3. list and describe the steps involved in interviewing and evaluating prospective staff members,

4. list and describe the steps involved in hiring a staff member,

5. list and describe the steps involved in supervising aquatic staff,

6. develop a comprehensive aquatic staff training program, and

7. list and describe methods of aquatic staff retention.

A mature, well-trained aquatic staff is crucial to the success of any aquatic facility or program. The recruitment, training, and retention of quality aquatic staff should be a top priority for aquatic managers. Poorly trained or ill-suited staff will reflect poorly on the facility as a whole; they may also place patrons in danger through inattentiveness to their duties. This chapter provides information about defining staff positions, interviewing potential staff, and hiring staff. Topics related to managing existing staff are also discussed, including orientation, supervision, scheduling, training, retention, and career development.

Aquatics is a field that is often short of employees. Recruiting enough employees of good quality becomes a high priority for your facility. There are many methods that you can use to recruit staff, including advertising, job fairs, and recruiting from classes. You'll need to plan carefully to make the most of the time and money you invest in this important project. To help you in this area, this chapter describes various methods and tools that you can use to recruit staff.

Once you've got your pool of potential employees, you must select those that will bring the most benefit to your facility. If you don't select the right employee, you might lower the quality of your programs and services. Therefore, this chapter also provides you with suggestions for screening, testing, interviewing, and hiring new staff. Included you'll find helpful hints for interview questions that you should and shouldn't ask.

The training that you provide to your staff is a key component in maintaining their skills and professionalism. There are many topics that your staff needs to review and many new skills to learn. To help you plan in-service training for your staff, this chapter provides a comprehensive list of topics and skills you may want to cover, along with a description of different methods that you can use to deliver this training.

STAFF POSITIONS

Aquatic facilities typically employ a variety of staff that have different job descriptions and duties. You must provide each employee with a specific description of his or her duties, and each employee must understand this description fully. The description should also identify who that staff member reports to and what qualifications the staff member is expected to have or obtain. This section includes position descriptions for aquatic director, assistant aquatic director, lifeguard supervisor, lifeguard, instructor, **pool operator,** and customer service staff.

> **KEY POINT**   *You must clearly define the duties and needed qualifications for all staff positions. This will help you select the proper staff and will help staff members know what is expected of them.*

Aquatic Director

The aquatic director is responsible for the overall operation of the aquatic facility and all of its programs. General duties include the following:

- Develops and manages the aquatics budget
- Recruits, hires, trains, and supervises aquatic staff
- Oversees the maintenance and cleanliness of the aquatic facility
- Develops and maintains aquatic programs
- Ensures that the facility is in compliance with the state and local codes, laws, and regulations
- Works with outside groups regarding use of the facility and cooperative programs
- Makes purchases related to aquatics
- Develops and implements marketing and promotions strategies related to aquatics

Required qualifications include certification in lifeguard training, CPR for the professional rescuer, standard first aid, automatic external defibrillation (AED), supplemental oxygen administration, and preventing disease transmission. Swimming instructor certification from a national agency (such as the American Red Cross or YMCA of the USA) as well as lifeguard training instructor,

CPR and first aid instructor, and pool operations certification, are also required. Other specialty instructor certification may be required by the facility. Several years experience as a lifeguard, swimming instructor, head lifeguard, or assistant head lifeguard should be required. Instructor trainer certification in lifeguard training, swimming instructor, and CPR and first aid are highly desirable. A bachelor's degree in physical education, recreation, or a related field is also required; a master's degree may be required at large institutions.

Assistant Aquatic Director

The assistant aquatic director aids the aquatic director and functions as the aquatic director in his or her absence. Specific duties include the following:

- Provides direct supervision and training of staff
- Assists with the development of the aquatics budget
- Maintains aquatic records, including employee files and incident and accident reports
- Identifies and reports maintenance and pool water chemistry problems to the aquatic director
- Provides direct supervision of aquatic programs

Required qualifications include certification in lifeguard training, CPR for the professional rescuer, standard first aid, automatic external defibrillation (AED), supplemental oxygen administration, and preventing disease transmission. Swimming instructor certification from a national agency (such as the American Red Cross, YMCA of the USA, or Ellis and Associates), as well as lifeguard training instructor, CPR and first aid instructor, and pool operations certification, are also required. Other specialty instructor certification may be required by the facility. Several years experience as a lifeguard, swimming instructor, head lifeguard, or assistant head lifeguard should be required. A bachelor's degree in physical education, recreation, or a related field is also required.

Lifeguard Supervisor

The lifeguard supervisor works with the lifeguard staff during their shifts, providing them with training, supervision, and direction. Specific responsibilities include the following:

- Performs duties as a lifeguard (supervising patrons)
- Performs rescues
- Completes basic record-keeping tasks
- Performs light cleaning duties
- Ensures that lifeguards are present for their shifts and that they are in uniform and at their stations
- Provides training for new staff
- Ensures that appropriate reports are correctly completed as needed (such as accident reports and payroll sheets)
- Ensures that the facility opens and closes according to posted schedules
- Identifies and reports maintenance and swimming pool water chemistry problems to the assistant aquatic director
- Assumes responsibility for lifeguard supplies, including first aid kits, rescue equipment, and office supplies
- Deals with initial patron complaints and takes action as required

Required qualifications include certification in lifeguard training, CPR for the professional rescuer, standard first aid, automatic external defibrillation (AED), supplemental oxygen administration, and preventing disease transmission. Head lifeguard training, swimming instructor certification, and lifeguard instructor certification are very helpful. A high school diploma and at least 2 years experience as a lifeguard round out the requirements for this staff member.

Lifeguard

The lifeguard's primary responsibility is to safeguard the patrons in the aquatic facility and to render assistance if they become injured, ill, or distressed. Other secondary responsibilities may be assigned (e.g., cleaning, completing reports, or testing water chemistry), but they must not interfere with the lifeguard's primary duty of maintaining supervision of the swimmers.

Qualifications that are required for this position include lifeguard training from a nationally recognized agency, CPR for the professional rescuer, and first aid training.

Instructor

The instructor's main responsibility is to deliver instruction to the students. Lesson preparation and planning are considered part of these duties. Although instructors are required to maintain supervision of their class from a safety standpoint, they can't watch every student at all times; therefore, a lifeguard should always be on duty during classes.

Required qualifications for instructors include lifeguard training, CPR for the professional rescuer, first aid, and a specialty instructor certificate appropriate for the area that they teach. This may be a swimming instructor certificate or instructor authorization in lifeguard training, water exercise, scuba, or small craft safety.

Pool Operator

Pool operators are unlike the other members of your staff. Their main responsibilities are technical in nature, and they may have little contact with the patrons themselves, yet everything they do directly affects your customers. The pool operators are responsible for the water chemistry and maintenance of the pool. Duties may include the following:

- Tests pool water chemistry
- Alters pool water chemistry (e.g., levels of chlorine or bromine and pH)
- Vacuums the pool
- Scrubs pool decks
- Maintains the filtration system
- Cleans pool fixtures such as diving boards and starting blocks
- Keeps accurate records of water chemistry and forwards them to the state regulatory agency
- Makes minor repairs to the facility
- Cleans and restocks locker and change rooms
- Maintains air and water temperature
- Works with contractors, including plumbers, electricians, and carpenters

A certification in pool operations—for example, the YMCA Pool Operator on Location, Aquatic Facility Operator (AFO), or Certified Pool Operator—is essential for this position. However, a good pool operator should also possess some intangibles, such as mechanical aptitude, ingenuity, and organizational skills. Pool operators must have a good understanding of the state **bathing code** because they will work with it daily. For safety purposes, pool operators must know how to swim in case they accidentally end up in the water while alone at the facility. A high school diploma should be the minimum education for this position. Pool operators should also be certified in CPR for the professional rescuer and first aid so that they will be able to assist in an emergency.

Customer Service Staff

Although they don't actually work in the pool area and may never get in the water, your customer service or "front desk" staff are crucial to your facility's success. A customer service staff member is often the first person a customer meets when entering your facility and may set the tone for that customer's opinion of your facility. Duties may include the following:

- Greets customers and potential customers
- Registers customers for aquatic programs (either by computer or on paper)
- Sells facility memberships and daily use passes
- Sells aquatics merchandise
- Distributes facility-related membership and promotional materials
- Answers customers' questions about aquatic facilities and programs
- Handles cash and makes correct change
- Answers telephone calls
- Refers inquiries to the proper staff member as needed

Your customer service staff should be friendly, outgoing, and well organized. They need to be well educated about your facility, programs, and services so that they can intelligently answer questions from the public. This can be on-the-job training and does not necessarily need to be a prerequisite for employment. These staff members should also have basic computer skills and the ability to easily make change and to be accountable for sums of money. Your customer service staff should also be certified in CPR and first aid so that they can respond immediately in the event that a customer becomes ill or injured in their area.

VOLUNTEERS

One way to augment your staff while cutting costs is to use volunteers. Volunteers can assist with registration, customer service, and swim lessons. Although volunteers should not be used to totally replace paid staff, they can work in conjunction with them.

Sources of volunteers include

- stay-at-home parents and retirees,
- high school or college students working on service projects,
- community service organizations, and
- Boy Scouts or Girl Scouts working on service projects.

Be sure that your volunteers receive training related to their assignments before they begin, including safety protocols and emergency procedures. Attempt to have all volunteers trained in first aid and CPR. Provide volunteers with the same name tags and uniforms that you provide for paid staff. You should also give your volunteers access to lunchrooms, fitness areas, and other staff-only areas of your facility. This helps increase their sense of belonging, develops a sense of professionalism, and reduces the distinction between paid staff and volunteers. Do not allow noncertified volunteers to assume duties that they are not qualified for, such as lifeguarding or coaching. Require your volunteers to record their hours just as your employees do. You can use these records to create awards for volunteers based on service.

Volunteers serve to reduce expenses incurred from payroll and employee benefits while still providing a service. Many volunteers have significant skills and provide a service to your facility that far outweighs any volunteer awards they may receive. Interview your volunteers to determine where their skills lie, and place them accordingly. When recruiting volunteers, you need to be very specific in outlining what the volunteer duties are, what populations are being served, and what training is being provided. Volunteers often perform unpaid work because it gives them a sense of contributing something to someone who needs them. Therefore, you should emphasize the intangible benefits to your volunteers. Prepare a well-thought-out and visual presentation to give to various groups that you want to draw volunteers from. Be sure to specify the time commitment required to volunteer (including time for training) and any prerequisites, such as background checks if working with children or CPR and first aid training.

RECRUITING

From aquatic directors to lifeguards, aquatics is a field with a shortage of applicants. Recruiting qualified applicants to become lifeguards, instructors, and supervisors at your facility is a critical step in ensuring the success of your programs, because a good staff is a key element in customer satisfaction. Identifying and attracting good candidates require time and inventiveness on the part of the aquatic director. Some suggestions for finding and recruiting aquatic staff follow.

> **KEY POINT** Successful recruiting is crucial to obtaining enough high-quality applicants to fill vacancies at your facility.

Sources of Candidates

Ready-made sources of potential employees are available to the employer who knows where to look. Potential sources of staff include lifeguard classes, swim teams, job fairs, college physical education departments, and college career centers.

Lifeguard Classes

You should offer your own lifeguard training classes if possible. This will create a pool of qualified candidates who are already predisposed to work for you because they are familiar with your facility. You are also given the opportunity to ensure the quality of their training and to include some facility-specific training during their course. This situation is really ideal—you know the candidates, you know their training is current, and you know they have knowledge of your facility.

You may also visit lifeguard courses offered at other locations, such as YMCAs, community pools, colleges and universities, and high schools. You can distribute information regarding vacancies at your facility, and you have the opportunity to see some of their training while you are there. Of course, you must obtain prior permission from the instructor and facility operator before you do this.

Swimming and Diving Teams

Swim teams at the high school, college, and older age group levels provide a prepared group of obviously competent swimmers. Many of these swimmers already possess lifeguard training and other certification. You can distribute employment information for those who are certified and distribute information about upcoming lifeguard training classes for those who are interested in becoming certified. Again, be sure to obtain prior permission from the coach before visiting, and always visit during practice, never during a meet.

Job Fairs

Many high schools, colleges, universities, and municipalities offer job fairs at selected times throughout the year. To take advantage of this opportunity, you'll need to contact the fair organizer and reserve a space. Most fairs provide a table, several chairs, and access to power for any appliances you bring. In preparing for a job fair, you should organize a display designed to attract potential applicants to your table. A stand-up display that shows action photos of your facility is helpful. Other materials that you should bring include application forms, job descriptions, business cards, and program information from your facility. You should also have materials available announcing upcoming classes in case prospective lifeguards show interest but tell you that their certification has lapsed or that they would like to become certified.

College Physical Education Departments

Many colleges and universities offer aquatics training ranging from lifeguard certification to a fully developed aquatics major. These institutions can be a source of lifeguards, instructors, pool managers, swimming and diving coaches, and aquatic directors. You should seek out the faculty members that teach the aquatics courses and ask them if employment vacancies can be announced in their classes or forwarded to interested students.

College and University Career Centers

Career centers at colleges and universities often collect vacancy announcements from the community and make them available to students seeking employment. You should contact the center director to see what the requirements are for announcing jobs.

Methods for Finding Employees

To ensure that you have the best pool of eligible employees, your employment vacancies must be announced to the widest audience possible. Avenues for announcing your vacancies include newspaper advertisements, trade magazines, radio announcements, flyers, and Internet postings.

Newspaper Advertisements

Despite developments in the realm of electronic communication, newspapers continue to be a popular source for employment seekers. Advertisements for jobs should include the following information: job title, job description, name of the company hiring, required qualifications, preferred qualifications, pay scale, benefits offered, whether the job is full or part time, length of employment period (temporary or permanent), application procedures (including mailing address if materials are to be mailed), and the deadline for application. In most cases, the best time to place newspaper employment advertisements is on Saturday and Sunday because the most widely read issues of the newspaper are printed on these days. You should place your advertisement in those newspapers with the highest circulation in the local area of the available job. Newspaper advertisements are priced by the word or by column inch of space; you should determine the pricing method when budgeting for your ads and preparing your copy.

Trade Magazines

Permanent professional positions such as aquatic director require a wider dissemination of information to draw qualified candidates. Trade magazines that are received by aquatic professionals are an excellent source for advertisement. Professional and trade magazines that you may want to advertise with include *Aquatics International, Athletic Business,* the *Chronicle of Higher Education,* and *Parks and Recreation Magazine.* You should contact the magazine or journal directly to determine if a fee is charged for advertising. You should include the same information in your trade magazine advertisement as in a newspaper ad.

Radio Announcements

Radio spots are a relatively cost-effective way to reach a large audience multiple times. Most radio ads are 20 to 30 seconds long, and the information communicated must be formatted accordingly. The cost for radio ads is determined based on the length of the spots and the number of times the spots are played. The time of day that the ads are run may also affect the price. The more potential listeners reached during a given time period, the more expensive the advertisement often is. The period with the largest listening audience of the day is called drive time. This period encompasses 6:00 to 9:00 A.M. and 3:00 to 6:00 P.M., when a large number of commuters are in their cars and are likely to listen to the radio. This time of day is the best for purchasing radio spots, and consequently, the most expensive. Consider the primary audience of the radio station that you will be advertising on. You'll want to select a radio station that your target audience will be listening to.

Flyers

One-page flyers announcing your part-time positions (such as swimming instructor and lifeguard) can be a cost-effective way of finding potential employees. Flyers can be mass produced cheaply using desktop publishing tools and color copiers. Once an eye-catching flyer announcing the job and containing pertinent information is produced, it can be distributed to high schools, colleges, and job placement centers. You can also post it in your own facility.

Internet Recruiting

The Internet is becoming an increasingly popular method for the recruitment of potential employees and the announcement of jobs. Announcements can be posted on your facility Web site or by utilizing another organization's Web site. Employment sites that specialize in aquatics or are likely to draw aquatics job seekers include the following:

- www.aquaweb.org
- www.bluefishjobs.com
- www.ncaa.org

You may want to develop a specific page on your Web site devoted to employment opportunities. This page can contain a list and brief description of all the jobs available at your facility, and the procedures for application.

INTERVIEWING POTENTIAL STAFF

Once you've identified candidates that you are interested in further investigating, you're ready to proceed to the interview process. You must act cautiously prior to and during the interview

> **KEY POINT** *Proper interviewing is an important factor in choosing the right candidate and adhering to labor laws. Be sure that all the questions you ask are within the bounds of the law.*

to ensure that you protect the rights of your prospective employees. This section provides some guidance.

Consult With Your Human Resources Department

Your human resources (HR) department can provide expert guidance regarding adherence to employment regulations and laws. You should always consult with this office prior to interviewing potential candidates. Your HR department will ensure that you are treating all candidates equally and that you are adhering to equal opportunity laws and agency regulations. You should provide your HR staff with a file of the candidates you want to interview, including application forms, resumes, letters of reference, copies of certification, and any other pertinent information. Your HR staff can then evaluate this information to ensure that the application package is complete and that you have abided by the appropriate laws and regulations. If your organization doesn't have an HR department, your senior staff should review the application package. Try to ensure that these senior staff members have some basic instruction regarding laws and regulations associated with hiring employees.

Have More Than One Candidate to Interview

Interviewing more than one candidate allows you to compare potential employees against each other to determine which one would be best suited to your facility's needs. Also, if the position is offered to one candidate, and that candidate declines the offer, you are able to offer it to your next highest ranked candidate with little delay because you have already completed an interview.

Prepare Your Questions in Advance

Questions should be open ended whenever possible to allow the interviewee to demonstrate his or her knowledge in a particular area. Ask questions or make requests that will elicit responses that show if the candidate possesses the needed skills in the desired areas. Here are some examples of these types of questions and requests:

- ▶ Please describe your previous work experience in positions similar to this job.
- ▶ Please describe the training that you've had to prepare you for this job.
- ▶ Describe typical duties that you've performed in the past that demonstrate the skills or expertise needed for this job.
- ▶ Describe examples of how you've offered suggestions, made improvements, or worked above and beyond your duties in other positions.
- ▶ How would you demonstrate your leadership skills and abilities if you were hired for this job?

Care should be taken to ensure that illegal questions are avoided. Examples of illegal interview questions include the following:

- ▶ Questions relating to the candidate's marital status.
- ▶ Questions relating to the candidate's religious preference.
- ▶ Questions relating to the candidate's ethnic background.
- ▶ Questions relating to the candidate's sexual orientation.
- ▶ Questions relating to the candidate's age (unless a minimum age is required to hold the position, in which case the question "Are you of legal age to hold this position?" may be used).
- ▶ Questions relating to the candidate's nationality. (You may ask, "Are you legally eligible to work in the United States?")
- ▶ Questions relating to whether the candidate has children or intends to become pregnant or otherwise have children.

If the candidate will be interviewed by a group or committee, all members of the group should be given questions to ask. The order in which the questions are asked should be predetermined, and all members should be briefed on questions that they may not ask.

Take Notes

Notes should be taken during a candidate's interview. When a committee is performing the interview, one member should be designated to record the questions and the candidate's responses; it doesn't have to be an exact word-for-word recording but can be a general account of the interview. Care must be taken to avoid subjective comments or personal opinions as part of the recording process. Once the interview is complete, the transcript should be typed and included as part of the candidate's application file.

Request Copies of Certifications

Be sure to ask the candidates to bring copies of all their current aquatic certifications with them to the interview, including lifeguard training, instructor certificates, CPR, first aid, and pool operator cards. This will enable you to verify that the candidates meet the certification requirements specified in your job description. You may also want to include specific questions related to their certification in the interview.

Adhere to the Americans With Disabilities Act

The Americans With Disabilities Act (ADA) specifies that you may not deny employment to a candidate based solely on the presence of a disability when the candidate is otherwise qualified for the position. You may, however, specify what the physical requirements are for a given job—for example, the ability to stand for long periods, the ability to lift a specific amount of weight, or the ability to successfully complete a rescue. You must consider the ADA when interviewing prospective employees. You may not ask if a candidate has a disability or inquire about disabilities that you perceive the candidate to have; you may inquire if the candidate can meet the physical requirements listed in the job description.

SKILLS AND KNOWLEDGE EVALUATION

Certification and experience alone do not give a clear picture of your potential employees' abilities. Certification cards only indicate that a person was able to perform certain skills and held certain knowledge at the time the test was taken. You must determine if a candidate still possesses those skills. Often the best way to do this is to require candidates to perform testing. Skills and knowledge tests are used for lifeguards and

instructors, and knowledge exams are used for administrative or managerial positions.

Skills Evaluation

Requiring your aquatic staff to perform a skills test prior to being hired allows you to determine their comfort level in the water and the proficiency of their rescue skills. Facilities that hire large numbers of staff at one time (such as at the beginning of a summer season) may want to schedule several testing dates and have potential staff members sign up for a given day. This allows the examiners to adequately prepare for administering the tests. Facilities that hire staff on an individual basis are able to perform tests on an individual basis.

Tests must be standardized to ensure fairness and consistency among all potential hires. Test items should focus on lifeguard fitness, technical proficiency, and skills performance. Staff members who are certified as lifeguard instructors by a national agency should administer lifeguard skills tests. Sample test items may include the following:

▶ **Distance swim (500 yards).** The candidate must swim 500 yards (457.2 meters) continuously using any stroke or combination of strokes. Set a minimum acceptable time standard for your facility (10 to 15 minutes is considered acceptable).

▶ **Deep water spinal injury rescue.** The candidate enters deep water and recovers a victim of a simulated spinal injury, treading water with the victim until told to stop.

▶ **Active victim rescue.** The candidate begins in the lifeguard stand with a rescue tube. Upon recognizing the victim, the candidate must properly signal an emergency, enter the water safely, perform a proper approach stroke, contact the victim, and tow the victim to the side. The candidate must remove the victim from the water.

▶ **CPR skills test.** The candidate is presented with a mannequin and prompted with various commands as he or she assesses the mannequin for breathing and pulse. The victim may be an adult, infant, or child. The rescuer should be asked to display **rescue breathing,** CPR, and choking rescue skills. Requiring the rescuer to demonstrate skills in the use of the **bag-valve mask** and **pocket mask** is also recommended. The CPR standards of a national agency, such as the American Red Cross or American Heart Association, should be used to evaluate rescuers in this area.

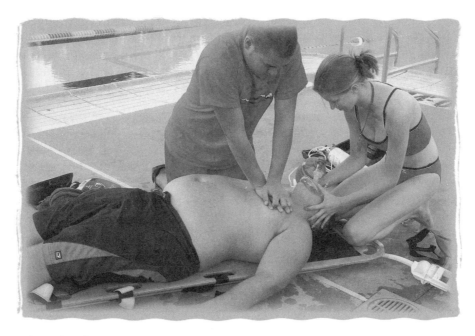

Lifeguards performing two-rescuer CPR.

▶ **Teaching demonstration.** For prospective instructors of any type (e.g., water exercise, swimming, or diving), you may want to ask them to demonstrate their skills by teaching a sample class with real students. Monitor them closely and have the regular class instructor standing by. Specify a set time period for them to teach (15 to 20 minutes). Prior to the session that they will be teaching, let the candidates know the topic, age and skill level, and duration of the class. This will allow them to properly prepare.

▶ **Water chemistry test (for maintenance personnel or lifeguards who will have responsibilities for water testing).** Provide the candidate with a test kit that you use at your facility. Ask the candidate to test for disinfectant level (chlorine or bromine) and pH level. Give candidates a brief period to become familiar with the test kit in case they have not used that particular type before; provide the instruction manual for reference.

Knowledge Evaluation

Knowledge evaluation may be used for lifeguards as well as administrative or technical staff, similar to the way the government uses civil service tests. Lifeguard knowledge tests should include items from (or may be taken entirely from) written tests administered by national lifeguard certifying agencies, such as the YMCA or American Red Cross.

Written tests for technical staff members such as swimming pool technicians and opera-

tors should emphasize filtration, maintenance, and water chemistry. Questions related to the state bathing code or the state pool operations certification are appropriate. These questions are usually multiple choice. Testing dates and sites should be scheduled, and they should be identified in the position announcements. Interviews are often not granted until the testing period has ended. The test scores can be used as criteria in interview selection—top scoring candidates are granted an interview. (See appendix D for a sample pool operator preemployment knowledge test.)

Knowledge-based tests for administrative or professional staff should be less technical and more subjective in nature. Open-ended questions dealing with personnel issues, program development, safety, and administration may be asked. These questions may be sent to the candidates in advance and either used as a prerequisite to the interview process or brought to the interview and added to the candidate's application package. (See appendix D for sample administrative test questions.)

HIRING

Once you've been through the prescreening process for your candidates and you've decided on your final candidate, you are ready to make an employment offer.

Notification

Make the offer of employment to the candidate who is your first choice prior to informing your other candidates that they have not been selected. If your first choice declines the offer, you can then continue to your second choice, who is not aware that she was not selected first. You should make your employment offer either in person or by phone. You should inform your candidate of the salary and other employment terms for the position. If the candidate accepts the offer, inform her that a written contract will be forwarded that she must sign and return. Be sure to also inform her of her start date. Top candidates who were interviewed for a professional position should be informed by phone that they were not selected. Since you have had personal contact with them in the interview process, a personal response is warranted. Letters should inform other applicants who were not granted an interview.

Orientation

New employees, whether professional staff or hourly wage employees, will require an orientation period. During this time, you should indoctrinate your new employees into your organization and attempt to make them as much a part of your "team" as possible. Facilities should develop a standard orientation program after consulting with their human resources department. If your facility does not have a human resources department, your senior staff members should develop or review the orientation program. Consult with your facility attorney to ensure that all legal issues are covered, such as your policy on sexual harassment. Whenever possible, orientations should be conducted for groups of new hires, with the exception of very senior management positions. The following sections discuss some of the items you may want to include in your orientation program.

Employment Forms

All employees must fill out I-9 employment eligibility forms as required by the federal government. This requires verification that an employee is legally eligible to work in the United States. You can verify this by asking employees to provide the appropriate form(s) of identification listed on the I-9 document; a valid driver's license and Social Security card are the two most common forms. Copies of the I-9 form and verification documents should be kept in the employee's file.

Other employment forms that may be completed during this time include tax withholding forms, emergency contact data, payroll deduction forms (for items such as savings bonds), payroll direct deposit forms, and insurance forms. Parking permits and employee ID cards can also be issued. Because employment forms can be confusing, a personnel specialist from the HR department should be on hand to assist new employees with this process. All forms should be filled out at one time to minimize confusion, duplication of effort, and wasted time.

Basic Orientation

During this phase, the new employees begin to become acclimated, and they learn more about what they will actually be doing. The orientation program should be held before the employees begin performing their actual duties. To do otherwise risks potential injury to the new employees and confusion on the part of patrons because the new employees are not aware of your policies. You should provide each employee with a written job description and discuss it with him to be sure that he understands it. The job description should state in some detail the employee's duties, who the employee reports to, and what other employees he is responsible for; a chain of command chart is helpful in explaining this. The employee's hours of work and scheduled breaks must be clearly stated. If your facility has a personnel manual, staff manual, or lifeguard manual, distribute it at this point.

Your orientation should include a review of your facility's major policies. These may include policies on sexual harassment and alcohol and tobacco consumption. Vacation and sick leave policies should also be discussed. After all policies and duties have been explained, the employee should sign a form stating that he has received a staff manual, job description, and policy explanation and that he understands and agrees to abide by those policies. This form should be kept in the employee's file.

Next, the employee should be given a working tour of your facility. If you are issuing facility keys to this employee, you should do it before the tour and allow the employee to verify that the keys are working properly as you tour the facility. The tour should include break rooms, locker rooms, offices, storage areas (including swimming pool chemical rooms), pool filter rooms, the pool itself, and any other areas the employee may need to go. During the tour, point out light switches, emergency exits, fuse boxes, security alarms, and doors that must remain secured. As you tour the facility, introduce the new employee to his coworkers, including secretaries, custodians, customer service staff, administrative staff, and aquatic staff.

You should issue staff uniforms and personal equipment (e.g., pocket masks, radios, and first aid supplies) at the completion of the orientation.

Probationary Evaluation

Every employee should be periodically evaluated. You should inform employees about your facility's evaluation policy, including how often evaluations will occur, what criteria will be used, and how evaluations affect an employee's pay and promotions. Many facilities place new employees on a probationary period lasting from 90 days to a year depending on the facility and the position the employee holds (lesser periods are used for part-time or seasonal employees). Evaluations conducted during this period often determine if the new hire will remain employed. If this is the case, you must clearly state that to the workers and specify what criteria are necessary to retain their job.

Copies of evaluation forms should be signed by employees and retained in their files.

✔ Employee Files

An employee file should be started once employment has been offered and accepted. An employee's file is confidential and should be available only to the employee, the employee's supervisor, and the human resources manager. Items that should be included in an employee's personnel file include the following:

- ▸ A current resume
- ▸ Grade transcripts (for professional positions)
- ▸ Copies of certification cards
- ▸ Completed employee evaluation forms
- ▸ Employment verification forms (I-9)
- ▸ Emergency contact sheets (identifying who you should contact in case this employee is injured)
- ▸ Letters of thank-you or commendation
- ▸ Records of any disciplinary actions taken against this employee
- ▸ A copy of the employee's current employment contract (if applicable)
- ▸ Copies of taxation forms

SUPERVISION

Employees should have regular, daily, and ongoing contact with their supervisor. This helps reinforce policies, gives the employee a sense of direction and belonging, and helps identify problems in their early stages.

Informal Supervision

Good supervisors practice "management by walking around." This practice involves regularly visiting employees at their workstations, whether at the pool, in the filter room, or at the registration desk. By doing this, the supervisor can answer questions that employees may have, lend assistance when the workload becomes heavy, correct small problems, and give encouragement. It also allows the manager to detect deficiencies in employee performance and plan steps to correct them, such as training or a conference with the employee. When visiting employees informally, managers should take the opportunity to give employees feedback regarding their performance. Whenever possible, this feedback should be positive. This helps the employee build a sense of confidence and accomplishment. If you detect a minor problem, correct it immediately with on-the-spot direction; be sure to tell the employee what she was doing incorrectly, why it is incorrect, and what to do to correct it. If you find a major violation, such as a lifeguard asleep on the stand or a cash register unattended, you may need to remove the employee on the spot and temporarily assume her duties. You can schedule a formal performance review or conference later to determine the final outcome of the employee's actions.

Aquatic Staff Evaluation

Employees should be formally evaluated regarding their work performance on a regular basis. You should have a set period for evaluations, perhaps annually or semiannually. For seasonal workers, you may opt for a midseason evaluation followed by an end-of-season evaluation. Formal evaluations should reflect the informal comments given on a daily basis, such as when you perform your daily visit to the pool deck and observe your lifeguards, instructors, and support staff at work. It is inconsistent and confusing to tell employees on a daily basis that their performance is good and then give them a poor written evaluation. Giving workers a true idea of their performance on a daily basis allows them to correct deficiencies before they become part of their formal evaluation and before those deficiencies are recorded in their employee file.

Evaluations should assess those things that are most important in an employee's job description, such as swimming supervision for lifeguards or quality of instruction for aquatic instructors. You may need to create different evaluation forms for different positions and ranks (e.g., entry-level lifeguard and supervisory swim instructor). Your assessments should occur on a regular schedule, whether they are every 6 months or annual. Employees must be aware of when their evaluations occur and should know what they are being evaluated on. An employee's direct supervisor should complete the performance evaluation because this supervisor is the only person who has direct knowledge of the employee's performance. You should not include information provided by other employees or third parties; do not include hearsay or any information about actions you have not witnessed.

After you have completed an employee evaluation, you should meet privately with the worker to discuss the results. You should highlight positive performance first, followed by a discussion of those areas in which you feel the employee requires improvement—for example, better enforcement of pool rules or improved scanning technique. Provide specific suggestions regarding areas needing improvement, such as "Try to be positive when you tell the kids what pool rule they're breaking" or "Be sure to sweep your whole zone, including the other guards, when scanning." If the evaluation will lead to specific action, such as terminating or promoting the employee, you must inform the employee of that as well.

After explaining the results of the evaluation, give the employee an opportunity to ask questions and make comments related to his performance. If he disagrees with the review, the worker should be given an opportunity to add a written rebuttal. Be sure to have the employee sign and date the evaluation. The employee's signature does not indicate acceptance of the results, only that he has seen the evaluation. After the employee and all appropriate supervisors have signed the assessment, it should be placed in the employee's personnel file.

If you suspect that an evaluation will cause an employee to become upset, you should ask another supervisor or your superior to be present when explaining it to your employee. This person can act as a witness and assist in the event that the employee becomes distraught or

violent. See appendix D for a sample employee evaluation form.

Disciplining Employees

Unfortunately, not all your employees will perform as you want them to on all occasions. If you determine that an employee is guilty of misconduct (e.g., tardiness to work, insubordination, theft, or vandalism), you must discipline the employee. This is particularly inexcusable for your lifeguards and safety staff because the safety of your customers rests with them. Failing to discipline an employee will result in the behavior recurring with this individual and possibly with other employees because they may think that they will not be punished. Since lifeguards tend to congregate in groups (due to the team-based nature of their job), you can expect news to travel fast. You must clearly define disciplinary actions in the personnel manual, and employees must be informed of them upon hire.

Many organizations have a "three strike" policy as follows:

- First offense for minor infractions (such as tardiness) results in a verbal warning.
- Second offense for an infraction results in a written warning being placed in the employee's file.
- Third offense results in immediate dismissal.

Major violations such as theft, vandalism, assault, uttering threats, drunkenness while on duty, and possession of illegal drugs should result in immediate dismissal and referral to local police. Because of the particularly sensitive nature of safety issues related to lifeguarding, certain behaviors that might not result in immediate termination for your other staff members might do so for lifeguards. These include the following:

- Reporting to work under the influence of alcohol
- Smoking on duty (particularly if they're doing it in the chemical storage area)
- Leaving the lifeguard stand or pool/beach area without permission or without being properly relieved by another staff member
- Failing to perform duties as directed, such as testing pool water, adding chemicals, or performing equipment checks
- Sleeping on duty (especially in the lifeguard stand)

These behaviors cannot be permitted in your life-guard staff. If a snack bar employee takes a nap in the storeroom while he's supposed to be on duty, most likely no one will be hurt as a result. But if a lifeguard takes a nap in his stand when he's supposed to be watching swimmers, someone could drown. Even if nothing bad happens and the lifeguard promises that he won't do it again—for any of the infractions listed above—you can't take the risk. If you give the lifeguard another chance and he repeats the same behavior, you might not be as lucky the second time, and injury or death could result.

If you issue a verbal warning to an employee, be sure to explain to him what he did wrong and ask him if he understands the policy. Refer him to the personnel manual and make sure he's aware that the next similar infraction could result in a written warning. In some cases, you may issue many verbal warnings before giving a written one (e.g., for very minor infractions such as tardiness on lifeguard rotation or forgetting to fill out the required checklist when opening the facility).

If a written warning is issued, a meeting should be held with the employee, supervisor, and one witness present. You should confront the employee with the rule violation and offer him an opportunity to explain his actions. In some cases, the employee's explanation may adequately excuse his actions or rebut the facts. For example, if you hold a disciplinary meeting for a lifeguard who was late to work, and he tells you that he stopped to administer care to an injured person on the way to work (and you verify this), you should reward the lifeguard, not punish him.

If the employee can't justify the violation and you end up issuing a written warning, you should have the employee sign the form before you place it in his personnel file. You should then try to engage the worker in a plan to ensure that his work habits improve. If you cannot create a mutually agreeable plan to improve his work habits, you may offer the employee the option to resign. This enables the employee to leave voluntarily and perhaps retain a reference from you. However, in the case of a lifeguard, if you truly believe that his skills are not good enough or that he is just not suited to be a lifeguard, you should be honest and tell him you would not give him a reference for future lifeguard jobs, but may for other types of employment.

Other tools you may opt to use at this juncture for an employee with work problems include reduction of work hours, demotion, temporary suspension from work without pay, or reassignment to other duties. Reassignment of problem lifeguards and instructors to maintenance duties, particularly cleaning rest rooms, is often a good lesson. Do not fail to inform them that the next disciplinary problem will result in their dismissal. Document all disciplinary actions and record them in the employee's file. See appendix D for an employee conduct form.

When an employee has progressed through the other disciplinary steps, or has committed a crime or violated a major facility policy, the employee must be dismissed. Before dismissal can take place, all of the employee's actions must be documented and reviewed; in this situation, the employee's personnel file is invaluable. All prior disciplinary actions must be reviewed and taken into account. If the employee has a history of work problems, then dismissal may be the only option. You should consult with your human resources department to make sure you are proceeding legally and appropriately. Dismissal should take place in person and always with a witness present. If you think the employee may become violent, make threats, or commit property destruction, you should alert security personnel and have them in the area. In this case, you may want to escort the employee to retrieve his personal belongings and escort him out of the facility. You may also elect to ban the individual from your facility if you think it is necessary. Collect any facility property (e.g., radios or keys) before the employee departs. Document the dismissal by placing a letter in the former employee's file. Although you do not need to tell other employees the reason for a dismissal, they should be informed of the dismissal so that they do not admit this person to the facility again or contact him about work-related issues.

SCHEDULING

Developing a fair and workable method of scheduling staff members for their shifts, and then ensuring that they adhere to it, is a major task for most managers. The larger the staff and facility, the more complex it becomes. Schedules can either be supervisor or staff created; they can also be made according to seniority.

Management-Created Schedule

A management-created schedule requires that all your staff members submit a schedule of their available times to the aquatic director. The director takes all these schedules and fills the available hours on the work schedule based on who is free and the number of hours they want to work. This method provides you with a great deal of control over who works together, allows you to reward good staff members with desirable shifts, and most important, makes sure that all shifts get filled. The disadvantages are that some staff members may not receive enough hours and may subsequently quit, or they may receive shifts they do not want and are more likely not to show up. Lifeguards tend to be very young in many cases, often as young as 16. Having a management-created schedule gives you, the supervisor, the oversight to ensure that they aren't overworked and that junior guards are scheduled with more senior guards.

Staff-Created Schedule

When staff create their own schedule, the procedure most often used is to place a master pool schedule on a chalkboard or poster board during a staff meeting and allow staff members to pick what shifts they want. The advantage is that you are relatively certain that staff members will show up for their shifts—after all, they selected the shifts themselves. The disadvantage is that you cannot control who works together, which may result in very junior staff members together on a shift, or the number of hours each member receives. Another problem is that certain members of your staff may not work well together as a group because they get along too well together, which might distract from their attention to their area of supervision or their classes. You can't control this dynamic when staff set the schedule.

Scheduling by Seniority

Scheduling by seniority requires you to keep a running total of all hours each staff member has worked. When shifts are allocated, those staff members with the highest number of hours select first. The least desirable shifts are given to the newer employees. This method rewards longevity and encourages experienced staff to stay, which is often an issue in the aquatics industry; however, it can be discouraging for newer staff.

Schedule Maintenance

Staff members will routinely require periods of time off for personal reasons or because they are ill. Lifeguards and swim instructors are often students in high school or college. These employees often seek leave from work during final exam periods, Christmas break for college students,

and the end of summer (approaching the start of fall semester). You should create a policy that is reasonable and enforceable for these eventualities. When staff members want to take a day off or miss a shift for personal reasons, they should be required to get their own substitute. If you involve management in this process, it becomes easy for the staff members to call and say they need a substitute. A good policy is to state that the shift belongs to the staff member it is assigned to until a substitute is found; it then becomes the substitute's responsibility. You should provide a substitution card that must be signed by both staff members—the person giving and the person taking the shift. This eliminates confusion regarding who is responsible for the shift. See appendix D for a sample staff substitute card. If a staff member fails to show up for a shift, you must record it on a written performance card and discipline the staff member. If you've had problems with seasonal aquatic staff leaving before the end of the summer, consider these possible solutions:

- ▶ Ask employees to sign an employment contract indicating a predetermined last day of work.
- ▶ Offer a cash bonus to those employees who stay to the end of their contract.
- ▶ Tell employees that they will not be rehired if they don't complete the term of their contract.

If extra shifts become available due to special events, such as pool rentals for birthday parties or proms, you can announce them in staff meetings and assign them to those who are interested, or you can post them in the office and allow them to be filled on a first-come-first-serve basis. You must always emphasize to your staff members that if they take a shift, they are responsible for it.

IN-SERVICE TRAINING

In-service training refers to the facility-specific skill and knowledge training that you provide to your aquatic staff. This is essential to ensuring that your staff members are familiar with the facility, its policies, and emergency procedures. This training also assists them in maintaining their fitness, reaction time, skills, confidence, and professionalism. Without in-service training, your staff can easily become complacent and lazy, and their rescue skills can quickly erode. Although in-service training is most often associated with lifeguards, other staff members (such as instructors and pool operators) may also benefit from regular training.

You should require all staff members to attend in-service training in order to ensure that training remains standardized. If some staff members cannot attend the scheduled training date, you should offer one alternate date. Those staff members who do not attend either time should be suspended until they make up the training. To assist your staff in planning for your training sessions, you should announce training dates and times on a quarterly basis. Create a flyer with the pertinent information and distribute it to each aquatic staff member. You should also post a copy in the lifeguard office.

Formal in-service sessions should last a minimum of 1 1/2 to 2 hours to allow adequate coverage of material. The frequency with which training is conducted often depends on the facility. Part-time hourly lifeguards may attend formalized training only once per week, while full-time seasonal staff may have training as often as twice per week. Training should be offered no less than once per month. You should schedule training at a time that is convenient for your staff to attend—for example, immediately before or after work shifts in which a large number of staff are present.

> **KEY POINT** *In-service training is essential to maintaining your staff's skills, fitness, and professionalism.*

Types of In-Service Training

There are several different forms of in-service training, including physical training, technical training, policy reviews, and social activities.

▶ **Physical training.** This is the most common form of training for lifeguards. It focuses on physical strength, stamina, and speed. Common physical training events include distance swims, distance running, and swimming and running sprints. You can break up the monotony by adding cycling, swimming relay races, the occasional game of Frisbee football, and even an intersquad minitriathlon. Staff can perform physical training individually or as a group. Many aquatic facilities require their staff members to swim a specified yardage each week and record it. Two timed 500-yard (457.2-meter) swims are considered standard. A 10-minute completion time is the goal for a 500-yard swim in flat water.

A lifeguard heads for a distressed swimmer.

▶ **Technical training.** Technical training involves the fundamental skills of aquatic safety. Topics that may be covered include spinal injury rescue, first aid skills, CPR, basic water rescue skills, and submerged victim recovery. Advanced technical sessions may focus on lifeguard teamwork, scuba rescue, situational training, and public relations scenarios.

▶ **Policy reviews.** Policy training is offered periodically to inform staff members about new information, such as blood-borne **pathogen** information, new facility rules, or the use of new equipment. This type of training involves information specific to the operation of your facility (e.g., the operation of equipment, such as hydraulic lifts, or the location of light switches, emergency exits, and storage areas).

▶ **Social activities.** It is important that your staff members know each other and are comfortable working together. In-service social activities foster camaraderie and help improve the work environment. Social events do not need to take place often, but events such as staff holiday parties should be held to maintain and improve morale.

There are a multitude of individual topics that can be included under each of the in-service training categories just described. The following sections provide you with some ideas for specific in-service training topics.

You can select topics from the previous list to develop appropriate training for your staff depending on their skill level and needs. Figure 5.1 shows a sample in-service training plan for a single session.

After training sessions have been held, minutes should be created documenting the topics covered. A list of staff members attending the training should be attached, and the minutes should be filed in an in-service log. A copy should also be posted in the aquatic staff office. This log provides proof that staff skills are current in the event of litigation. See appendix D for a sample in-service training log.

Spinal Injury Immobilization

To cover the topic of spinal injury immobilization (head splint and head and chin support), conduct a review that includes an in-water demonstration to your staff on the correct method of performing these skills. After the demonstration and review, the class (i.e., your staff) should divide into teams of two and practice each immobilization method a minimum of three times each. Training supervisors or senior staff should evaluate the performance of the skills and offer constructive feedback.

Full Spinal Injury Rescue

Training for a full spinal injury rescue should include back boarding and removal in deep and shallow water. Ask a group of experienced staff members to practice full boarding procedures in advance and to demonstrate these procedures to the whole staff. While the demonstration is being performed, the training director should explain to the staff what is being done. After the demonstration, the staff should divide into teams and perform the full boarding procedure. Training supervisors

---

I. Staff arrive and are greeted by aquatic director, head lifeguard, and other senior staff (15 minutes before start time).

- Staff sign in as they arrive for purposes of pay and attendance; one senior aquatic staff member supervises. After signing in, staff are seated on pool deck or on bleachers. All staff should be in swimsuits and have towels.

II. At selected time for in-service to begin: Ensure that everyone has signed in. Make general announcements (10-15 minutes).

- Describe what is happening at in-service today.
- Provide an opportunity for staff to find substitutes for shifts they will be absent for (record on sub card).
- Provide an opportunity for staff to give up shifts they can't keep, and allow other staff to take them.
- Announce upcoming special events, particularly any you will need extra staff for.
- Announce any staff promotions or staff departures.

III. All staff swim 500 to 1,000 yards (457.2 to 914.4 meters) timed. Appoint one staff member to record times (15-20 minutes).

IV. Divide into groups for station practice (15 minutes each).

- Group 1: Spinal injury rescue shallow water; turnovers; full boarding procedures; review of equipment
- Group 2: CPR/rescue breathing; adult CPR, one rescuer; use of a bag-valve mask; child CPR; adult choking
- Group 3: Rescues; active victim rescue at the surface; passive victim rescue at the surface; recovery of a submerged passive victim not breathing from deep water
- Group 4: Policy review; staff rules; facility rules; working with the press

V. Conclusion. Around the horn: air a concern or make a comment (not personal) (10-12 minutes).

Figure 5.1   A sample outline for an in-service training session.

or senior staff should evaluate the performance of the skills and offer constructive feedback.

Recovery of a Victim With a Spinal Injury From Deep Water

Review and demonstrate the proper technique for the recovery of a victim with a spinal injury from deep water. Be sure to remind staff to use the slip-in entry for this skill. After the review and demonstration, the class should divide into pairs and practice the skill. Provide individual feedback as the students practice the skill.

Active Victim Rescue

Demonstrate the proper method of performing an **active victim** rescue, including entry from the side or lifeguard stand and the use of the rescue tube. After the demonstration, the class should divide into teams and perform the skill. Training supervisors or senior staff should evaluate the performance of the skills and offer constructive feedback.

Passive Victim Rescue

Demonstrate the proper method of performing a **passive victim** rescue, including entry from the side or lifeguard stand and the use of the rescue tube. After the demonstration, the class should divide into teams and perform the skill. Training supervisors or senior staff should evaluate the performance of the skills and offer constructive feedback.

Recovery of a Nonbreathing Victim From Deep Water

When discussing and demonstrating the recovery of a nonbreathing victim from deep water, be sure to review the use of pocket masks and other breathing devices. You should also cover your facility policy regarding the use of pocket masks in the water. After reviewing and demonstrating the skill, have the group divide into pairs for practice. Provide individual or group feedback during this practice.

Rescue of Two Victims at Once

Demonstrate the proper method of performing a rescue of two victims (grasping each other) at once, including entry from the side or lifeguard stand and the use of the rescue tube. After the demonstration, the class should divide into teams and perform the skill. Training supervisors or senior staff should evaluate the performance of the skills and offer constructive feedback.

Jumps Into the Pool From the Lifeguard Stand

Emphasize safety when explaining and demonstrating the proper technique for jumping into the pool. Remind your staff to ensure that the rope for the rescue tube is gathered in their hand so it doesn't become entangled in the chair while the lifeguard is jumping in. Remind your staff to check for swimmers below their stand and to ensure that chairs stationed over water have sufficient water depth under them for the guard to safely enter the water. After reviewing safety precautions, demonstrate the skill and then have the staff practice. Evaluate your staff as they perform the skill.

Rescue of a Scuba Diver Submerged in Deep Water

This drill is only required if scuba classes are conducted at your facility. Only certified divers should be used as the "victim." A safety diver wearing skin diving gear should be in the water to assist the diver and to ensure that the diver is not brought up too fast. Perform a safety briefing regarding the speed at which a scuba diver should be brought up from the bottom of the pool—1 foot (30.5 centimeters) per second. Caution your staff that bringing the diver up any faster could damage the diver's lungs. After the safety briefing, deliver a brief lecture demonstrating and describing the diver's equipment, including the weight belt and buoyancy compensation device. After the equipment lecture, the safety diver should demonstrate how to release the diver's weight belt and bring the diver safely to the surface, inflating the buoyancy compensator and securing the victim. After this demonstration, you should allow time for questions and then have your staff practice the skill.

Rescue Breathing for an Adult, Infant, and Child

Demonstrate the proper rescue breathing technique to use for an adult, infant, and child. After the demonstration, the class should divide into groups and practice the skill using mannequins. Training supervisors or senior staff should evaluate the performance of the skills and offer constructive feedback. You can also show a training video if you think it's needed.

CPR for an Adult, Infant, and Child

Demonstrate the proper technique for performing CPR on an adult, infant, and child. After the demonstration, the class should divide into groups and practice the skill using mannequins. Training supervisors or senior staff should evaluate the performance of the skills and offer constructive feedback. You can also show a training video if you think it's needed.

Obstructed Airway Maneuver

Demonstrate the proper performance of the obstructed airway maneuver on a conscious and unconscious victim (adult, infant, and child). After the demonstration, the class should divide into groups and practice the skill using mannequins. Training supervisors or senior staff should evaluate the performance of the skills and offer constructive feedback. You can also show a training video if you think it's needed.

Use of a Pocket Mask or Other Rescue Breathing Barrier

Review the use of the pocket mask or similar device carried by staff at your facility. Staff members should then practice using the device on a CPR mannequin. You can combine this with the practice of CPR or rescue breathing.

Use of a Bag-Valve Mask Manual Resuscitation Device

Demonstrate and review the use of a bag-valve mask manual resuscitation device. Staff members (in pairs) should then practice using the device on a mannequin.

Oxygen Administration

Show the oxygen administration video from your certifying agency. Demonstrate the proper use of the device that your facility uses. If possible, allow your staff to practice using this device.

Use of an Automatic External Defibrillator

Show the AED video from your certifying agency. Demonstrate the proper use of the device that your facility uses. If possible, allow your staff to practice using this device.

Bandaging

Demonstrate and review the proper procedure for bandaging, including pressure points and elevation of the affected part. Remind your staff of the need to wear latex gloves to prevent infection from blood-borne diseases. After the demonstration

and review, the class should divide into groups for skills practice.

Splinting

Demonstrate and review the proper procedure for splinting. After the demonstration and review, the class should divide into groups for practice. Provide feedback to your staff as you watch them perform the skill.

Blood-Borne Pathogen (Body Substance) Isolation

Review your facility procedures for blood-borne pathogen control and disposal. Demonstrate to your staff the proper method of putting on gloves as well as taking off and disposing of contaminated gloves. You may also want to show the blood-borne pathogens video produced by your certification agency.

Dealing With Fights in the Facility

Review your facility policy for dealing with violence in your facility. If you have security personnel at your facility, you may want to ask them to deliver this lecture. Emphasize to your staff the importance of protecting their own safety first.

Dealing With Domestic Disturbances at the Pool

Deliver a brief lecture regarding your facility procedures for dealing with domestic disturbances. If your facility has security personnel, ask a representative to participate in this discussion. Remind your staff that any time violence takes place, law enforcement must be called.

Dealing With Theft

Review with your staff the procedure for contacting police and filing a theft report. Remind them to fill out a facility incident report form for this event and explain how to route it to the proper staff members. You may even want to fill out a sample form with the proper information and distribute it to the staff so they will know how to properly complete the form.

Responding to Fire Alarms

This training topic has several parts. First, you'll need to review the emergency evacuation plans with your staff, including emergency exits and muster points outside the building after evacuating. Second, you'll need to teach your staff how to lead an evacuation, including what to say to patrons, use of the PA system, and so on. You can begin staging a scenario in your in-service session and later run a full drill with patrons in the pool. (Be sure to give the patrons notice prior to the drill.) You should also cover rules for reentering the facility after the alarm is over. Discuss with your staff those fires that they can fight and when it is more prudent to evacuate. Only small, relatively contained fires should be fought; otherwise, let the firefighters do it. An employee should never be at personal risk when fighting a fire. A side topic is also the correct operation of fire suppression equipment such as extinguishers and fire hoses.

Facility Evacuation Procedure

Review your facility's emergency evacuation plan. You may also want to stage an evacuation before the facility opens (or after it closes) so that your staff can actually go through the motions of carrying out an evacuation.

Use of a Fire Extinguisher

The use of a fire extinguisher is best demonstrated by fire department personnel (or security personnel if they are specifically trained in the use of fire extinguishers). You'll need to conduct this training outside by setting a controlled burn in a burn pit or other safe area. The training officer should describe the various types of fire extinguishers and what types of fires they are used for. Next, a demonstration should be conducted showing how to properly activate and use the extinguisher. If possible, give each staff member a chance to practice with the extinguisher under the direct supervision of the training officer. Be sure to include instruction regarding how to check if a fire extinguisher needs to be recharged and when to abandon fire extinguishers in favor of allowing firefighters to fight the fire.

Interaction With Emergency Medical Services

EMS paramedics or **EMTs** should conduct this session as guest lecturers. Review which entrances to your facility are most appropriate for EMS personnel to enter, taking into account their need to bring in equipment. Your guest lecturers should tell your staff what information they will need about the victim when they arrive on scene. Clarify whether EMS personnel will enter the water to assist with patient care when needed or if they will require your staff to have

the victim delivered and extracted to the side of the pool. Also determine if your staff will need to accompany the victim in the ambulance. Be sure to ask your visiting EMS personnel how to reclaim facility equipment in the event that it goes to the hospital with the victim.

Opening and Closing the Aquatic Facility

Review facility procedures with your staff regarding the correct steps in opening and closing the facility.

Handling Complaints and Unhappy Customers

Give your staff some helpful hints for dealing with unhappy customers, such as never raising their voices, asking the patron what can be done to resolve the problem, and remaining positive at all times. Remind staff members to call for a supervisor if the customer becomes agitated or violent. To practice these situations, one of your senior lifeguards can simulate an unhappy customer, and your staff can simulate dealing with that customer. Offer constructive comments after these simulations.

Working With the Press

One of the best ways to conduct an in-service training session about working with the press is to set up a simulated interview and videotape the participants. After the simulated interview, review the tape with the group and offer constructive criticism. Before discussing the tape, review some basic principles of dealing with the press. This session adds a new and fun twist to regular in-service sessions.

Lifeguard Stress

Lifeguards can experience stress for a wide variety of reasons, including posttraumatic stress disorder from rescues seen or attempted. Stress can also come from the stress of the responsibility of watching many swimmers coupled with heat, sun, and high operational tempo. You'll need to discuss coping strategies with your staff, including working out, eating properly, getting enough sleep, and talking their problems out.

Basic Swimming Pool Water Chemistry

Provide a lecture to your staff on the basic elements of water chemistry, including pH and disinfection. You should use visual aids such as Microsoft PowerPoint or chalkboards.

Applying Chemicals to the Pool

Review the manufacturer directed method for proper application of swimming pool chemicals. Demonstrate the proper method to your staff, emphasizing safety procedures and equipment (e.g., eye protection, footwear, protective clothing, and gloves).

Pool Chemical Safety

Take your employees for a visit to your pool chemical storage area. Explain to them how chemicals must be properly stored, including what chemicals cannot be stored together, where **material safety data sheets** are stored, and where eye wash stations and safety showers are located.

Operating Special Equipment

Perform a demonstration and provide instruction on the various equipment that your facility owns (e.g., lifts, ramps, slides).

Setup for Special Events

Review with your staff the standard setups for events (e.g., swim meets, water polo matches, and so forth). Provide a checklist to assist them. Explain where equipment and supplies are stored and approximately how long setup takes.

Facility Rules

Review facility rules with your staff while gathered around a facility rule board. Point out each rule and explain the policy or safety consideration behind it. Explain to your staff the proper method of informing adults and children that they've broken a rule and what to do if they don't change their behavior.

Methods of Training Delivery

There are multiple methods that you can use to deliver in-service training. When selecting a method, consider the topic to be taught or practiced and the abilities of your staff. Whatever method you use, you must organize your time effectively to minimize wasted time and maximize training opportunities.

Mass Practice

The mass practice method is most often used for physical and technical training. In mass practice, all staff members carry out the same skill at the same time. This method works well for lap swimming and basic skills such as entries and rescues. It does not work well for advanced skills such as spinal injury rescue where individual feedback and attention to detail are required.

When using mass practice, the trainer should explain the skill to be practiced, demonstrate it, and allow the staff to practice it until they are performing it correctly. While the staff practices, the trainer should observe them and offer as much individual feedback as possible.

The advantages to this method are that only one or two trainers are required and that wasted time is minimized. The major disadvantage is the lack of individual feedback.

Station Practice

In station training, you select several skills to be practiced and offer small group activities to practice all the skills simultaneously. The staff divides into teams of four or five, which distribute themselves to the stations. A trainer meets the teams at each station, and a skill is practiced for 20 to 25 minutes; then the groups rotate. Rotation continues until all groups have attended all stations. A lead trainer should monitor the groups' progress and coordinate the rotation between stations.

This method works best for highly technical skills that require close observation and feedback. Skills such as spinal injury rescue, CPR, and the use of advanced equipment (e.g., AEDs and supplemental oxygen) are best suited to this style. Advantages to station practice include individualized practice and observation, a variety of skills being practiced in one session, and small group interaction. The major disadvantage is the need for several trainers—at least one trainer per station and a lead trainer coordinating the session. Station practice sessions also require more preplanning. You must ensure that you have the right number and types of stations for your staff, that each station has a trainer, and that each trainer knows what the participants need to do and how long they need to do it.

Scenario-Based Training

The scenario-based method attempts to add realism to training by requiring lifeguards to practice their skills in situations they will encounter while performing their duties. You should divide your staff into teams of the same size they would be in while on duty. The first team of guards should then take their positions as they would while on duty at the facility. The remainder of your staff act as "patrons," swimming and playing in and around the water. During the course of their "shift," the team should encounter rescues, first aid events, public affairs scenarios, and major emergencies. Three or four events should be encountered by each team, with the most major event, such as a simulated spinal injury, happening last. By simulating the most major event last, you can debrief the team on it while they are together immediately after the pool has been cleared from their final scenario. While a trainer is debriefing one team, other trainers can direct the next team to get set up and can brief the "swimmers" on their next set of roles. If possible, several trainers should be involved to keep things running quickly and to allow multiple evaluations to be given to each team.

The key to this method is requiring the staff to recognize the emergency and to work as a team while they respond. They must not know what the scenarios are before assuming duty or the element of forcing them to recognize the emergency is lost. Preparing a number of scenarios in advance assists in running the training session more quickly and smoothly. You should prepare a standardized evaluation sheet so that you can easily judge the teams on their performance. See appendix D for a sample in-service scenario evaluation sheet.

This method is best used for more advanced staff members who have mastered the basic skills. Advantages include teamwork building, realism, and fun. Disadvantages include its time-consuming nature, and that only a few staff members can participate at any one time.

Lecture

The lecture method is often the least desired because it is nonparticipatory and can be boring. However, in some cases, the transmission of new material can't be done any other way. For information such as how to clean up blood spills, how to fill out forms and reports, or other administrative issues, a lecture may be the best training method.

If you do select this method, use a room that is comfortable and suitable for sitting and listening. Pool decks are usually poor choices because the sound quality is often bad and there is often no good place to sit. Using a visual aid—such as a videotape, transparencies, or a PowerPoint presentation—helps make the lecture more interesting. Always prepare your presentation in advance and have notes to help you stay on task. Never talk for longer than an hour without a break; after that point, even avid listeners become bored or tired and begin to lose interest.

An advantage to this method is the ability to transmit large amounts of information to a large number of people quickly. The major disadvantage is that lectures are often boring and people don't enjoy them.

Games and Competitions

While still focusing on helping the staff sharpen their skills and gain new knowledge, you can use games and competitions to inject more fun into training by playing on your staff members' sense of competition. This method can be used in many different ways: intersquad swim meets to build up fitness, first aid quiz shows, aquatic or first aid trivia games, lifeguard competitions to foster improved skills, or water polo games to strengthen treading skills.

The only limit to this form of training is your imagination. The advantages of increased interest and fun on the part of the staff are readily apparent, and the only disadvantage is the somewhat intensive preparation time required to organize a good competition.

New Certification

New certifications are frequently becoming available in aquatics. In 1999, certification in preventing disease transmission, automatic external defibrillation (AED), and supplemental oxygen became available.

Offering this training to your staff as an in-service session is an efficient way of ensuring that they all receive the new training, rather than requiring them to procure it on their own and hoping that they will do so. This becomes critical if you intend to implement the use of AEDs or supplemental oxygen at your facility.

Training Seminars

There are a wide variety of aquatic consulting and training firms that offer seminars and courses. Many of them will come to your site provided you have enough staff to fill a class and are willing to pay the costs involved. Training sessions focus on all types of topics, including basic lifeguarding skills, accident prevention, risk management, scuba rescue, and ice rescue. Before selecting an external agency for training, you should ask yourself several questions:

- Does my staff need the training the agency is offering?
- Do I have someone on my staff or in my organization who has the expertise to conduct this training?
- Can I afford the fees required for this training?

▸ Is the training agency a reputable one?

▸ Will my staff receive certification or course completion letters for this training?

▸ Can the agency certify a member of my staff to offer this training in the future?

▸ What texts, videos, or resources are provided with this training and is there an extra cost for those?

See appendix A for a list of some aquatic agencies that offer training seminars.

In-Service Training for Instructional Staff

Ongoing training is often seen as necessary only for lifeguards. However, to keep your instructional staff fresh and up-to-date, you should offer training for them as well. Because instructional skills are used more frequently than rescue skills and don't tend to degrade, this form of training is not required as often (one training session per month is adequate). Activities you may offer during in-service sessions for instructional staff include the following:

▸ **Game time.** Each instructor teaches a game she uses with her classes to the other instructors, allowing everyone to learn a new lesson.

▸ **Guest instructor.** Invite an experienced instructor from another facility to teach a sample lesson to your staff.

▸ **New materials.** Bring your staff up to speed on new programs offered by the YMCA of the USA or American Red Cross by showing new instructional videos and reviewing the new manuals together.

▸ **Equipment and toys.** Explore new teaching equipment and toys the facility has purchased (such as flotation devices, pull buoys, and water exercise devices) to see how they can be implemented into instructional plans.

Staff Audits

You can use staff audits as an advanced mechanism for training your staff and evaluating their skill level. An audit involves an unannounced drill, which requires staff to demonstrate their skills (such as active victim rescue, CPR, or spinal injury rescue) under stress that is similar to an actual event. Audits are often conducted during an open

swim to provide the realism of forcing the lifeguard to recognize the simulated victim among the other swimmers. Post signs at your facility informing your patrons that a drill may be occurring that day so they will not become alarmed.

For an audit program to be effective, staff should be fully trained through in-service sessions before implementing the program. You should inform your staff that audits may occur, but not the specific day or time. Audits differ from scenario-based training in that they primarily test the skills of a single staff member and occur during duty hours (not during a training session).

Advance preparations for audits include developing an evaluation sheet that grades the lifeguard on those items that you want to test, such as reaction time, skill proficiency, and communications. You can share this form with your staff so that they are aware of those critical skill areas. (See appendix D for a sample audit evaluation sheet.) Once you've developed your form, ask for volunteers to act as "victims" during the audit; if possible, use persons not known to your staff. Clearly instruct your volunteers on how to perform during the audit.

During the actual audit, select one staff member to be audited. Brief your "victim" out of sight of the lifeguard about when and how to perform. Station yourself at a location where you are able to see and evaluate the audit. Ensure that the pool is well supervised by other lifeguards during the drill so that patron safety is not compromised. If possible, after the drill is completed, remove the evaluated staff member from the stand and provide immediate feedback. Place a copy of the completed evaluation form in the staff member's file. You should have a plan in place for those staff members who perform poorly or cannot respond to the skills challenge. You may want to require staff members who perform the skills below standards to attend remedial training until they meet standards. Staff members who are unable to perform at all should be immediately removed from duty until they can satisfactorily perform the skills.

STAFF RETENTION

Hiring the best staff in the world will be useless if you can't retain them. Although you should implement a plan of tangible rewards to convince good staff members to stay, it's often the intangibles that really make a difference. You should strive to create a positive work environment, one in which the employees feel that they are a valued part of the team. Treat your employees fairly; discipline those who require it and praise those who deserve it. These seemingly small things will go a long way toward making your employees want to stay employed at your facility.

> **KEY POINT** *It's important to retain the staff that you've invested in and worked hard to train and develop.*

A recognition program is another excellent way to ensure that your staff remains motivated and happy. Think about instituting an employee of the week or month program. Outstanding staff members can be nominated by their supervisors based on their work performance. Recipients should be selected by a panel of supervisors to ensure fairness and eliminate favoritism. The employee selected should have her photo and a bio listing her employment history and the reason for her selection placed in a location where it can be seen by all patrons and staff. Presenting the employee with a certificate in a staff meeting provides her with a nice keepsake and serves as encouragement to other staff members. You may also want to place this information in a monthly newsletter.

An employee of the year award can be similarly granted from the ranks of the monthly winners. This award carries more prestige due to the length of high performance required to win it. You may want to give these awardees a small plaque and present it at a ceremony, awards dinner, or other such prominent occasion.

CAREER DEVELOPMENT

You should provide opportunities for your staff to grow and develop. Doing so will increase their interest in their job, make them more competent at their duties, enable them to assume new duties, and possibly prepare them for promotion. Some methods that you may want to use for the career development of your staff include training opportunities, promotion opportunities, and mentoring.

Training Opportunities

Training opportunities that may be beneficial for your staff include training to be a lifeguard instructor, CPR and first aid instructor, swimming instructor, water exercise instructor, pool operator, and

aquatic facility manager. By providing this training for your staff at low or no cost, you show the employees that they have value and that you are interested in them. From a practical standpoint, staff members who receive this training develop new skills and can perform additional tasks for you; you've created a valuable resource. This also improves job satisfaction for the employee.

Promotion Opportunities

Good employees often want to advance to new and more challenging assignments once they have been employed for a while and have learned their job well. Giving senior lifeguards and instructors the opportunity to become supervisors allows you to take advantage of their skills and knowledge and keeps your facility running more smoothly. It is also a great form of retention. Here are some positions you can create for experienced lifeguards:

▶ **Crew chief.** This staff member still performs lifeguard duties but is accountable for the supervision of all the other lifeguards on a shift. The crew chief is responsible for ensuring that the doors are locked and unlocked on time and that all staff are present and in place. This staff member can also be helpful in acclimating and training new staff members. Crew chiefs can deal with the small problems (such as lifeguards failing to wear the appropriate uniform or being late on rotation), freeing managers for other larger issues. Lifeguards should have at least 1 year of experience at the facility before being promoted to crew chief.

▶ **In-service trainer.** Leaders in this position help plan, administer, and deliver in-service training. They should be experienced lifeguards who are certified as lifeguard training and CPR instructors. This is essentially a collateral duty; when not performing this task, the staff member can function as a crew chief or lifeguard.

▶ **Administrative assistant.** This staff member may no longer work as a lifeguard or may do so only part time. This person works in the aquatics office on projects such as maintaining records, ordering supplies, answering phones, assisting with payroll, scheduling the pool and lifeguards, taking program registrations, and miscellaneous other office tasks. An aquatics administrative assistant should have good organizational skills, work well with people, and have several years of lifeguarding and crew chief experience.

▶ **Program supervisor.** Program supervisors take on-deck responsibility for large programs,

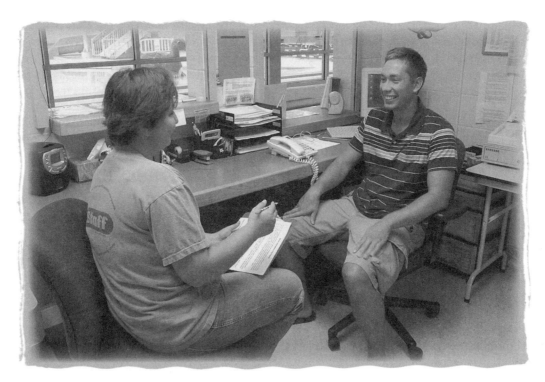

A candidate for promotion is interviewed by the facility supervisor.

such as swimming lessons, where many classes run simultaneously. They answer questions from parents, prepare class lists, ensure that instructors begin class on time, and other supervisory tasks. This position requires instructor certification and several years of experience as an instructor in the program they will supervise.

Provide an opportunity for your staff to apply for and be interviewed for these positions. Although you should already know them because they work for you, interviewing them formalizes the process, lends legitimacy, and makes them feel that the positions were not arbitrarily given away. Interview experience is also good for young staff members to prepare them for professional interviews later in life.

Mentoring

Most lifeguards are in their mid to late teens, and for many lifeguarding is their first job. Take the opportunity as a supervisor to spend time with your staff members individually and to learn what their goals and desires are. You may be able to offer some wisdom and guidance beyond just work-related feedback. The interest that you show in your staff members is often important in their lives. From a work-related standpoint, you can also help mold your young staff members' work

habits and provide a positive influence. Here are some examples of opportunities you can use to mentor your staff:

- ▶ Talk with members of your staff and find out what their goals are. Try to find opportunities for them at the workplace to begin to develop in those areas, even if it means letting them take on responsibilities in other departments of your organization.

- ▶ Encourage promising staff members to apply for positions of increasing responsibility, such as crew chief or head lifeguard.

- ▶ Ask more experienced staff members to watch out for and help junior staff members with tasks they might find difficult. Regularly check back with the senior member to see how the junior member is doing, to offer suggestions, and to listen to the senior member's input. By doing so you're really mentoring both staff members because this helps the senior member develop leadership skills.

- ▶ Learn staff members' goals for higher education and their career aspirations. Be sure to point out opportunities in aquatics for those who you think would do well in the field. Encourage those who have realistic higher education aspirations. Point out that employment in aquatics can continue to provide income for them during school (on breaks and in the summer). Remind them that they can come back to work at your facility when school is out!

By mentoring your staff, you develop a more personal bond with them. This creates a better work environment, builds personal loyalty from your staff, and creates a better sense of accomplishment for you. You will also find that your staff members stay employed at your facility longer, recommend employment to their friends, and provide a better atmosphere for the patrons. Employees who feel that their supervisor cares about them and is attempting to help them achieve their goals are more content, motivated, and positive.

SUMMARY

Selecting the correct staff and developing them appropriately are key to the success of your aquatic facility. To do this, you will need to create clear and accurate position descriptions and then recruit people to fill the positions you've created. Once you have your pool of candidates for a position, you'll need to screen them and select the correct one. After you've hired your staff, you must train and supervise them to ensure that they perform as you want them to. Retaining your staff is the final step in maintaining the group of well-trained and hardworking staff members you've assembled.

REVIEW QUESTIONS

1. List the duties performed by a lifeguard supervisor.
2. List and describe three methods for recruiting aquatic staff.
3. List questions that are illegal to ask in a job interview.
4. List the items that should be kept in an employee's file.
5. Describe three methods for delivering in-service training.
6. Describe three methods that may be used for lifeguard retention.

BIBLIOGRAPHY

Anderson, S. (1982, April). *Training lifeguards.* Focus on Lifeguarding, Saskatoon, SK.

Ellis and Associates. (n.d.). Ellis and Associates lifeguarding certification agency home page. Retrieved September 9, 2003, from Web site: www.jellis.com/ programs/lifeguarding/default.html.

Fawcett, P. (1999, January/February). Aquatics: Where the jobs are. *Aquatics International,* 10(2), 16-22.

Palm, J. (1986, May). *Lifeguard preparation and continuing education.* Rescue '86 Symposium, Vancouver, BC.

RESOURCES

De Rozario, F.J. (1999). Human resource management. In S. Brown & L. Schoonmaker (Eds.), *Managing the collegiate recreational facility* (pp. 175-204). Eugene, OR: National Intramural Recreational Sports Association.

Fawcett, P. (2000). *Aquatic management handbook.* Eugene, OR: National Intramural Recreational Sports Association.

Fawcett, P. (2001). Managing lifeguards effectively. *Parks & Recreation,* 36(2), 72-75.

Lifeguarding

Chapter Objectives

After reading this chapter, you should be able to

1. understand the qualifications needed to be employed as a lifeguard,
2. list and describe the technical aspects of lifeguarding,
3. describe methods for stationing lifeguards,
4. list the essential items to include as part of the lifeguards' uniform,
5. list and describe safety systems, and
6. plan for special situations that lifeguards may encounter.

The foundation of aquatic safety at any facility is sound lifeguarding practices provided by well-trained and well-equipped lifeguards. The failure to provide lifeguards or to properly train or equip them is negligent and dangerous to a facility's customers. This chapter assists aquatic facility managers by outlining lifeguard responsibilities, guarding procedures, lifeguard stations, and safety procedures (including **buddy systems** and **buddy boards**).

Alphabet soup. That's probably what you think when you hear about all the agencies that offer certification in lifeguard training: ARC, YMCA, BSA, USLA, E&A, and so on. But what does it all mean? Are all agencies created equal? To help you sort this out, this chapter explains who these agencies are and what makes them different from each other.

This chapter also provides information about the job description and desired qualifications for a lifeguard. What exactly do lifeguards do? How is it that they do it? You'll find answers to these questions and find out about methods of surveillance for lifeguards.

One of the keys to effective lifeguarding is communication. A lifeguard must be able to pass along information to other staff members at your facility. This could mean life or death for a victim. This chapter also discusses the many ways that lifeguards can share information and helps you determine which way is best for your facility and situation.

LIFEGUARD POSITION DESCRIPTION

A lifeguard's primary responsibility above all others is to prevent accidents and injuries at an aquatic facility. In the event that the lifeguard cannot prevent the accident, he or she must make an appropriate rescue in the shortest possible time. Lifeguards are expected to be expert swimmers capable of swimming long distances comfortably and short distances quickly. Your lifeguards' technical proficiency in aquatic rescue should include rescue of active victims at the surface, rescue of passive victims at the surface and

Lifeguarding Equipment

Equipment common to all aquatic facilities

- Rescue tube
- Reaching pole
- Ring buoy
- Shepherd's crook
- Heaving line
- Rescue breathing pocket mask or similar barrier for CPR rescue breathing
- Bag-valve mask for rescue breathing
- Portable manual or automatic suction device for obstructed airway victim
- First aid kit
  - Personal lifeguard first aid "waist packs" worn while on duty
- Backboard
- Cervical collar
- Head immobilizer
- Towels
- Blankets
- Flashlights
- Whistles
- Notepad and pen
- Weather radio (for outdoor facilities)
- Automatic external defibrillator
- Portable supplemental oxygen
- Water bottles (for use by lifeguards on the stand)
- Lifeguard uniforms (not all are appropriate for every facility; all should be clearly labeled "lifeguard")

- Distinctive swimsuits
- Jackets
- Sweatshirts
- Sweatpants
- Hats
- Shoes or sandals
- Lifeguard chairs or stands

Equipment specific to open water facilities

- Diving mask
- Snorkel
- Swim fins
- **Rescue board**
- Rescue kayak
- Rescue boat
  - Fire extinguisher
  - Life jackets
  - Distress flares
  - Marine band radio
  - Sheath knife
  - Oars or paddles
  - Motor (if nonmotorized boats) or gas cans (if motorized boats)
  - Area nautical charts (if boat is used offshore)
- Two-way radios and chargers
- Semaphore flags (if semaphore signaling is used at the facility)
- Lifeguard vehicles
- Rescue Jet-skis

submerged, and rescue of spinally injured victims at the surface and submerged. A lifeguard's CPR skills should encompass one- and two-rescuer CPR, as well as adult, infant, and child rescue breathing and choking rescue skills (Clayton & Thomas, 1989).

Although lifeguards may be assigned other tasks—such as teaching, coaching, or cleaning—they should never be assigned those tasks while supervising the pool. During the course of their duties, your lifeguards may also be assigned tasks such as unlocking and locking the facility before and after their shift, performing safety

inspections of the facility before opening, and completing inventories of supplies. Almost all lifeguards carry out basic administrative tasks (e.g., counting patrons each hour, recording water chemistry, filling out accident reports, and completing time sheets).

LIFEGUARD QUALIFICATIONS

Giving someone employment as a lifeguard does not make him one; certification and training do. Lifeguards must possess certification in lifeguard training, first aid, and CPR from a nationally recognized training entity before you allow them to begin working a shift. The following list identifies many of the lifeguard training certifications currently available and provides a brief overview of their content:

▸ **American Red Cross.** This agency offers an approximately 30-hour program that includes first aid and CPR for the professional rescuer in addition to water rescue skills. Modules in automatic external defibrillation, supplemental oxygen, and preventing disease transmission, as well as water park and waterfront, are optional. This certificate is valid for 3 years as long as the CPR certification, which must be recertified every year, remains valid. Participants in this program must be 15 years of age by the conclusion of the program.

▸ **YMCA of the USA.** The YMCA of the USA program differs from the others in that it includes units on leadership and child abuse prevention. Although CPR training is required, it is not included as part of the 33 hours of training time counted in the class. The course is designed to be used for staff at YMCA facilities, and it espouses the YMCA philosophy. However, it is acceptable for use at other facilities and is identified as such in most state bathing codes.

▸ **Ellis and Associates.** Ellis and Associates (E&A) was originally developed specifically for the water park industry and continues to be an industry leader in that respect. However, with the development of their National Pool and Water Park Lifeguard Training (NPWPLT) program, they have expanded into traditional swimming pools. The E&A program is unlike others in that it offers a "license" and not a certification; as such it is revocable by the company. Facilities that offer E&A instruction must be contracted E&A clients. Staff who are employed by E&A contracted facilities may have their skills audited at any time; if they fail the audit, their license will be revoked. E&A licenses are valid for only 1 year and require annual retraining. The E&A program integrates CPR/first aid and AED into its lifeguard training course. The E&A program includes options for licensing seniors (55 and over), and a junior lifeguarding program is available to those not old enough for the NPWPLT program. Advanced training offered by this company includes the aquatic rescue professional course designed for public safety personnel (Ellis, 2000b).

▸ **United States Lifesaving Association.** Unlike the other agencies, the United States Lifesaving Association (USLA) does not directly certify lifeguards. Instead, the USLA sanctions programs that abide by the guidelines contained in its materials. The USLA is an open water lifeguard training program and does not have a pool training element. This program is used mostly by beach patrols on the coasts and Great Lakes. The USLA course includes 40 hours of open water and lecture instruction in addition to first aid and CPR training.

▸ **Starfish Aquatics Institute.** This newest of lifeguard agencies offers a training program that certifies staff in CPR, first aid, emergency oxygen, preventing disease transmission, and lifeguard training. Their certification is known as STAR: Safety Training and Aquatic Rescue. This certification is valid for 1 year.

▸ **Boy Scouts of America.** The Boy Scouts of America (BSA) lifeguard training program is primarily designed for Scouts and for meeting the water safety needs of the Boy Scout program. The BSA course is therefore very open water focused, as opposed to focusing on swimming pools. The primary piece of rescue equipment used in this course is the ring buoy (not the rescue tube). Only certification in adult CPR (as opposed to professional rescuer CPR) is required.

Web site addresses for many of the previously listed agencies are included in the resources section at the end of this chapter. Also see appendix A for contact information for many of these agencies.

USE OF NONCERTIFIED STAFF IN AN AQUATIC ENVIRONMENT

There are two major advantages to using non-lifeguard-certified staff at aquatic facilities: They are less expensive to hire due to their lower level of training, and there is a larger pool of eligible candidates to hire. Noncertified staff can be used effectively for tasks such as ID checking, maintenance and cleaning tasks, clerical duties (e.g., program registration), and cash management. However, under no circumstances should nonlifeguards be given lifeguard duties. This places both the patron and the staff member at great physical risk. Justification used for doing this is often that there are not enough lifeguards available for employment and that the "monitors" would only notify lifeguards of an emergency. This is dangerous and faulty reasoning because it assumes that these untrained staff members can recognize an aquatic emergency and know what response is required. If they fail to recognize the emergency or fail to take the correct action, the consequences may be catastrophic for the victim. If you do not have enough lifeguards to adequately staff your facility, take other actions until you can recruit more lifeguards—for example, close selected sections of your facility, curtail operating hours, or have supervisory staff members who are lifeguard certified work as lifeguards.

However, noncertified observers can be used in addition to, or to supplement, lifeguards during particularly busy times. This is often done at camp waterfronts during camp swims. If you elect to use observers to supplement your lifeguard staff, it is very helpful to offer some form of lifesaving training that teaches the observer how to recognize a victim and how to signal for assistance. Certifying these assistants in first aid and CPR also adds greatly to their value. Again, these assistants must never be left to supervise swimmers on their own; they may be used in addition to but not in place of lifeguards. If noncertified staff are used in place of lifeguards, you will be in violation of the state bathing code in most states, and you will definitely be in violation of the professional **standard of care.** This leaves you open to sanction by the state or litigation by injured parties.

> **KEY POINT**   There are a myriad of agencies that offer certification programs for lifeguards. It's crucial that you only hire lifeguards with current certification from a nationally recognized agency. The agency's program must include certification in CPR and first aid at a minimum.

LIFEGUARD PROFESSIONALISM

In terms of aquatic safety, the lifeguard represents the "face" of your aquatic facility. Your lifeguards are responsible for greeting guests, providing information, enforcing rules, and providing rescue and emergency care services as needed. To successfully carry out these tasks, your guards will need to behave professionally. You, as the manager, must foster a sense of professionalism in your lifeguard staff.

Uniforms

Your lifeguards must be clearly identified to the public so that patrons will notify them of an emergency. Uniforms perform this function in addition to giving your staff a sense of identity and a feeling of professionalism. The type of uniform issued to your staff will depend on your facility. However, regardless of the type of facility, the guards' uniform should clearly say "lifeguard." Matching off-the-rack swimsuits will not substitute for uniforms because they provide no identification, and a swimmer could easily have the same suit. Elements of a lifeguard's uniform may include the following:

▶ **Shirts.** Tank tops or T-shirts can be used for lifeguards, and collared polo shirts for supervisors. The word *lifeguard* should be clearly spelled out on the back, and your company logo can be on the front.

▶ **Swimsuits.** One-piece suits should be used for females, and trunks for males. A lifeguard crest or silk screen should be placed on the swimsuit.

▶ **Hats (only needed at outdoor facilities).** This item is necessary to protect the face and scalp from exposure to the sun. Your company logo or the word *lifeguard* should be on the band. Visors should not be substituted for hats because they do not protect the scalp. Hats should always be worn bill forward. Do not allow the hat to be worn sideways or backward; this is unprofessional and can be viewed as a gang symbol.

▶ **Warm-up suits (only needed at outdoor facilities).** Warm-up suits that include a jacket and pants help protect your lifeguards against cold and rainy weather. Suits can either be lined with nylon or Gore-Tex. Although Gore-Tex is much more expensive than nylon, it repels water up to 250 pounds (113.4 kilograms) per square inch and provides excellent insulation. This fabric is recommended for outdoor lifeguard uniforms in more northern climates.

▶ **Footwear.** Tennis shoes or sneakers may be worn at outdoor facilities to protect lifeguards' feet from rocks, glass, and hot sand or asphalt. Lifeguards at indoor facilities may want to consider aqua socks or shower sandals to protect their feet and provide traction on slippery decks.

▶ **Sunglasses.** Many lifeguards from earlier generations have damaged their eyes by guarding outdoors without adequate eye protection. Sunglasses with UVA/UVB and infrared (IFR) lenses are necessary when guarding outside. The direct light and glare are harmful to the eyes and make it difficult to see the water.

▸ **Sunscreen.** Sunscreen really is part of the uniform at outdoor facilities. Failure to wear sunscreen can result in painful and debilitating burns and eventually skin cancer. Facilities may want to provide sunscreen to their staff to be sure they will wear it.

▸ **Waist packs.** In recent years, these items have become part of many lifeguards' uniforms. These kits are worn on the lifeguard's waist and include a rescue pocket mask, latex gloves, and basic first aid supplies such as adhesive bandages, tape, and gauze.

Dress and Grooming

As just discussed, uniforms are an essential part of identifying lifeguards so that they can be easily found in an emergency. But having a uniform isn't enough—it must be worn properly. Don't allow staff members to cheapen their professional image by altering uniforms to suit their individual style. Alterations such as tearing sleeves out of shirts, cutting parts out of swimsuits, or ripping the bills out of hats present an unprofessional image. You must require your staff to wear their uniforms at all times while on duty. It's helpful to have a plan in place for what you will do when a staff member forgets or does not bring her uniform. You may want to keep extra "loaner" shirts or jackets stored in the guard office for such a case.

You should encourage your staff to present a neat, well-groomed appearance. Here are some guidelines you may want to enforce for your staff:

▸ Lifeguards may not wear any piercings of the tongue, lips, or mouth. (This is an infection control issue for rescue breathing as well as a professionalism issue.)

▸ Males or females with long hair must wear their hair in a neat ponytail or bun. (This is also a safety issue because long hair can be tangled in equipment.)

▸ Jewelry (including chains, rings, toe rings, and earrings) is not permitted on duty because it may injure patrons or become caught on equipment during rescues.

▸ All tattoos must be covered while on duty.

▸ Long nails (real or artificial) are prohibited due to the possibility of injuring a victim during rescues.

▸ Uniforms must be neat and clean at all times.

▸ Men's facial hair must be neatly trimmed.

▸ Makeup worn must be modest in nature and not attract attention to the staff member.

Staff Rules

You must set standards of behavior for your staff. You cannot expect them to know what level of professional behavior is expected from them unless you tell them explicitly. Here are some suggestions for aquatic staff rules:

▸ Food and drinks (except water) may only be consumed in the break room, not on the lifeguard stand or in the first aid room.

▸ Staff members must refrain from public displays of affection, such as kissing or inappropriate touching, with other staff or patrons.

▸ When answering questions from patrons while on duty, lifeguards must be brief; if further discussion is required, refer the patron to a supervisor.

▸ When seated in the lifeguard stand, the lifeguard must face the pool and place both feet on the stand, and he should not slouch.

▸ Rescue tubes should be placed in the lifeguard's lap, with the strap worn across the shoulder. The lifeguard should not sit on the tube or place it under the feet.

▸ The playing of musical instruments on duty is prohibited.

▸ Except for the break room or other staff areas, only music selected by the management and played on facility equipment may be played.

▸ Visitors are not permitted in the lifeguard office, first aid room, storeroom, or filter room.

▸ Telephones in the first aid room or offices are for official use only.

▸ Lifeguards may not carry personal cell phones while on duty. (Cell phones may be kept with a lifeguard's personal gear.)

▸ Staff members are expected to be courteous and polite to patrons at all times. Adult males should be addressed as "Sir," and adult females should be addressed as "Ma'am."

▸ Staff must treat their coworkers with respect and care, and should be alert for their welfare.

▶ Staff must refrain from using profanity while on the facility premises.

▶ Any staff member found committing vandalism, theft, violence or threats of violence, or any other illegal act will be fired on the spot and ejected from the facility immediately, and the police will be immediately informed.

▶ Alcohol and illegal drugs are banned from the facility.

▶ Sales of merchandise, as well as political, religious, or ideological statements, are prohibited from the facility.

TECHNICAL ASPECTS OF LIFEGUARDING

Lifeguarding is a highly technical skill that requires the application of individual and team skills and techniques to be performed properly. This section includes information regarding area coverage, rotations, scanning, and signals.

Area Coverage

Area coverage refers to the method your guards use to ensure that each part of the swimming area is assigned to a particular person and to reduce confusion regarding who is watching what. There are three types of coverage: zone, total, and backup.

Zone Coverage

When using **zone coverage,** you divide the swimming area into designated sections or "zones." Each zone is assigned to a particular lifeguard to supervise. Zones should overlap to ensure that no part of the swimming area is missed. Guards should scan their entire zone and into the zones adjacent to them to ensure that there is no confusion regarding the overlap areas. When creating zones, you should not place a lifeguard in a position where she has more than 180 degrees of coverage. This means that you should not place lifeguards at inside corners of L-, T-, or Z-shaped pools where they will have to completely turn around to complete their surveillance. The zones must be small enough that each lifeguard can easily see all the patrons she is supervising. Zones that usually contain large numbers of patrons should be smaller; this will increase your lifeguard-to-patron ratio (American Red Cross, 2004). Your staff must understand this concept well enough to be able to adjust the zones themselves with the addition or subtraction of guards in the rotation.

Create diagrams of your aquatic facility with your zones drawn in and color coded (see figure 6.1). Put these diagrams in your staff manual and hang them up in the lifeguard office. This will help eliminate confusion about where your zones are.

The advantage to zone coverage lies in its division of coverage areas among your staff. Some confusion can arise over where zones begin and end, with swimmers "on the line" between zones. This is particularly true if your facility doesn't have an easily identifiable boundary such as a float line to identify zones. Zones also require multiple lifeguards to be effective; you need one or more lifeguards per zone. If your facility only has a few staff members, you may not be able to effectively use zone coverage. Zone coverage is the safest, most efficient method of lifeguarding.

Total Coverage

Total coverage is used when only one lifeguard covers an entire swimming area. This is more often the case at smaller pools with fewer patrons attending at any given time.

Total coverage is dangerous because it assumes that the single lifeguard can see the entire area at all times, that he will remain alert at all times, and that he can rely on others to assist him with an emergency in the absence of other lifeguards. If total coverage is used, the lifeguard should make continual or regular walking rounds of the swimming area to ensure that all areas of the facility are being seen, and to interact with patrons in all areas of the facility. You must make sure that this single staff member has adequate rest breaks; this may necessitate closing the pool for a 10- to 15-minute period every 2 hours. You must also create a mechanism for summoning assistance from other staff members in single lifeguard facilities. An emergency alarm button or a direct line to other staff must be installed. Otherwise, the lifeguard could be forced to perform a rescue without anyone else available to contact EMS or assist with the rescue.

Backup Coverage

Backup coverage is needed whenever one or more of your lifeguards must leave their stations for any reason, such as to perform a rescue or speak with a patron. If this occurs, you must still maintain safety coverage of the aquatic facility. Backup coverage is the act of one lifeguard shifting zones temporarily to cover her own zone and a neighboring zone for

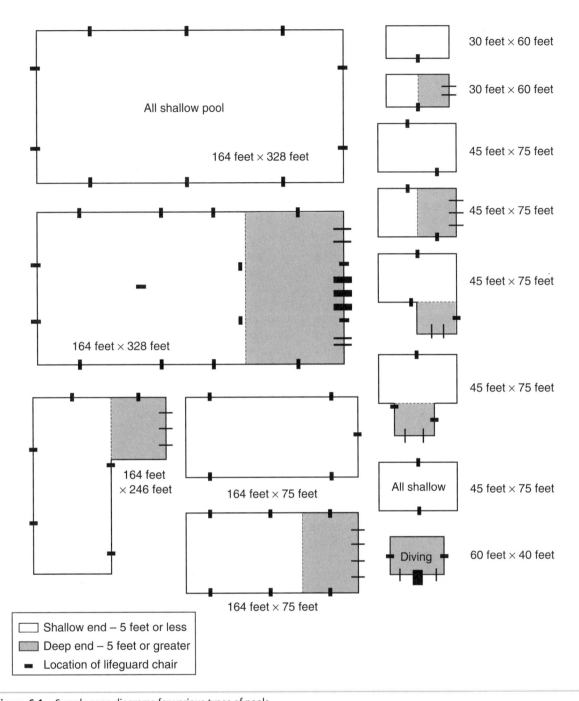

Figure 6.1 Sample zone diagrams for various types of pools.

From *Swimming Pools: A Guide to Their Planning, Design and Operation* (p. 114) by M. Alexander Gabrielsen (Ed.), 1987, Champaign, IL: Human Kinetics. Copyright 1987 by the Council for National Cooperation in Aquatics.

another guard. It is only temporary, until the original lifeguard can resume scanning. Many facilities require all staff on duty to stand up during backup coverage to get a better view of the swimming area; they sit down again when the absent guard returns and the zones return to regular coverage. Other facilities have staff members hold up their hand indicating with their fingers how many guards are

on duty at that particular pool during backup coverage. This is done so that there is no confusion about how many guards are on duty and what the coverage factor is; hands are put down when all staff return to their stations.

The practice of having an extra staff member in the rotation—one who mans the phone and performs first aid as needed—provides a buffer in the event backup is needed. This "extra" staff member can come out to handle patron problems, handle minor cleanups, or pick up a guard's zone if a rescue happens. This eliminates the need for the other lifeguards on duty to pick up the zone of the guard making the rescue, and it preserves optimal coverage of the swimming area.

Rotations

Lifeguarding is an activity that requires long periods of intense surveillance of swimmers, often in hot sun or warm, humid indoor pools. Your lifeguards can easily become mentally fatigued by the intense concentration required over long periods; eyestrain, dehydration, and fatigue are also common complaints due to bright sun and glare off the water surface. Another frequent complaint is boredom. Lifeguards are required to scan endlessly, with little interaction with other staff or patrons so that they will not be distracted from their duties. By regularly rotating your staff from station to station, you give each guard a chance to rotate out of high glare stations, reducing eye fatigue, as well as giving the guards a chance to see a new zone, reducing boredom.

Staff should be rotated every 15 to 20 minutes, with no more than 2 hours on the rotation without a break. An optimal rotation is for staff to have a 1- to 2-hour rotation that includes a 15-minute break and a first aid station in the rotation. If the first aid station at your facility is very busy and lifeguards don't get any rest during that period in the rotation, you should not count that as the lifeguards' break (Palm, 1987).

When your lifeguards rotate, a new lifeguard should come out from the lifeguard office and go to the first station. He should have a rescue tube or another rescue device with him. He should assume a position next to the lifeguard or the lifeguard stand and take over coverage; the lifeguard in the stand then gets down and assumes coverage while the oncoming lifeguard gets in the stand. The outgoing lifeguard stops coverage and leaves only when the oncoming lifeguard is in position and states that he has assumed coverage of the zone. By making the transition from guard to guard this way, the facility is never unguarded. During the transition, the outgoing lifeguard should relay to the oncoming lifeguard any special concerns or problems in the coverage area. The outgoing lifeguard should not leave until he is sure the new guard is in position and has resumed scanning.

Rotation is also an opportunity for you to send out water for your guards to stay hydrated or to pass information among your staff.

Scanning

Scanning is the act of a lifeguard systematically watching the swimming area. Proper scanning requires the lifeguard to sweep her eyes over her entire zone every 20 to 30 seconds. While scanning, lifeguards should be alert for tired and weak swimmers, **near drowning** victims, spinal injuries, or dangerous behavior that can lead to any of these. Scanning should encompass the bottom of the swimming area as well as the water's surface. Scanning the bottom allows lifeguards to detect swimmers who have sunk without being heard or seen. Every few minutes while scanning, the guard should view the entire pool to retain situational awareness of what's going on in the entire area. Similarly, the lifeguard should also check the other guards every few minutes to ensure that they are alert and not in need of assistance.

Signals

Communication between staff in aquatic facilities is often difficult due to the poor acoustic qualities of the facility, high noise volume generated by large numbers of swimmers, and large distances between lifeguards. Because of these factors, your lifeguards can't rely entirely on verbal communications. There are several other methods of relaying information that lifeguards can use, including hand signals, **semaphore,** whistles, and radios.

Hand Signals

The hand signal method involves creating a standardized set of signals that lifeguards can use to send and receive messages. Each facility can create its own set of signals as long as they are understandable and appropriate for that staff. Signals that are commonly used include major rescue, minor rescue, spinal injury, heart attack, first aid, cover my area, clear the pool, rotate, stop, go, and OK. Signals should be sent clearly using arms and hands, not just hands, so they can be easily seen at a great distance (Palm, 1987). The receiving lifeguard should signal back to the sending lifeguard to be sure the message was received correctly. A chart showing the facility signals should be contained in the lifeguard staff manual and should be posted on the staff room wall (see figure 6.2).

Cover my area:
One hand held up
for attention. Other
hand points to pool
and sweeps.

First aid:
Arms held to side
in shape of a cross.

Spinal injury:
One hand points to
victim in pool, second hand
taps back of the neck.

OK:
Arms held above
head to form large O.

Heart attack:
One arm points to
victim. Other hand
taps chest with
a closed fist.

Major emergency:
Rescue tube held
horizontally over head.

Lost child:
Both hands held
to one side indicating
a child.

Clear the water:
Arms held in front
and to the side.
Beckon for patrons to
clear the water.

Figure 6.2 Commonly used lifeguard hand signals.

Semaphore

Semaphore is a method of communication that re-creates the alphabet using hand or flag signals (see figure 6.3). The flags are used to gain the receiver's attention and to extend the distance from which the signals can be read. If flags are used, they are normally half red and half yellow squares that are divided diagonally with the red portion in the upper corner. Semaphore is used almost exclusively at large beaches because its usefulness at pools is diminished by the short distance between

Figure 6.3 The semaphore alphabet.

lifeguards. Semaphore is somewhat difficult and time consuming to learn, but it relays information very accurately once you have done so. One of the main advantages to using semaphore is that it is relatively inexpensive as opposed to other forms of communication such as radio or telephone. Aside from training, the only cost associated with this method is the flags, which are relatively inexpensive. Semaphore flags can be purchased from MrFlag.com (see appendix C).

Whistles

Whistles are by far the most commonly used mechanism for communication between lifeguards and from lifeguards to patrons. Unfortunately, they are the most abused form of communication as well. Many lifeguards overuse their whistle, making patrons almost immune to hearing it. The whistle should be used sparingly and only when absolutely necessary. To do otherwise runs the risk of being ignored in an emergency. Lifeguards may wear whistles secured to their wrist or neck. However, if a lifeguard will be working in very close proximity to patrons, such as servicing patrons on a water ride, wearing the whistle around the neck may constitute a hazard. Patrons have been known to grasp the whistle around the guard's neck, pulling the guard into the slide or ride. Although it's not a common occurrence, it is a risk eliminated by wearing the whistle on the wrist. Whistles can be purchased from many of the aquatic supply companies listed in appendix C.

You should create a standardized set of whistle signals for all your staff members to use. A copy of your whistle signals should be in your lifeguard staff manual. A sample set of signals may include the following (YMCA of the USA, 2001):

- ▸ One blast: Lifeguard to patron.
- ▸ Two blasts: Lifeguard to lifeguard.
- ▸ Three blasts: Rescue in progress.
- ▸ One extremely long blast: Clear the pool (whether for an emergency or for the end of the day).

Radios

Radio communication is the most expensive form of communication and is therefore used somewhat less among lifeguards. It is used most commonly at water parks and large beaches due to the long distances involved. Facilities with extensive boat or vehicle patrols should consider two-way communication radios an important feature for these units. Marine band radios should be used for lifeguard operations with extensive boat patrols or for lifeguard operations on open water. Marine band radio channel 16 is the international hailing and distress frequency and provides immediate access to the U.S. Coast Guard (Fawcett, 2001b).

For facilities with less prevalent boating operations, often only selected staff members have radios due to their high cost. Staff members and locations that should be issued radios include the first aid station, security officers, the facility manager, head lifeguards, pool operators, maintenance supervisors, cashiers, and front desk staff. Some facilities issue radios to strategic lifeguard stations based on their view of the swimming area. These lifeguards are responsible for relaying information up the chain of command if an emergency occurs.

Radios must be placed on their charger at the conclusion of the day in order to have a full battery charge for the next day. They must be "off" while in the chargers or they will not retain their charge. If your facility has radios that aren't rechargeable, you should check the radios for battery strength each night by performing a radio check to test their signal. Be sure to have a supply of batteries on hand to replace dead ones. Be sure to turn the radio off when not in service to preserve the limited battery life. You must purchase radios of adequate quality to ensure that their range and sound quality are appropriate for what you want them to do. Good quality radios are expensive; you must be prepared to invest in them. If you are unwilling to pay for quality equipment, you should not purchase radios. Cheap radios will not do what you want, and you will have wasted the money you spent.

As with the other forms of communication, a standardized communication code is necessary. The Federal Communications Commission regulates all radio traffic on public airwaves. A radio communications station certificate may be required for your facility. You must caution your staff that playing with the radios, false distress messages, and profanity cannot be tolerated and may be a crime. Any misuse of radios must be punished by immediate removal of that staff member's radio and possible suspension.

The RID Factor

Frank Pia, aquatic specialist and former chief lifeguard for the city of New York, has identified three major causes for lifeguards' failure to respond properly to a **distressed swimmer** in their area of supervision. He has summarized these factors under the acronym RID: Recognition, Intrusion, Distraction (Pia, 1986).

Recognition

Your staff won't be able to respond to and rescue a distressed swimmer if they can't recognize one. The problem is that most flat water swimming pool lifeguards can go years without seeing one. This problem is not as acute at water parks and open water beaches, where the frequency of rescues is often higher. You must spend time training your lifeguards to scan properly and teaching them what factors to look for when scanning. Active drowning victims may not call out for help; they may exhibit a vertical position in the water, flail their arms at their sides, and face shore. In your in-service training sessions, emphasize drills that focus on the lifeguard recognizing distressed victims. Situational training is one way to accomplish this. You may also show videos, such as *On Drowning,* that show actual victims in distress and the rescues of those victims.

Intrusion

Intrusion refers to nonsupervision activities taking the lifeguard's attention away from watching the pool. These activities might include maintenance or cleaning tasks, folding towels, checking IDs, or giving instruction. Regardless of the task, the effect is the same—your guard isn't watching the pool when she is supposed to be. The equation is clear: Less time watching the pool equals more opportunity for a distressed swimmer to drown unnoticed. The solution is simple: Don't assign lifeguards other duties when they're supposed to be watching the pool. This is an unpopular idea with many facility managers because they think of lifeguards in the stand "doing nothing" as wasted manpower. However, lifeguards are like insurance; you pay for them hoping not to need them, but if you do, you'll be very glad you have them.

Distraction

Lifeguards tend to be young, and in many cases, they are experiencing the world of work for the first time. They often develop poor work habits that can distract them from their primary duty of supervising swimmers. Here are some poor habits that they may develop:

- Talking to friends or patrons while in the lifeguard stand
- Playing musical instruments while on duty

- Eating while on duty
- Reading while on duty
- Daydreaming
- Talking on the telephone while on duty (particularly cell phones)
- Listening to music other than that played over the facility PA system

As a supervisor, you must take steps to redirect your lifeguards' attention back to their duties. Begin by removing distractions such as cell phones, radios, televisions, and other electronic devices from the lifeguard office. You should also pay frequent visits to the pool area to check on your staff. Make random walk-throughs to correct distractions as you see them—for example, asking lifeguards' friends to see them *after* work, redirecting staff attention back to the pool, and reminding them to only eat on breaks. By doing so you will increase the safety factor of your facility by ensuring that your staff members are vigilant.

LIFEGUARD–EMS CONNECTION

Lifeguards are, in effect, the first link in the emergency medical services chain. Lifeguards are the first responders who arrive quickly to the scene of an emergency, begin initial rescue procedures, and administer lifesaving first aid. Because of this, you'll need to establish contact with EMS personnel before an emergency occurs to foster seamless care for victims. Ask the local EMS crew to visit your facility, talk to your staff, and bring in their equipment. There are several questions you will want to address during this meeting, including the following:

- If EMS personnel are called to your facility, which entrance will they be met at?
- Are your backboards and stretchers compatible with EMS gurneys and ambulances? (Will your backboard fit into their gurney? Can the ambulance doors close with your backboard inside?)
- What procedures do EMS personnel expect when transferring patient care from lifeguards to EMS? What information will they want?
- If your equipment goes with EMS to the hospital, how will you get it back?
- Will EMS personnel enter the water to assist with back boarding a victim, if needed?

- Does EMS allow or want lifeguard staff to ride in the ambulance with the victim to assist with care and reclaim facility equipment?
- Is your equipment compatible with that of EMS? For example, will oxygen bottles from EMS hook up to your rescue breathing devices? Will the AEDs used by EMS hook up to your paddles?
- If an air **medevac** is needed for an emergency at your facility, where is the nearest location that a helicopter could land?

Try to set up a meeting with your county medical director to determine the protocols for issues such as the use of oxygen and automatic external defibrillators. You may also want to explore training opportunities for your staff if you think it would benefit them. Ask if your staff can accompany EMS personnel on ride alongs to broaden their knowledge. (This is recommended only for older, well-trained staff members.) You may also explore opportunities for advanced certification such as first responder or emergency medical technician.

For larger beach operations, you may want to look into having your facility placed on the 911 system. If you do this, when near shore marine emergencies are reported to 911, your command center (along with other emergency agencies) will be contacted and given the information.

LIFEGUARD HEALTH AND SAFETY

Lifeguarding as an occupation can be physically challenging for your staff. There is a risk of injury from a variety of sources, ranging from overexertion to injury from rescues to exposure to the elements. It's incumbent upon you as the supervisor to take steps to ensure the health and safety of your staff.

Guarding the Guards

Your lifeguards are supervising the swimmers, constantly providing surveillance to protect against drowning and injury and to respond to any situation that arises. But who's watching them? The answer is that you are, and that they should also be watching each other. As mentioned earlier, lifeguards can suffer from dehydration, loss of concentration, and eyestrain. Your staff can also experience a wide range of other physical difficul-

ties, including but not limited to sunburn, **heat exhaustion** or **heatstroke,** nausea, hypothermia, fatigue, and muscle strain or sprain. These problems are more common and may be more severe in outdoor facilities.

As a supervisor, you should make frequent visits to your staff to ensure their welfare. Learn to recognize the signs of potential problems, both physical and mental, with your staff. If you determine a lifeguard is ill and unable to effectively continue working, you should remove him from his duties. If the problem is temporary and can be solved by a rest period or fluids, you may allow the lifeguard to continue his shift when you both think he is able. If you think that a staff member is too sick or injured to continue working, relieve him from duty.

Consider the implications before simply "sending him home." If the lifeguard is very ill or seriously injured, he may require medical attention. In other cases, it may be appropriate to have another staff member take him home or to call family and friends to provide transportation for him if you think he is too sick to drive. Do not rely on staff members to give you an accurate or truthful impression of their physical condition. Your staff is your responsibility; trust your own good judgment.

Another method that you can use to ensure the welfare of your staff is to instruct them to check on each other as part of their scanning routine. This ensures that your staff is monitored every few minutes. It also gives them the opportunity to signal each other if they have a need such as water or the need to use the rest room.

You should also have a contingency staffing plan for when you determine that a staff member is injured or ill to the point that he will not be able to complete his shift. Your contingency plan might include calling in replacement staff, closing areas of your facility, or functioning with reduced staff. Regardless of what action you take, you must not compromise patron safety through reduced lifeguard coverage.

Lifeguard Personal Needs

Seasonal lifeguards in particular often work longer consecutive hours and more often outdoors. The combination of hot weather, sun, and longer hours creates the need for you to give special consideration to their personal needs.

Water is undoubtedly the primary concern above all others, particularly at outdoor facilities.

Your lifeguards must remain well hydrated or they will become susceptible to heat-related illnesses such as heat exhaustion or heatstroke. You must ensure that your staff members have easy access to fresh, cool drinking water. Preferably, your staff office or first aid area will have a sink or water cooler that your staff can use to draw water from; if you can't provide this option, ensure that water jugs or bottles are available. Staff at remote stations should take water with them. As mentioned in the discussion of rotations, during hot weather, you should send a water bottle with the guard beginning the rotation cycle to pass from guard to guard for each to take a drink from. In cases of extreme heat or long shifts, place a water bottle on each chair and ensure that the guards are drinking regularly.

Staff at outdoor facilities are also very susceptible to sunburn, particularly early in the season. Remind your guards to wear the appropriate level of sunscreen and to reapply it throughout the day. If possible, have a large bottle of high SPF sunscreen available in the guard station for those who did not bring any. You should also encourage guards to wear hats at outdoor facilities to protect them against overexposure from the sun.

Lifeguards often work long hours during busy seasons, particularly during the summer months. You should make sure that they have access to food while working at your facility. On a basic level, you can make a refrigerator available and encourage them to bring their lunch and store it there. An inexpensive microwave will expand the possibilities of what they are able to make for themselves at meals. Larger facilities can explore options such as vending machines and access to on-site food vendors, possibly at reduced rates. Whatever route you choose, be sure to plan adequate time in the lifeguard's shift rotation for meals.

> **KEY POINT** *Lifeguards are people too! If you're not looking out for them, they'll be unable to supervise your patrons. You need to ensure that they get sufficient water and rest breaks as well as protection from the sun.*

STATIONING GUARDS

Where you place your guards will determine how much of the swimming area they can see and how well they can see it. There is no one correct way to station your staff; it will depend on the type of facility, the number of patrons, and the activity being performed. Some of the methods that can be used are raised stands, deck level stations, roving guards, guards stationed in the water, boat patrols, and vehicle patrols.

Raised Lifeguard Stands

Raised lifeguard stands are the most common form of station currently in use. They are popular at pools, beaches, and water parks for their ability to get the lifeguards above the swimmers and deck level congestion so that they can see more of the swimming area. Another advantage to raised stations is that they allow the lifeguard to see more of the bottom and any swimmers who may be there in distress. The lifeguard in the stand is also clearly visible and identifiable to the swimmers in case the lifeguard is needed.

However, there are disadvantages to the raised stand. If the raised stand is projected out over the pool, the lifeguard will have a blind spot underneath the stand. To remedy this problem, guards in stations opposite each other should be told to watch the area underneath each other's stand.

You should direct your guards to keep their rescue tubes either on their lap if seated or held

A raised lifeguard stand gives lifeguards a better view of the pool.

in front of them if standing. The rescue tube line must be collected and held in front of them. If these steps are not followed, the tube or strap may become tangled in the stand when the guard enters the water for a rescue. This has seriously injured lifeguards.

Care must also be taken when positioning raised stands and when instructing staff in how to use them. Lifeguards should not jump from stands into shallow water of 5 feet (152.4 centimeters) or less because they may be injured. Portable stands must be kept close enough to the pool for lifeguards to easily enter the water, and the wheels must be in the locked position. Lifeguards at wave pools should be taught how to time their entry from the stand to hit the crest of the wave, not the trough, in order to provide as much shock absorption as possible. You should caution your staff never to dive off raised stands due to the increased risk of spinal injury.

Deck Level Stations

Lifeguards at deck level may be standing or seated. The advantage to deck level guards is in their closeness to the patrons and the water. They can interact with the swimmers more easily to enforce rules and answer questions. Guards stationed at deck level can also see facial expressions of the swimmers more easily and may be better able to detect distress.

The major disadvantage of deck level stations is their poor vantage point. Guards stationed in these positions are more likely to have their view obstructed by patrons on the deck. They are also unable to see as much of the swimming area and may have a more difficult time seeing the bottom. Lifeguards at deck level stations should stand at waterside, meaning with feet almost in the water. This reduces the likelihood of obstructed views and of missing a distressed swimmer on the bottom immediately in front of the guard.

Roving Guards

"Rovers," as these guards are often called, do not have a set position; they roam a swimming area at will. This is particularly effective in providing lifeguard presence throughout a swimming area, which increases rule enforcement capability. Rovers are helpful in early intervention, such as directing weak swimmers toward shallow water and reuniting wandering children with their parents (YMCA of the USA, 2001).

Because the nature of their tasks is more interactive with the swimmers, it is difficult for rovers to exercise surveillance over their entire area simultaneously. Therefore, you may want to combine rovers with guards in other types of stations.

Guards Stationed in the Water

Stationing guards in the water is most commonly done at water parks, usually in catch pools at the bottom of body slides. The advantage to using this method is that the lifeguard is in very close proximity to the swimmer and can respond immediately if needed. If you station a lifeguard in the water in a catch pool, be sure to tell her to position herself where she will not be struck by sliders as they exit.

The disadvantage to this method is that the lifeguard cannot see or respond to anything behind her and that her view of the larger swimming area is poor. For these reasons, stationing staff in the water is not recommended for areas larger than a catch pool.

Boat Patrols

Boat patrols are used only at open water beaches and waterfronts. The best use of boat-stationed lifeguards is to have them patrol the sides or far reaches of the swimming area. Boats may be either powered or unpowered depending on the services needed and the size of the area to be patrolled. For smaller inland beaches, lifeguard kayaks or rowboats may be used. Large open water areas may require large boats with high horsepower.

All lifeguards using rescue boats must be instructed in their proper use. This is particularly true of powerboats. You must ensure that powerboats do not enter swimming areas, except in extreme emergencies, because swimmers could be struck and injured by the boat's prop. If assistance is needed from a boat patrol, you can direct the boat's crew to send one of its members over the side with a **rescue can** or tube to make the rescue.

Equipment that should be kept aboard large lifeguard rescue craft includes the following:

- Rescue cans or tubes
- First aid kit (comprehensive)
- Backboard
- Fire extinguisher (if motorized)

▶ Marine radio (for contacting the Coast Guard and other marine agencies)

▶ Distress flares

▶ Life jackets of various sizes, including children's sizes

Federal regulations require that all boats carry enough life jackets for each person on board. You should direct your lifeguards on boat patrols to wear their life jackets for their own personal safety.

Vehicle Patrols

Vehicle patrols are also only used at open water swimming areas. Vehicles commonly used for this purpose are all-terrain vehicles (ATVs), quad runners, and four-wheel drive trucks and jeeps. These types of patrols are particularly useful along long, sparsely used beaches in the off-season. Beaches in southern climates that are still warm enough for swimming during the off-season (yet are only sparsely used) can be patrolled from a vehicle; this provides better coverage at a cheaper cost than regularly stationed lifeguards. During peak season, the vehicles can deliver immediate assistance in the form of advanced medical equipment (e.g., AEDs and supplemental oxygen) and from additional staff in the vehicle. Victims can often

be transported off the beach to meet the ambulance more quickly and easily in the vehicle than by carrying them.

Lifeguard emergency vehicles should be painted red or yellow and should be clearly marked with the service crest and the word *lifeguard* on the side so that the vehicles can be easily identified by the public. You should also equip them with a light bar and siren in order to be able to alert the public that they are in the area. Vehicles should be driven at slow speeds on the beach to reduce the risk of hitting someone. Use of these vehicles should be limited to supervisors with good driving records.

SAFETY SYSTEMS

Safety systems are methods employed by aquatic staff to assist in maintaining accountability for swimmers and ensuring safety. Safety systems discussed in this section include buddy boards, the buddy system, **safety stops,** and swim tests.

Buddy Boards

A buddy board is a safety aid that is most often used at camp waterfronts. A large marine plywood board is placed at the entrance to the swimming area. The board is divided in half with the word

A lifeguard rescue vehicle patrols a beach.

© Will Funk/Alpine Aperture

In painted at the top of one side and the word *Out* at the top of the other. A series of hooks, one for each swimmer, are arranged in rows on each side of the board. Each swimmer has a tag with his name on it (the tag is color coded to indicate his swimming ability). This tag is hung on a hook on the buddy board. As the swimmer comes into the swimming area, he moves his tag from "out" to "in." This assists the staff in maintaining accountability for all campers. It is helpful to have a counselor stationed at the board to ensure that all campers properly move their tag. Before swimmers are allowed to enter the water on their first day, you should explain the board and why it is important to the campers. At the end of a swim period, if you note that one or more tags have not been moved to the "out" position, you must assume that you have a missing swimmer and initiate your emergency action plan. Because of this, you must ensure that swimmers move their tags as required or you will be continually performing searches for lost swimmers.

The Buddy System

The buddy system is also a safety aid that is used at camp waterfront settings. Before swimmers enter the water, they are required to choose a "buddy" and must stay with their buddy at all times. A counselor or lifeguard records the number of buddy pairs. At 15- to 20-minute intervals, a "buddy check" is called by a lifeguard, and the number of buddy pairs is counted and compared against the number recorded. If the number does not match, or if a swimmer does not know where her buddy is, the emergency action plan must be activated.

The advantage to using the buddy system is that it provides another measure of accountability for the swimmers besides the lifeguard. However, you must assume that the swimmers are able to be accountable for each other and that both members of a buddy pair will not get into distress at the same time. For this system to work effectively, a staff member must monitor it closely, and the swimmers must be old enough to be responsible for each other.

Safety Stops

Safety stops can be used at camp waterfronts, pools of all types, and beaches. When a safety stop is initiated, all swimmers are cleared from the water. The purpose is to check the pool bottom

and to give the lifeguards and swimmers a brief rest. This is particularly helpful on very high use days, especially at those facilities without enough staff to provide lifeguards with a break. Safety stops can be called whenever needed but are usually called once per hour for a period of 5 minutes. Lifeguards may want to take the opportunity to visit the rest room, drink water, or get cooled off by swimming during a safety stop. Safety stops are easy to implement and provide a measure of rest for both swimmers and staff. Before implementing this safety option, be sure to educate your swimmers by posting signs and by using public address system announcements (Palm, 1987).

Swim Tests

Swim tests are normally used to determine if swimmers possess enough swimming skill to be allowed in deep water. In operating swim tests, one or two lifeguards may set aside a lane or a deep water area that swimmers must swim without stopping. The required distance is normally 15 to 20 yards (13.7 to 18.3 meters). If a swimmer successfully completes the test, he may swim in the "deep end." Swimmers who have passed the test may have their names recorded, or in the case of resident summer camps, they may be issued a plastic strip to wear around their wrist.

Swim tests help eliminate the problem of nonswimmers or weak swimmers in the deep end. Swimmers performing the test must be watched closely because many weak swimmers are unaware of their ability; they may attempt the test but be unable to complete it and become distressed swimmers.

SPECIAL SITUATIONS

Lifeguarding often results in exposure to a variety of situations aside from rule enforcement, rescues, and the prevention of injuries. These situations can range from the amusing, such as frogs in the pool, to the traumatic, such as assault on a staff member. Special situations discussed in this section include spinal injuries, facility evacuation, guarding persons with disabilities, and guarding water attractions.

Spinal Injuries

Aquatic spinal injuries are one of the most catastrophic events that can happen at your facility. Spinal injuries can occur almost anywhere in your facility, including the pool deck, locker areas, deep water, shallow water, and on apparatuses such as diving boards, slides, and starting blocks. Spinal injuries are horrific because an injury to a patron's spine can render her paraplegic (without the use of her legs) or quadriplegic (without the use of both arms and legs) for the rest of her life depending on the type of injury.

The most common cause of spinal injury is diving into shallow water of a depth of 5 feet (152.4 centimeters) or less; victims most often strike their head on the bottom, causing a flexion or extension injury. The diver is often injured in the fourth through sixth cervical vertebrae, in the neck region. These accidents often happen because the diver is not aware of the dangers of diving in shallow water or is not a trained diver. Spinal injury victims in the water often float facedown at or just below the surface and may show very little movement. Even if they are conscious, they may not be able to cry out for help (Pike, 1980).

Public education is the first step that you can take to minimize the occurrence of this injury. Post signs that state no diving in shallow water at both pools and waterfronts. You may even use contrasting color tile to incorporate a "no diving" message into the tiles of your pool deck. Remind your staff to emphasize this rule to rental and special use groups. Your staff must also be constantly vigilant to prevent patrons from diving in shallow water.

You may also want to take steps to reduce the possibility of injuries by physically altering your facility. If a hazard exists at your facility and you take no steps or insufficient steps to eliminate or mitigate the risk (e.g., warning signs or physical alteration), your facility will be legally responsible for any injuries sustained to patrons as a result of that hazard. Here are some examples of steps you can take:

▶ Remove your starting blocks from shallow water and place them in the deep end to prevent shallow water diving injuries.

▶ Use traction strips or sand in the paint at spots on pool decks that you know are slippery and may cause falls. Spinal injuries may also occur from slips and falls.

▶ Place railings and hand grips in lavatories and showers.

▶ Paint a line several feet behind the low (1-meter) diving board. Ask divers waiting their turn to wait at the line until they are told it's their turn. This will reduce the risk of one diver diving on another.

▶ Regularly inspect diving boards, **restraining bolts,** and diving standards to ensure that they are in good condition.

In the event that a spinal injury does happen, your staff must be well trained and prepared to respond, whether the injury occurs on the deck, in shallow water, or in deep water. They must regularly practice using the backboard and the various turnover methods used to roll a spinal injury victim, such as the head splint and head-chin support method. Your staff should also practice more challenging special rescues once they've mastered the basics, such as recovery of a spinal injury victim from deep water, back boarding in deep water, and back boarding a spinal injury on the pool deck (or in the sand if at a waterfront facility). Particularly challenging scenarios that an advanced lifeguard team might practice include the following:

▶ Victim on stairs

▶ Victim facedown on the pool deck

▶ Spinal injury victim simulating vomiting or choking

▶ Nonbreathing spinal injury victim

Any of these scenarios could happen at your facility, and they require additional training of the lifeguards beyond what they receive in their basic lifeguard training courses. You should also ensure that your staff members are fully trained in the use of spinal injury rescue equipment, including

▶ backboards,

▶ cervical collars,

▶ head immobilization devices, and

▶ pediatric backboards.

A combination of a well-trained staff and a prepared facility can assist in preventing most spinal injuries and professionally treating those that cannot be prevented.

Facility Evacuation

A facility may be evacuated for any of the following reasons: fire, fire alarm, severe weather (such as a hurricane or tornado), chlorine gas leak, or power outage. An emergency evacuation plan should be included in your emergency action plan and should be drilled at least once annually, more often for fire drills. A map of emergency evacuation routes should be posted in the lifeguard office and on the pool deck.

Whenever the pool must be evacuated, lifeguards should signal to clear the area by blowing their whistles and directing customers to the emergency exits. Swimmers must not be allowed to return to the locker room to retrieve personal belongings, because this will delay the evacuation and could result in injury or death. If possible, lifeguards should count the swimmers as they evacuate, so that after they meet at the evacuation point, accountability for all swimmers can be made. Lifeguards should be the last to leave the swimming area. The doors should be locked behind them to prevent anyone from reentering the area and drowning in an unguarded pool. The evacuation point selected must be far enough away from the building to allow emergency vehicle access. In winter in the northern climates, an alternate indoor site must be selected to avoid exposure injuries. An "all clear" signal must be established to let staff know when to allow customers back into the facility. The swimming area must not be reopened until the lifeguards have taken their stations and are ready for swimmers.

Guarding Persons With Disabilities

For the purposes of this book, the term *people with disabilities* refers to any segment of the population with physical, mental, or emotional needs. This may include people with arthritis; people with ADHD; and people who are mobility impaired, visually impaired, hearing impaired, or mentally impaired. You should try to find out as much information as you can about people with disabilities before working with them. Some information that you may need to know includes the following:

- Their level of swimming ability
- Their ability to understand and follow directions
- If they will require assistance entering and exiting the pool
- If they will require assistance showering and changing (and if this will require same sex attendants in the locker rooms)
- If there are any medical issues, such as **seizures,** that you should be aware of
- If parents, spouses, or attendants will be attending to personal needs

Some patrons will require one-on-one instruction in the pool due to their level of physical or mental impairment. If this is the case with the group that you will be supervising, you must determine if they will be bringing assistants with them to help in the water or if you will need to provide assistants. In many cases, as long as you have lifeguards and some certified instructors, not every student will require her helper to be a certified instructor. You may use uncertified assistants if you provide some basic safety training for them and if you provide an adequate number of lifeguards and supervisors.

Your staff should be aware that the body motions of patrons with special needs may be erratic and may look like the motions of an active drowning victim (Priest, 1986). Staff members will need to recognize the specific signs of distress for these swimmers. You should also review information related to medic alert tags, including what information is recorded on them, where they are worn, and the importance of that information to the victim in an emergency. Also discuss with your staff the need to alter the way information is communicated to this group. Some swimmers may have mental impairments and may function mentally at a lower age level despite physically being an adult. Therefore, techniques for communicating rules, regulations, and other information may need to be changed. However, caution your staff that physical impairment is not necessarily an indication of a mental impairment (Moon, 1983).

If you determine that your patrons with disabilities cannot enter the pool by themselves, you must create a plan to assist them. One of the best methods is to provide aids that enable them to assist themselves. Here are some methods you may use:

- **Easy ladders/steps.** This device is a removable set of stairs with rails on both sides. The steps are wide and have traction strips. This system works well for clients who can walk with some assistance.

- **Hydraulic lifts.** Either a staff member or the swimmer, depending on the swimmer's level of mobility, can operate this system. The lift attaches to a hole drilled into the deck and is powered by a standard water hose; it can be removed from the pool as needed.

- **Ramps.** Ramps can either be permanently or temporarily installed in the pool. Permanent ramps should be built so that they do not project into the pool; this will keep them from obstructing swimmers when lap swimming. Ramps normally require a staff member or assistant to help the user into the pool.

If you do not provide some form of a physical aid, you will have to resort to physically lifting patrons who cannot otherwise enter the pool. This method is not recommended because there is the potential for injury to both lifter and patron from improper lifting technique. Many patrons also dislike this method because it takes away any sense of independence that they have.

Guarding Water Attractions

Water attractions used to be mainly the domain of water parks, but they are now found at all types of aquatic facilities. Water attractions you may encounter include diving boards, body slides, tube slides, speed slides, **Tarzan swings, zip lines,** and **mushrooms.**

- Body slides are rides made of fiberglass "flumes" or chutes in which the riders use a current of water to carry them to the bottom without the aid of any other device such as a mat or inflatable device. Body slides may be of various heights with turns and tunnels.

- Tube slides are rides made of fiberglass "flumes" or chutes in which the rider uses an inflatable raft or tube to ride down a current of water to a pool waiting at the bottom.

- Speed slides are water slides ridden without tubes or mats. They often do not have turns or tunnels. Speed slides start at a greater height than body slides and have a more sheer vertical drop. They are often constructed of fiberglass, and they carry the riders on a cushion of water and deposit them in a catch pool of water several feet deep.

- Tarzan swings are thick cords of rope suspended over the water that swimmers can use to swing on and then propel themselves into the water.

- Zip lines are ropes arranged horizontally over a pool and set at a down angle. The rider grasps a handle that is attached to the line by wheels. When the rider picks up his feet, gravity carries him rapidly at a downward angle toward the pool; at an indicated point, the rider lets go and falls into the pool.

- Mushrooms are play structures normally set in children's pools. A mushroom consists of a large metal pipe normally 8 feet (2.4 meters) high topped with a dome-shaped top approximately 12 feet (3.7 meters) in diameter. Water is pumped up the pipe and flows off the sides of the mushroom, creating a cascade effect all around the structure. Children enjoy standing under the water, hiding under the mushroom, or running back and forth between the water flow and the mushroom.

A lifeguard waits in a catch pool at a water park.

© Bruce Coleman

Riders must wait for the lifeguard's signal before using the water slide.

Attractions should be inspected each day before they are opened for use to ensure that they are safe. Slides and diving boards should be inspected for cracks, loose or missing bolts, and other damage. You should create an inspection sheet for your staff to use and file it each day. (See appendix D for a sample attraction inspection form.) When a new attraction is installed in your facility, you should always test it before allowing it to be used by the public.

You should follow the manufacturer's suggestions for operation and maintenance procedures, and you should ensure that your staff members are aware of these procedures. Create safety rules specifically for the attractions you have and post them where they can be clearly seen by the users. You should survey the attraction to determine the number of lifeguards needed to safely operate it and where they should be positioned. Some rides and attractions will require a lifeguard or attendant to instruct riders on how to use them and to assist the riders. You should always place a lifeguard at or near the bottom of any slide because some slides create a pressure effect that pushes small sliders to the bottom and holds them there. An assistant should also be placed at the top of zip lines and slides to control the flow of users and ensure there is enough time between them.

PREVENTING DISEASE TRANSMISSION

Your aquatic staff works in an environment where transmission of disease is a possibility that must be considered and guarded against. Diseases that may possibly be transmitted include HIV/AIDS, tuberculosis, meningitis, and hepatitis. Diseases are transmitted through pathogens, or agents that cause disease. Body fluids such as blood, saliva, stools, and urine are of particular concern as carriers of pathogens for disease transmission. Lifeguards are at risk from disease transmission while treating bleeding victims and while performing rescue breathing and CPR.

For a disease to be transmitted, the following factors must be present:

▶ Enough of the pathogen to cause the disease must be present.

▶ The new host must be susceptible to the disease.

▶ The pathogen must pass through a proper portal of entry.

Pathogens enter the body through one of four methods (American Red Cross, 2004):

▶ Direct transmission (body to body contact with pathogen carrier)

▶ Indirect transmission (the infected substance, such as blood, is transmitted to a surface and is transmitted from there to the new host)

▶ Airborne transmission (droplets bearing the pathogen are carried through the air)

▶ Vector borne transmission (insects such as mosquitoes, ticks, or flies)

There are several precautions that you can institute to protect your staff from exposure to disease transmission:

▶ **Education and training.** Train your staff on how to recognize risks of disease transmission and what steps they can take to protect themselves.

▶ **Personal protective equipment.** Equipment that your staff members need includes latex gloves, rescue breathing devices (e.g., pocket masks and micro shields), eye and face protection, and gowns for large blood spills.

▶ **Work practice controls.** Implement workplace practices that minimize the opportunity for disease transmission. Some work practice controls may include

- ▶ placing used bandages in biohazard bags and bins,
- ▶ requiring all staff to wear latex gloves while performing first aid or cleaning duties,
- ▶ requiring all "sharps" (such as needles and glass) to be disposed of in a sharps container, and
- ▶ creating and implementing a biohazard cleanup protocol (see figure 6.4).

▶ **Engineering controls.** Provide tools and physical changes to the workplace to minimize the opportunity for disease transmission. Examples of engineering controls include

- ▶ sharps containers,
- ▶ biohazard bags and bins, and
- ▶ biohazard cleanup kits.

Due to the nature of their work, lifeguards should have constant easy access to personal protective equipment. They should carry rescue breathing devices and latex gloves on their person at all times while lifeguarding. They may do this by carrying them in a waist pack or by attaching them to rescue equipment in some logical fashion. Replacement items should be readily available at lifeguard headquarters (Fawcett, 1996).

LIFEGUARDING IN OPEN WATER ENVIRONMENTS

Lifeguarding in open water environments, which include surf beaches, nonsurf waterfronts, rivers, lakes, and any other nonpool body of water, creates special challenges. These challenges require facility-specific training and procedure development. Some of the special considerations to be aware of include the following:

- ▶ **Water clarity.** Water clarity can often be less than crystal clear due to stirred up sand, algae, or other causes; this can make it difficult to see swimmers below the surface.
- ▶ **Currents.** Currents can sweep away unwary swimmers and make it difficult for rescuers to follow them.
- ▶ **Rip currents.** This is a form of current that sweeps unsuspecting swimmers far out to sea.

Biohazardous Spill Cleanup Procedure

1. Get the biohazard cleanup kit from _____.
2. Kit includes disinfectant, protective gown, gloves, absorbent paper, a biohazard waste bag, protective eyewear, and a mask.
3. If the spill is in a common area, mark it off with a "Wet Area" sign available in the janitorial closet, or use barrier tape.
4. Put on the gloves and protective gown. If splashing is anticipated, protective eyewear and a mask should be worn.
5. The area should then be decontaminated with disinfectant solution or a 1:10 solution of household bleach for 10 minutes.
6. Remove visible material with absorbent towels.
7. Dispose of towels in the biohazard bag provided.
8. Dry the area with absorbent towels and dispose of the towels in the biohazard bag.
9. Dispose of gloves in the biohazard bag and wash hands well.
10. Dispose of protective gown in the biohazard bag.

If you think you might be exposed to blood or other potentially infectious bodily fluids, you should get the hepatitis B vaccine series, which is available at the Health Center.

Figure 6.4   A sample protocol for cleaning up biohazardous spills.

Adapted, by permission, from Norris Health Center.

- **Water depth.** Water depth can be much deeper or shallower than thought by swimmers. This can contribute to spinal injuries or distressed swimmers.
- **Surf.** High-breaking waves can overwhelm swimmers and cause drowning or injury.
- **Drop-offs.** Drop-offs cannot be clearly marked (as they are at pools) and may catch weak swimmers unaware.
- **Changing bottom conditions.** Weather and tides can create holes or shallows and can bring up limbs and trees.
- **Severe weather.** Electrical storms, heavy rain, and high winds are all a particular danger to swimmers at open water facilities.

You should direct your staff to spend extra time and effort educating your patrons about these special concerns. Also, you must post signs marking the hazards you are aware of. Make regular surveys of your open water area to identify new hazards. The bottom of your beach should be surveyed by scuba divers at the start of each season to see if conditions have changed. You should also instruct your staff on how to recognize the signs of oncoming severe weather, which is a particular danger at open water facilities (Brewster, 2001).

LIFEGUARDS AND LAW ENFORCEMENT

Lifeguards may find themselves in situations where law enforcement personnel are needed, such as when a crime is witnessed or when violence is occurring or imminent. Your staff should know exactly what their role is in terms of law enforcement. Some larger beach operations deputize their full-time year-round lifeguards; more commonly, lifeguards are told to have as little to do with police duties as possible. You should arrange a briefing from your facility lawyer to explain exactly what the lifeguards' powers and legal responsibilities are in this area. It may also be appropriate to have a local law enforcement officer come to address your staff during in-service training to determine what they can and should do in the event a crime is witnessed or danger of violence is imminent. Try to foster a sense of cooperation between lifeguards and the local police. Encourage officers to visit the facility often. Consider offering incentives for police officers to frequent your facility; the benefit of having law enforcement personnel at your facil-

ity, even during their off-duty hours, will offset any small cost you may expend.

JUNIOR LIFEGUARDS

Junior lifeguarding is a program offered at aquatic facilities that helps to prepare youth (ages 14 to 16) who have strong aquatic skills for future certification and employment as lifeguards. These junior guards are given an opportunity to refine their strokes and other aquatic skills while participating in lifeguarding operations under the supervision of certified lifeguards. They can be permitted to stand next to the lifeguards on the pool deck and learn scanning and victim recognition techniques. Off the pool deck, junior guards can learn basic administrative skills such as filling out forms and filing. They may also assist with minor cleaning tasks. Both the American Red Cross and Ellis and Associates offer packaged junior lifeguard classes; you can use these programs as a starting point and build other activities around them to fit the needs of your students and facility. Junior lifeguards should never be used in place of lifeguards but only in addition to certified staff.

A junior lifeguard program provides an excellent mechanism for feeding motivated and partially trained youth into your lifeguard training program. After these potential employees have been through your junior lifeguard and lifeguard training programs, they will be predisposed to employment with your facility. They will also come with a store of knowledge from their experiences as a junior lifeguard. Figure 6.5 provides a list of activities you may include in your junior lifeguard training program.

LEGAL ASPECTS OF LIFEGUARDING

Lifeguarding is an area where the law and the effects of lawsuits and regulation have become more and more prevalent. Therefore, you and your staff must be educated about the types of legal issues you may encounter.

Attractive Nuisance

Let's face it, swimming pools, water parks, and beaches are attractive places to be, particularly on hot days. That's really what you want, isn't it? But you only want people in the facility when you control it—when you're open for business and your

Course title: Junior Lifeguarding

Minimum age: 14 at time of first class

Skill prerequisites: Must be able to swim 300 yards (274.3 meters) continuously, demonstrating freestyle, backstroke, breaststroke, and sidestroke. Must be able to tread water with the aid of the hands for a minimum of 1 minute.

Instructor: Certified swimming instructor or lifeguard instructor

Recommended course length: 1 to 1.5 hours a week for as long as the facility wishes

- Stroke correction and refinement:
  - Freestyle
  - Backstroke
  - Breaststroke
  - Sidestroke
  - Elementary backstroke
  - Increase stroke endurance
- Reaching rescues:
  - Using equipment
  - Using arms and legs
- Throwing rescues:
  - Heaving jugs
  - Heaving lines
  - Ring buoys
  - Kickboards
- Entries:
  - Shallow dive (done in deep end only)
  - Stride jump
  - Slip in
- Fitness activities:
  - Treading water
  - Endurance swims
  - Sprints
- Basic first aid:
  - Care for bleeding
  - Care for fractures
  - Care for burns
- Use of mask/fins/snorkel: A basic introduction, to be done mainly in the pool; the goal is to teach students to clear the mask and snorkel.
- Rules of the pool: Must be able to recite from memory and give reason behind each.
- Facility tour: Give students a tour of the facility, including lifeguard offices, break rooms, storage areas, filter rooms, administrative offices, and first aid spaces. Point out special features of the facility, such as ramps, lifts, hydraulic bottoms, rescue equipment, and so on.
- Guest speakers: Lifeguard supervisors or aquatic directors, for example, to talk about their jobs.
- Clinical/Practical experiences:
  - Shadow guarding: junior guards assist senior guards with their shift
  - Swim lesson assist: junior guards assist certified swimming instructors with instruction of younger children
  - First aid room assist: junior guards observe minor first aid cases under supervision of certified staff
  - Administrative assist: junior guards assist/ observe administrative staff in processing common aquatic forms, such as registration forms, accident reports, and timesheets
- Possible activities:
  - Discuss the need for lifeguards and what would happen without them.
  - Break into pairs and identify all rescue equipment found in the pool. Ask lifeguards what the purpose of each is. Share results with class.
  - Each student designs (draws) own pool and stations lifeguards where they would be needed.
  - Create a water safety poster.
  - Write a paragraph about why you want to be a lifeguard.
  - Role play situations you may encounter as a lifeguard and how you would deal with them.
- Suggested videos:
  - *Water, the Deceptive Power,* American Red Cross
  - *The Reasons People Drown,* Pia Enterprises
  - *On Drowning,* Pia Enterprises

Figure 6.5 A sample training program for junior lifeguards.

lifeguards are in place. When this is not the case, you can't protect the facility or the swimmers.

But the facility doesn't stop being a desirable place to be just because you're closed. If it draws people to it in violation of your wishes, it becomes an attractive nuisance in legal terms. Potentially, if a trespasser becomes injured or dies at your facility due to the fact that you did not properly secure it, you could be civilly liable. The most likely culprits for this catastrophe are young children and teens. To prevent this from happening, there are several steps you can take:

- Ensure that the doors to your facility are securely locked when the facility is closed.
- If your facility is an outdoor facility, ensure that it is adequately fenced and that the fence is a minimum of 8 feet (243.8 centimeters) in height.
- Put **sentry lights** at all indoor and outdoor facilities to ensure that all pools and water attractions are lit at night.
- Create a checklist of security procedures for your staff to follow at closing.
- Direct your staff to check all locker rooms and each individual stall in each rest room at closing.
- Always keep filter rooms and storerooms locked when not in use.
- Post signs when the pool is drained.
- Always lock doors when the pool is closed but other parts of the facility are still open.
- Never leave an unlocked pool unattended, even for a minute.

Standard of Care

Although most states have laws that regulate the operation of swimming pools, there are also industry standards that affect the operation of your facility. These industry standards are unenforceable in the sense that your pool can't be closed if you don't adhere to them. However, if a patron is injured or killed at your facility, you will undoubtedly be asked at trial why you did not adhere to them. Ignorance is generally not an excuse; if your answer is that you simply did not want to or that you ignored them, the jury will likely feel that you disregarded known safety procedures maliciously and that the injury could have been prevented had you followed those procedures. Therefore, you can expect to be punished by a large settlement

against you. Conversely, if you can show that you followed industry standards to the best of your abilities, you may shift the burden of liability back to the plaintiff.

Standards of care are set by common industry organizations. In aquatics, this includes the American Red Cross, YMCA of the USA, Ellis and Associates, United States Lifesaving Association, and other aquatic agencies. You, as a manager, should regularly attend certification courses and professional seminars so that you stay current on industry standards (Clement, 1997). If you volunteer to assist agencies such as the American Red Cross with aquatic program development, you can help develop industry standards. Some commonly held aquatic standards of care include the following:

- Lifeguards must be currently certified in lifeguard training, CPR for the professional rescuer, and first aid.
- Lifeguards must be at waterside and equipped with a rescue tube or other flotation device.
- Lifeguards must have no other duties except swimmer supervision while on duty.
- A lifeguard must be on duty at all times that the pool is open.
- Lifeguards must have access to a telephone and first aid equipment while on duty, including adequate personal protective equipment such as latex gloves.
- Lifeguards must receive recurring and regular in-service training.

Duty to Warn

Regardless of how safe a facility you try to operate, you're bound to have some hazards that are inherent to aquatics. Swimming pool decks are naturally slippery when wet, particularly when patrons are running. Shallow water is inherently hazardous to untrained divers. In some cases, facilities have other hazards that are inadvertently built in. Whatever the reasons for the hazards at your facility, you have a **duty** to warn your customers about them. Failure to warn your users constitutes negligence. There are several methods that you can use to fulfill your duty to warn:

- Post rule boards at your facility both on the pool deck and in the locker rooms. You should specifically forbid running on deck or diving in shallow water.

- Paint or tile in signs stating "SHALLOW WATER, NO DIVING" on the pool deck in shallow areas.

- Place stickers on the back of starting blocks indicating that they should only be used by trained divers and explaining how to dive properly. (These stickers can be purchased from vendors listed in appendix C.)

- Instruct lifeguards to enforce facility rules at all times and equally for all patrons.

- Inform students of safety rules and facility rules at the beginning of all classes.

- Review facility rules and safety rules with rental groups before they are permitted to enter the pool.

- State facility rules and safety rules on rental agreements and require rental groups to sign stating that they have read them.

You should include your facility legal counsel in your in-service training sessions at least once annually to review these legal issues (and other legal topics included in chapter 7). This will help your staff understand what their responsibilities are and how they can adhere to them.

LIFEGUARD COMPETITIONS

Lifeguard competitions are an excellent way to improve fitness and skills while providing an opportunity for competition, networking, and just plain fun. Lifeguard competitions normally include several physical events, such as short-distance sprint races or long-distance iron guard events, and skills events, such as CPR, first aid, and lifeguarding scenarios. You should carefully consider the skill and fitness level of your staff before entering or hosting a competition. Your staff should be given a chance to practice and develop before the event. Entering your staff in a competition before they are ready will be counterproductive because it will lower morale.

Hosting a lifeguard competition represents a major commitment of facility space, effort, staff planning time, and funds on the part of your facility. You'll need to carefully weigh the benefits and costs to your facility before deciding to host one. Although there are agencies that sponsor lifeguard competitions (such as the United States Lifesaving Association and Ellis and Associates), there is no requirement to adhere to any established pattern of events or rules. You may create your own or borrow liberally from these agencies as you choose.

© Bruce Coleman

Lifeguards race to the rescue in a beach competition.

Sample Staff Description

The number and type of officials that you need for a competition will depend on the size and scope of your event. You can organize officials however you choose because there are no set standards. Here is a suggested list of officials, their duties, and recommended qualifications.

▸ **Competition coordinator.** This is the administrator who oversees the entire event. The competition coordinator chooses competition locations, assists in event selection, publicizes the competition, ensures that proper equipment is in place, orders supplies, directs volunteers, takes registration, and secures sponsors (if needed). This person should be an experienced event coordinator certified as a lifeguard instructor trainer.

▸ **Event coordinator.** An event coordinator directs competition for a given event, oversees volunteers, makes final officiating decisions for that event, sees that the event stays on schedule, ensures that equipment is in place and accounted for at a given event, and oversees safety for that event. This person should be an experienced official with certification in lifeguard instructor training. You'll need one per event. In smaller competitions, one person may be able to coordinate several events. Coordinators can only oversee one event at a time and should not oversee two events occurring simultaneously.

▸ **Event judges.** Event judges officiate an event or part of an event. They should be subject matter experts for that event. They refer officiating challenges to the event coordinator. Judges should have a background in lifeguard training, CPR instruction, or competitive swimming officiating, depending on the event to be officiated. Several judges are needed for each event.

▸ **Marshals.** These officials are responsible for ensuring that competitors move from location to location at the appropriate time. In the case of scenario-based events, marshals ensure that the events remain secure from competitors who have not been in them yet. No special qualifications are necessary. At least two marshals are needed for each competition venue; more may be needed for larger events.

▸ **Timers.** Timers keep and record time for speed events. At least one timer is needed for each entrant (team or individual) in races. One overall timekeeper is needed for scenario-based events. Regional or national competitions should provide at least two timers per entrant for race events. No special qualifications are necessary.

▸ **Runners.** Runners take scores from event judges to the event coordinator for tally. They also deliver equipment and directions from higher officials as needed. At least one runner should be assigned to each event. No special qualifications or training is needed.

▸ **Victims.** You need people to play the role of injured victims, drowning victims, or bystanders at scenario-based events. Swimming ability is required. Victims must be instructed on the roles they will play and how and when to play them before the beginning of the event they will participate in. A large number of victims may be needed for scenario-based events.

In most cases, officials and victims are volunteers. Officials are often senior aquatic staff members from area facilities. Other sources for competition officials include American Red Cross and American Heart Association instructors. It's helpful to have an application process for potential volunteers so that you'll know their qualifications and how to best use them. (See appendix D for a sample lifeguard competition volunteer application form.) Once you've selected your volunteers, be sure to send them a letter confirming their participation and telling them where and when to report for duty. (See appendix D for a sample lifeguard competition volunteer assignment letter.) If your competition is being held outside, you may want to remind them to dress appropriately for the weather and to bring along sunscreen.

Hold an officials meeting on competition day to review assignments and to distribute clipboards, pencils, and officiating sheets. Review the time line for the day and emphasize the importance of keeping events moving. Identify the area where your officials can go to rest. Finish the meeting by thanking all volunteers and officials. A separate meeting should be held to explain roles and responsibilities to victim volunteers.

Since your officials are volunteers, try to make every effort to make the experience enjoyable for them. Provide an officials' and volunteers' area where they can relax without the presence of competitors; this is particularly important if your event will take much of the day. Provide water and access to rest rooms in this area. If possible, provide snacks.

Be sure to thank your officials at the closing ceremonies of your event. Sending thank-you letters to them after the event is also a nice touch. (See appendix D for a sample volunteer thank-you letter.) If your competition budget permits it, provide your officials with identifying shirts to wear during the event. This serves to identify them to the competitors and is a nice keepsake when the event is over.

Team Composition

You can set the male-female ratio of the teams however you want. Some competitions are open to women only. Others specify that there must be a minimum of one female on each team. Another option is to specify that there must be at least one member of each sex on the team.

Teams may be made up of members of varying skill level and experience. As much as possible, skills should be standardized through team practice. Many competitions do not permit every team member to compete in every event. Assign team members to events based on their strengths and abilities. You may also assign less experienced members to teams as alternates, allowing them to attend the competition and experience it firsthand without the stress of competing in the first event they attend. This also provides the team captain or coach with a trained alternative if a team member is unable to compete for any reason.

Team captains are necessary for interaction between the team and the officials. It's helpful to ask captains to attend a precompetition meeting held about an hour before competition starts. During the meeting, you can explain rules, the time line, and appeal procedures. Only team captains should interact with officials regarding rule disputes.

Competition Types

There are several types of lifeguard competitions. You may select an existing type or create your own style of competition to fit your needs. Here are some common types of lifeguard competitions:

▶ **Invitational.** The competition is open only to selected agencies, such as state beaches or municipal pools.

▶ **Open.** All facilities or independent teams can participate; no affiliation with an aquatic facility or type of facility is required.

▶ **Regional competition.** Although a competition winner is the result of this event, the purpose is to declare eligibility for a higher level competition.

▶ **National competition.** A competition to declare a national winner from a given agency.

▶ **International competition.** Sponsored by the International Life Saving Federation or the Commonwealth Lifesaving Society, these competitions are held periodically and are designed to draw together lifeguard teams from various countries to share information and engage in competition.

Sample Events

The only limits to the number and type of events for a lifeguard competition are the time you have available and your imagination. Events should be both realistic and useful. The purpose is to challenge the lifeguards to perform needed skills better. The following is a list of suggested events. Select the events that would be most beneficial for your staff.

▶ **Rescue tow relay.** Each rescuer swims 25 yards (22.9 meters) and tows a victim 25 yards using a rescue tube. Swimmers may not enter the water until the previous competitor has touched the wall. One victim is required for each rescuer. Total team time is used to determine placement in the event. Fastest time wins this event.

▶ **Pool or beach situations.** This is a subjectively scored event. Teams of two to four lifeguards are placed in a pool or on a beach to lifeguard as if working a normal shift. The competitors may bring any equipment or supplies they want, such as first aid gear or rescue equipment. The pool or beach has a standard number of swimmers for each team. During the 10- to 20-minute period that each team is on duty, three or four scenarios will occur. Scenarios may include public relations incidents (e.g., angry parents), minor rescues, and major events such as a simulated spinal injury. The same scenarios are used for each team to preserve fairness. Scenarios occur one after another, rather than simultaneously, to avoid overtaxing the lifeguards. To prevent competitors from having prior knowledge of the scenarios, the competitors must not be allowed to watch this event prior to competing in it. Competitors are graded on recognition of each scenario, speed of response, communication with each other, maintenance of surveillance of the pool during the rescue, and appropriateness of response. An aggregate score is given to each team in this event.

▶ **CPR skills.** Each competitor is scored on an individual CPR skill. Judging is based on the standards of a national agency such as the American

Red Cross. Each competitor draws a skill out of a hat to see which one he will perform (e.g., adult CPR, infant choking, child rescue breathing).

▶ **First aid skills.** Teams are dispatched to a first aid emergency, such as a car accident in the parking lot, a fight in the locker room, and so forth. Multiple victims are present with multiple injuries. Competitors must take control of the situation, triage, and treat victims. The same scenario is used for each team. Competitors may bring their own equipment, or you may provide a "standard" first aid kit. Scoring is subjective, and competitors are judged on their treatment of victims based on the standards of an organization such as the American Red Cross or National Safety Council.

▶ **Spinal injury rescue.** This event combines the technical aspects of spinal injury rescue with speed. Points are awarded for the technical proficiency of the rescue as well as the time in which it is performed.

▶ **Run-swim-run.** Rescuers run over a given course, then swim, and then run again. This event is often done in open water competitions but can also be done at pools. Distances can be whatever the event coordinator chooses. Placement is determined by the fastest time.

▶ **Tauplin.** This event is a combination of running and rowing over a marked course. **Tauplin** is used at open water facilities only.

▶ **Beach flags.** Competitors lie side-by-side, facedown, with their heads resting on their hands and their toes in a line in the sand. A series of flags are planted in the sand a set distance away. Flags are mounted on 2-foot (61-centimeter) sticks. At a whistle signal, competitors get up and sprint down the beach to retrieve a flag. One less flag is provided than there are runners. The runner who does not secure a flag is eliminated. If two runners come up with the same flag, the lowest hand on the stick is given the flag. The event is run until only one competitor remains. In larger competitions, "blocks" or "heats" are run with winners of heats combining into a final (champions) heat.

▶ **Iron guard.** If run in open water, you can prepare a course of running, swimming, paddling, rowing, and victim towing over a marked course. If run in a pool, you can combine swimming and towing.

▶ **Priority assessment.** Teams encounter a large number of victims (25 to 30) in an area such as a pool deck, gymnasium, or open area. Victims are made up with various injuries. Team members are given 5 minutes to scatter and identify each victim's injury correctly. At the end of the identification period, teams are given 1 minute to list victims in the order of priority in which they would be treated. Victims are allowed to answer three yes or no questions. Points are awarded for correctly assessing the victims and for properly prioritizing the order of treatment.

▶ **Priority treatment.** Twenty-five to 30 victims are placed in the pool area. Various victim types and injuries are used, such as active victim, unconscious victim, nonbreathing victim, fractures, seizures, or choking. Rescuers are given 5 minutes to treat as many victims as possible correctly. Points are awarded for the number of victims treated and for treating them correctly.

Not all events are used in every competition. Select events from the list based on whether your competition is in open water or a pool, the length of time available, and the expertise and experience level of teams and officials. You can give each event a percentage of the total score and add all scores from individual events together to determine the winner. Think about which events you consider to be the most crucial parts of the lifeguard skill set when assigning weight to events. In larger competitions, winners of individual events are often awarded prizes in addition to the winners of the total competition.

Competition Package

On arrival at the competition, teams should receive a package that contains a competition program. The program should list all teams, team members' names, and the facilities they represent. If you're going to list team members' names in the program, you will need to require advance registration. (See appendix D for a sample competition registration form.) The names and titles of officials should be included on a separate page of the program. A description of events and scoring procedures is also helpful. Include a time line for the day that allows for officials meetings, captains meetings, warm-up periods, and time for competitors to become familiar with the facility. Be sure to list all sponsors in the program and thank them. If your competition has a history, it's also appropriate to include a brief description of its history in the program.

It's customary after many competitions to host an awards dinner. The formality of this event will vary depending on the scope of the competition. If tickets are required, include them in the competition package along with directions to the dinner, the dress code, and the start time.

Competition T-shirts are often a sought after premium item. You can include the cost of the shirt in the registration fee or seek sponsorship from aquatic suppliers or local aquatic facilities to offset the cost. Try to have additional shirts available for purchase on competition day because spectators will often want to purchase them.

Equipment

You can determine whether you will allow competitors to bring their own equipment or require them to use standard rescue materials that you provide. If you do allow teams to bring their own equipment (such as rescue tubes, first aid kits, and backboards), the equipment should be inspected by officials to ensure uniformity with standard issue equipment. Many teams have trained extensively with their equipment and are very comfortable with it.

Uniforms

For judging purposes, it is very helpful to have competitors wear uniforms for ease of identification. International open water lifeguard competition rules require that all competitors wear a "beanie" style cap with a chin strap and contrasting quartered colors. Colors are assigned by country or club to prevent duplication. Appendix C provides a list of aquatic suppliers that offer lifeguard uniforms and "beanie" caps.

The "Sit Kit"

The situation kit, commonly known as the "sit kit," is a box containing props that are commonly used in simulations during lifeguard competitions or training. Here are some items you may want to include in your sit kit:

- Rubber knife—to simulate the weapon used in stab wounds or by assailants
- Empty pill bottle—for simulating overdoses
- Electrical extension cord (tied off, nonfunctional)—for simulating electrocution in locker rooms or on pool decks
- Empty beer cans—for simulating alcohol abuse or drunkenness

- Toy gun—for simulating assaults or attacks
- Tissues—for simulating burned skin and blisters (by placing a single ply of tissue over petroleum jelly on the skin)
- Cigarettes—to make ash for simulating burns
- Petroleum jelly—to simulate burns (by placing it on a body part)
- Flesh-colored plasticine—to simulate wounds
- Simulated blood
- Mannequins—for performing CPR skills

Sample First Aid Scenarios

You can use the following four scenarios to test the competitors in different areas of skill.

Scenario A: The Fight

Read the following to each team immediately before the event: You are dispatched to a fight in the men's locker room. You have 12 minutes to respond to any and all victims you find, including assessment, treatment, contacting emergency services, or completing any forms.

- **Scenario setup and background:** There are two victims. They were intoxicated and began to fight; one pushed the other down. The one who was pushed struck his head and is unconscious and not breathing. The other victim is wandering the locker room carrying a can of beer and laughing. The conscious victim has a simple fracture to the forearm.

- **Key points for rescuers:** Secure scene; assess unconscious victim; begin rescue breathing; manage cervical spine; remove beer from conscious victim; obtain information about what happened; call EMS and police; treat conscious victim's fracture.

- **Props needed:** Beer cans, simulated blood for head wound, resuscitation mannequin for rescue breathing.

Scenario B: Chlorine Gas Leak

Read the following to each team immediately before the event: You are dispatched to the pool chemical storage room with a report of "person down."

- **Scenario setup and background:** A lifeguard has entered the chemical storage area and has become overwhelmed by the fumes from granular chlorine. The victim is unconscious, not breathing, and without a pulse. Rescuers must avoid being similarly overcome while attempting the rescue.

▶ **Key points for rescuers:** Scene safety; enter room without being a victim by means such as **self-contained breathing apparatus (SCBA)** or other breathing protection; assess victim; begin CPR as needed; contact EMS.

▶ **Props needed:** CPR mannequin.

Scenario C: Lost Child

Read the following to each team immediately before the event: You have been approached by a hysterical mother requesting help looking for a lost child.

▶ **Scenario setup and background:** A young child has wandered away from the mother and has become lost. Hide a junior CPR mannequin somewhere in the facility that is not conspicuous, such as a sauna, storage room, or showers. The victim will be **vital signs absent:** no breathing and no pulse.

▶ **Key points for rescuers:** Organize search; assign areas; assess victim when found; begin CPR; communication among rescuers; contact EMS.

▶ **Props needed:** CPR mannequin.

Scenario D: Injured Employee

Read the following to each team immediately before the event: You have been dispatched to the facility garage with a report of an injury.

▶ **Scenario setup and background:** A maintenance employee was performing work on a snowblower and had his hand and arm severely cut by a power surge of the blades. The victim is bleeding profusely and is in great pain. A second employee is in shock from watching the first.

▶ **Key points for rescuers:** Scene safety; treat primary victim for bleeding; treat both victims for shock; contact EMS.

▶ **Props needed:** Simulated blood.

SUMMARY

Lifeguards are the key to safety operations at any aquatic facility. Selecting lifeguards with the proper certification will ensure that high-quality supervision of patrons is maintained. Your lifeguards must be certified by a nationally recognized agency and

must be prepared to respond to a variety of special rescue situations. It's important that your staff members are properly identified by uniform as a lifeguard. Lifeguards must be stationed so that they can easily see all swimmers in their area of responsibility and can respond quickly to any emergency that may arise.

REVIEW QUESTIONS

1. Describe the typical duties of a lifeguard.
2. What certifications are required for employment as a lifeguard?
3. Describe the proper method of performing "scanning."
4. Why might you evacuate an aquatic facility?
5. List the recommended lifeguard staff rules.
6. Describe three events that could be included in a lifeguard competition.

BIBLIOGRAPHY

American Red Cross. (2004). *Lifeguard training.* Teterboro, NJ: Staywell.

Branche, C.M., & Stewart, S. (Eds.). (2001). *Lifeguard effectiveness: A report of the Working Group.* Atlanta: Centers for Disease Control and Prevention, National Center for Injury Prevention and Control.

Brewster, B.C. (2001). *The United States Lifesaving Association manual of open water lifesaving.* Old Tappan, NJ: Brady Publishing.

Clayton, R., & Thomas, D. (1989). *Professional aquatic management* (2nd ed.). Champaign, IL: Human Kinetics.

Clement, A. (1997). *Legal responsibility in aquatics.* Aurora, OH: Sport and Law Press.

Ellis, J. (2000a). *Aquatic rescue professional.* Sudbury, MA: Jones and Bartlett.

Ellis, J. (2000b). *National pool and water park lifeguard training* (2nd ed.). Sudbury, MA: Jones and Bartlett.

Fawcett, P. (1996, May). Handling biohazards. *Athletic Management,* 8(5), 16.

Fawcett, P. (2001a, February). Managing lifeguards effectively. *Parks and Recreation Magazine,* 36, 72-75.

Fawcett, P. (2001b, Spring). Coast Guard–lifeguard interface. *American Lifeguard Magazine,* 12-13.

Gabrielsen, M. (1981). *Diving injuries: Prevention of the most catastrophic sport related injuries. A research product of the Council for National Cooperation in Aquatics.* Indiana, PA: Indiana University of Pennsylvania.

Lee, J. (1983, May). *Lifeguarding the disabled: Techniques and considerations.* Focus on Lifeguarding Symposium, Saskatoon, SK.

Moon, B. (Ed.). (1983). *Focus on lifeguarding.* Ottawa, ON: Royal Lifesaving Society Canada.

Palm, J. (1987). *Alert aquatic supervision in action* (7th ed.).Toronto, ON: Royal Lifesaving Society Canada.

Pia, F. (1986, May). *The RID factor as a cause of drownings.* Rescue '86 Symposium, Vancouver, BC.

Pike, B. (1980). Aquatic Spinal Injury Symposium. Sudbury, ON.

Priest, L. (1986, May). *Lifeguarding the disabled.* Rescue '86 Symposium, Vancouver, BC.

United States Lifesaving Association. (1993). *Guidelines for open water lifeguard training.* Chicago, IL: USLA.

YMCA of the USA. (2001). *On the guard II: The YMCA lifeguard manual* (4th ed.). Champaign, IL: Human Kinetics.

RESOURCES

Carney, B. (2000). *In-service training for aquatic professionals.* Sudbury, MA: Jones and Bartlett.

The following Web sites provide helpful information about lifeguarding:

American Red Cross Web site: www.redcross.org/services/hss/aquatics/lifegard.html.

California Junior Lifeguard Programs Web site: www.jrlifeguards.com.

Ellis and Associates Web site: www.jellis.com.

Hawaiian Lifeguard Association home page: www.aloha.com/~lifeguards/hla.html.

Starfish Aquatics Web site: www.starfishaquatics.org/safety_training_aquatic_rescue.php.

United States Lifesaving Association Web site: www.usla.org/Train+Cert/agenciescert.shtml.

The following Web sites provide information about lifeguard competitions:

International Life Saving Federation Lifeguard Competition Rules: http://php.dsnsports.com/lifesaving/content.php?name=sports&file=sports_rules.

Lifesaving Society Canada Lifeguard Competition Manual: www.lifesavingsociety.com/default.asp?PageId=145.

United States Lifesaving Association Lifeguard Competition Rules: www.usla.org/events/rules.asp.

Managing Risks and Planning for Emergencies

Chapter Objectives

After reading this chapter, you should be able to

1. list and describe the types of emergencies you may encounter at an aquatic facility;

2. understand how to identify and reduce security concerns;

3. create a plan for special situations such as natural disasters, fire, or mechanical problems;

4. understand how to use the state bathing code;

5. list and describe emergency equipment needed at aquatic facilities;

6. create forms needed at aquatic facilities in the event of an emergency; and

7. understand legal terms associated with risk management.

As an aquatic facility operator, your primary duty must be to ensure the health and safety of the swimmers in your facility. You must first understand the basic theory of risk management in order to create a frame of reference for your risk management program. This chapter begins by explaining the concepts of **transfer of risk** and hazard identification and explaining how you can apply these concepts at your facility to reduce the incidence of injury and resulting legal action.

Risk management is an exercise in mental gymnastics. You have to anticipate every possible bad event that can occur at your facility and plan for each of them. You need to consider the structure of your facility, the types of customers your facility draws (including their ages), and the types of activities your customers undertake at your facility. Next, you must translate planning into actions that include supervision, training, purchase and use of safety equipment, and development and enforcement of facility safety policies.

The number and types of incidents and accidents that can occur are as varied as the individuals that visit your facility. After the discussion of risk management theory, this chapter outlines and defines those potential emergencies that may happen in aquatic facilities. It then provides strategies that you can use to reduce the likelihood of those incidents occurring.

RISK MANAGEMENT THEORY

Risk management focuses on reducing the probability that an accident, injury, or other harmful incident will occur at your facility, and on reducing your liability if one does occur. There are several methods you can use to do this: hazard elimination, hazard identification, transfer of risk, and risk avoidance.

Hazard Elimination

The first step in hazard elimination is locating those hazards; if you don't know what they are, you can't do anything about them. Locating hazards at your aquatic facility enables you to mitigate those hazards, thereby reducing your liability and the risk of future accidents or injuries.

One mechanism for locating hazards is the injury chart (see figure 7.1). When accidents occur at your facility, the accident report forms should be filed by fiscal or calendar year. At the conclusion of the year, create a spreadsheet categorizing each type of injury: cuts, rescues, bites and stings, slips and falls. Assign a code for each type of injury or accident: A = minor rescue, B = cut, and so on. Draw a diagram of the facility that shows the swimming area and locker areas. Using the assigned codes, map out on the diagram where each injury or accident occurred in the facility. This matrix will allow you to visualize the groupings of injuries. If a large number of injuries or accidents have occurred in a given area of the facility, you have identified a particular hazard area. You can then inspect the hazard area for ways to minimize the danger, such as increased signage or more supervision. Retain the chart and repeat the process again the next year; compare the results to see if progress has been made.

The other mechanism for identifying hazards is an inspection of the facility. You should assess all aspects of your facility, including the following:

▶ Filters—for cracks and leaks

▶ Swimming pool basin—to ensure it is free of leaks and cracks

▶ Fixtures, including ladders, diving blocks, diving boards, and slides

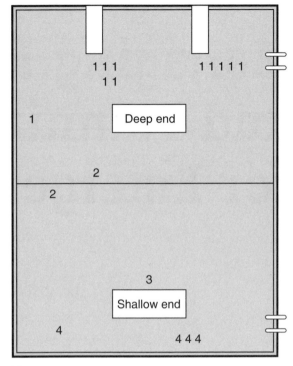

Key:
1: Distressed swimmer rescue
2: Weak swimmer
3: Spinal injury
4: Cuts/scrapes

Figure 7.1   A sample pool injury chart.

▶ Decks—to ensure they are clean, nonskid, and clear of obstructions

▶ Lighting, including emergency lighting

▶ Electrical safety—exposed wires or overloaded plugs

▶ Water chemistry and clarity

▶ Security—damaged locks or propped doors

Create safety checklists for your facility and use them daily (abbreviated lists) and weekly (full list); file your results. A full list directs you through an in-depth inspection of all equipment at your facility and is more geared toward long-range maintenance projections. An abbreviated checklist, which is compiled daily, simply requires you to check to see if the equipment at your facility is functional; this list is more geared toward answering the question, "Can I use this today?" Immediately correct any deficiencies noted, or if you cannot correct them, mark them and close that area of the facility if necessary. See appendix D for a sample facility safety checklist.

Once you've located the hazards present in your facility, you should set out to eliminate any that you can. You can eliminate hazards through several means—for example, removing equipment known to cause injury or to create significant risk of injury; repairing broken equipment or facilities; or closing hazardous facilities, rides, or attractions.

Hazard Identification

Of course, your most desirable option is to eliminate the risks you discover at your facility. If you can't do that, your next option is to label or identify the hazard so that it can be avoided or made safer (Johnson, 1994).

One method you can use to do this is signage. You can place signs on the actual object itself as well as on the general facility signs. For example, an assessment of your facility might reveal that you have starting blocks in the shallow end of your pool and that it is dangerous for untrained divers to use them. However, you can't remove the blocks because they are permanently anchored in your deck or you need them for swim meets. You can, however, place stickers on the rear of the blocks that identify the hazard and state, "No Diving."

Another way to identify hazards is to use physical obstructions. In some cases, the hazard is part of your facility and cannot be removed, so you must prevent access to it.

Transfer of Risk

Transfer of risk involves shifting responsibility from the facility to the patron or to suppliers or other parties. One of the most common methods for doing this is through the use of a statement of understanding that patrons are required to sign before being permitted to take part in physical activities. (See appendix D for a sample statement of understanding.) The understanding states that the patron agrees that there are inherent risks that are involved in physical activity, that the patron agrees to accept risk for her personal readiness to participate in the activity, and that the patron agrees to abide by safety guidelines provided by instructors. This should not be confused with waivers or hold harmless agreements, which have been used to attempt to absolve facilities of liability. The waiver states that the patron agrees not to sue the facility or its agents as a result of injuries received while at the facility. A hold harmless agreement differs in that it asks the participant to hold the owner, manager, employees, and agents of the facility not responsible for injuries incurred at the facility regardless of reason or cause. The courts have not upheld these documents on the grounds that a person cannot be required to surrender his or her right to bring litigation for a wrong suffered; therefore, the waiver is useless. The hold harmless agreement has been similarly found unworkable because in

Aquatic Safety Equipment

Safety equipment is an essential ingredient in ensuring that your emergency preparations and plans will function properly. For sources of supply for this equipment, see appendix C. Lifeguard equipment is not included in this list but is listed separately in chapter 6.

- Fire extinguishers
- Fire blankets
- Smoke detectors
- Fire alarms
- Escape ladders
- Eye guards
- Hard hats
- Emergency eye wash stations
- Self-contained breathing apparatus
- Blankets
- Sleeping bag
- Latex gloves
- Splints
- Triangle bandages
- Closed-cell, latex-covered seizure mat
- Weather radio
- First aid kit

some cases the facility owners or employees are responsible for injuries to participants, and legal action is justified. Prior surrendering of the right to bring legal action without advance knowledge of facts has not been upheld in court.

Another method of transferring risk is to require rental groups to provide proof of their own insurance prior to being allowed to use the facility. This limits the facility's insurance liability for accidents occurring to rental group members. It also has the added benefit of making the rental group more proactive regarding their own safety.

Risk Avoidance

Risk avoidance is a facility policy of eliminating those opportunities, elements, and behaviors that contribute to injuries and death at your facility. Creating and enforcing reasonable safety rules are a mechanism of risk avoidance. To focus on risk avoidance, you should select attractions such as slides and diving boards based significantly on their safety factor. When you are considering allowing activities in your aquatic facility, you must determine what actions you can take to reduce and avoid risk: Are special rules required for this activity? Are additional staff members required? Do those staff members need special training? Will special equipment be needed?

Thinking professionals won't reject new programs out of hand, but they will think through the risk avoidance steps to determine if and how the new program can be undertaken safely.

TYPES OF EMERGENCIES

As an emergency planner, you have to take into account Murphy's Law: "If anything can go wrong, it will." This isn't to say that you should be a pessimist, but that you should prepare for every possible emergency at your facility. It is much easier to react to the anticipated emergencies than to the unanticipated. Types of emergencies discussed in this section include **drowning,** medical emergencies, missing persons, chemical emergencies, mechanical failures, security emergencies, bomb threats, and natural disasters. Emergency preparations can require you to maintain various types of equipment; to help you with this, a comprehensive safety equipment list is provided (page 141).

Drowning

Drowning is defined as death by suffocation while immersed in liquid (usually water). There are actually several forms of drowning and related injuries. Drowning can be caused by many different things, such as inability to swim, entanglement of

A drowning victim struggles in the water.

the swimmer, or entrapment of the swimmer. In the Centers for Disease Control *Injury Fact Book 2001-2002*, statistics for 2001 to 2002 indicate that 80 percent of all persons drowning were male and that alcohol was a factor in 25 to 50 percent of all cases (Centers for Disease Control, 2002).

You can help prevent drowning through the use of well-trained and well-equipped lifeguards assigned in appropriate numbers to the swimming area. However, proper water chemistry is necessary to enable lifeguards to see the swimming area (see chapter 8).

Wet Drowning

Wet drowning refers to the type of drowning in which water has entered the victim's lungs. There are several stages that a victim progresses through when drowning:

- **Surprise.** The victim experiences fear and surprise at his predicament and begins to struggle.

- **Involuntary breath holding.** This occurs until the amount of carbon dioxide stimulates the respiratory center of the brain.

- **Gasp reflex.** A small amount of water is inhaled into the lungs due to the stimulation of breathing. This provokes a coughing reflex, which results in inhalation.

- **Unconsciousness.** This is brought about due to lack of oxygen in the circulating blood (known as **anoxia**).

- **Hypoxic convulsions.** These may also include gasping and vomiting.

- **Death.** Death is preceded by a change in blood chemistry known as **hemoconcentration,** a thickening of the blood due to saltwater drowning, or **hemodilution,** a thinning of the blood due to freshwater drowning. **Ventricular fibrillation,** a twitching of the heart muscle, also occurs immediately before death. Actual death occurs when breathing and pulse cease.

Near Drowning

Near drowning occurs when a victim begins the drowning process but is rescued before a fatality occurs. Although a near drowning does not result in immediate loss of life, when correlated with **secondary drowning,** it can be fatal. As discussed in the upcoming "Secondary Drowning" section, the most important question to ask any victim of a near drowning is, "Did you swallow any water?"

Near drowning victims should also be assessed for cuts, scrapes, bruises, broken bones, and other trauma-related injuries. This is crucial for victims in open water, particularly in rivers and tidal areas. Near drowning can be quite violent, and the victim may become injured due to contact with the bottom or sides of swimming pools or with rocks, branches, or other objects in open water situations. Near drowning victims who are otherwise injured or who have swallowed water should be turned over to EMS (emergency medical services) for further treatment and evaluation.

Staff members should be cautioned when reporting on or completing records regarding near drowning incidents not to erroneously mark them as drowning. This may cause a reader to assume loss of life and can draw undue attention (including media attention) to the case.

Secondary Drowning

Secondary drowning occurs after a near drowning case when the victim has been safely removed from the water. Secondary drowning occurs when water is present in the lungs, causing suffocation and death of the victim due to water in the alveoli of the lungs. Secondary drowning can occur up to 48 hours after the victim has been rescued from a near drowning situation. This is why the determination of aspiration of water into the lungs during near drowning is so crucial. Any victim thought to have swallowed water must be referred to EMS for transportation and a chest X ray. If the chest X ray indicates no water in the lungs, the victim is often released.

Dry Drowning

Although a **dry drowning** also indicates death by suffocation through immersion in water, it differs from a "wet" drowning. The major difference between these two types of cases is that dry drowning victims will have no water in their lungs. This type normally occurs in saltwater settings. The presence of salt water causes a **laryngospasm,** which causes the vocal cords to close off the upper airway. Victims then have no air exchange from the lungs, and they suffocate.

Medical Emergencies

The term *medical emergency* describes a multitude of emergencies ranging from the minor to the life threatening. Identification and care of these emergencies are normally taught in first aid certification courses. Although this book provides basic information regarding these emergencies, it is not intended to replace certification from a nationally recognized agency. Aquatic managers should ensure that all aquatic staff members, including pool operators and front desk staff, have current certification in both first aid and professional rescuer CPR.

Fainting

Fainting is normally caused by poor circulation to the brain from standing for long periods, excessive heat, or even exposure to traumatic sights. The onset of fainting is usually preceded by sweating and pale skin. If you notice these symptoms and think the victim may faint, direct the person to sit down immediately. Fainting causes the victim to fall, which may result in additional injuries.

Fainting victims should be placed on their back with their legs slightly elevated to increase blood return to the brain. Loosen any tight or restrictive clothing and keep the victim comfortable. Cover the victim with a blanket if you believe she will become chilled; do not do so if the blanket will cause her to be overheated. Do not give a fainting victim anything to eat or drink until she is fully conscious. Place her on her side if she begins to vomit.

Diabetic Emergency

A diabetic emergency can be caused by one of two things: failure of the victim to take insulin as needed or not enough sugar in the bloodstream. Victims of diabetic emergencies are often characterized by unusual smelling breath, erratic behavior, and eventually unconsciousness. Left untreated, a diabetic emergency is fatal.

When you are attempting to determine if a victim is having a diabetic emergency, check to see if he is wearing a medic alert bracelet or necklace that indicates he is a diabetic. If possible, question the victim to see if he is a diabetic, and if so, try to find out the time of his last insulin injection and meal. If the victim cannot respond, ask these same questions to anyone who is with him or knows him. If you determine that the victim needs sugar and is conscious, administer the sugar mixed with water. You should keep sugar packets in your first aid kits for this purpose. Do not give him candy bars or other food because you are unaware of this victim's potential allergies. If the victim requires insulin, EMS or a physician must administer it. Do not administer insulin yourself. Lifeguards are not trained or certified to administer medicines of any kind, including injections. Aside from the legal

implications arising from administering insulin, if an injection is administered improperly, it could potentially be fatal.

Cerebrovascular Accident (Stroke)

A cerebrovascular accident or CVA is commonly referred to as a stroke. A CVA is brought on by a clogged blood vessel in the victim's brain. The blood vessel swells and eventually bursts, causing pressure on tissues in the brain. Victims of CVA will lose muscle control on one half of their body; this is known as **hemiplegia.** Their facial features on the affected side of the body will droop due to loss of muscle control. At the onset of the stroke, the victim will fall, potentially causing other injuries.

EMS should be called immediately in the event of a CVA. While awaiting EMS arrival, place the victim on his affected side. This will permit the drainage of saliva from his mouth and will still allow him to use his unaffected limbs. Make the victim as comfortable as possible and cover him with a blanket as needed. Reassure the victim and do not leave him unattended.

Heart Attack

Heart attacks can range from massive and immediately life threatening to minor. Victims of heart attack may exhibit any or all of the following signs and symptoms: sweating; nausea; pain from the chest radiating into the arms, jaw, and stomach; flushed skin; and difficulty breathing.

Immediately call EMS for any victim of a heart attack, no matter how minor you suspect it may be. Place the victim in a comfortable position (most often this is semireclining). Administer supplemental oxygen to this victim if you are trained and your facility has the equipment.

Anaphylactic Shock

Anaphylactic shock is a severe allergic reaction brought on by contact with a substance the victim is allergic to. The danger of **anaphylaxis** is due to the swelling of tissues in the airway, which can prevent the victim from breathing and can be fatal. Common causes of anaphylaxis include food items such as fish or peanut oil and insect stings, particularly bees.

A victim who is in anaphylactic shock must have antidote administered as soon as possible; most often this is in the form of a syringe. Many people prone to severe allergic reactions are aware of the danger and carry antidote with them. Assist the victim in getting the antidote as quickly as possible. However, you cannot administer the medication for the victim. It is illegal for lifeguards and first aiders to issue medication at their level of certification. The potentially fatal result of wrongly or improperly administering the medication outweighs the potential benefits. Contact EMS and maintain an open airway for victims of anaphylactic shock.

Seizure

Seizures may be brought on by several different causes, including head injury, sudden illness, high fever, or epilepsy. There are several different types of seizures:

▶ **Grand mal.** A **grand mal** seizure is characterized by general and uncoordinated twitching of all the muscles in the body. The victims cannot control themselves during the seizure and may injure themselves from contact with objects or the ground. You should attempt to cushion the victim as much as possible, particularly the head. Do not put anything in the victim's mouth, especially not your fingers; victims cannot "swallow their tongue" as is commonly believed. They may also injure you inadvertently by biting your fingers. After the seizure, the victim will often be tired and confused. Provide a private place for the victim to clean up and rest, and treat any injuries. If this is the first seizure of its type, call EMS. If the victim regularly has seizures due to an illness she is aware of, she may only need assistance in getting home.

▶ **Petit mal.** A person in **petit mal** seizure often stares into space with unfocused eyes, or the person's eyes roll back into her head. The victim remains conscious and often has no other symptoms or injuries. However, a swimmer having a petit mal seizure may slip noiselessly below the surface and may be difficult to detect due to the lack of a struggle.

▶ **Focal motor seizure.** This type of seizure is a localized involuntary twitching of a muscle group. It is not life threatening.

The greatest concern in any seizure case is identifying the cause. If the victim is prone to seizures and is aware of what causes them, your level of concern is much lower. If the victim has never had a seizure before and is unaware of what caused it, this victim must go to advanced medical care as soon as possible. You should consider purchasing a closed-cell, latex-covered seizure mat for your facility. You can place a victim having a seizure on the mat, and it will prevent injury from contact

with the pool deck. You should also include grand mal seizure drills in your in-service training for lifeguards.

Heat Emergencies

The two major types of heat emergencies are heat exhaustion and heatstroke. They are caused by the same factors: overexposure to a hot environment and the inability of the body to replace fluids as fast as they are lost from sweating. In the initial onset, the victim will be suffering from heat exhaustion; if left unchecked, it will become heatstroke. These cases are particularly common outside in the summer months. The elderly, children, and anyone working or playing outside are susceptible to these illnesses. Alcohol is a contributing factor to heat emergencies because it dehydrates the body, yet the victim thinks he is taking in fluids. It also impairs judgment at a critical time. For these reasons and others, you should prohibit alcohol at aquatic facilities.

Lifeguards are particularly vulnerable to heat emergencies because they often work in direct sunlight for long periods without a break. You must help prevent heat illnesses in your lifeguards by insisting on several precautions:

▶ Require staff to wear brimmed hats while on duty outside.

▶ Strongly encourage staff to wear sunglasses while on duty outside.

▶ Provide sunscreen for staff use. Strongly encourage all staff members to wear it and to reapply it throughout the day.

▶ Insist on regular intake of cool water by staff members. Provide water bottles for this purpose and regularly check to see that they are filled.

▶ Encourage staff members to swim while on breaks to give them a chance to cool off.

Heat Exhaustion

Heat exhaustion is characterized by cool, moist, pale skin; headache; nausea; dizziness; and weakness. This victim should be removed immediately from the hot environment to a cool place. Remove excess clothing and begin the cooling process. You can do this by placing cool, wet towels on the victim's chest, under his arms, and around his head (not face). Give the victim small sips of cool water to drink. Do not allow him to drink large amounts of water at one time or he may vomit. You should ensure that this victim is lying down or he may fall down. You can also fan the victim to speed up the cooling process. Monitor the victim's pulse and breathing and do not leave him alone. Place him on his side if he vomits, to keep the airway clear. If the victim is not improving or if the case is severe from the beginning, contact EMS.

Heatstroke

Victims of heatstroke will have red skin and will be warm and dry to the touch. They are often unconscious or in a stupor. This victim is in a life-threatening situation. His body's thermostat has shut down, and he is in jeopardy of overheating his brain from lack of fluids. The victim must be treated immediately and transported to emergency medical care as soon as possible. Remove any excess clothing. Cool the victim by spraying him with cool water from a garden hose, placing him in a cool bath, or sitting him in a lawn chair in the shower while being held on either side by lifeguards. The victim will have little or no control over his body and must be supported at all times. Do not attempt to get an unconscious victim to drink water. Monitor the victim's breathing and pulse and begin CPR if necessary. Continue cooling the victim until EMS arrives or the victim begins to respond to the treatment and his body temperature returns to a normal level. Inform EMS of the patient history and turn over any vital sign information you have recorded.

Cold Emergencies

There are two main types of cold emergencies: frostbite and hypothermia. Both are brought on by exposure to a cold environment. While frostbite is a rare occurrence at most traditional aquatic facilities, hypothermia may happen early or late in the season at outdoor facilities and can happen in infants at indoor facilities at any time.

Frostbite

Frostbite is the freezing of tissues that have been overexposed to cold. It most commonly affects the fingers, toes, nose, cheeks, and ears. The body part may appear waxy white and feel hard to the touch in severe cases. Less serious cases may swell and become reddish purple in color. You should cover the injured part. Do not try to rewarm the part using direct heat sources; you may burn the victim. Do not rub snow on an affected part (which some people mistakenly believe will help). For severe cases, the victim should seek medical attention. For minor cases, gradually rewarm the affected area using room temperature water (hot water may cause pain).

Hypothermia

A victim is considered to be in hypothermia when her body core temperature has dropped to 96 degrees Fahrenheit or below. Victims of

EMS personnel performing a rescue.

hypothermia exhibit symptoms such as shivering, poor coordination, poor judgment, and inability to speak clearly. If untreated, the victim will eventually become unconscious and will die. Treatment for this victim includes removal from the cold environment and rewarming. You can rewarm the victim by removing wet clothing, wrapping the victim in warm blankets, and placing her in a sleeping bag. Place a winter hat on the victim's head to hold heat in. Offer sips of warm, nonalcoholic, noncaffeinated drinks if the victim is fully conscious. Monitor the victim's breathing and pulse and administer CPR if necessary.

Fractures

The two major types of fractures are open (or compound) and closed (or simple). Open fractures protrude through the skin and will result in associated bleeding; the risk of infection with this type of injury is high. Closed fractures will not come through the skin but may result in swelling, discoloration, pain, and deformity at the site of the injury.

Treatment for fractures consists of immobilization of the injury through the use of splints. You may use commercially made splints or may make your own from prepared boards and triangle bandages. You should splint fractures in the position of injury; do not attempt to straighten an injured limb. Be sure to assess the pulse of the injured limb below the site of the injury; this will determine if the splint is too tight and must be loosened.

Fracture of the vertebrae, a spinal injury, requires special treatment. The victim may exhibit a variety of symptoms, including tingling of the fingers and toes, pain at the site of the injury, or inability to move the arms or legs. You should try to keep the victim as still as possible and secure him to the backboard. Contact EMS as soon as possible.

Bleeding

Bleeding is one of the most common aquatic emergencies. It can range in seriousness from a minor scrape, which results in very little blood loss, to major arterial bleeding of life-threatening proportions. Bleeding can be external or internal.

External Bleeding

External bleeding results from a break in the skin. Initial treatment consists of direct pressure and elevation of the wound. Latex gloves and other appropriate body substance isolation protective equipment should always be worn. After initial direct pressure and elevation, you should apply dressings and bandages to the wound. Dressings should be clean and of sufficient size to cover the entire wound. You should make sure that self-adhesive dressings do not stick to any part of the wound. Do not remove blood-soaked dressings; reapply new ones as needed over the old ones.

Internal Bleeding

Internal bleeding results from ruptured blood vessels where there is no break in the skin. Signs and symptoms include softness in the area of the injury and discoloration of the skin. Victims of severe internal bleeding will also exhibit excessive thirst and pain at the site of the injury. Very little first aid can be given to this victim. The victim should be transferred to EMS care immediately.

Missing Persons

When dealing with missing persons cases, the reporting source is the most important asset available. You should ask the reporting person for the following information:

- ▶ Name of the missing person
- ▶ Age of the missing person
- ▶ Physical description, including height, skin color, and hair color
- ▶ Description of clothing the person was wearing when last seen
- ▶ Where the missing person was last seen or where she was going
- ▶ What the person was doing when last seen
- ▶ When the person was last seen
- ▶ Who the person was with when last seen

You must determine if the missing person might be in the water. If this is suspected, you must begin your search immediately. For swimming pools, clear the water and do a visual search of the bottom. If you have a bulkhead or any other structure in the water that may obstruct your view, have a lifeguard enter the water to search under it. If the subject is not found during the visual search, while the swimmers are out of the water ask if the subject is present or if anyone has seen her recently or knows where she is. Allow the swimmers back into the pool, supervised by lifeguards, and continue your search. Be sure to inform all staff of your search, including front desk staff, concessions staff, and custodians. Search the entire facility—lavatories, locker rooms, concession areas, storage areas, and activity areas.

If you don't find the subject at this point, consider that she may have departed the facility. Get a description of her vehicle and check the parking area to see if the subject or the vehicle is there. Obtain the subject's home phone number and call her residence. You may also try to determine if she may have gone to a friend's or relative's home.

If you have exhausted all possibilities at this point, and the subject is a child, contact the police. If possible, keep the reporting source with you during your search; this will eliminate the possibility that the subject is found and it is not reported to you.

If the missing person is at an open water facility, such as a lakefront or beach, the search becomes more complicated. Open water searches require coordination of a large number of lifeguards and volunteers. For shallow water searches, organize a line search—volunteers and staff form a line from shore outward and link arms. The line moves forward, and the searchers sweep with their feet until the shallow water area is covered. Line searches of this type should only be conducted up to chest deep water, with the best swimmers being in the deepest water. Deep water searches require several lifeguards to perform line **surface dives** to cover the swimming area and beyond. Be sure to account for currents and riptides or other environmental factors in determining your search area.

If you determine that your missing person is in the water but potentially outside your swimming area, notify other agencies for assistance, such as police, fire department, marine patrol, or Coast Guard. If all other possibilities are exhausted, contact the local authorities to have the dive rescue team search the bottom of your search area.

Chemical Emergencies

Aquatic facilities require a large number of chemical products to maintain cleanliness and sanitation. These include but are not limited to chlorine, bromine, muriatic acid, soda ash, cleaning supplies, gasoline for vehicles and lawn equipment, and machinery oil. Many of these chemicals are flammable, and many are toxic if swallowed or inhaled. Some chemicals may also become volatile when mixed with each other. You must be aware of the properties of all the chemicals that you use. Each chemical comes with a material safety data sheet (MSDS) that contains essential information regarding that chemical, including its toxicity, properties, and first aid procedures. You must

collect all MSDSs for all chemicals you use and store them in a binder either in the room where the chemicals are kept or in your aquatics office, preferably both.

All chemical storage areas should be cool and well ventilated to lessen the risk of a buildup of gases or combustion. Equip these areas with eye wash stations and emergency showers to be used in the event of contamination of a worker. If your facility uses chlorine gas for disinfection of pool water, you must store it in a separate locked and ventilated room. You must also provide your employees with access to a self-contained breathing apparatus (SCBA)—and instruct them on how to use it—in case a gas leak occurs.

Prepare and test an emergency action plan for a chlorine gas leak. Include the local fire department in your planning because they will be your primary responding agency. Always have your meeting point for evacuees upwind of the leak and well away from the site to prevent further exposure to the gas. Your fire alarm should be the primary mechanism for signaling evacuation of the building due to a gas leak. Your emergency action plan should include a map of your facility and surrounding area, along with an assessment of prevailing winds. This will indicate where the gas cloud will settle after a leak.

You must also plan for spills of liquid and solid chemicals of any significant amount, particularly if they enter the water table. The entrance of chemicals into the water table can contaminate the local drinking water supply, so this must be prevented at all costs. Liquid spills are the greatest risk for contamination of this type. Deployment of absorbent materials and containment booms, and immediate contact with local HAZMAT teams, are the best responses to a spill of significance, such as one that threatens the water supply.

Mechanical Failures

Mechanical failures can affect many types of machinery at aquatic facilities, including filters, heaters, air handling units, air conditioners, and generators. When planning for mechanical emergencies, you should consider prevention the first step in preparation. Follow all manufacturers' specifications for the care and maintenance of mechanical devices; when necessary, have factory-trained technicians service mechanical implements. The cost of properly servicing these devices will save money by extending the life of the device and saving replacement costs.

To prevent unauthorized tampering with mechanical devices, you should lock mechanical rooms and mark them with "Authorized Personnel Only" signs. Always post cautionary warning signs and operating instructions in a conspicuous location adjacent to the device. Regularly inspect all mechanical devices to ensure that they are functioning properly and that instructions are still in place. When new staff members are being trained in the use of mechanical implements, be sure to provide a thorough safety lecture and inform them of any safety equipment that must be worn while using the device, such as eye guards and hard hats.

Try to envision the impact that the failure of a given mechanical device may have on your facility. The failure of some devices, such as pool filter motors, would completely incapacitate your facility. You may want to consider purchasing redundant systems for essential devices such as these. You may want to keep essential parts on hand for other devices or have a standing maintenance contract in place with a local dealer.

From a safety standpoint, ensure that all manufacturer recommended safety guards are in place.

Security Emergencies

Security emergencies include such occurrences as assault, rape, murder, riot, civil disturbance, fights, domestic disturbance, abduction, and threats of violence. Although these events may be rare at your facility, and some may seem unlikely, it's best to be prepared.

You may want to have local law enforcement personnel conduct in-service training for your staff regarding violent crimes. They can address prevention, dealing with violence, and reporting procedures. You must have a plan in place to deal with violent or potentially violent circumstances. The safety and protection of your staff and customers must always take precedence in your planning. If your facility has a security force, they must take the lead in planning for this type of emergency.

Survey your facility for security gaps. Your first consideration should be the access control point, which allows customers into your facility. A customer service area should be arranged in such a way that customers must pass by it before entering the facility. All members should be issued an identification of some form that they must show or surrender before being admitted. You may want to have your entrance to the activity areas secured with a locked gate or door that can only be opened by an employee with a **solenoid switch**—the familiar practice of "buzzing" someone in—or by a magnetic strip on member ID cards. By using this method, you can reduce the incidence of unauthorized entries and unsupervised children entering the building. Guests to your facility should be signed in by members and escorted by them (if your facility is on a membership system).

Your security survey should next focus on exits and entrances other than the main entry point. Assess all doors and windows for locks and latches. Windows should latch in such a way that they cannot be opened from the outside. Doors should be tight fitting, in good repair, and should lock securely from the inside. Emergency exits should be equipped with panic bars on the inside—horizontal bars that you lean against to open the door quickly and easily—and should never be locked from the inside so that they could not be opened without a key.

Review your security procedures from a daily standpoint. Here are some basic precautions you can take:

▸ Secure access to activity areas such as swimming pools and gymnasiums when unsupervised and not in use.

▸ Lock custodial and storage closets when not in use.

▸ Lock filter, electrical, and mechanical spaces.

▸ Never leave cash registers and cash boxes unattended.

▸ Keep accurate logs of what keys are issued to what employees.

▸ Ensure that employees turn in their keys when employment ends for any reason.

▸ Arrange for cash drops to a central safe during busy times of the day so that large amounts of cash don't build up in the till, presenting a tempting target for thieves. Have two employees transport cash to the safe or bank any time a drop is made.

▸ Lock display cases containing merchandise such as swim goggles and towels.

▸ Try to place vending machines in an area where they can be seen by staff. This reduces the possibility of theft and vandalism.

▸ Install a security alarm system in the building and issue the access code to a limited number of staff members.

- Have staff members make random walk-throughs of the building, including locker rooms, at least once an hour.
- Ensure that all areas of the building are well lit.
- Place flashlights in offices in case there is a blackout.
- Encourage your patrons to lock their belongings in lockers. Provide rental locks and daily pay lockers for this purpose.
- Post signs in the locker rooms reminding patrons to secure their valuables.
- Place lighting controls on a key control system that only staff members have access to. This prevents lights from being turned out by unauthorized parties.
- Always require two staff members to open and close the building together. This reduces the possibility of assault during the most vulnerable time of the day.

Closing the building is one of the most security sensitive times during the day. Thieves, vandals, and vagabonds may try to hide in the building after it has closed for a variety of reasons. You must ensure that your staff members thoroughly check all areas of the building and lock these areas behind them as the building is closed. Whenever possible, have two staff members do this together to reduce the risk of assault. If your staff members separate during the process, be sure to issue them radios to facilitate communication.

If security concerns are a major issue at your facility, you may want to consider installing a closed-circuit camera system. These systems enable you to mount multiple cameras to survey several different areas of the building simultaneously. A monitor capable of showing many camera views at once can be stationed in an administrative office. The recorder can be set to tape the camera views for a 24-hour period. Although systems such as these tend to be very expensive, they are very useful in identifying and prosecuting thieves and vandals. Over time the incidence of criminal activity in your facility may decline due to the effectiveness of the cameras.

Prepare a plan for dealing with violent or potentially violent intruders or patrons. You may want to develop a signal to be used between staff members whenever the police or security need to be called, one that does not alert the subject to what you are doing. Never leave an employee alone with a potentially violent person. If you are having a meeting with a patron or employee that could potentially become emotionally charged, always have another employee with you. You should leave the door open and arrange the meeting so that the subject is never between you and the door. Alert other staff members that the meeting is taking place and may become heated. You may want to ask a staff member to check in on you after a set period of time.

If a violent intruder enters your facility, immediately call the police. Evacuate the facility and monitor where the intruder is so that you can inform law enforcement when they arrive. Do not try to subdue the intruder yourself; you are likely to become injured.

In the event of a riot, close and lock down the facility if the riot is outside the building. You may need to keep the patrons in your facility to ensure their safety. If the riot is inside the building, evacuate nonparticipating patrons and contact police. Remove all staff from the building.

If a crime has occurred, care for the victim in any way possible and contact the police. Try to preserve any evidence and restrict access to the crime scene as much as possible. If a rape or sexual assault has occurred, try to have a same sex rescuer with the victim at all times. Never leave the victim alone and do your best to ensure that the assailant has left the area. You should not try to catch the assailant; treatment of the victim should be your primary concern.

Bomb Threats

All bomb threats should be treated as serious. Bomb threats can be received by phone, fax, e-mail, or in person. If the bomb threat is received by phone, try to get as much information from the caller as you can before the person hangs up. See appendix D for a sample bomb threat checklist that can be used during the call.

Once you've gathered as much information about the threat as you can, evacuate the facility in an orderly fashion. Have customers and staff meet at a predetermined point well away from the building. While the evacuation is taking place, contact the police and give them the information you have. Tell the police that you are evacuating the building and ask if they have any instructions. Ask the police if they want you to contact the fire department. When evacuating the building, ensure that the pool area is locked and that all safes and cash registers are closed and locked. Send one staff member on a quick pass through the building to ensure that all groups have heard the evacuation signal and that everyone has left the building. Once you have evacuated the building, do not return for any reason until given the all clear by emergency response personnel.

> **KEY POINT** *Having a security plan that reads "call police" isn't enough. Your best policy is preparation and prevention. Remember, protect your people first and your property second.*

Natural Disasters

Natural disasters include but are not limited to hurricanes, earthquakes, tornadoes, electrical storms, and blizzards. All facilities should be equipped with a weather radio that is monitored at least hourly. Severe weather can appear very rapidly and leave very little time to react.

Prepare a designated shelter area at your facility. It should be large enough to accommodate all staff and a large number of patrons. Preferably, this shelter will be underground to provide protection against tornadoes.

In the event of the forecast or onset of severe weather, such as a hurricane or tornado, evacuate all staff and patrons to the shelter as rapidly as possible. If possible, secure all cash and valuables and lock access to the swimming areas before entering the shelter. Account for all staff members before closing the shelter. Take the weather radio, a cell phone, and first aid equipment into the shelter with you.

If the onset of a blizzard or other such long-term weather emergency is predicted, make an informed decision about whether to close the facility or not. The highest levels of your organization should make this decision. If you do decide to close for a snow emergency, be sure to announce this information over local radio stations. Contact all staff members and tell them if they need to report to work. If possible, contact patrons who have registered for classes and tell them if the classes will be canceled or rescheduled. Your primary concern should always be for the safety of your staff and customers; therefore, the predicted road conditions should drive your decision to be open or not.

ALCOHOL AND THE AQUATIC FACILITY

The presence, or absence, of alcohol in aquatic facilities seems to be a constant subject of discussion and debate. The best policy is to prohibit the mixing of alcohol and aquatics. Although there are many legitimate reasons for such a policy, the primary reason is safety.

Alcohol is known to have several effects on people, both physiologically and psychologically. These effects include

- lowered social inhibitions,
- impaired decision-making and judgment skills,
- reduced reaction time,
- lowered coordination skills, and
- poor balance.

Although it takes varying amounts of alcohol for these effects to become apparent in people, depending on their size and tolerance to alcohol, these are the prominent effects. Similarly, not all of these effects will be present in every person affected by alcohol.

Knowing that these are common effects of alcohol, you can begin to see the types of problems that a person exposed to too much of it may present at an aquatic facility:

- Alcohol impaired patrons are more likely to disregard facility rules due to their lowered social inhibitions and poor judgment.
- Alcohol impaired patrons are more likely to engage in high-risk behavior, such as diving in shallow water, due to poor judgment.
- Alcohol impaired patrons are more likely to be unable to get up after falling in shallow water due to loss of balance, increasing the risk of their drowning.
- Patrons who are consuming alcohol are more likely to suffer from dehydration and other heat illnesses. Alcohol promotes dehydration due to its content, yet the consumers feel they are warding off thirst because they are consuming liquids.

In addition to these concerns, there are several others unrelated to safety:

- The need to prevent **minors** from consuming alcohol.

- The potential for the facility to be liable if consumers injure themselves due to the alcohol they consumed in the aquatic environment.
- The increased chance for drinking and driving due to the consumption of alcohol at the pool.
- The potential for increased "morality issues"—such as unwanted romantic advances, sexual activity, profanity, vulgarity, and indecent exposure—due to the lowering of social inhibitions associated with alcohol consumption.

As mentioned, the best policy is never to allow alcohol in an aquatic environment due to the potential for injury or death to one of your customers (to say nothing of the potential legal action against the facility and its employees). However, if you have decided to allow or sell alcohol at your facility, consider these safeguards:

- Ensure that your facility is appropriately licensed to sell alcohol.
- Do not allow employees less than 21 years of age to serve or handle alcohol.
- Keep alcohol sales and consumption separate from the pool area.
- Strictly enforce the minimum age requirement for consumption of alcohol in your state or province. Ask for identification bearing photo and date of birth before selling alcohol to a customer.
- Do not allow staff to consume alcohol while at the facility. Lifeguards and other safety staff, especially, should never even be in the vicinity of alcohol due to the negative impact it can have on their professional image.
- Do not allow patrons who have been drinking to enter the pool. This is difficult to enforce, and lifeguards will have to watch the behavior of patrons carefully.

Be sure that you have carefully researched the laws regarding alcohol at your specific type of facility. Federal reservations, for example, including national parks, military bases, and nature preserves, strictly control alcohol. Also, the facility charter or covenant that guides your facility may specifically forbid alcohol on the premises. You must know these facts in advance. And remember that the dangers associated with alcohol usually far outweigh the benefits.

AREAS OF SPECIAL CONCERN

The public nature of aquatics and the presence of large numbers of people at your facility mean that your staff may encounter difficult and disturbing situations. These might include theft, violence, substance abuse, suspected child abuse, or sexual activity in the aquatic facility. Your staff members should be prepared and trained so that they can respond well in the event that one of these special situations arises.

Theft

You should attempt to reduce theft at your facility by encouraging patrons to secure their valuables in locked lockers. To facilitate this, you may want to provide locks for sale, daily pay lockers, and rental locks for a nominal fee. Security cameras installed within the building also assist with theft prevention. Staff should never agree to "hold" or "look after" valuables for swimmers because they then become responsible for them.

Once a theft is reported, a supervisor should interview the customer and fill out an incident report. Information gathered should include the customer's name and contact information, last known location of the item, and a description of the item or items taken. Any amplifying information, such as if the locker was forced open or if the items were marked, should be recorded as well. If the items were of sufficient value and the customer desires it, you should file a police report. If you do so, be sure to get a copy of the report and keep it with your incident report.

Periodically, you should review your incident reports to see if you can determine a pattern or any common factors. If you determine that your thefts are happening during a certain time of day, on a certain day of the week, or in a certain area, you may want to increase random patrols based on that information. If you catch a theft in progress, you should not attempt to physically stop the thief; the thief may decide to resist, and you may be injured. You should make note of the thief's physical appearance and clothing to report to the police. You should also make note of where the thief goes when she leaves. If possible, summon your facility security to apprehend the thief. If you do not have security, report it to the police.

Violence

Violence is a serious issue that not only results in harm to the victim but also can cause fear and trauma to the staff and other patrons who witness it. You must do everything possible to prevent violence from occurring at your facility. The presence of alcohol is a large factor in violence. Preventing intoxicated patrons from entering your facility and forbidding alcohol will assist greatly in reducing violence. You should also have a controlled entry point that requires all swimmers to show identification or check in. This allows you to refuse entry to belligerent, drunk, or problem patrons before they enter and can cause problems. Staff members at the entry point must be confident enough and prepared to deny entry to problem patrons. You should also devise a method for them to call for assistance if they need it, such as an emergency alarm or an emergency phone.

If you observe violence in progress, you must carefully consider whether or not to intervene. Although you do not want any patrons to become injured, you must also consider the risk of injury to yourself. To prepare for this type of situation, you should seek guidance from your facility director, legal counsel, and local police before you're faced with the problem. If you are informed of violence after the act has been committed, your first tasks should be to prevent further harm to the victim and perform any necessary first aid. You should also notify the lifeguards on duty as soon as possible and contact the police immediately, as well as security personnel and senior management. Determine if the assailant is still in the area, and if so, monitor him so that you can direct police to his location when they arrive. Be sure to complete accident and incident reports, and collect a description of the assailant. Pass any information that you gather to the police upon their arrival. Due to the sensitive nature of violent incidents, you should not make a statement to the press without first clearing it with senior management or your public affairs officer.

Substance Abuse

Substance abuse may be in the form of alcohol or drugs. As previously mentioned, you should prevent alcohol in your facility as much as possible. Intoxicated or impaired swimmers can endanger themselves and others by disregarding safety rules, using poor judgment, and committing violence against others. When you identify an intoxicated or impaired individual in your facility, you should direct the person out of the pool area. If the patron is cooperative and of age, you may want to arrange transportation home for the person by contacting family or friends. You should also try to remove any alcohol that the subject has in her possession to prevent further intoxication from occurring. If the swimmer is a minor, you must report the incident to the minor's parents and to police.

If the substance abuse involves illegal narcotics, you should immediately contact local law enforcement and monitor the patron. If the patron is injured or ill, administer emergency care as required, taking particular care of the victim's airway. If the victim becomes violent or threatening, you should not attempt to restrain her but should clear the area of other patrons. Try to remove anything that could be used as a weapon so that she does not use it to hurt herself or others. Do not leave the victim alone; attempt to calm her by speaking calmly until police and EMS arrive. Provide EMS with a full report when they arrive, including a description of any substances you found. Turn over any narcotics to the police.

Suspected Child Abuse

Child abuse can come in many forms, including physical abuse, neglect (often characterized by hungry or poorly kept children), sexual abuse, and psychological abuse. You should provide training for your staff regarding how to recognize signs of abuse. If a staff member believes she has recognized the signs of abuse, she should immediately contact her supervisor to report it. If the staff member and supervisor agree that abuse may be occurring, the case should be referred to law enforcement and child protective services. If the child is in immediate danger, the child should be removed from the abusive situation immediately and taken to a safe place. Do not leave the child unattended. Attempt to calm and reassure the child, while providing for any basic needs and providing any emergency first aid that may be required. You should attempt to determine the child's name and age and any other information that may be helpful to police when they arrive.

Sexual Activity

Sexual activity must be forbidden at aquatic facilities. If a patron reports witnessing it, or a staff member encounters it, the participants should be immediately ejected from the facility. You may want to report it to law enforcement as a public indecency incident.

If the incident involves abuse or assault, follow these guidelines:

- Always refer the case to police.
- Remember that your primary concern is to protect and care for the victim, not catch the perpetrator.
- Never leave a victim of sexual abuse unattended.
- Always have a staff member of the same sex present for the victim's own sense of security.
- Never make judgmental statements about the victim's clothing or character.
- Provide the victim with as much privacy as possible (except for the presence of staff giving treatment).
- Do not examine the victim's genital area.

CODES AND LAWS

Regulations and laws of several state and local agencies affect the operation of swimming pools. These regulations include the state bathing code, Blood-Borne Pathogen Standard, and Hazard Communication Standard.

The State Bathing Code

Most states and many counties and cities have regulations governing swimming pools and bathing beaches under their jurisdiction. These regulations are commonly known as "the bathing code." (See appendix B for a listing of where state bathing codes can be obtained in each state.) The strength and scope of these regulations vary markedly from state to state. Most states differentiate between public pools—usually taken to mean those pools owned and operated by government entities such as towns and counties—and semipublic pools, which refers to those operated by membership agencies such as YMCAs and country clubs. State bathing codes do not regulate private swimming pools or beaches.

Most states require that public and semipublic pools obtain and post a swimming pool permit. Obtaining a permit requires application to the appropriate state agency, normally the health department, sanitation department, department

of natural resources, or water department. A fee is often required for the permit. Many states examine the pool for structural integrity and compliance with the bathing code prior to issuing the operating permit. Once you obtain your pool permit, you must display it according to state law. Usually the permit is valid for 1 year and must be renewed; often the state will automatically send renewal application packages to facilities licensed the previous year. Upon receipt of the application, the state is aware of the facility being in operation again, which will trigger an inspection.

Maintaining your permit often requires passing an inspection administered by the state office responsible for swimming pools in your area. If your city or county issues permits, you may have to be inspected by and display permits from these agencies as well as the state. The frequency of the inspection depends on the availability of inspectors but often ranges from quarterly to annually. Items that inspectors typically check include the following:

- Water chemistry is in compliance with state code, including pH and chlorine.
- Water clarity is acceptable. The standard test is the ability to see a 6-inch (15.2-centimeter) contrasting red and black disc at the deepest point of the pool.
- Rules are posted according to state code.
- An adequate number of lifeguards are on duty.
- Rescue equipment is stationed and maintained properly.
- Lavatories and locker rooms are clean and sanitary.
- Trash is contained properly.
- Filters are functioning properly.
- Water chemistry records are on file and maintained properly.
- Swimming pool or bathing beach permit is displayed properly.

You should keep a copy of the most recent edition of the state bathing code at your facility and refer to it often to ensure that you are operating under the law (see figure 7.2). Remember that the law is a minimum standard. If agencies such as the YMCA or the American Red Cross recommend a higher standard than your state law, follow the higher standard; it will make your facility safer and reduce liability.

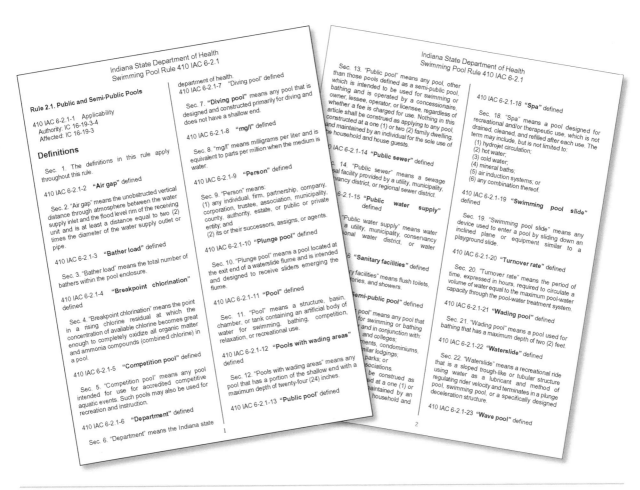

Figure 7.2 Excerpts from the Indiana bathing code.

From Indiana State Department of Health.

Some states require the pool operator to receive some form of formalized training. Some states offer this training, while others rely on courses such as the National Recreation and Parks Association Aquatic Facility Operator course to fulfill the requirement. Read the bathing code to determine if your state requires this, and if so, register for the correct course. Keep a copy of your certificate posted for the inspector to see.

The exception to the rule regarding the jurisdiction of state enforcement of the bathing code is aquatic facilities on federal lands. Swimming pools, beaches, and waterfronts on lands owned by the U.S. military, National Park Service, Bureau of Land Management, or any other federal entity are not subject to the laws of the state in which the federal reservations exist. However, most federal agencies have some kind of regulations regarding the operation of their own facilities, and managers at those reservations are responsible for knowledge and enforcement of these regulations.

The Environmental Protection Agency (EPA) publishes information related to recreational water quality standards. Many states have used this EPA document in developing their own bathing beach guides and regulations. This document includes information related to safe bacterium levels in recreational water as well as the methods for achieving and maintaining that level. If you manage a waterfront or beach, obtaining a copy of this information from the EPA may be helpful. You can write the EPA to request a copy or download the information from their Web site (see appendix A).

The Blood-Borne Pathogen Standard

The Occupational Safety and Health Administration (OSHA; see appendix A) is the government agency that regulates safety at the workplace. OSHA rules determine what personal protective equipment is mandated for employees, what safety equipment must be in place, and what the appropriate work-to-rest ratio is, among other things. The most common OSHA regulation affecting pool operators is the Blood-Borne Pathogen Standard (29 CFR 1910.1030). This regulation states that "employers are responsible for identifying job classifications in which there is a reasonable anticipation that workers will come in contact with blood and other potentially infectious materials in the course of accomplishing their assigned work tasks." Lifeguards, first aid workers, and other aquatic staff clearly fall within this grouping. Because of this, aquatic staff members are entitled to training regarding the prevention of disease transmission, access to personal protective equipment (such as latex gloves and rescue masks), and vaccination against hepatitis.

The Hazard Communication Standard

OSHA also promulgates the Hazard Communication Standard (HCS; 29 CFR Parts 1910, 1915, 1917, 1918, 1926, and 1928RIN 1218-AB02), which requires that all employees receive information regarding the hazards of the chemicals they use to perform work tasks. This information must be transmitted through correct labeling of products, material safety data sheets, and training programs. According to the standard, if chemicals are transferred from their original container, you must label the new container and include information regarding what the dangers of that chemical are. The standard applies to swimming pool chemicals, cleaning supplies, and pesticides used on lawns and fields.

AQUATIC FACILITY RULES

You must have a clearly defined and easily understood set of aquatic facility rules (see figure 7.3). If you don't, you increase the potential for injury and illness at your facility because the swimmers aren't aware of what constitutes dangerous behavior. You can have an excellent set of rules, but if the patrons don't know what they are, they're useless.

You must post your rules in your swimming area so that they are clearly visible to all swimmers. You may want to consider having two rule boards to ensure that they are seen. Rules should be painted in contrasting colors on marine plywood, steel, or Plexiglas. Signs should be of significant size in

1. Please shower before entering the pool area.
2. Walk, don't run, on the pool deck.
3. Dive only in designated areas.
4. An adult must accompany children under the age of 12.
5. Food and drinks are not permitted in the pool area.
6. Infants must wear swim diapers.
7. Only one person is permitted on the diving board at a time.
8. Starting blocks are not to be used except during swim team practice.
9. Pool privileges can be revoked at any time by lifeguards.
10. Lifeguards must be obeyed at all times.
11. Bathing suits are required.

Figure 7.3   Suggested aquatic facility rules.

order to be easily seen—a 5-by-4-foot (152.4-by-121.9-centimeter) rule board is not uncommon for indoor pools; beaches may have signs double that size. Consider the clientele that visits your facility. If you serve a large number of young children or customers who cannot read, or who do not speak English well, consider using picture rules. These make rules understandable even to those who cannot read. You should also post rule boards in the locker rooms so that patrons see them before entering the swimming area. The message "No Diving" should be tiled into the pool deck in areas of the pool where diving is prohibited. Letters should be 4 to 6 inches (10.2 to 15.2 centimeters) high.

Here are some other strategies that you can use to communicate rules:

- Hold safety briefings with rental groups before they enter the pool.
- Review safety rules on the first day of swim classes.
- Print facility rules on swim lesson registration forms.
- Include facility rules on facility reservation forms.
- Sponsor a coloring contest for children in swim lessons to illustrate pool safety rules. Announce the winner in the newspaper and post the entries around the building.

► Have lifeguards enforce rules in a positive manner.

You should be sure that all aquatic staff members are aware of all facility rules. Include this information in their pre-service orientation and in their staff manuals. Work to ensure that your staff is enforcing the rules uniformly.

EMERGENCY EQUIPMENT

Well-developed emergency plans are undoubtedly important, but in order to implement those plans, you must have the required emergency equipment. You should ensure that all staff members have the proper equipment in the appropriate amount, and that they know where the equipment is located and how to use it. The emergency equipment needed for your facility is dependent on its size, bather load, activities taking place, staff training, and proximity to emergency services. You should consider these factors when deciding what equipment is needed at your facility. The following is a list of suggested emergency equipment for aquatic facilities. (See chapter 6 for a complete list of all suggested lifeguard equipment.)

Latex Gloves

Latex gloves are mandatory for all aquatic facilities. They come in single, double, and triple ply. Single ply is effective for treating most minor injuries. Thicker gloves should be used for injuries at vehicle accidents or in industrial settings. Nylon gloves are available for rescuers with a latex allergy. Gloves should be purchased by the box. Boxes should be placed in first aid stations and guest services areas. Lifeguards on duty should carry a minimum of two pairs of gloves on their person at all times.

Rescue Breathing Devices

There are many types of rescue breathing barriers: pocket masks, seal-easy, micro shield, rescue-key. The device should be transparent so the rescuer can observe the victim's mouth in case of vomit. It should also have a one-way valve to prevent the exchange of air between rescuer and victim, as well as a flexible face piece to allow it to mold to the victim's face. Each lifeguard on duty should have his or her own mask and should be trained in its use. Retraining should occur at least annually.

First Aid Kits

Large, comprehensive first aid kits should be stationed at strategic locations around the facility (see figure 7.4). The pool area, first aid station, and all other activity areas should have a well-stocked kit. Lifeguards and building supervisors should each be issued a small waist pack containing latex gloves, a rescue pocket mask, and minimal first

- Adhesive bandages, assorted sizes: one box.
- Gauze pads, assorted sizes: several boxes.
- Triangle bandages: 10.
- Roller gauze: six rolls.
- First aid tape: assorted width, several rolls.
- One bottle water.
- Sugar packets: several.
- Three-ounce paper cups: several.
- Blunt-tipped scissors/shears: one pair.
- Paper: one small pad.
- Pen: two.

- Pocket-sized first aid book: one.
- Chemical cold packs: two.
- Sanitary napkins: several.
- Disinfectant wipes: one box.
- Tweezers: one.
- Trauma dressing: two.
- Pen light: one.
- Latex gloves: several pairs.
- Face shields for anti-exposure protection: two.
- Pocket mask: one.
- Space blanket: one.

You should not stock painkillers, even over-the-counter ones such as aspirin or acetaminophen, because basic first aiders are not authorized to distribute these items. If they are administered and the victim becomes ill because of them, the first aider bears the liability of issuing medication without proper training.

Figure 7.4 Suggested items for a comprehensive first aid kit.

aid equipment (such as gauze pads, roller gauze, and adhesive bandages). These smaller packs allow for immediate treatment of minor injuries without waiting for the larger kit to be brought to the victim.

Supplemental Oxygen

Supplemental oxygen requires specific training and certification for your staff to be able to use it. However, that training is readily available and easy to obtain from agencies such as the American Red Cross. A minimum of one supplemental oxygen unit is recommended for any given site. It must be stored away from direct heat or open flame. Care must be taken not to drop it, or the expelled gas can propel it, potentially injuring anyone nearby. The tank should be inspected and serviced according to the manufacturer's instructions. Oxygen is particularly useful for victims of heart attack and breathing difficulty.

Automatic External Defibrillators

Automatic external defibrillators (AEDs) can regulate a victim's irregular heartbeat by means of an electrical shock. Although specific training is required to operate them, this training is short in duration (2 hours if certified in CPR) and easy to obtain. AEDs significantly increase the survivability of victims of heart attack and are fast becoming the standard of care. One unit is recommended for each facility. It should be stored in its container, with laminated instructions and a small towel. Do not store it where it is accessible by the public; an available office is recommended. Special care is required when operating these devices in an aquatic environment due to the risk of shock to the rescuer. Many counties require approval from a medical director before they will approve AEDs for use (Fawcett, 2000).

Backboards

Backboards are used for immobilization of spinal injuries and fractured lower extremities, and for transport of any nonambulatory victims. A minimum of two backboards per aquatic facility is recommended. Two are required in case a victim is sent to medical care on one board; the facility can remain open with the spare. Backboards should be a minimum of 6 feet (182.9 centimeters) long and 18 inches (45.7 centimeters) wide. They should be constructed of varnished marine plywood or poly-

ethylene. All boards should be adjustable for use with children and adults. Additionally, they should be equipped with a set of at least four straps made of either Velcro, cloth, or nylon. The board should have runners or be curved at the handles to allow the rescuers to set it down without crushing their fingers. Label the board with your facility name to prevent its loss in a hospital equipment room.

Head Immobilization Devices

Head immobilization devices (HIDs) are constructed of closed-cell foam covered in a latex skin. They consist of a base and two triangular foam pillows. The pillows attach to the base (with Velcro) to hold the victim's head in position. The entire device is attached to a backboard. A minimum of one device is recommended for each backboard. Staff members require at least quarterly practice with the combination HID and backboard to remain proficient.

Cervical Collars

Cervical collars, or C-collars, work in conjunction with the HID and backboard to immobilize the victim's neck. Currently, several major lifeguard training agencies do not include this device in their training, although it has been included in the past. This doesn't mean it cannot be used, but most staff members will have to be trained from scratch how to use it. Implementation of the use of C-collars is at the discretion of the facility manager.

Splints

Splints can be constructed from a variety of materials, including metal, wood, cardboard, and plastic. Premade splints can be purchased, or splinting materials can be used to create them as needed. Splints can be used for fractures, sprains, and dislocations. Splints for several fracture sites (elbow, lower arm, upper arm) of the upper and lower extremities are recommended for each aquatic facility.

Water Rescue Devices

Water rescue devices include rescue tubes, rescue cans, ring buoys, heaving lines, heaving jugs, shepherd's crooks, and reaching poles. Most lifeguard agencies use the rescue tube as their standard training implement. Keep this in mind when purchasing equipment. Be sure to check state bathing code requirements for rescue equipment; many states still require a ring buoy. Each pool should have several pieces of rescue equipment, including reaching equipment and flotation devices. Rescue equipment should be accessible from all sides of the swimming area. Each lifeguard on duty should carry a piece of rescue equipment, preferably a rescue tube at indoor facilities and inshore beaches and a rescue can at surf facilities.

Rescue Cans

Rescue cans are hard, red plastic flotation devices ranging from 28 to 33 inches (71.1 to 83.8 centimeters) in length. The can has a shoulder strap and a 10-foot (3-meter) tow line attached. A rescue can is most often used in open water environments due to its high level of flotation—several victims can grasp it and still stay afloat. It's not a popular device at pools and water parks because the hard structure can easily injure people if you have to jump into a crowded pool with it and you accidentally strike someone.

Heaving Lines

Heaving lines are heavy-duty braided poly lines with a large knot attached at one end for weight. Heaving lines are often used in 50-foot (15.2-meter) coils. The line is used to throw to victims from shore. Heaving lines are generally not used in pools.

Heaving Jugs

Heaving jugs are similar in form and function to heaving lines except that they have an empty jug attached to the end for added flotation. Milk jugs or large household bleach jugs often serve this purpose well. Be sure to add a small amount of water to the jug for weight when it's being thrown. Also secure the cap in place or the jug will fill with water after it's thrown, defeating the whole purpose. Heaving jugs are generally used in open water situations.

Shepherd's Crook

A shepherd's crook is a 7-foot (213.4-centimeter) aluminum pole with a blunt-ended hook on the end. The crook is used to assist victims at swimming pools.

Telephone

All aquatic facilities should have a telephone that is accessible at all times the facility is open. In the event that the phone becomes inoperable or is inaccessible, the facility must be closed. The phone should be included in an aquatics office located near the swimming area. Cell phones can be used at remote beaches or waterfronts as long as batteries remain charged and service is not interrupted. Emergency phone numbers and emergency phone scripts should be posted immediately adjacent to the telephone. Emergency phones should be kept free for emergency calls at all times. See appendix D for a sample emergency phone script and also an emergency phone list that you can fill out and keep handy.

Two-Way Radios

Two-way radios are recommended for use by supervisors and lifeguards at large facilities. Good radios can be very expensive, costing hundreds of dollars per unit, including charging bases. Radios should be used only for emergency traffic and must be kept charged at all times. Lock the units in a cabinet when not in use.

Manual Suction Devices

Suction devices are a recent addition to the aquatics toolbox. They are used to remove lodged items from a choking victim's airway. The tube of the device is inserted in the victim's airway and the rescuer, squeezing a handle containing a plastic bottle, applies low-pressure suction. The obstruction is sucked into the bottle. These devices are very effective in upper airway management. A minimum of one manual suction device is recommended for each aquatic facility. Specific staff training is required for this device.

Bag-Valve Masks

Bag-valve masks (BVMs) are used to ventilate nonbreathing victims. The BVMs are more effective than standard rescue breathing because they use environmental air (which has a higher oxygen content) instead of the victim's expired air. The BVM requires two rescuers to operate: one to hold the mask in place and one to squeeze the bag (supplying air). Most BVMs have the capability to be attached to supplemental oxygen bottles, further increasing the oxygen content. Training in the use of the BVM is included in CPR for the professional rescuer courses. A minimum of two BVMs is recommended for each aquatic facility, more for larger facilities such as state beaches.

EMERGENCY REPORTING FORMS

There are two commonly used emergency report forms: accident reports and incident reports. At the conclusion of any emergency, report forms should be completed and forwarded through the supervisor on duty to the aquatic director. Report forms should contain facts only and never conjecture or opinions. In the event of legal action regarding a response to an emergency, reports serve as documentation of what measures were taken to remedy that emergency. If reports are not completed, you have no proof that you did anything in response to the emergency. Report forms involving minors should be retained on file until the child turns 18 plus 5 years. After this period, the statute of limitations enabling the individual to bring legal action has expired. Accident reports involving adults should be retained for a minimum of 5 years.

Accident Reports

Accident reports are used to record information regarding the condition of and treatment given to injured victims. The victim should be identified by name, address, and telephone number. The activity the person was undertaking coupled with the location in the facility where the accident occurred should also be noted. You may want to include an outline view of the human body so that the location of the injury can be noted. Include any names and telephone numbers of witnesses. The date and time of the incident and the name of the person preparing the report must be on the form. See appendix D for a sample accident report form.

Incident Reports

Incident report forms are used to record information about noninjury events such as theft, fights, domestic disturbance, and assault. The majority of the form should be devoted to a case narrative. The affected party's name and contact information should be included as well as the date, time, and location of the incident. If police, fire department, or EMS are called, be sure to get the case or trip number from them and record it on the form. See appendix D for a sample incident report form.

DEVELOPING EMERGENCY PLANS

#3

Before you begin to actually write an emergency action plan, there are certain steps that you should take: obtain floor plans for your facility, assess your safety equipment, consult with EMS, and set up a chain of command.

Obtaining floor plans for your facility enables you to identify emergency exits and routes that EMS can use to access indoor areas. These floor plans don't need to be actual blueprints but can be line drawings drawn to scale. Once you've identified emergency exits and access to the pool for EMS, go and physically inspect the entrances and corridors to ensure that they are suitable for use. Entrances and corridors must be wide enough to accommodate a gurney, and the route planned for EMS should include few turns.

Make a list of the safety equipment that your aquatic facility owns, the condition of each piece of equipment, and where it's stored. This will enable you to include this information in your emergency planning. It will also help in identifying deficiencies that your facility has so that you can purchase the correct equipment to meet your needs. You may also decide after this step that the location where you have your equipment stored is not appropriate for where it will be needed in an emergency, allowing you to move it and adjust your plan accordingly.

Consult with local EMS agencies. EMS must be aware of what your plans are. They must know where to enter your facility in an emergency and if the entrance that you have chosen is appropriate for them. They will also answer other important questions, such as what the transition procedures will be for turning over a victim to EMS once they have arrived on scene. Will they want your staff to assist? Will EMS take over completely? You should also consult with local law enforcement and fire officials in much the same way to determine if your evacuation plans are appropriate, and to provide copies of the plans to these agencies.

Your staff members have to know whom they report to and who is authorized to make certain decisions (see figure 7.5). They will need to know who is authorized to call EMS and who can order a facility evacuation or closure. They must also know who the media officer and attorney are and how they relate to them in command authority. If they don't know this information, you cannot

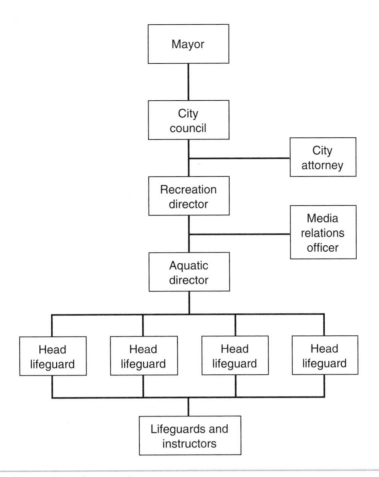

Figure 7.5   A sample chart showing chain of command.

expect them to respond appropriately when dealing with these coworkers.

Once you've performed the basic information-gathering steps just described, such as getting floor plans for your facility and identifying all your emergency equipment, you're ready to begin writing your emergency plans.

How to Develop a Plan

In the early stages of emergency planning, you should make a list of all possible emergencies that could happen at your facility and divide them into two categories—major and minor emergencies. You should next determine how many staff members you will have on duty at any given time, both in the aquatics area itself and in the building as a whole. The number of staff members on duty will affect the way emergency procedures are carried out. Next, create a diagram of your facility, including where the telephone is and where emergency equipment is located.

Once you have done this, you can begin to visualize accidents and what response you would like to have happen based on the information you have available. Determine how staff members will communicate with each other (e.g., whistles or radios). Consider the following points when developing your plan:

- ▶ The staff member who recognizes the emergency should signal the other guards that there is an emergency and what type.
- ▶ The staff member closest to the emergency should respond to the victim.
- ▶ The staff member closest to the phone should call EMS.
- ▶ Secondary guards should clear the pool and bring equipment to the scene once the pool has been cleared.
- ▶ Patrons should be evacuated to the locker rooms or at least out of sight of the incident while it is occurring.

▸ During minor emergencies, the water does not need to be evacuated, but a second guard must pick up the zone that is not supervised while the rescue is being made.

Figure 7.6, a and b show sample emergency plans.

You should post your emergency procedures in your lifeguard office and include them in your staff manual. You should require all staff members to read and understand your emergency procedures before they begin work.

Testing Emergency Plans

Once you've written your emergency action plan, you should test it to see how well it functions. Begin by walking through the plan with your staff in a controlled manner so that everyone understands the basic procedures. Perform this step when the facility is closed so that you do not disrupt facility operations. Next, practice executing the emergency plan at normal speed during an in-service training session. When your staff members have become comfortable with your emergency

procedures, you should inform them that you will be testing emergency procedures unannounced. When you do perform these drills, be sure to post announcements so that your patrons are aware that a disruption to their day may occur. While performing the drills, you can also take the opportunity to make constructive changes to your emergency plans.

> **KEY POINT** *The planner's motto is "fail to plan, plan to fail." If you have made no plans for how to act in an emergency, your response will be disjointed and ineffective. Develop a well-thought-out plan specific to your staff and facility, and then practice it.*

INFORMING NEXT OF KIN

Whenever an emergency has occurred involving injury, illness, or death, you should inform the victim's family members as soon as possible. Failure to do so may mean that the family finds out

(a)

1. Guard #1 recognizes emergency. Signals other guards, using one long blast of his whistle and hand signal for the appropriate victim type, and enters water to perform rescue or begins treatment.

2. Guard #2 calls EMS. Alerts other building staff via radio or phone and goes to meet EMS and escort them to the scene.

3. Guard #3 clears the pool using one long whistle blast. Brings equipment to assist Guard #1. Patrons should be directed to the locker rooms, and doors should then be locked.

4. Guard #4 clears the pool using one long whistle blast. Assists Guard #1.

The pool is not reopened until EMS has departed, all reports are complete, and guards have returned to their stations. You can also include the emergency phone script as part of the emergency action plan and incorporate them into one document.

(b)

1. Guard recognizes emergency, blows whistle, triggers emergency alarm, and enters the water to rescue the victim.

2. Other facility staff respond to the pool area and assist in clearing the pool.

3. Lifeguard directs staff to call EMS, meet them at the designated entrance, and assist with the rescue as needed.

This plan requires an emergency alarm, such as a bell, to be installed in the pool area for the purpose of summoning assistance.

Figure 7.6   Sample emergency action plan for *(a)* a four-lifeguard facility and *(b)* a one-lifeguard facility.

from the media or another third party. This may cause them great distress, and they may receive wrong information. If you know that relatives are in the building, send a responsible staff member to summon them to the scene. If the family is not with the victim, you must determine the appropriate method to summon them. For minor or non-life-threatening emergencies, you may call them and explain the situation, including where the victim is and what care is currently being given.

If the victim is deceased, you must consider many more factors. You must be certain that notification of next of kin is the responsibility of your facility. In cases involving other agencies, such as the police, those agencies may automatically assume notification responsibilities. If your organization becomes part of the process, keep the following points in mind:

- Be very gentle and do not tell graphic details that the family member does not need to know. Be prepared with basic details, such as what happened and when and where it happened. Be prepared with information regarding where the body is or is being taken.

- Consider that this may be very traumatic and that the family may require medical assistance or grief counseling.

- Provide a contact number from your facility that they can call if they have questions.

- Never make death notifications to family members over the phone; always go in person. If the family is geographically distant, try to contact local law enforcement in that area to deliver the notification for you.

- Think about having a uniformed law enforcement officer accompany you when making notification.

- Always send a senior staff member to deliver the notification. Never send anyone alone to make the notification.

- Make yourself as presentable as possible for this process; dress appropriately.

- Bring identification with you indicating who you are and where you work.

Victims' families will often go through a grieving process that may include denial or anger. The family may blame rescuers or lash out against them. The notification team should be prepared and should not take it personally.

DEALING WITH CRITICAL INCIDENT STRESS

Any time an incident involving violence, severe injury to a patron or staff member, death, or a dramatic rescue occurs at your facility, staff members may experience critical incident stress. The risk of this is increased by the fact that most lifeguards are very young, many in their teens. Left unchecked, stress from incidents such as these can cause a variety of physical and psychological problems for a staff member.

As soon as the incident is over and victims have been treated and evacuated, the process of helping staff members deal with the stress should begin. A professional critical incident stress debriefing team should be brought in after major events; many police departments can assist in identifying such a team. These #6 professionals will counsel affected staff members, allow them to constructively vent their feelings, and assist them in returning to function. As a supervisor, there are steps you can take to assist staff members suffering from post-traumatic stress disorder:

- Make yourself available for them to talk to; be nonjudgmental.

- Never place blame.

- Do not allow them to return to work until you think they are fully fit.

- Encourage them to get rest and exercise.

- Encourage them to eat properly.

Do not allow staff members who have experienced such a traumatic situation to return to work until you are sure that they are able to function properly. Doing so would place patrons under their supervision in jeopardy because of their inattention. It also does the staff member no good. You can require staff members to seek counseling before they return to work.

LEGAL ISSUES

To fully understand legal issues as they apply to aquatics, it's necessary to understand some basic legal terms. These terms include negligence, **abandonment,** standard of care, expressed **consent,** implied consent, and **in loco parentis.**

Negligence

There are two types of negligence: **negligence of omission** and **negligence of commission.** Negligence of omission refers to not doing something that you were required to do. For example, if you were required to be on duty lifeguarding the pool and you were asleep in the lifeguard office instead, you have committed negligence of omission.

Negligence of commission refers to committing an act that you were not supposed to. For example, if you store pool items where they block the emergency exits from the pool, thereby denying use of the exits, you have committed negligence of commission (Clement, 1997).

Abandonment

Abandonment refers to beginning treatment for a victim and then ceasing that treatment before surrendering the victim to another rescuer. Lifeguards are considered professional rescuers, and when on duty, they have no choice regarding whether they will treat a victim in their area of responsibility. They are not legally obligated to treat victims outside their facility and its grounds when on duty or to treat victims anywhere when off duty (although they may feel morally obligated to do so). Therefore, lifeguards and other aquatic staff must be prepared to respond to all emergencies in their area and are responsible for the victim until turned over to EMS (Schottke, 2001).

Volunteer rescuers who have no legal responsibility to help a person in distress are often called Good Samaritans. Although no legal responsibility exists to help a victim, it is illegal to stop rendering assistance once you have begun. Treatment is considered to have begun when you move toward the victim with the appearance of intending to treat. By starting and stopping, you may have denied the victim assistance from others who may not render assistance because they believe it is already being done. By stopping assistance, you have crossed over from passively exercising your right not to be involved to actively hurting the victim through denial of service. Therefore, if you begin moving toward the victim and then stop, assistance to the victim may be denied, and abandonment has occurred.

Standard of Care

Standard of care refers to the body of information put out by professionals and professional agencies in the field. In aquatics, information from the YMCA of the USA, the American Red Cross, and the United States Lifesaving Association would be considered standard of care. In many cases, the standards published by these agencies are higher than those required by law in most state bathing codes. For example, the state bathing code may not require that lifeguards be on duty in all aquatic facilities in all cases, whereas a YMCA publication may recommend that lifeguards always be on duty. Where standards do not conflict with the law, always adhere to the higher standard. Courts expect you, as an aquatic professional, to provide the highest standard of care and will hold you to that standard (Clement, 1997). (See "Standard of Care" in chapter 6, page 131.)

Consent

Rescuers may not treat a victim without permission from that victim. Minor children who are entrusted to the care of another are an exception to this. Parents or guardians may give permission to treat a minor child if they are present. Permission to treat the victim must be expressed either verbally or in some other form, such as a head nod or gesture; this is referred to as expressed consent. Treating a victim without consent is considered unlawful touching. Restraining a victim for the purposes of treating that victim is considered false imprisonment.

Victims who are unconscious are considered to have given their permission for treatment. A victim who refuses treatment while conscious and then becomes unconscious is considered to have given consent on becoming unconscious. This is referred to as implied consent.

Adults have the right to refuse consent for their own treatment, even if they appear to be acting erratically. Involuntary treatment cannot be given unless directed by law enforcement in conjunction with EMS. Treatment cannot be refused on behalf of another adult, such as a husband or wife refusing treatment for a spouse (Schottke, 2001).

In Loco Parentis

In loco parentis is a Latin term meaning "in the place of the parent." Any child care worker, instructor, or staff member entrusted with the care of a child is expected to take reasonable care of that child (as the parent would). This includes protecting the child from harm, exercising supervision over the child, and providing appropriate care if the child becomes injured or ill. Lifeguards are considered in loco parentis while on duty supervising children (McGregor & MacDonald, 2000).

KEY POINT *Your lifeguards don't need a law degree to do their jobs, but they do need a basic understanding of legal concepts that affect them. Have your facility legal counsel visit periodically to review legal concepts appropriate for lifeguards. Discuss with your counsel beforehand what level of information and topics you want him to cover.*

SUMMARY

The first step in risk management and emergency planning is to understand some basic principles of risk management, including how to locate risks and ways to eliminate, transfer, or avoid risk. After you've grasped the basic tenets of risk management, you can continue on with planning for the various types of emergencies that you may encounter at your aquatic facility. Further risk management tactics that you can employ include planning for special situations such as security concerns and mechanical malfunctions. Understanding and properly using the state bathing code are not only key to risk management but to your facility operations as a whole. Choosing the proper safety and emergency equipment gives your staff members the tools they need to effectively carry out their emergency management tasks. Creating the appropriate forms enables you to accurately record the facts of an emergency at your facility and provides you with documentation and some measure of protection in the event of litigation. Understanding the legal terms and framework involved in risk management and emergency planning provides you with a better understanding of the reasons for your planning. Although accidents and emergencies cannot be totally prevented at even the best-managed aquatic facility, using these steps can help mitigate and prepare for them.

REVIEW QUESTIONS

1. Compare and contrast near drowning versus wet drowning.
2. Explain the concept of "consent" and list its various forms.
3. What steps will you need to take before developing an emergency action plan?
4. How does a statement of understanding differ from a waiver and a hold harmless agreement?
5. Describe some basic media relations tips that you can give to your staff.
6. What role does a critical incident stress debriefing team play after a traumatic event?

BIBLIOGRAPHY

American Red Cross. (1993). *Preventing disease transmission*. St. Louis: Mosby Lifeline.

Centers for Disease Control. (2002, July 17). *Injury fact book 2001-2002*. Retrieved May 19, 2003, from Web site: www.cdc.gov/ncipc/fact_book/30_WaterRelated_Injuries.htm.

Clement, A. (1997). *Legal responsibility in aquatics.* Aurora, OH: Sport and Law Press.

Fawcett, P. (2000, August). Automatic external defibrillation: What's the standard? *From the Gym to the Jury, 12*, 6-7.

Johnson, R. (1994). *YMCA pool operations manual* (2nd ed.). Champaign, IL: Human Kinetics.

McGregor, I., & MacDonald, J. (2000). *Risk management manual for sport & recreation organizations* (2nd ed.). Corvallis, OR: NIRSA.

Schottke, D. (Ed.). (2001). *First responder.* Sudbury, MA: Jones and Bartlett.

Teather, R. (1994). *Encyclopedia of underwater investigations.* Flagstaff, AZ: Best Publishing Company.

Williams, K. (1995). *Aquatic facility operator manual* (2nd ed.). Hoffman Estates, IL: National Recreation and Park Association.

Wynn, B. (1984, February). *Drowning: A programmer's nightmare.* Aquatic Programming Symposium, Ottawa, ON.

YMCA of the USA. (1997). *On the guard II: The YMCA lifeguard manual* (3rd ed.). Champaign, IL: Human Kinetics.

RESOURCES

Garner, B. (Ed.). (1999). *Blacks law dictionary* (7th ed.). Berkley, CA: West Group.

The following Web sites provide information related to risk management:

Environmental Protection Agency Web site: www.epa.gov/OST/beaches.

Foundation for Aquatic Injury Prevention Web site: http://aquaticisf.org/resources.htm.

Managing Water Chemistry and Filtration

Chapter Objectives

After reading this chapter, you should be able to

1. understand the basic concepts of pool filtration and circulation,

2. list and describe the elements of water chemistry,

3. properly perform a pool water test,

4. properly perform a langlier saturation index,

5. explain the concept of total dissolved solids, and

6. safely and correctly store swimming pool chemicals.

Maintaining proper water chemistry is an important part of a well-run aquatic facility. Well-maintained water chemistry can result in clear, clean water that is attractive and pleasing to your customers. Poorly maintained water can be a conduit for disease and illness.

Filtration is the aspect of your water chemistry plan that removes solid material from your water. Particles of dirt, deodorant, perfume, soap, dust, pollution, and anything else solid you can think of are screened out by the filters. There are a variety of types and styles of filters available, each with its own advantages and disadvantages. This chapter includes a list and description of the different types, and it helps you choose which type might be best for your facility by explaining the advantages and weaknesses of each.

This chapter also covers the dizzying array of factors that affect the chemistry of your pool water—disinfectant, pH, **alkalinity**, hardness, and **total dissolved solids,** just to name a few. Each of these factors is explained in detail, and information is provided to help you understand how the factors relate to each other. The section on the **langlier saturation index** is especially helpful in this area.

Water testing is a particularly important topic in this chapter. Simply put, if you can't determine what's happening with your pool water, you won't know how to fix it. This chapter explains where, when, and how to test pool water. You'll also learn whom you need to report your findings to and why that's important.

Giardia, cryptosporidium, nagleria, pseudomonas aeruginosa. If they sound bad, they are; they're all diseases. What's worse, they could be in your pool! This chapter helps you learn what they are, how to recognize their effects, what to do if you've got them in your pool water, and how to prevent them in the first place.

CIRCULATION

Circulation refers to the way in which water transits from the pool to filtration and chemical treatment and back again. Elements of circulation include pipes, pumps, motors, and the hair and lint strainer. You can think of the circulation system of the pool as similar to the circulation system of the body—the pump is the "heart" that keeps the system going, and the pipes are like blood vessels that move water instead of blood. You need to understand how and why your pool circulation system works. This will enable you to identify problems, such as leaks or poor water pressure, and take steps to correct them.

At the top of the circulation system, gutters (troughs on the pool decks) run parallel to the pool. These gutters are connected to pipes that carry water into the filtration system. The gutters come in many shapes and sizes. Some are open and 3 inches (7.6 centimeters) deep and 6 inches (15.2 centimeters) wide. Other types are very shallow, only an inch or so deep, but several feet wide and covered in sturdy plastic slats. The type of gutter isn't necessarily important, as long as it's functional for your facility. Gutters should run completely around the pool. Water flows from the pool basin into the gutters. The water level in the pool should be high enough to keep a constant flow of water just skimming over the edge of the pool and into the gutter. If this is not happening, you will have poor circulation, which could result in poor water quality.

After water exits the gutter, it is carried by piping, usually PVC or steel. Exposed piping that you can see in the filter room is called **face piping.** Prior to reaching the filter, water passes through a hair and lint strainer. This is a receptacle in the pipeline that is lined with a steel or plastic mesh basket and a screw-down top. The purpose of the hair and lint strainer is to remove large objects (such as jewelry, adhesive bandages, and, of course, hair and lint) in order to prevent them from damaging the filters. Once a day, you should shut down the water flow and remove the basket for cleaning. It's helpful to have a spare basket to use while you're cleaning so that the filter is not shut down for any length of time. If you do not regularly clean the skimmer basket, pressure will build up as water is being held back by debris built up in the basket. Eventually the basket will break, allowing debris to reach the filters.

The heart of the circulation system is the pump and motor. These two items move the water through the pipes and into the filter. If the motor breaks down or the pump burns out, water will stop moving, and your filters will not be able to run. The pump has an impeller, which is used to draw water into the pipes and keep it moving. You should perform periodic maintenance on the pump in accordance with the manufacturer's instructions. If operation of your pool is essential and you are willing to incur the expense, redundant pumps can be mounted side by side in the recirculation system. Doing this allows you to simply activate the redundant pump if the primary pump fails. You lose no filtration time, meaning your pool would never close. It is an expensive option, but a good investment for large-volume facilities.

The water is returned to the pool through a series of return jets. These should be spread around the perimeter of the pool so that treated water is returned evenly throughout the pool.

> **KEY POINT** Good water circulation is a central factor in ensuring that the pool water is clean, filtered, and sanitary.

FILTRATION

Filtration refers to the removal of dirt and other undesirable substances from the water. The dirt to be removed is usually particulate matter of very small size that is in suspension in the water. The more effective the filtration system used, the clearer and cleaner the water will become due to the removal of more dirt.

> **KEY POINT** Selecting the right size and type of filter is crucial to achieving clear, clean pool water.

There are two major types of filters: permanent and temporary media. Media is the term used for the element that actually filters the water. Sand and gravel filters are considered permanent media, while **diatomaceous earth** and cartridge filters are considered temporary media. Temporary media must be replaced on a periodic basis, while permanent media can last for years before replacement. Each filter type has its advantages and disadvantages depending on the type of facility and the needs of the operator.

Permanent Media

Sand and gravel filters are essentially a steel tank—up to 10 feet (3 meters) high and usually about 6 feet (about 2 meters) across—with stacked layers of sand and gravel inside. The topmost layer is fine silica sand, and the descending layers progress to coarse sand and to gravel at the bottom of the tank. After the media has been in place for 12 hours or more, a naturally occurring layer called "floc" appears on the top layer. Floc assists in water filtration. Water comes from the pool through a pipe at the top of the tank. As it enters the filter, it strikes a pipe called a "baffle plate." The baffle plate spreads the water flow evenly over the filter surface so that channels are not formed in the media. Debris of various sizes is left in the media as it passes through. Once water reaches the bottom, it is collected in a series of pipes called laterals that extend through the bottom of the tank. Water is then returned to the pool through recirculation lines. As more dirt is left in the media, it becomes difficult for water to pass through. This creates a pressure differential between incoming (influent) and outgoing (effluent) water. A well-organized filter will have gauges for incoming and outgoing pressure mounted together for easy evaluation. When the pressure difference reaches 5 pounds per square inch **(PSI),** you should **backwash** the filter; this may occur as infrequently as once per week or as often as daily, depending on your bather load in the pool and the size of your filter in relation to your pool water volume.

Backwashing filters requires running water backward through the filter from the bottom up. Water is redirected to waste instead of back to the pool after backwashing. Backwashing removes built-up dirt and reduces pressure differential. Most filters have a **sight glass** that allows the operator to see the water as it passes from the filter to waste. Early in the backwashing process, the water will be brown because it contains dirt from the media. When the water in the sight glass is clear, the filters are clean and you can stop backwashing.

Sand and gravel filters are made predominantly from two materials: carbon steel and stainless steel. Stainless steel is more expensive but lasts longer. Carbon steel is not as durable but tends to be less expensive. Most filters are now coated with a rubber or epoxy internal coating. This helps prevent the tanks from rusting from the inside out. You can purchase the filter in many different styles: a single tank, many small tanks, or anything in between. Your choice will often depend on the available space in your filter room. If space is limited, you should purchase filters stacked on top of each other to maximize vertical space. Purchasing one large filter can be risky because if the filter becomes inoperable for any reason, you must close the pool. If three or four smaller filters are purchased, and one malfunctions, water quality can often be maintained until repairs are made on the damaged filter.

Filters are selected based on the number of gallons of water in the pool and the rate of flow of the water through the filter. The state bathing code will dictate the turnover rate for water in the pool. Turnover rate is the time it takes for all the water in the pool to pass through the filters. Often 6 or 8 hours is the required turnover rate. The appropriate filter sizes are determined by computing the required gallons per minute (GPM) flow. **GPM** is calculated by dividing the total volume of the pool by the number of minutes required for turnover. When selecting filter and pump sizes, this information is needed. The GPM figure is needed to assist in selecting filter size because the higher your desired GPM, the more filter capacity your facility will require.

Sand and gravel filters are classified as either pressure or vacuum. Pressure filters have the pumps before the filters, "pushing" the water through. Vacuum filters have the pump after the filter, drawing the water through.

Sand and gravel filters (figure 8.1) provide clear, clean water at a reasonable cost. One drawback is that they must be backwashed (as described). Each time you backwash the filter, you lose water that has been heated and chemically treated. This results in lost money each time because you must add makeup water, which you must then heat and chemically treat.

The media in a sand and gravel filter must be replaced at periodic intervals. Normally the run life is a period of 5 to 7 years depending on bather load, water chemistry quality, and the number of months per year that your filter is used. The filter media is replaced by opening a small access hole in the top or side of the filter tank, removing the media, and repacking new sand and gravel. To do this, you'll need to shut down the filters and drain them of water. Depending on the piping configuration of your pool, you may also need to drain the pool itself. If you have to totally suspend filtration during media replacement (which depends on your filter and piping setup), you'll have to close the pool. Try to schedule media replacement for a

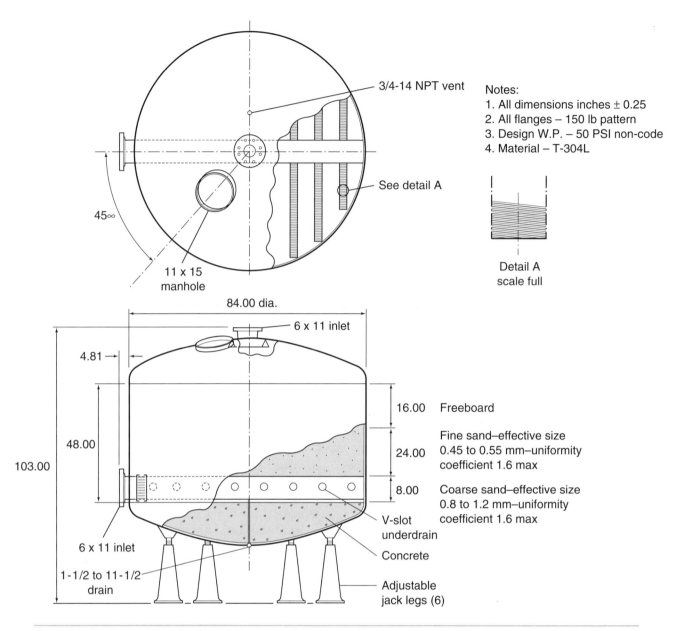

Notes:
1. All dimensions inches ± 0.25
2. All flanges – 150 lb pattern
3. Design W.P. – 50 PSI non-code
4. Material – T-304L

Detail A
scale full

Figure 8.1   A diagram of a sand and gravel filter.

Adapted, by permission, from R.L. Johnson, 1994, *YMCA pool operations manual,* 2nd ed., (Champaign, IL: Human Kinetics), 7.

time of the year when it will be less disruptive for your patrons. The longer you go between media replacement, the more you will see a degradation of water quality over time as the sand in the tanks becomes saturated with grime, hair, and lint that it cannot backwash out. You must take great care when repacking the media or the filter will not function properly.

Temporary Media

Diatomaceous earth (DE) is a commonly used form of temporary media. Diatomaceous earth is a white powder that is a naturally occurring substance. It

is rich in fossilized microscopic sea creatures. The individual fossils are called diatoms. The diatoms form a latticework that works very well to trap dirt as it passes through. When handling DE, care should be taken not to breathe it in because it can become lodged in the lungs. A respiratory protection mask should always be worn when handling DE. A synthetic form of DE is also available.

Diatomaceous earth filters provide clean, clear, and sparkling water. DE filters can remove particulate matter as small as 1 micron in size. This produces a sparkling effect. Although diatomaceous earth filters are often more expensive in initial purchase cost than other types of filters, they are less expensive to operate. Diatomaceous earth filters do not require backwashing, eliminating the loss of water, heat, and chemicals from the process. Although you must purchase DE for regular recoating, judicious operation will extend filter runs between media replacement, saving money.

There are two main types of DE filters: regenerative and vacuum.

Regenerative Diatomaceous Earth Filters

Regenerative diatomaceous earth filters are large metal tanks—6 to 10 feet (about 2 to 3 meters) high and 3 to 5 feet (about 1 to 1.5 meters) across—that contain a series of cords hanging from a metal plate (see figure 8.2). The size of the tank may vary from only a few feet in diameter to as wide as 8 to 10 feet (2.4 to 3 meters) across. The cords are coated with diatomaceous earth. As water flows into the tank, it comes in contact with the DE and deposits particulate matter. Periodically, the DE will become saturated with dirt. You can then initiate what is known as a "bump cycle." The bump cycle agitates the cords, which causes the DE to separate from them. When the DE settles back onto the cords, the "dirty" DE will settle on the bottom, with the clean DE on top of it. The filter process can then be continued because the useful

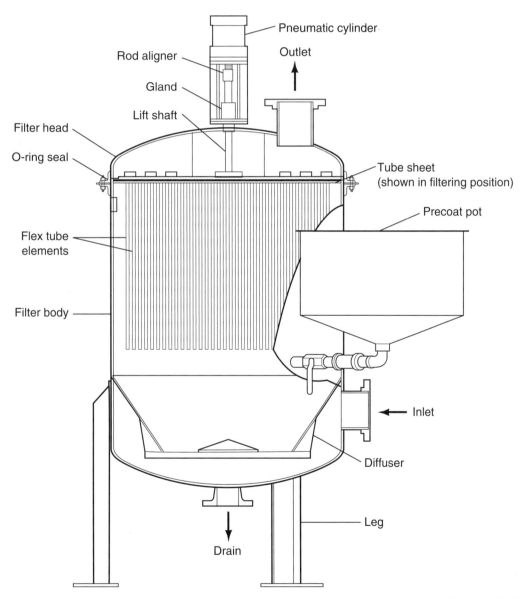

Figure 8.2 A diagram of a regenerative DE filter.

Reprinted, by permission, from R.L. Johnson, 1994, *YMCA pool operations manual,* 2nd ed., (Champaign, IL: Human Kinetics), 11.

DE is now exposed to the water. Bump cycles can take place automatically or can take place at the touch of a button. Periodically, new DE will need to be added through a precoat pot—an open-topped box on the filter that allows DE to feed directly into the filter.

Vacuum Diatomaceous Earth Filters

Vacuum DE filters are large open boxes, as large as 6 feet (almost 2 meters) square, normally constructed of concrete (see figure 8.3). Inside the box, there is a series of screens covered with a synthetic cover. The DE forms a filter cake, which is coated to the sides of the screens. As water passes through the screens, it deposits dirt in the DE. As the filter cake becomes clogged with dirt from use, the boxes are drained of water and refilled. On refilling, the DE recoats the filters with the unused DE on top, allowing the filter run to continue. New DE is periodically fed into the system through a slurry feeder.

Filter Replacement

Like any other item of swimming pool equipment, filters have a life span after which they become ineffective. The life span of your filter depends on several factors:

▶ The bather load in the pool.
▶ The level of pool water quality you maintain.
▶ The number of months the filter is in operation each year. (If your pool is seasonal and filters only run for a few months, they should last longer.)
▶ The size of the filter versus gallons of water in the pool. (If you have a low number of gallons per square footage of surface area of filter media, your filters are not as stressed because the filter load is being distributed.)
▶ The type of filter you use.

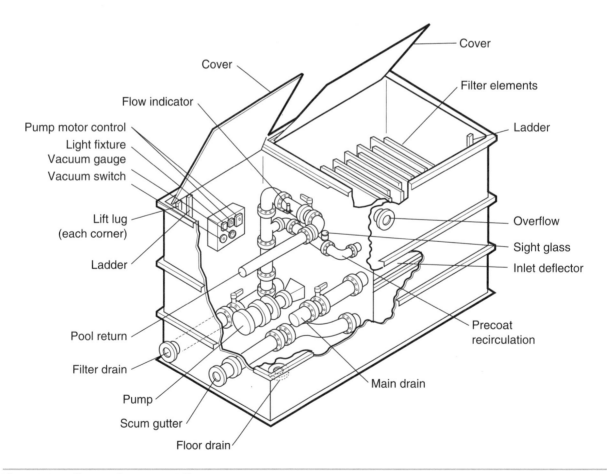

Figure 8.3 A diagram of a vacuum DE filter.

Adapted, by permission, from R.L. Johnson, 1994, *YMCA pool operations manual,* 2nd ed., (Champaign, IL: Human Kinetics), 9.

▸ The frequency and quality of maintenance you perform on your filters.

Effective filter life can range from 10 to 25 years depending on these factors. You should regularly inspect your filters to see that they are in good repair. See appendix D for a sample filter inspection form.

Signs that you need to consider filter replacement may include the following:

▸ Poor water clarity even after backwashing or media replacement

▸ Clogged pipes or burned-out pumps due to calcium buildup

▸ Presence of rust or other particulate matter in the pool due to corrosion of filter or pipe interior

▸ Filter cracks

▸ Filter leaks

▸ Leaking pipes

▸ Broken hardware such as gauges

Filter replacement is a major project that can cost into the hundreds of thousands of dollars. Filter companies build filters specifically for a given project; you can't buy them "off the shelf" for commercial pools. With that in mind, you need to know your requirements and other data before calling the supplier or manufacturer. The customer service or sales representative will want to know the volume of your pool in gallons (see figure 8.4), your desired turnover rate, the configuration of your filter room, and what type of filter you'd like. If you don't know your turnover rate, check your state bathing code. The filter room configuration will determine the style of filter you need.

Actual replacement of the filters requires considerable planning because most filter units are quite large and cannot be disassembled for installation. This may require a wall to be taken down, a roof removed, or some other major renovation done to your facility in order to install the filters.

Filter installation may take several weeks, during which time your pool will be unable to operate. Because of this, you should plan to per-

form this task during times of low usage for your facility. Pre-staging equipment and parts as well as careful advanced planning for this project will help you expedite the process. Be sure to give advance notice to your patrons so that they will be aware of the disruption to their schedule.

CLEANING THE POOL BOTTOM

You can keep your pool bottom clean mainly through the use of a vacuum. There are two main types of swimming pool vacuums: automatic and manual. The type of vacuum you select will depend on the amount of money you want to spend and the amount of work and time you want to put into vacuuming. If your facility has an automated vacuum, you may want to have your staff place it in the pool every evening after closing (or every other evening depending on bather load) so that it can run during the hours the facility is closed. If you are using a manual vacuum, you may only vacuum once or twice a week due to the high intensity of labor and the amount of time required. Vacuums range in price from $1,500 to $4,000. (See appendix C for suppliers.)

Automatic Vacuums

Sometimes called "aquabots" or "frogs," automatic vacuums clean the pool bottom simply by being plugged in and placed in the pool. The device is powered by a small internal electric motor and is set on tracks or wheels. The vacuum travels across the pool bottom, collecting dirt until it comes into contact with a wall. Most automatic vacuums have a sensor that allows them to turn and continue working when they come into contact with a wall. Most vacuums use a paper filter to remove dirt and debris from the water. The filter must be periodically changed to maintain the effectiveness of the vacuum.

Swimmers should not be permitted in the pool when the automatic vacuum is in operation. Although the electrical cords powering the vacuum are insulated, there is a risk of electrocution to the swimmers if the insulation becomes damaged or

Pool length (feet) × Pool width (feet) × Pool average depth (feet) = Volume in cubic feet

Volume in cubic feet × 7.5 = Pool volume in gallons

1 cubic foot of water = 7.5 gallons

Figure 8.4 A method for calculating swimming pool volume.

worn. To reduce the downtime associated with vacuuming the pool, you can put the vacuum in the pool after closing and allow it to run during the night. This eliminates the need to close the pool for vacuuming. The average automated vacuum is 3 feet long and 2 to 3 feet (61 to 91.4 centimeters) high, and varies from 1 to 3 feet wide.

Manual Vacuums

Manual vacuums have a long hose connected to the pool filter on one end and an intake at the other. A long pole attached to the intake end allows the user to direct the vacuum. A pool worker must move the manual vacuum slowly across the pool bottom. This allows water and dirt to be sucked off the bottom and directed to the filter. You must move the vacuum slowly; otherwise, the dirt will be stirred up, and you will have to wait until it settles out to begin vacuuming again.

Although manual vacuums are much cheaper than automatic ones, they require a great deal of tedious labor to operate. The quality of the cleaning will be dependent on the skill and attention of the worker performing the task.

WATER TESTING

Testing your pool water correctly and keeping accurate records are essential to maintaining clean, clear water. If you don't know what your water chemistry is, you can't manage it properly. Outdoor aquatic facilities should be tested each hour, and indoor facilities every 2 hours. Tests should be completed in both deep and shallow water. Water chemistry can change rapidly as a result of weather and bather load; if you don't test frequently, you will have a problem before you can react. Be proactive about water chemistry, not reactive.

You should always record the results of your water tests and retain the records. Many states require that the results be recorded on a state-approved form and submitted to the state monthly. Check your state code for the requirements in your state. Regularly review your records so that you can determine patterns based on weather or bather load and can prepare accordingly. See appendix D for a sample monthly water chemistry report form.

Water test kits of various types are available; the brand is not as important as the tests the kit performs. A comprehensive test kit that performs tests for free chlorine, free bromine, pH, alkalin-ity, and hardness is essential (see figure 8.5). The reagents used for most kits have a shelf life of no more than a year. Phenol red, the reagent used for pH, has a shelf life of only 6 months; after that point, readings are not accurate. You should buy a new test kit at least once per year. You can purchase the phenol red reagent separately at the end of its usefulness to avoid the unneeded cost of purchasing an entirely new test kit every 6 months. The test cells and color comparators are often bleached by exposure to sunlight, high humidity, and chemicals; when this occurs, they will give inaccurate readings. Record the purchase date of chemicals on the bottle with indelible marker as soon as they are bought. This allows you to track their freshness and discard them when they are no longer effective. Use only the type of reagents designed for the type of test kit you purchased; doing otherwise will give inaccurate test results. (See appendix C for suppliers of test kits, color comparators, and test reagents.)

Water tests should be taken in both deep and shallow water. Place your thumb over the vial and submerge it at least 12 inches (30.5 centimeters) underwater; take the sample from there. Do not take the sample in front of the water return inlets because this water has just been chemically

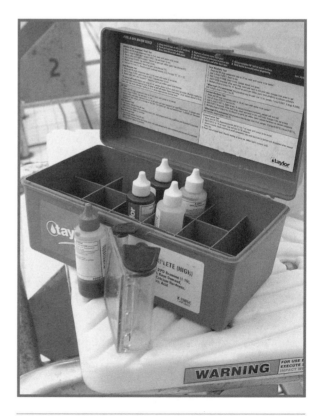

Figure 8.5 A pool test kit.

treated and is not representative of the entire pool. Likewise, the water at the surface contains a high concentration of body oils, which will skew the results. Once you have your sample, add the test reagents as directed in the kit instructions. If your kit uses liquid drops, do not place the dropper bottle in the sample vial because you will contaminate the sample. Hold the dropper directly over the top of the sample vial and squeeze out even drops. If your test kit uses tablets, tear open the pouch and do not touch the tablet with your hands because your body oils will get on the tablet and alter the test.

After you've added the reagent to the vial, secure the cap on top and shake the vial to evenly mix the sample. Do not cap the vial with your finger, because your body chemistry will alter the test results. Next, compare the color of your sample against the color comparator by holding the sample and comparator up to the light. Direct sunlight is best for reading test results, followed by incandescent light and fluorescent light (in that order). When you have completed your test, record your results and discard your sample into the drain, not the pool. Discarding test samples in the pool contributes to the buildup of solids and just plain makes the water taste bad to the swimmers. If possible, water testing should be delegated to aquatic facility operations staff who have facility maintenance and cleanliness as their primary expertise and duties. If this is not an option for your facility, try to assign this duty to senior staff who have more experience with facility operations.

Although more expensive than commonly used test kits, minicomputers with digital readouts of pH are available. These palm-sized devices require the operator to put a probe in the pool water and take the reading off the miniscreen. If you're thinking about purchasing one of these, you should consider if the cost will be offset by the ease and accuracy. Variants of this model are pen shaped and require the operator to place the nib end of the "pen" into a test cup of water. Some of these automatic test systems can also perform tests for total dissolved solids and **oxidation-reduction potential (ORP).**

Newer pools often contain "test sinks" or nozzles on the pool's circulation pipes that are located in the filter room (see figure 8.6). The thought is that the water in the test sinks will be representative of the total volume of water in the pool. It's often easier to take tests at these sinks because you are not in the flow of traffic on the pool deck

Figure 8.6   The filter room at an aquatic facility.

and do not have to worry about where to dispose of your test water when complete. If you doubt your readings from the test sink, take an additional sample from the main body of pool water.

WATER CHEMISTRY

Clear and sanitary swimming pool water depends on several interrelated factors: disinfectant (most commonly chlorine or bromine), pH, alkalinity, **calcium hardness,** and total dissolved solids. These factors are interconnected, and adjustment of one factor will affect the others as well as the overall operation of the pool. You should make adjustments to water chemistry in small increments over time. Radical changes to water chemistry can cause unwanted extreme changes such as drastic rises in disinfectant level and drastic rises or drops in pH.

Disinfection

Disinfection refers to maintaining the water in a disease and bacteria free state. The most commonly used chemicals for disinfection are chlorine and bromine, which are explored in some detail in this

A lifeguard performs a water chemistry test.

chlorine. Free chlorine and combined chlorine are added together to indicate total chlorine.

Gas (Elemental) Chlorine

Gas chlorine, or **elemental chlorine,** is the most cost-effective form of disinfection available for swimming pools. Gas chlorine is 99.9 percent actual chlorine, meaning you are not paying for other chemical additives that may adversely affect your water chemistry and don't assist in killing bacteria.

Gas chlorine is packaged in spun cylinder containers with the gas stored under pressure in the cylinder as a greenish liquid. The chlorine resumes its gaseous form when emitted from the cylinder. A scale and feeder system allows the gas to be fed through tubing from the container directly into the pool's circulation return lines (see figure 8.7). The scale indicates how much chlorine remains in the tank, so you can estimate when the tanks will need to be changed. Gas chlorine is sold by weight.

The use of gaseous chlorine requires some safety measures. Chlorine gas is a deadly poison that could cause widespread illness and death if the canisters were ruptured. However, this eventuality is rare and unlikely if the canisters are handled properly. Use of chlorine gas is outlawed

section. Although other forms of disinfection are available—such as iodine, dichloroisocyanurates, silver salts, ozone, and chlorine generation—their market share is dwarfed by chlorine and bromine. Failure to maintain the proper disinfection of your aquatic facility can result in the transmission of disease to your swimmers.

Chlorine

Chlorine is the most popular chemical on the market for the disinfection of swimming pools. The reason is simple: You can't beat the cost and reliability. Chlorine is available for use in either solid, liquid, or gas form. Chlorine is an excellent bactericide, algaecide, and oxidizer. The amount of chlorine present in water is measured in parts per million (PPM). Most states require a minimum of 1.0 free chlorine (chlorine that has not yet bonded with any other ions in the water and is available to destroy bacteria). A level of 2.0 to 2.5 PPM of free chlorine provides ample amounts of chlorine to kill bacteria and algae. You should be aware that very high levels of chlorine in the water can be hazardous to swimmers. Pool water with chlorine above 3.0 PPM should not be swum in. Chlorine that has bonded with other chemicals in the water and is unavailable for killing bacteria is called combined

© Steven Jahnke

Figure 8.7   Chlorine gas apparatus.

in some states; you should review your state bathing code when considering the use of this system to make sure it is allowed in your state. Many state legislatures have become afraid of chlorine gas due to the fear of poisoning a large number of people if an unexpected and uncontained leak of poisonous chlorine gas ever occurred. However, chlorine gas is perfectly safe for use at aquatic facilities provided safety precautions are taken, such as the following:

▶ Chlorine gas canisters should never be lifted by the valve or bonnet. Use a dolly or hand truck to move the canisters.

▶ Chlorine gas canisters should be chained against the wall while stored or in use.

▶ The chlorinators and chlorine gas should be stored in a separate room that has a continuously running fan. If a gas canister leaks, a buildup of gas will not occur in the chlorine gas room. (Chlorinators are devices used to inject the chlorine gas into the water return lines, which will carry the chlorinated water to the pool.)

▶ A self-contained breathing apparatus (SCBA) should be available for staff use. Your staff can don the SCBA to enter the chlorine room and shut off the chlorinator in an emergency. Although other types of breathing devices are available, the SCBA is the most desirable. The SCBA should not be stored in the chlorine room, but in an adjacent area, readily accessible in the event of an emergency.

Liquid Chlorine (Sodium Hypochlorite)

Liquid chlorine, or **sodium hypochlorite,** can be purchased in bulk (packaged in barrels) or in smaller quantities (packaged in gallon bottles). This is the least cost effective of all the forms of chlorine. Liquid chlorine contains no more than 16 percent actual chlorine by volume. This means that you are paying for a large volume of other chemicals that you don't want.

Liquid chlorine is most effectively fed into the circulation system through the use of a chlorine feeder placed on top of a barrel. Periodically, the feeder should be removed and cleaned to prevent the buildup of calcium from impairing the feeder function. The plastic tubing attaching the feeder to the circulation line should similarly be cleaned by running muriatic acid through it.

Liquid chlorine can be hand-fed into the pool if chlorine levels need to be raised quickly due to high bather loads or high heat. However, hand-feeding cannot be used in place of a chlorinator; all state bathing codes require the use of an automatic

disinfection device. If you do add chlorine directly to the pool, ensure that no swimmers are in the water because they may be burned by exposure to the partially diluted chemical. Chemicals added directly to the pool should be poured in front of the recirculation return inlets to allow for even distribution of the chlorine throughout the water.

Even if you don't use liquid chlorine as the primary form of disinfection at your facility, you should always keep several bottles on hand. You can use liquid chlorine to disinfect floors and pool fixtures (e.g., diving boards and starting blocks).

Keep the following safety tips in mind when handling liquid chlorine:

▶ Store liquid chlorine in a cool, dry place away from direct sunlight. The chlorine content of sodium hypochlorite dissipates if it is exposed to direct sunlight or high heat.

▶ Don't store liquid chlorine bottles in an area where they can be exposed to cold temperatures. The plastic bottles become brittle in the cold and can easily shatter when handled, creating a splash hazard for staff and patrons alike.

▶ Always store liquid chlorine in its original container with the label clearly visible.

▶ Do not store liquid chlorine on shelves above other chemicals. If the container leaks, it will drip onto other chemicals, potentially creating toxic fumes or other hazards.

▶ Do not mix chlorine with other chemicals for application to the pool because it may cause toxic fumes, explosions, or fires.

▶ Always wear safety goggles, rubber aprons, rubber gloves, and shoes or boots when handling liquid chlorine. Bare skin can be burned when in direct contact with liquid chlorine.

Granular Chlorine (Calcium Hypochlorite)

Calcium hypochlorite is a granular form of chlorine normally sold in barrels. Granular chlorine is 65 percent chlorine by weight. Although granular chlorine is more cost effective than liquid sodium hypochlorite, it does add unwanted chemicals to your water that are necessary to stabilize the granular chlorine in its solid form.

To ensure that granular chlorine is applied as effectively as possible, you should mix it with water in a plastic barrel (with a tight-fitting lid) using a slurry feeder. A slurry feeder is a small motor that attaches to the top of the barrel and has a rod protruding from it into the mixture. The rod agitates the mixture so that the granular chlorine doesn't settle to the bottom but instead creates an even mixture. The nonchlorine particulate matter is not dissolved in the water and settles out because it is heavier. This creates a highly concentrated chlorine mixture. Allow the calcium present in this mixture to settle out; then draw off the liquid into a second barrel using plastic tubing. Pump the chlorine-rich mixture from the second barrel into the circulation return lines using a chemical feeder. If you do not allow the calcium to settle out, it will begin to build up in the circulation pipes, reducing flow and impairing the function of your circulation and filtration system.

Granular chlorine can be hand-fed directly into the pool in an emergency if needed. High temperatures and heavy bather loads can rapidly deplete free chlorine available to fight bacteria. This is particularly common at outdoor facilities during summer months. In situations such as these, automatic chlorinators are often unable to keep up with the demand. If granular chlorine is added directly, it should be mixed with water and siphoned into the pool after the sediment has settled out. As with liquid chlorine, you should not add granular chlorine directly to the pool while swimmers are in the water; the undiluted chemical may poison the swimmers if swallowed, or burn them when in contact with exposed skin. Pour the granular chlorine mixture in front of circulation return jets to help ensure even distribution of the mixture throughout the pool. Allow 1 hour for circulation before swimmers are permitted to return to the pool.

Keep the following safety tips in mind when handling granular chlorine:

▶ Store the chemical in a cool, well-ventilated, and dry place. This will prevent the buildup of noxious fumes and the combustion of the barrels.

▶ Store the chemical in its original container with the label clearly visible.

▶ Use the measuring scoop that came with the barrel for its intended purpose (many companies include plastic scoops with the barrel). Do not substitute paper cups or other devices. Calcium hypochlorite burns and explodes when it comes into contact with organic substances such as paper or sweat.

▶ Store the chlorine barrels on pallets in your storage room. This will eliminate rusting of the barrels due to standing water on the floors.

▶ Ensure that lids and restraining bands are in place on the barrels when the calcium hypochlorite is not in use. This will cut down on dust drift, which is very irritating to the lungs.

▶ Ensure that workers always wear eye and respiratory protection when handling granular chlorine directly.

Calcium hypochlorite can make an excellent cleaning solution for decks and swimming pool fixtures. Mixing a small amount of calcium hypochlorite with water creates a strong chlorine solution that is great for killing algae and mold. Be sure to wear gloves when using calcium hypochlorite in this way.

Super Chlorination and Breakpoint Chlorination

Super chlorination and breakpoint chlorination are often mistakenly thought to be the same. Super chlorination involves the use of a concentrated chlorine agent to raise the chlorine level rapidly to 5.0 to 6.0 PPM. This is often used when filling the pool to rapidly destroy bacteria and algae with high chlorine concentration. The chlorine level is then allowed to settle to an acceptable 2.0 PPM before swimmers are permitted back into the pool.

As chlorine is added to the pool over time, more and more chlorine combines with chemical compounds in the water, creating a condition called "chlorine lock." Chlorine that is locked into solution is ineffective at killing bacteria and algae. Breakpoint chlorination raises the chlorine level to 7.0 to 10.0 PPM, which oxidizes organic compounds and releases combined chlorine from solution, returning it to free chlorine.

Hydantonin Bromine

Hydantonin bromine is sold as a brown stick when used as a swimming pool disinfectant. Bromine is often touted as the alternative to chlorine. Some swimmers object to the smell of chlorine or have allergies to it. However, some swimmers also have allergies to bromine. Bromine is good at killing bacteria and algae. It is not, however, as cost effective as using chlorine. Despite some possible drawbacks in its use, bromine is as effective as chlorine as a disinfectant.

Bromine is applied to the pool by placing the stick in a receptacle in the return line, where it erodes away slowly, gradually feeding into the pool. The bromine stick must erode evenly to be effective. There is no mechanism to hand-feed bromine directly into the pool. Bromine cannot be used as a direct cleaning agent as can calcium hypochlorite and sodium hypochlorite.

Disadvantages to using bromine include that it may stain the pool basin brown and that the water may exhibit a greenish tint. Bromine is also usually more expensive to purchase than chlorine.

> **KEY POINT** *There are a variety of methods that you can use to disinfect your pool. Most disinfectants are derivatives of chlorine or, less common, bromine. When selecting the type that's best for your facility, focus on safety, effectiveness, and cost.*

pH

pH is an abbreviation for potens hydrogen, which stands for potential hydrogen. pH is not a substance that can be added to the pool; it is a measure of the acidic or basic (alkaline) nature of water (or any substance for that matter). The pH of water is measured on a scale from 0 to 14 (see figure 8.8). Water measuring 0 to 6.9 is considered acidic, and water from 7.1 to 14 is considered basic. Water with a pH of 7.0 is considered neutral.

Most state bathing codes require swimming pool water pH to be maintained between 7.2 and 7.8. You can determine the pH of your pool water through regular testing using water samples, reagents, and comparison against a color comparator. The pH test is included in most standard water tests. Outside of this required pH range, water will be irritating to swimmers' eyes and skin and will be much more likely to transmit disease. The ideal pH range for swimmer comfort and for maximizing the effects of disinfectant is 7.4 to 7.6. Maintaining pool water in this range will also assist in regulating other aspects of water chemistry, such as alkalinity and hardness.

You can regulate the pH of your water through the use of two main chemicals: soda ash to raise it and muriatic acid to lower it. Soda ash **(sodium carbonate)** is a grayish powder that is sold by the bag and is very chemically similar to baking soda. Muriatic acid is a liquid that can also be used to clean piping and tubes for chemical feeders.

You need to know the natural pH of the water you use to fill your pool. If your pool water is coming out of the tap above or below the ideal range, you may adjust it through the continuous addition of muriatic acid or soda ash. These chemicals are added directly into the return line from a barrel using a chemical feeder.

Total Alkalinity

Total alkalinity is a combination of materials such as carbonates, bicarbonates, and hydroxides. Total alkalinity reflects water's resistance to change in pH. You must balance the alkaline nature of your pool water. Rapid changes in pH occur when alkalinity is too low. The pH of pool water can be difficult to adjust when alkalinity is too high. High alkalinity may also cause water to corrode metal surfaces. You can raise the alkalinity of your pool water through the addition of sodium bicarbonate, and you can lower it through the addition of sodium bisulfate or muriatic acid. The acceptable range for total alkalinity is 100 to 150 PPM. Most comprehensive swimming pool test kits contain a test for total alkalinity.

Calcium Hardness

Calcium hardness indicates the amount of dissolved calcium in water. The target level of calcium hardness for your swimming pool should be 250 PPM. Low calcium hardness in water will cause calcium to be drawn out of surfaces such as copings and walls, which will pit and weaken the surface. High calcium hardness will cause a buildup of calcium deposits on pipes and pool fixtures and will also cause cloudy water. Calcium hardness may be raised through the addition of calcium chloride and lowered through the addition of anhydrous trisodium phosphate.

Total Dissolved Solids

Total dissolved solids (TDS) refers to the buildup of dirt, body oil, urine, hair spray, perfume, lotion, sunscreen, and cosmetics that are left in the water by swimmers. If you could evaporate all the water out of a pool, you would be left with a pile of debris that would be TDS. Total dissolved solids build up over time; one way to slow down the buildup is to ensure that all swimmers take showers with soap

```
|------------------------------------|------------|------------------------------|
0.0 Acidic                      7.0 Neutral                      14.0 Basic
                  [Ideal pH range for swimming: 7.4-7.6]
```

Figure 8.8 The pH scale.

before entering the pool. This removes much of the dirt, cosmetics, and body oil before they enter the pool. High TDS creates an unpleasant odor and taste to your pool water. High TDS also makes chemical adjustment of pool water difficult.

You should test for TDS weekly and record your results. Separate test kits are normally required, because many kits do not include this function. A total dissolved solids reading of 2,000 PPM or above requires the pool to be drained and refilled. This will eliminate unpleasant odors and tastes and will allow for proper chemical balancing of pool water. To prevent your pool from reaching this point, you can drain off some water and refill with makeup water. Makeup water is water drawn from the local water supply by hose or pipe and is used to replace pool water lost through leaks, evaporation, and splash out. You must add additional chemicals to disinfect makeup water, and you must heat the new water to the desired temperature. Because of these factors, you should try to only add makeup water at night when the pool is closed, giving you hours to get the pool chemically balanced and properly heated before swimmers arrive in the morning. Although this does not totally eliminate the TDS problem, it will reduce the amount.

Regulation of Swimming Pool Chemicals

States vary widely in their regulation of swimming pool chemicals. Some states, such as Pennsylvania, strictly regulate who can apply chemicals and how it must be done. Some states prohibit the use of gas chlorine because of perceived safety concerns.

Many swimming pool chemicals, such as chlorine and muriatic acid, are considered hazardous materials (HAZMAT). As such they must be properly placarded during transport as regulated by the U.S. Department of Transportation. If an appreciable quantity of hazardous pool chemical is spilled, you must report it to the National Response Center (NRC; see appendix A) at 800-424-8802. The NRC is staffed 24 hours a day and 7 days a week. You must file reports within 24 hours of a spill. Be prepared to provide the name of the chemical, amount spilled, spill location, your information as reporting party, and the number of injuries, fatalities, and evacuations as a result of the spill. The NRC will notify all other necessary parties, such as the Environmental Protection Agency (EPA; see appendix A) and your state EPA.

DISEASE TRANSMISSION

If they are not maintained properly, swimming pools and open water facilities can be an opportunity for patrons to contract a range of infectious diseases. Some diseases that can be contracted from a swimming pool or waterfront include the following:

▶ **Giardia.** Giardia is a parasite that causes giardiasis, a gastrointestinal illness. The bacteria enters the pool through fecal matter introduced into poorly disinfected water. It takes up to 10 days for symptoms to appear after **ingestion.** Symptoms include diarrhea, gas, bloating, weight loss, fatigue, and fever. To determine if giardia is in the pool, take water samples to a state or private laboratory. If you suspect giardia in the pool, remove fecal matter and perform super chlorination. Do not allow swimmers in the pool for at least 30 minutes. If the fecal matter is loose and watery, close the pool and allow the water to turn over three or four times. Superchlorinate and allow the water to return to normal.

▶ **Legionella.** Legionella is a rod-shaped bacterium that causes bronchial diseases (contracted through airborne droplets). Symptoms include body aches, headaches, diarrhea, fatigue, stomach cramps, cough, and weight loss. To determine if Legionella is in the pool, take water samples to a state or private laboratory. Spas are good transmitters because spa jets can aerosolize the bacteria. Super chlorination will kill Legionella, but disinfection of filters is necessary. The spa will need to be drained and disinfected.

▶ **Escherichia coli (E. coli).** This is coliform bacteria living in the digestive tracts of humans and animals. Swimmers who swallow contaminated water can contract the disease. Symptoms include severe, bloody diarrhea, abdominal cramps, and fever. The bacteria enter the pool through fecal matter introduced into poorly disinfected water. To determine if it's in the pool, take water samples to a state or private laboratory. If you suspect E. coli in the pool, remove fecal matter and perform super chlorination. Do not allow swimmers in the pool for at least 30 minutes. If the fecal matter is loose and watery, close the pool and allow the water to turn over three or four times. Superchlorinate and allow the water to return to normal.

▶ **Pseudomonas aeruginosa.** This bacterium is found in human skin and gastrointestinal tracts. Symptoms include a red, itchy rash, flulike symptoms, coughing, sore throat, urinary tract infections, and nausea. The bacteria are passed through the skin, nose, throat, and feces of infected individuals. To determine if it's in the pool, take water samples to a state or private laboratory. Super chlorination will remove the infection.

▶ **Cryptosporidium.** Cryptosporidium is a protozoan parasite that can live in human and animal intestines. Effects of "crypto" include diarrhea, upset stomach, cramps, and fever. Transmission occurs through fecal matter in the water. Crypto is particularly resistant to chlorine as a pesticide. The parasite's strong outer shell makes it all but impervious to normal swimming pool disinfectant levels. If you suspect it's in your pool, take a water sample to a state or private laboratory. For confirmed or suspected crypto contamination, remove swimmers from the pool, remove fecal matter, and perform super chlorination. If the fecal matter is loose and watery, close the pool and allow the water to turn over three or four times. Superchlorinate and allow the water to return to normal.

▶ **Cercarial dermatitis.** This illness is commonly known as "swimmer's itch" and is usually contracted at outdoor facilities. It is caused by parasites released into the water through the feces of infected animals and birds. Symptoms may include tingling, burning, or itching skin that may develop into pimples or blisters. Swimming pools with adequate amounts of disinfectant are at low risk for carrying this disease. Patrons who contract this illness may receive relief from cool compresses and baking soda paste applied to the rash. The parasitic infection of the pool can be eliminated through super chlorination.

▶ **Nagleria.** Nagleria is an illness caused by an amoeba found in warm bodies of fresh water, including swimming pools with no chlorine. Although rare, this illness can cause death if untreated. Symptoms include headache, fever, stiff neck, vomiting, and confusion. Maintaining swimming pool disinfection within state bathing code limits can prevent the outbreak of this illness in your facility.

Note that the introduction of fecal matter into the pool is a major factor in many of the waterborne diseases just described. There are several things that you can do to guard against these and other **recreational water illnesses (RWIs),** as they are referred to by the Centers for Disease Control and Prevention:

▶ Maintain water disinfectant or sanitizer at 1.2 to 2.5 parts per million.

▶ Require all children who are not toilet trained to wear swim diapers or tight-fitting plastic pants.

▶ Regularly backwash sand and gravel filters.

▶ Enforce the shower before swimming rule required by most state bathing codes.

▶ Prohibit entry to the pool of any swimmers who have experienced symptoms of diarrhea in the previous 2 weeks. This is a difficult rule to enforce. In reality, the best you can do is post the appropriate sign; you should not question swimmers about this issue.

The possibility of contracting the HIV/AIDS virus in a swimming pool is a concern for many. However, the HIV virus is not hardy and does not survive well outside the body. Normal levels of swimming pool disinfectant would easily kill the virus.

> **KEY POINT** *There are a lot of really nasty diseases that can be carried by, and contracted in, swimming pool water. However, you can drastically reduce the potential for disease transmission by simply maintaining water chemistry, such as pH and disinfectant, within the levels set by your state bathing code.*

WATER TEMPERATURE

Water temperature is a source of constant debate among pool user groups. Swim team coaches tend to want the water at a cooler temperature; seniors and children's groups tend to want warmer water; and lap swimmers tend to want something between the two. As a pool operator, you should attempt to find the middle ground, realizing who your primary constituent group is and that for each degree you raise your pool water you are spending money.

For general pool use, 80 or 81 degrees Fahrenheit is a good compromise temperature among groups. It is a bit cold for children and a bit warm for the teams, but not unmanageably so for either. However, pools that mainly serve people with arthritis or therapy patients should be as warm as 84 to 86 degrees. Any cooler and the users' muscles will lock up, making use of the pool impossible. Post your water temperature on a blackboard in your facility each day. It may be helpful to explain to some of your user groups that water temperature for volumes the size of swimming pools takes days to raise or lower a single degree and that adjustment on short notice is not possible. You should never alter your water temperature if you can avoid it. It is simply too costly and makes it more difficult to adjust water chemistry.

Temperatures of 88 degrees and above represent a significant change in the way water reacts to chemical treatment. Swimming pools should not be heated to this point because they essentially become large hot tubs, with corresponding significant changes in water chemistry. Pool water temperature should not be kept below 75 degrees at the coolest. Most swimmers find any temperature below 80 degrees to be too cool.

LANGLIER SATURATION INDEX

The langlier saturation index is a formula that utilizes pH, temperature, alkalinity, and hardness to give you a picture of the corrosiveness of your pool water. Values on the scale are given between –3 and +3. A saturation index (SI) reading of zero is considered perfect because it indicates that your pool is neither building up calcium deposits on pipes and fixtures nor being eroded by acidic water. Readings below zero indicate corrosiveness that eventually will devour pumps, motors, and fixtures. A saturation index reading above zero indicates the buildup of calcium deposits on pipes and fixtures; if not corrected, this could eventually cause the pipes to become totally plugged, resulting in a burnout of the pump and motor from lack of water. A saturation index in the range of –0.5 to +0.5 is considered acceptable.

Adjustments to water chemistry can be made based on the results given from the saturation index. You should run the saturation index on your pool weekly and record the results. Adjustments to raise or lower the langlier saturation index are dependent on the readings. For example, if you want to raise pH, you'll add soda ash; lowering the pH will require muriatic acid. Changes in temperature will require reducing or lowering water temperature by adjusting the boiler. See appendix D for a langlier saturation index worksheet.

COMMON WATER PROBLEMS

As a swimming pool operator or manager, you can encounter many water problems. When considering possible factors that may have affected water chemistry, remember this: Everything affects water chemistry. Your first step when confronted

with a problem should normally be to perform a comprehensive water chemistry test, including the langlier saturation index. Test for temperature, disinfectant, calcium hardness, alkalinity, pH, and total dissolved solids. After you have tested and analyzed these elements, you can begin to take action. If you determine that the problem is chemistry related and not mechanical, make your chemical adjustments gradually and in small increments to avoid causing wild unwanted changes in water chemistry. A list of common problems and their potential causes follows.

> **KEY POINT** *Many factors affect the water chemistry of your pool, including pH, alkalinity, hardness, temperature, and disinfectant. But you can sum it all up in one question and answer: What affects water chemistry? Everything.*

▶ **Turbid (cloudy) water.** If the pool has a vacuum diatomaceous earth filter, a tear in the filter cover may cause DE to leak into the water, causing cloudiness. The water will appear clear when the pool is empty. The DE will be stirred up when there are swimmers in the pool, and this will cause **turbid** water. Vacuum the DE from the bottom of the pool and replace the damaged filter cover while the filter is shut down. Other causes of cloudy water may include high TDS, high calcium hardness, and pH that is out of the proper range. Acid rain can also drop ash into the pool and cause turbidity. Vacuuming the ash off the bottom should remove the problem.

▶ **Swimmer eye or skin irritation.** This may be caused by a pH level that is too low or too high. The disinfectant level may also be too high. Run pH and disinfectant tests on the pool and adjust accordingly.

▶ **Colored water.** Water can take on any number of colors: green, red, brown, blue. Causes may include metals in the pool water (copper for brown, iron for yellow, manganese for purple and black) from rust in the pipes entering the water. Try to determine the cause of the metals in the water, and adjust pH to the ideal range. Consider the use of a metal sequestering agent. Too much metal content in pool water can cause discolored pool water and staining of the pool basin. To prevent this, a sequestering agent is used to "buffer" the metal ions so that they don't cause staining and discoloration. (See appendix C for suppliers of sequestering agents.)

▸ **Difficulty in adjusting pH.** This may be due to high alkalinity. Run the appropriate test, and lower alkalinity through the use of sodium bisulfate.

▸ **Rapid changes in pH.** This is normally due to low alkalinity. Run an alkalinity test, and add sodium bicarbonate if necessary.

▸ **Difficulty maintaining disinfectant in the pool water.** This may be due to an old or expired product, high heat and humidity "burning off" the product, high bather load, or a malfunctioning chlorinator (or brominator). Check dates on chemicals and check the attachments on the chlorinator. Add liquid chlorine directly to the pool while empty.

▸ **Algae.** Algae is a slimy organic substance that commonly appears in swimming pools. Algae can make water cloudy and pool surfaces slippery. It can appear in black, red, or green forms. Algae growth is promoted by hot weather, sunlight, and a low level of disinfectant. Algae can be controlled through sufficient amounts of disinfectant. For spot cleaning of algae, use liquid chlorine applied directly to the spot or mix granular chlorine with water and scrub affected surfaces.

POOL OPERATOR TRAINING

The quality of the operation of your aquatic facility is partly dependent on the training that your pool operations staff receives and the expertise that they develop. Although a certain amount of knowledge can be gained through on-the-job training, formalized instruction is required to ensure that your staff members are fully aware of all regulations and codes as well as technical information not covered in on-the-job training. There are a number of agencies that offer pool operations training. The agency that you choose should be based on the needs of your staff. Here is a list of some of the agencies that offer pool operations training as well as a description of their courses (see appendix A for contact information):

▸ **National Recreation and Parks Association (NRPA): Aquatic Facility Operator (AFO) course.** The AFO certification course is a training program specifically designed to meet the needs of those working in public, semipublic, and municipal pool or water park facilities. The AFO program offers a unique discussion of risk management, which is not usually directed toward operations personnel. The course is designed to provide information and training for both supervisory and operations personnel. Course length is 2 days. (Course description taken from NRPA Web site.)

▸ **National Swimming Pool Foundation (NSPF): Certified Pool Operator (CPO) course.** This course covers pool and spa chemistry, testing, treatment, filtration, maintenance, automatic feeding equipment, government requirements, and many other areas related to pool and spa maintenance. After completion of the 16 hours of classroom instruction, the candidate must successfully pass an open-book, written exam. NSPF CPO certification is valid for 5 years from the date of certification. (Course description taken from the NSPF Web site.)

▸ **YMCA of the USA: Pool Operator On Location (POOL).** This is an 8-hour course specifically designed for YMCA pool operators but open to anyone. It includes information regarding filtration, circulation, water chemistry, aquatic safety, cost reduction, and energy conservation. After successfully completing a standardized multiple-choice test, participants receive a certificate.

▸ **State certification.** Many states require or suggest that a pool operator complete a state sponsored and sanctioned program. The programs vary widely: Illinois offers a self-study program free of charge; Nebraska offers a 4-hour program for a small fee; Pennsylvania offers an 8-hour program that includes certification as a swimming pool pesticide applicator. Some states require that a state-certified pool operator be on duty whenever the pool is open. Check your state bathing code to determine if a state course is available or required in your state, and if a commercial course such as the CPO or AFO is an acceptable substitute.

The courses just described are essential to an understanding of the principles of water chemistry and maintenance as well as the codes, laws, and licenses related to pool operations. However, well-organized and well-developed on-the-job training is also important in preparing a good pool operator. Here are some topics and tasks that you may want to include in your on-the-job training program:

▸ The flow of water through the pipes and filters in your filter room. (Have the employee diagram this water flow.)

▸ Backwash of sand and gravel filters. (Have the employee perform a backwash under the supervision of trained staff.)

▸ Water chemistry tests. (Have the employee perform tests under the supervision of trained staff.)

► Use of personal protective equipment such as SCBA, eye protection, gloves, and boots. (Discuss and then let the employee practice with the equipment.)

► First aid for exposure to chemicals through inhalation, contact with the eye, and ingestion.

► Certification in CPR.

► How to read material safety data sheets.

► The langlier saturation index—what it is and how to use it.

► Safe storage and handling of chemicals.

► Application of swimming pool chemicals.

Plan your training program with the strengths and weaknesses of your particular pool technician in mind. Don't forget to include regular refresher and update training.

SUMMARY

Water chemistry is an essential part of ensuring the health, safety, and comfort of your patrons. To properly regulate the chemistry of your pool, you'll need to understand the principles of filtration and circulation as well as the elements of water chemistry. You must also be able to administer accurate water tests and interpret their results. Performing the langlier saturation index and understanding its results will also help you properly regulate the chemistry of your pool water. Safely storing your pool chemicals will help ensure the safety of your staff and will enable you to operate your pool more efficiently. Properly training your pool operations staff will help to ensure the cleanliness and safety of your facility. Remember, in some states, this training is required; check your state bathing code.

REVIEW QUESTIONS

1. What are the two major types of filter media available for commercial pools?

2. What interrelated factors affect water chemistry in swimming pools?

3. List the chemicals commonly used for swimming pool disinfection.

4. Define the term pH as it applies to swimming pool water.

5. What elements can make up total dissolved solids?

6. List several agencies that offer certification for swimming pool operators.

BIBLIOGRAPHY

Andreotti, P., Osinski, A., Sweazy, J., Tate, C., & Young, R. (1999). Identifying and combatting waterborne diseases. *Aquatics International,* 11(1), 32-34.

Centers for Disease Control. (2003, June 11). *Healthy swimming.* Retrieved November 29, 2003, from Centers for Disease Control Web site: www.cdc.gov/ healthyswimming/fact_sheets.htm#3.

Fawcett, P. (2001). *Aquatic directors' handbook.* Corvallis, OR: National Intramural Recreational Sports Association.

Fawcett, P. (2001). Planning annual facility maintenance. *Parks & Recreation,* 36(11), 46-51.

Fawcett, P. (2001). Proceed with caution: Operators must ensure safe chemical storage and handling. *Aquatics International,* 13(8), 18.

Foster, L.N. (1999). Got pools? Got problems? Get a plan! *Parks & Recreation,* 34(2), 56-66.

Johnson, R. (1994). *YMCA pool operations manual.* Champaign, IL: Human Kinetics.

Johnston, K. (1999). *The encyclopedia of aquatic codes and standards.* Hoffman Estates, IL: NRPA Aquatic Section.

Monahan, P. (2001). The smell tells: Busy indoor parks district and school pool enhances air quality. *Parks & Recreation,* 36(11), 58-62.

National Recreation and Parks Association. (n.d.). AFO Course Content. Retrieved November 4, 2002, from Web site: www.nrpa.org/content/default.aspx?docu mentId=756.

National Swimming Pool Foundation. (n.d.). NSPF Certified Pool/Spa Operator Training. Retrieved November 4, 2002, from Web site: www.nspf.com.

Tamminen, T. (2001). *The ultimate pool maintenance manual: Spas, pools, hot tubs, rockscapes and other features* (2nd ed.). New York: McGraw-Hill.

Williams, K. (1999). *Aquatic facility operations manual.* Ashburn, VA: National Recreation and Parks Association.

RESOURCES

Centers for Disease Control and Prevention Web site: www.cdc.gov.

Chlorine Chemistry Council Web site (provides some excellent information regarding chlorine): www.c3.org/chlorine_knowledge_center/#2.

National Response Center Web site: www.nrc.uscg.mil/ nrchp.html.

U.S. Department of Transportation Office of Hazardous Materials Web site: http://hazmat.dot.gov.

Managing Facility Operations

Chapter Objectives

After reading this chapter, you should be able to

❶ develop security procedures for an aquatic facility,

❷ develop safety and sanitation procedures for an aquatic facility,

❸ develop a chemical safety plan for an aquatic facility,

❹ develop an electrical safety plan for an aquatic facility,

❺ plan for aquatic facility inventory and maintenance, and

❻ create an aquatic facility energy conservation plan.

A well-operated aquatic facility will be clean, efficient, and attractive to patrons. To create these qualities in your facility, you will need to develop operations and maintenance procedures. You must then implement these procedures in your facility. This chapter includes information regarding general cleaning, chemical and electrical safety, equipment inventory and maintenance, and energy conservation.

Cleaning and maintenance are everyday, all-the-time activities. If you let them slide even briefly, your facility can become a very dirty and unpleasant place to be. The key is to plan and organize tasks so that you're spending more time accomplishing the right task at the right time instead of reacting to cleanliness emergencies and complaints as they arise. To help you do this, this chapter lays out tasks that need to be conducted daily, weekly, monthly, and yearly. Sample checklists are provided to make your planning process easier and faster.

As an aquatic specialist, you're probably well aware of safety issues such as enforcing rules and making remedial rescues. But have you thought about electrical and chemical safety? Water and electricity don't mix well, and yet you need that electricity on your deck to power your stereos, lights, and speakers. The trick is to have the electricity and water coexist safely. You'll need to understand some specific electrical safety procedures and how to apply them. This chapter includes sections that will help you with that.

The chapter also covers chemical safety. Chemicals are everywhere in an aquatic environment. They are used for cleaning the pool deck, washing towels, killing weeds, and disinfecting the pool water. But many chemicals don't mix well with each other, and even combined fumes can be deadly. Improper use and storage of your chemicals can spell disaster for your staff. This chapter helps you by explaining proper marking, storage, and application methods, as well as the required personal protective equipment for your staff.

Inventory plans are also discussed in this chapter. You've spent a lot of money purchasing equipment for your facility, everything from lawn mowers to pool toys. To protect your investment, you need to know what you've got versus what you're supposed to have, and you need to know what shape it's all in. An inventory plan helps you answer these questions. This chapter guides you through the process.

SECURITY

You must maintain security of your facility for several reasons. Your facility will be attractive to persons who would like to swim even when you're not open. Maintaining security helps prevent drowning by keeping these uninvited guests out. Facility security also helps prevent after-hours theft of facility equipment and supplies and reduces incidents of vandalism. No security program is foolproof, but you can close gaps in your security screen by taking proactive steps.

> **KEY POINT** *Your facility is an investment. You need to take steps to protect it, including fencing, alarms, or security cameras.*

If your facility is outdoors, it should be fenced. The minimum standard for fencing at swimming pools is a 6-foot (182.9-centimeter) minimum height fence, with 8 feet (243.8 centimeters) preferable (Gabrielsen, 1987). However, a 7-foot (213.4-centimeter) fence or higher provides a much greater deterrence against unauthorized entry. Fences should be secured to the ground so that they cannot be easily crawled under. Fence gates should be secured with a lock when not in use. A self-closing, self-latching gate will close on its own each time the gate is reopened. This provides an added measure of security by ensuring that the fence gate is always closed. You should have your staff make regular fence checks to ensure that the fence has not been cut or otherwise tampered with.

If your aquatic facility is indoors, you should control access by limiting it to as few doors as possible. All doors leading to the pool should be locked when the pool is not open for business. Keys to these locks should be issued to manage-

ment level personnel only. Lifeguards should sign keys out for use or have the pool opened for them by management. If you issue keys to anyone other than facility management, you run the risk of the pool being used when it is unsupervised. A drowning or other injury may be the result. Emergency exits at indoor facilities should open from the inside only. Panic bars should be placed on these doors. All emergency exits should be labeled with a glow-in-the-dark exit sign.

Preferably, windows at indoor aquatic facilities will not open at all. Opening windows violates the building's environmental envelope, expels heat, and reduces ventilation effectiveness, which means you're wasting heat, not to mention money. Windows that open also create another opportunity for unauthorized entry. Windows that do open should be secured shut at the close of business each day.

Another mechanism that you can use to secure your facility is alarm systems. Alarms provide an electronic barrier that sends out an audible or silent signal when breached. The purpose of the audible alarm is to scare away intruders and draw attention to the scene. Silent alarms send their signal only to police or security forces with the goal of not alerting the intruders so that they can be caught. Alarms are often active only at night or other hours when the aquatic facility is closed. To be active, an alarm usually must be "armed" by an employee as she is leaving the facility; the alarm must then be deactivated by returning employees when they enter the facility. Although alarm systems are expensive, they do provide a measure of protection for the large investment you have made in your facility.

Closed-circuit security cameras are a method that is gaining increased popularity in indoor aquatic facilities. In this security system, cameras are mounted in the swimming pool area, in hallways, at entry points, and at cash transaction points. (Cameras are never placed in locker rooms or rest rooms.) All cameras feed into a central viewing point where they are also recorded on a continuously running tape. The camera viewers can be set up with the feeds from all cameras shown on a split-view screen or to cycle between each camera showing greater detail. Cameras can also be set to move or "pan." Recording tapes generally run for 24 hours and are then replaced with a new tape. You should save tapes for a minimum of a week in case you determine there is material on a tape that you need to access. Tapes can only be viewed on a special viewer. Although video surveillance systems are expensive, they provide a deterrent against illegal activity. You can also use these tapes as evidence against vandals, thieves, and violent criminals.

If your facility has large open areas such as beaches, waterfronts, and parking lots, you may want to consider the installation of emergency call boxes. Emergency call boxes are direct dial telephones mounted on lighted poles situated on walkways and parking lots. Picking up the receiver directly connects the caller to the police without dialing. These items are particularly useful after dark in locations where patrons may immediately need assistance.

You should have a standardized checklist for your staff to complete at the opening and closing of business each day. These checklists should direct your staff to check all equipment, the pool itself, and entrances and exits. The purpose is to determine if the facility is ready for operations in the morning and is secured at night. Checklists should include a section to note problems or needs. Your staff should be directed to report any immediate concerns—such as broken equipment, improper lighting, or doors unable to be secured—to management or maintenance staff. All completed opening and closing checklists should be retained for at least a month. A supervisor should check each day to ensure that these forms are being completed. See appendix D for a sample opening and closing checklist.

SAFETY AND SANITATION PROCEDURES

If your facility is not cleaned regularly, you run the risk of disease transmission. You can also expect a drop in attendance and revenue, because patrons will not want to visit an odorous and unsightly facility. You should develop a daily and weekly cleaning schedule to be carried out by your staff. You need to be very specific in identifying what items must be cleaned, what chemical solutions must be used to clean them, and when it must be done. Preferably, the majority of your cleaning will take place when the patrons are not in the facility so that their activities will not be disrupted. You should avoid cleaning the pool deck when the pool is open because this creates a slip hazard. To maintain cleanliness, some cleaning will have to be carried out while customers are in the facility.

> **KEY POINT** *You'll need a systematic plan for regular daily, weekly, and annual maintenance and cleaning. If you don't have a plan, your facility will quickly deteriorate, and your patrons will go elsewhere.*

Daily Cleaning

Daily cleaning should consist of those items essential for the prevention of disease, elimination of odors, and general cleanliness. Schedule your cleaning activities for either before the facility has opened or after it has closed. You may want to create a checklist (particularly if your staff is junior level) so that you are assured all tasks have been completed. Assign a supervisor to assess cleanliness at the beginning of each day to determine the readiness of your facility for business. It's also a good idea to have regular inspections of rest rooms and locker rooms throughout the day to see if replacement of supplies or spot cleaning is required. One way that you can institute this is to have the lifeguard coming off rotation walk through the appropriate sex locker room before proceeding to his or her break or other duties. This spot check will help catch spills, plumbing problems, and other maintenance issues early—before they become large problems. Regular and periodic staff presence in your locker rooms also helps reduce opportunities for theft and other mischief to occur. You can also task maintenance staff, security personnel, program staff, or management personnel to assist with these spot checks. You may want to ask each employee to do one walk-through per day to spread the effort and to get different perspectives. Each person viewing your facility will see something different. Appendix D contains a sample daily cleaning checklist.

Weekly Cleaning

Weekly cleaning should focus on items that are not essential to the daily operational cleanliness of the facility but must be cleaned periodically to ensure that they remain clean. (See appendix D for a sample weekly cleaning checklist.) You can schedule weekly duties so that a few are done each day or schedule them all on one day. If you schedule them all on one day, you should have extra cleaning staff on that day, because both weekly and daily tasks will need to be done.

Annual Cleaning and Maintenance

You should drain your swimming pool and perform heavy maintenance and cleaning each year if possible. (The exception to this rule is during years of drought, when you should not drain the pool to help conserve water.) Although you can buy swimming pool water that is prefiltered and pretreated with chemicals, in most cases water is drawn directly from the local water supply and fed into the pool through existing stand pipes or through fire and garden hoses fed into the pool. Failure to drain and clean regularly can lead to a buildup of total dissolved solids in the water, which can cause an unpleasant taste, feel, and smell. It can also make water chemistry difficult to regulate. Over time, if the pool is not drained and repaired for several years, the basin can become stained and develop cracks and leaks.

Before performing your annual maintenance, you should develop a maintenance schedule and plan. Involve your pool operators, aquatic management, and senior facility management in the scheduling process. When selecting a time of year to carry out the maintenance, consider major events that are scheduled. Collect swim meet schedules, major rental agreements, and class schedules to determine the time of year that is the most feasible. Inform all groups that will be affected by the pool closure well in advance so that they can make appropriate plans. Annual maintenance can take from 2 to 4 weeks depending on the projects scheduled.

Determine what budget is allotted for the annual maintenance program. Create a project list in order of priority, select projects to be accomplished, and plan accordingly for those projects. Determine if your staff can complete the projects scheduled or if contractors will be required. If contractors are needed, contact them to get a cost quote and time estimate for the project. Once all projects are selected and costs have been determined, create a time line of events and plan them in the order in which they should occur. Common tasks that are carried out during annual maintenance include the following:

- Acid washing the basin to remove stains
- Regrouting tile decks and basins
- Restringing lane ropes
- Painting plaster basins and deck walls
- Replacing burned-out lightbulbs in the basin and deck
- Replacing ceiling tiles

Facility staff members clean a drained pool.

- Buffing deck tiles
- Repacking sand and gravel filter media as needed (See "Filtration" in chapter 8.)
- Repairing and performing maintenance on pumps and motors
- Cleaning chemical feed motors
- Cleaning air circulation fans
- Cleaning and repairing diving boards and starting blocks as needed
- Making plumbing repairs

Acid Washing the Pool Basin

Acid washing the pool basin requires you to drain and scrub down the basin using an acid solution followed by rinsing the basin with clean water. You can accomplish the actual acid bath by mixing a 1:1 ratio of muriatic acid and water, and spreading small amounts of this mixture on pool basin sections prewetted with hose water. You can then use brushes to spread around the mixture. The acid mixture normally requires approximately 1 minute to eat away grime before it can be rinsed away by a running hose. Be sure to post signs in the pool area when it is drained and to continue to maintain security as if the pool were filled. It is potentially deadly for a trespasser to assume the pool is filled and dive in. Also, you should ensure that workers in the diving well are provided with a ladder or climbing rope to get out. The steep slope can often be very difficult to climb up when it is wet.

You should ensure that your staff members have the proper protective equipment to carry out this task. Equipment they will need includes

- eye protection,
- rubber boots,
- long-sleeve shirts,
- long pants, and
- respiratory protection (a mask designed to protect against acid fumes).

If possible, maintain air circulation vented directly to the outside (if acid washing an indoor pool). You may want to prop open doors and set up fans to avoid a buildup of fumes in the pool. Never allow a staff member to acid wash a basin alone, and always post a staff member on deck to keep watch and ensure that fumes do not overcome staff members working in the basin. In the event that staff members are overcome, do not send unprotected personnel in to rescue them; use of a self-contained breathing apparatus (SCBA) will be required.

Regrouting Tiles

Regrouting the deck tiles involves removing loose or damaged tiles that are no longer held in place by the adhesive or "grout" that sticks them to the deck. In some cases, the grout will begin to wear away, leaving visible gaps between tiles. You should be able to easily remove loose tiles by hand or pop them out easily with a screwdriver. Replace the empty spaces with tiles to match the color of your deck. Your pool manufacturer or pool supply company should carry this item. Once you've removed all loose and damaged tiles and replaced them with new ones, you'll regrout the tiles into place by spreading grout (a thick putty-like mixture) over the tiled area with a trowel and patting it into place in the creases between the tiles. You'll then scrape the excess off the tile face with the trowel, leaving grout only in the creases. This is a tedious and painstaking process that can only be accomplished on hands and knees. You'll need the following items:

- A trowel
- A board to spread the grout on and scoop it off of to put on the deck
- Grout
- Replacement tiles (match colors to your existing tiles)
- Knee pads

Restringing Lane Ropes

During the course of a year's use, your lane ropes can take a beating: Wires begin to fray, take-up reels break, and floats break. Take-up reels are the part of lane ropes that set the length and tension of the rope while in the water. Inspect your lane ropes before annual maintenance to determine what parts (and in what quantities) you'll need for lane rope repair. You should order the parts far enough in advance to have them on hand during maintenance season (see appendix C). While the pool is being cleaned and repaired, you can take the floats off the lines, replace broken and damaged lane floats and take-up reels, repair frayed wires, or replace the wires if needed. Caution your staff to be careful when working with the wires because damaged wires may be sharp enough to cut them.

Repainting the Pool Basin and Walls

Plaster basins should be repainted each season to maintain a fresh, clean look and to help seal the plaster against leaks. The basin should be painted a light color, such as white, so you can easily see swimmers against it. However, you can outline hazards (such as stairs) and paint lane markers in black paint. You can repaint the pool walls, with murals if you want, to add to the fresh, new feeling of your facility.

Replacing Burned-Out Lightbulbs

Replacing burned-out lightbulbs above the pool may require the use of a "cherry picker" or "scissors lift" raiseable platform to reach the ceiling. These devices have an enclosed platform or basket that is controlled by levers powering an hydraulic lift. When activated, it carries the operator to a height that allows him to make repairs or perform other tasks that he can't reach with ordinary ladders. Be sure to have the correct lightbulbs on hand to install when you've arranged for the cherry picker to be on scene. These types of lifts can often be rented from construction or equipment rental companies, much as you would rent a backhoe or a truck. Replacing bulbs in the pool basin requires pulling the fixture from the wall and removing the watertight seal and gasket to access the actual bulb. After replacing the bulb, the fixture must be reassembled and put back into the wall.

Replacing Ceiling Tiles

Replacement of ceiling tiles requires identifying (before the maintenance season) those tiles that have been damaged or stained by water, age, vandalism, or other causes. After identifying the number of needed tiles, you should order them well enough in advance to have on hand during the maintenance period. You can order the tiles from the pool manufacturer or a building supply store. You'll need the cherry picker or scissors lift, as described earlier, to install the tiles.

Buffing Deck Tiles

You can buff deck tiles by using a standard electric floor buffer. Buffing the tiles helps remove dirt and grime from the deck, and it restores the well-worn paths of "high-traffic areas" to the same color as surrounding tiles. When buffing, be careful not to let the electric buffer come too close to your pool, whether the pool is empty or full. Contact with a full pool could result in electrocution of the operator or swimmers. When the pool is empty, the buffer could fall into the pool and sustain damage.

One way to avoid these dangers is to tether the buffer to a deck fixture with a rope that comes just short of the pool. Move the rope to different fixtures as you move your buffer area.

Repairing and Maintaining Pumps and Motors

While the filters are shut down and the pool is drained, check your pumps for signs of rust and damage. If possible, open the pump and motor to check impeller blades for damage. If you note corrosion or damage, replace the impeller blade. This device is responsible for drawing water through the pipes, and circulation will be slowed if it is damaged.

Cleaning Chemical Feed Motors

Cleaning your chemical feed motors involves detaching plastic water lines from the motors and running a muriatic acid solution through them to prevent a buildup of calcium in the lines. The motors themselves should be scrubbed with a bristle brush and clean water to remove any built-up calcium deposits, which would impair their function.

Cleaning Air Circulation Fans

When cleaning air circulation fans, be sure that you shut them down (and that they remain off) to eliminate the possibility of a worker becoming injured. Remove dust and grime buildup by wiping down the blades or using shop vacuums to suck up dust and dirt. This process will help eliminate dust in the circulating air and will make your fans function more effectively, thus improving your air quality.

Cleaning and Repairing Diving Boards and Starting Blocks

Inspect your starting blocks and diving boards for cracks on surfaces and for rust and decay in metal parts. Scrub the surfaces with liquid bleach and water to remove algae. Clean metal parts of these fixtures with steel wool. Be sure to replace any broken or rusted out restraining bolts or pins.

Making Plumbing Repairs

Plumbing repairs involve identifying those parts of your facility with leaking pipes and seals, and then replacing, patching, or caulking the affected part. If you do elect to replace a gasket or pipe section, be sure to shut down the water in that area and drain the pipe before taking off the part. Don't attempt plumbing repairs without specific training in that trade. If you don't have a trained person on your staff, hire a pool contractor to make the repairs.

Exterior Facility Maintenance

Whether your pool is indoor or outdoor, you must maintain a clean, safe, and pleasing facility exterior. You should regularly inspect the parking lots, walkways, fences, lawns, and other exterior areas to ensure that they are safe and clean. Establishing a regular maintenance and cleaning protocol for exterior facility care will help to ensure that this important area of your facility is not overlooked. See appendix D for a sample checklist for exterior facility maintenance.

> **KEY POINT** *Keeping your facility clean and well prepared is a large and never ending task. You'll need to plan and organize tasks carefully to ensure that they're all done properly and on time. Checklists and maintenance plans can help you do this.*

CONTRACTED MAINTENANCE AND CLEANING

Aquatic facility maintenance and cleaning—whether annual, weekly, or daily—can be contracted to pool management and maintenance companies. A spectrum of options are available, from contracting all cleaning and maintenance services to contracting only those large yearly tasks requiring special expertise. By using contractors for these tasks, you free your staff from much of the training, risk, and distraction from other duties often associated with cleaning and maintenance. Another benefit is that you are taking advantage of the experience and expertise that a contractor of these services should provide. This frees your staff to concentrate on other duties, such as interacting with your patrons and supervising the facility. Contract maintenance is often performed at set periods of the day when no permanent staff are left on-site; this can present problems if a maintenance or cleaning emergency arises. Although the contractor can respond, response may not be immediate, and additional costs may be involved.

You should communicate regularly with the contract maintenance company to ensure that they have specific directions regarding your needs and that they are meeting them. Remember that the facility operator is ultimately responsible for ensuring that the facility is in compliance with state regulations relating to cleanliness and water quality; it is therefore your responsibility to ensure that your contractor's work is within standards.

CHEMICAL SAFETY

Chemicals are a large part of the safety concern at an aquatic facility. Your staff works with them every day—applying them to the pool, storing them, and moving them. Your staff must be well trained and educated regarding what they are handling so that they can take the proper safety precautions. Some chemicals, such as chlorine or bromine, are used for regulating water chemistry, while others are used for cleaning or maintenance. Many of these chemicals can be volatile if mixed together. Some burn or explode under certain conditions. Others are toxic if inhaled or ingested.

The Occupational Safety and Health Administration's (OSHA) Hazard Communication Standard (29 CFR Parts 1910, 1915, 1917, 1918, 1926, and 1928) states that all chemical containers must have their contents clearly labeled. Your staff members must be aware of the types of chemicals that they will be handling, the ways that these chemicals can enter their body, and the respective dangers of those substances (Johnson, 1994). This information is contained in material safety data sheets (MSDS), which are included with chemicals when they are sold (see figure 9.1).

Chemical Safety Training

You should include chemical safety training as part of your staff in-service training program. This training should provide information regarding

- what chemicals are in use at your facility,
- the proper use or application of those chemicals,
- what protective equipment must be worn when applying those chemicals,
- how and where the chemicals should be stored,
- first aid procedures to take if exposed to those chemicals, and
- safety precautions to take when handling the chemicals.

A wide variety of chemical safety training is available from commercial sources. When selecting a commercial training agency, you should ensure

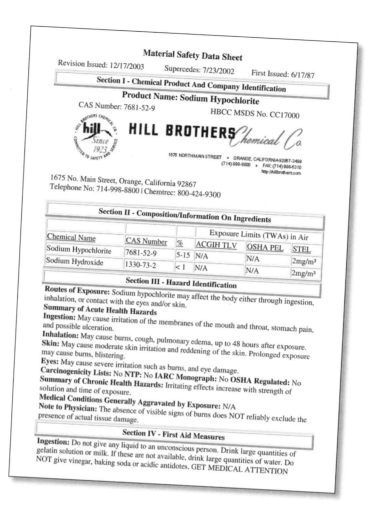

Figure 9.1   An excerpt from a sodium hypochlorite MSDS.

Reprinted, by permission, from Hill Brothers Chemical Company.

that the training agency materials are written to OSHA standards. Training modules offered by commercial sources often include the following:

- Hazard Communication Standard
- Material safety data sheet training
- Safety shower and eye wash training

OSHA (see appendix A) offers safety training through 30 OSHA Training Institute (OTI) centers around the country. Mainly located at colleges and universities, these OTIs offer resident training related to a variety of chemical safety topics, such as

- respiratory safety,
- hazardous materials,
- indoor air quality, and
- air sampling for toxic substances.

In some cases, these courses are available in an online format, eliminating the added expense of

potentially having a staff member travel to a training site. When determining which staff members to send, consider who will benefit most from this training. The training may be best suited to maintenance staff (if they handle pool chemicals). Usually, these employees also work with chemicals in several other areas of the facility and can apply the training to many parts of their work. Additionally, maintenance staff may be more permanent in their employment as opposed to lifeguards, who are often students and whose employment may be more temporary in nature.

> **KEY POINT** *Swimming pool chemicals can be stored and used safely if the proper precautions are taken. Be sure to read the manufacturers' safety instructions and store your chemicals in the proper environment.*

Methods of Entry

There are several routes through which chemicals can enter the body. Those methods include the following (Johnson, 1994):

▶ Orally—through ingestion of the substance by eating or drinking it

▶ Dermally—through the skin, by touching the object

▶ Optically—by having the substance splashed in the eye

▶ Inhalation—by breathing in toxic fumes

▶ Injection—by having the substance taken directly into the bloodstream

Personal Protective Equipment

As an employer, you are required by OSHA regulations to provide appropriate personal protective equipment to your employees while they are working with chemicals as a part of their work duties (29 Code of Federal Regulations Part 1910). You must also instruct them on how to properly use the equipment and then enforce its use. Personal protective equipment includes eye protection, gloves, boots, masks, proper clothing, and aprons.

▶ **Eye protection.** Eye protection should be worn any time staff members are working with liquid chemicals or corrosive solids. Eye protection should protect the eye from the front, sides, and bottom. Safety eyewear should be ventilated to prevent fogging and must be the appropriate size to fit the wearer. You should store the safety eyewear in a location that staff members must pass on their way to the chemicals. Do not store eyewear in the chemical room, because vapors from the chemicals can build up condensate on the glasses, causing irritation to the eyes.

▶ **Gloves.** Staff members should wear gloves whenever handling liquid or corrosive solid chemicals. Gloves should be rubber, nonporous, and unlined. Lined gloves can soak up water and chemicals, bringing them close to the skin. Gloves of any material other than rubber also soak up liquids and may contaminate the wearer. When gloves become torn or otherwise unusable, discard and replace them. To see if a glove has a hole, fill it with water and hold it by the wrist.

▶ **Boots.** Footwear protects your staff members from liquids being spilled on their feet and also from stepping in puddles of chemical. Leather or canvas footwear is not recommended because it may soak up water or chemical and hold it next to the skin. Rubber boots repel most liquids and will provide an appropriate measure of protection.

A staff member in protective equipment works with chemicals.

▶ **Masks.** Masks should be worn any time your staff handles granular chemicals, gases, or any chemicals that give off fumes. The type of mask will depend on the chemical being used. Filter masks should always be used with any chemical that produces irritating or corrosive fumes. Dust masks may be used for chemicals that produce inert fumes. Filter masks provide a higher level of respiratory protection due to a more stringent barrier level designed to trap fumes before they reach the lungs. Dust masks provide only a single unfiltered layer of material to stop fumes from reaching the nose and mouth. The mask selected should fit properly to the user's face and should be in proper working order. When a mask becomes damaged or otherwise ineffective, discard it and replace it with a new one.

▶ **Clothing.** Any staff members working with chemicals should wear clothing suitable to protect them from splashed or dropped chemicals. The traditional bathing suit worn by most lifeguards when lifeguarding doesn't qualify. Long-sleeve shirts and long pants should be worn for this purpose. Loose clothing should be avoided because it can become accidentally soaked with chemicals. Clothing such as nylon or rayon should also be avoided because it provides very little protection.

▶ **Aprons and rain suits.** Repellent aprons or rain suits are recommended for tasks that require heavy activity with chemicals, such as hand-feeding liquid chlorine (adding the chemicals directly to the pool water from the deck, instead of through the filtration/circulation process) or acid slugging (adding an acid and water mix directly to the pool water, bypassing the circulation process).

See appendix C for suppliers of personal protective equipment.

> **KEY POINT** *Chemical handling and application can be a hazard to staff members if they're not equipped properly with personal protective equipment. It's the responsibility of management to identify hazards, train staff appropriately, and provide the appropriate protective equipment.*

Chemical Storage

When determining the proper storage methods for chemicals, you should first check the container label for instructions. Many chemicals have restrictions regarding ventilation, storage near other types of chemicals, and exposure to heat or cold. All chemicals must be stored in their original container with the label and safety precautions clearly legible. Do not remove chemicals from their original containers and store them in other containers. If you do this, you can expect a staff member to make a chemical application error.

You should store material safety data sheets that accompany chemicals in the chemical storage area. Place the MSDSs in plastic sheets and keep them in a red binder that is secured in a highly visible location.

See appendix D for a chemical storage area inspection form that you can use to help ensure the safety of this area. Other things you can do to store chemicals safely include taking steps to protect your staff, watching expiration dates, storing items separately, and controlling the environment.

Protect Your Staff

Do not allow your staff to eat, drink, or smoke while handling chemicals; this greatly increases the risk of poisoning the staff member.

You should post permanently mounted first aid procedures in the chemical storage area. First aid procedures should include skin exposure, eye exposure, and ingested poison procedures. Also, equip the area with emergency showers and eye wash stations to be used in the event that a staff member suffers a chemical exposure incident.

Always insist that the measuring device provided with a chemical be used and not replaced with another device. Chlorine burns and explodes when it comes into contact with organic substances such as paper. Using a paper cup to measure granular chlorine instead of using the provided plastic one may cause this to occur.

For staff safety, a self-contained breathing apparatus (SCBA) should be stored adjacent to, but outside of, the chlorine storage room (so that a staff member won't be exposed to the gas while trying to reach the SCBA). This device can be worn by staff to shut off the gas supply in an emergency (i.e., a gas leak). It can also be worn when performing maintenance on the gas cylinders. Only an SCBA should be used for these purposes; other respiratory protective devices require a minimum amount of oxygen in the atmosphere to be functional. This minimum oxygen content is not present when chlorine has been leaked.

Watch Expiration Dates

If your facility is seasonal, do not store pool chemicals over the course of the winter. Many chemicals have limited shelf lives, and the chemical would be useless at the beginning of the next season.

Also, the increased moisture and cold could cause cracks in the container and leak the product. Properly dispose of chemicals when they have reached their expiration date. Contact the supplier for instructions; if they are unable to assist, you may contact the manufacturer. Do not dispose of expired chemicals in the storm or sanitary sewer. This is illegal and creates an ecological hazard.

Store Items Separately

Store chemicals separate from each other. Do not stack chemicals of different types together. Many chemicals are combustible when mixed together. If one container leaks onto another, an explosion may result. Mark areas of your storage room with signs indicating where different chemical types are to be stored; this will help eliminate confusion (Fawcett, 2001).

In addition, don't store gasoline, oil, or petroleum products with swimming pool chemicals. Chlorine and gasoline are explosive when they come in contact with each other. The fumes from the two chemicals can also be toxic when combined. Gasoline and other petroleum products should be stored in a separately ventilated room.

Control the Environment

Post a permanent sign on the door of your chemical storage area that states "Authorized Personnel Only." The sign should be constructed of painted metal to withstand the effects of chemical exposure. In addition, post "No Smoking" signs in conspicuous locations in the storage area, and post "Poison" signs as needed above the chemicals themselves.

Close and lock the door to the chemical storage area when it is not occupied to reduce the possibility of children entering the room and handling or even eating the chemicals.

Be sure that your chemical storage area is cool and does not have direct sunlight exposure. Many chemicals can explode when heated or can break down when exposed to direct sunlight.

Ensure that your storage area is continuously ventilated to the outside with a fan. This will reduce the possibility of the buildup of noxious fumes and gases.

Store chemicals off the floor on wooden pallets. This will prevent bags and canisters from becoming wet with standing water and eventually leaking their contents from container deterioration.

After a chemical container has been opened for use, instruct your staff to replace caps, lids, and restraining bands each time they open the container. This will help prevent spillage.

Be sure to station at least one large fire extinguisher in your chemical storage area. Use a dry chemical extinguisher, not water. Many chemicals will react with water, causing additional danger.

ELECTRICAL SAFETY

Electricity and water are a potentially deadly mix. You must institute an electrical safety plan to ensure that your staff and customers are protected. The most important aspect of electrical safety at your facility is the **ground fault circuit interrupter (GFCI)** on an outlet. GFCIs automatically shut off power to an outlet if water enters the socket. You will recognize that your power outlets have GFCIs if there are "test" and "reset" buttons between the sockets. All power outlets on the pool deck and in the locker area should be GFCI protected. All outlets in these areas should also have a spring-loaded cover to protect them from exposure to water.

Circuit boxes and electrical panels should be locked at all times to prevent unauthorized access. Preferably, all electrical panels will be located in locked service rooms so that they are inaccessible to unauthorized users.

Keep in mind the following electrical safety tips:

▶ Make sure that any appliances (such as radios and stereos) brought onto the pool deck are waterproof to prevent an electrical shock hazard. If possible, only allow appliances owned by the facility to be brought onto the deck; then you will be sure that they are in compliance with this rule. If you can't do that, post a sign indicating that all appliances must be inspected by facility management before being allowed on the deck.

▶ Never permit swimmers to be in the pool when the pool vacuum is in the water. These vacuums are operated by an external power source drawn from the deck outlets.

▶ Only place the automatic vacuum in the pool after operational hours. Although the cords are insulated, there is a risk of shock.

▶ Be sure everyone in the building is aware when electrical work is to take place. If a circuit is shut down to be worked on, you should station someone at the breaker to ensure that it is not turned back on while being serviced.

▶ Know where the electrical shutoff switch for the entire building is located so that you can shut the power off in an emergency.

▶ Do not allow patrons in the area where electrical work is being performed (due to the electrocution hazard).

See appendix D for a sample electrical safety checklist.

FIRE SAFETY

Fire safety and prevention are often overlooked at swimming pools because it's often thought that fire is unlikely there due to the presence of a large volume of water. This couldn't be less true. Swimming pools require a large amount and variety of chemicals for the water to stay chemically balanced and free from disease. Many of these chemicals burn or explode when they come into contact with each other or with petroleum products or organic substances. (Read each product's label for specifics.) This is to say nothing of the presence of other flammable substances at the pool, such as wood or paint.

The basic elements to your fire safety plan should include training, equipment, and signage. Train your staff on the basic principles of fire suppression and facility evacuation. Arrange for the fire department or other qualified personnel to instruct your staff regarding how to operate fire extinguishers, fire hoses, and fire alarms.

At least once per year, hold a seminar in which staff members are able to learn to operate a fire extinguisher correctly. Many people have never done so and are unable to operate the extinguisher properly during a fire. The seminar can be coordinated with local fire departments or can be taught by a knowledgeable security officer in your organization. The training should focus on not only how to operate the extinguisher but also how to direct the spray at the fire for maximum effect.

Hold regular fire drills, first for your staff only to allow them to walk through the process, and then with the patrons to add realism and to instruct patrons on your process. (Be sure to warn your patrons that a fire drill will be happening on a given day.) Record the drill in your training log and discuss with your staff the ways that the evacuation could be improved. Implement the suggestions immediately if they are suitable. Holding the drill will help ensure that your fire exits are unlocked and adequate and that all staff members know where the exits are and know what their roles are in the event of a fire.

Inspect your facility to make sure that you have the proper number and types of fire suppression equipment. If possible, have a representative from the fire marshal's office assist you with this. Items you may need include fire hoses, dry chemical extinguishers, water extinguishers, sprinkler systems, and fire axes. Once you've determined that you have what is required, you'll need to regularly inspect and test your extinguishers. Fire extinguishers should be periodically recharged and marked when they are tested.

Facility staff members learn to use a fire extinguisher.

Smoking is always a significant factor in increasing the risk of fire at a facility. Smoking should never be permitted near chemicals of any kind. If you permit smoking at your facility, restrict it to an area free from any flammable materials such as stored paper products, paint, or fuels.

All fire exits must be clearly marked. Also ensure that all fire exits can be opened from the inside, preferably with a panic bar, and are not locked. An evacuation plan for fire should be developed and posted in the pool area, locker rooms, and other activity areas in the building. The posted plan should include a building map that clearly marks where the reader is, where the nearest exit is, and how to get to it.

The state fire marshal's office is also responsible for setting rules regarding maximum capacity for rooms. This includes swimming pools. Once a maximum capacity has been designated for your swimming pool, post a sign on the pool deck indicating that number. Train your staff to enforce the maximum number of persons allowed. Exceeding this amount can place everyone in danger if the building needs to be evacuated due to fire (not to mention the added difficulty in supervising swimmers).

SPECIAL ATTRACTION SAFETY

Special attractions include water slides, inflatable attractions, and sprays. Before purchasing an attraction, research the item to determine what type of customers and facility it is designed for. If your facility does not meet the requirements in terms of needed water depth or deck space, you should not purchase the item. You should check the manufacturer's instructions for installation, maintenance, and operation of the attraction. If possible, have major permanent attractions, such as water slides, installed by the manufacturer to ensure it is done properly. After initial installation is complete, test the attraction thoroughly to be sure that it is operating properly. Do not allow customers to use the attraction until you have done so. You should create safety precautions for the attraction based on the manufacturer's instructions. Post all safety regulations so that they can be seen by all patrons. When the attraction is first opened, you should spend time educating the patrons about it in order to instill safety habits early.

Incorporate any new attractions into your emergency action plan so that you know how you will respond to an emergency involving them. You

A dual water slide.

should also perform emergency drills involving the attractions.

Include your attractions in your daily inspections. Check to ensure that they are functioning properly and that they are undamaged.

EQUIPMENT INVENTORY AND MAINTENANCE

You must be aware of what equipment and supplies your facility owns. If you don't know what you have, it's easy to run out of a crucial item at a time when you absolutely have to have it. You should complete an inventory of all items in your aquatic facility each year. Expendable items, such as first aid supplies and cleaning items, should be inventoried more frequently, even weekly if needed.

If possible, you should centralize your supply inventory and manage the records with a computer. A good computerized inventory will include a description of the item, its part number, supplier, location in the storage room, and the quantity of the item remaining. In most cases, you can use an off-the-shelf software program, such as Microsoft Excel®, to fill this need. Listing the part number and supplier will make reordering the part much easier. You must train your staff to update the spreadsheet so that it reflects the current number of supplies in the inventory when one is removed. If possible, designate only one or two staff members to operate the program; that way, you're sure that you have good data and that the data is up-to-date (if these staff members are doing their jobs correctly). Also, if the data is bad, you'll know whom to see.

Organize your supply room into a series of shelves and bins to hold various size items. Your supply room should also be cool and well ventilated to prevent moisture from forming and destroying paper products. Label each bin with the item it should contain and its part number. Including the part number makes it easier when you are reordering the item. Ensure that your storage room is locked when not in use and that key control is restricted to only a few staff members. This will help prevent pilferage and theft.

Many supplies have a limited shelf life. Recording the date that supplies were ordered helps prevent products from expiring before use. For chemicals, write the expiration date in permanent marker on the bottle. Order your supplies in sufficient quantities so that you do not run out, but don't order so much that the products expire. Use your previous usage reports to estimate the amount of supplies you need in a given period.

Label expensive items when they enter your inventory so that they are more difficult to steal. Metal items can be engraved with your facility name; other items can be marked using permanent marker or paint. You may also want to assign an inventory control number that is noted on the item and in the property list. Some large facilities use a bar code reader system for this. A bar code sticker is placed on the item and is read by a scanner during inventory to make the process easier.

When you perform annual inventory, be sure to note the condition of the items you check as well as the number and location. At the end of your inventory, reconcile the inventory list with the list from the previous year. If you determine that items are missing, try to find out their location or why they are no longer in stock. If you determine that the condition of some of the items inventoried makes them no longer usable, you can use that information to purchase new supplies.

The environment created at aquatic facilities by high humidity, moisture, and chemical fume buildup can be damaging to aquatic equipment. Items such as water exercise equipment and life jackets should be regularly rinsed with fresh water to remove pool water that contains chlorine. If items such as these are not rinsed, they will begin to rapidly deteriorate. Whenever possible, hang equipment to air dry in a well-ventilated area to reduce the possibility of mildew and mold.

Other pieces of equipment should be cared for in accordance with manufacturers' instructions.

FECAL AND VOMIT CONTAMINATION CLEANUP PROCEDURES

The presence of large numbers of young children in swimming pools makes fecal and vomit accidents almost a certainty. The introduction of these substances into the pool water is dangerous due to the possibility of disease transmission. Diseases that can be contracted include cryptosporidium, giardia, shigellosis, hepatitis A, and E. coli (see "Disease Transmission" in chapter 8, page 180). The risk of transmission of these diseases in swimming pool water varies with the chlorine level at the time of the contamination incident. Aquatic facilities with higher chlorine levels at the time of the incident run less risk of contamination of their patrons from a majority of these diseases. Although most states recommend a minimum of 1.0 part per million (PPM) of free chlorine, a 2.0 to 2.5 PPM level is much more effective in killing bacteria while remaining comfortable for swimmers.

Recently, the disease cryptosporidium has become recognized as one of the more common waterborne diseases. This illness is of particular concern due to its resistance to chlorine. "Crypto," as it is commonly called, is transmitted through fecal contamination of the water. Figure 9.2 contains decontamination procedures for fecal accidents as recommended by the Centers for Disease Control and Prevention (CDC; see appendix A).

Prevention of fecal and vomit accidents is the best method for preventing disease transmission. Here are some steps you can take to reduce the likelihood of transmission:

▶ Require that all children who are not toilet trained wear tight-fitting swim diapers.

▶ Do not permit the changing of diapers on the pool deck or at poolside. Provide baby changing stations in locker rooms of both sexes for the purpose of facilitating this.

▶ Disinfect lavatories using bleach several times per day.

A. Formed stool (solid, nonliquid)

1. Direct everyone to leave all pools into which water containing the feces is circulated. Do not allow anyone to enter the contaminated pool(s) until all decontamination procedures are completed.

2. Remove as much of the fecal material as possible using a net or scoop and dispose of it in a sanitary manner. Clean and disinfect the net or scoop (e.g., after cleaning, leave the net or scoop immersed in the pool during disinfection). Vacuuming stool from the pool is not recommended.

3. Raise the free available chlorine concentration to 2.0 mg/L, pH 7.2-7.5, if it is <2.0 mg/L. Ensure this concentration is found throughout all co-circulating pools by sampling at least three widely spaced locations away from return water outlets. This free available chlorine concentration was selected to keep the pool closure time to approximately 30 minutes. Other concentrations or closure times can be used as long as the CT inactivation value is kept constant.

4. Maintain the free available chlorine concentration at 2.0 mg/L, pH 7.2-7.5, for at least 25 minutes before reopening the pool. State or local regulators may require higher free available chlorine levels in the presence of chlorine stabilizers such as chlorinated isocyanurates. Ensure that the filtration system is operating while the pool reaches and maintains the proper free available chlorine concentration during the disinfection process.

5. Establish a fecal accident log. Document each fecal accident by recording date and time of the event, formed stool or diarrhea, free available chlorine concentration at the time or observation of the event and before opening the pool, the pH, the procedures followed to respond to the fecal accident (including the process used to increase free chlorine residual if necessary), and the contact time.

B. Diarrhea (liquid stool)

1. See A1.

2. See A2.

3. Raise the free available chlorine concentration to 20 mg/L and maintain the pH between 7.2 and 7.5. Ensure this concentration is found throughout all co-circulating pools by sampling at least three widely spaced locations away from return water outlets. This chlorine and pH level should be sufficient to inactivate cryptosporidium and should be maintained for at least 8 hours, equivalent to a CT inactivation value of 9600. A higher or lower free available chlorine level/inactivation time can be used as long as a CT inactivation value equaling 9600 is maintained for cryptosporidium inactivation. State or local regulators may require higher free available chlorine levels in the presence of chlorine stabilizers such as chlorinated isocyanurates. If necessary, consult an aquatic professional to determine and identify the feasibility, practical methods, and safety considerations before attempting the hyperchlorination of any pool.

4. Ensure that the filtration system is operating while the pool reaches and maintains the proper free available chlorine concentration during disinfection.

5. Backwash the filter thoroughly after reaching the CT value. Be sure the effluent is discharged directly to waste and in accordance with state or local regulations. Do not return the backwash through the filter. Where appropriate, replace the filter media.

6. Swimmers may be allowed into the pool after the required CT value has been achieved and the free available chlorine level has been returned to the normal operating range allowed by the state or local regulatory authority. Maintain the free available chlorine concentration and pH at standard operating levels based on state or local regulations. If necessary, consult state or local regulatory authorities for recommendations on bringing the free available chlorine levels back to an acceptable operating range.

7. See A5.

Figure 9.2 Fecal decontamination procedures.

From CDC. www.cdc.gov/mmwr/preview/mmwrhtml/mm5020a7.htm.

► Disinfect pool decks using bleach water at the close of each day.

► Discourage patrons from drinking or spitting water.

You should include information regarding changing of diapers and proper swimwear for children in your swim lesson information packets. Reviewing this information during parent orientation meetings will also assist in reinforcing it.

SPAS AND HOT TUBS

Spas and hot tubs are different from swimming pools in their operation and maintenance, and they present a special challenge for the pool operator. The presence of warm, moving water creates water chemistry and safety challenges not present in traditional swimming pools.

The high water temperature associated with spas and hot tubs rapidly burns off any disinfectant added to kill bacteria. This makes maintaining any disinfectant level a constant difficulty and contributes to the transmission of disease. Disease and bacteria are prone to growth in hot tubs and spas due to the warmth, darkness, moving water, and the presence of a food source—the swimmers. To assist in guarding against disease, the hot tub or spa should be regularly drained, cleaned, and refilled with clean water. The maximum bather load should be strictly enforced; this assists in lowering TDS and maintaining disinfectant level in the tub.

Spa and Hot Tub Safety

Hot tub safety is often overlooked due to the mind-set that "It's only a few feet deep, no one will drown in there." This is a dangerous and false assumption; patrons do die in hot tubs for a variety of reasons. Warm water magnifies the effects of alcohol, prescription drugs, and illegal drugs. This could cause sleep or unconsciousness that may result in the patron drowning. Other hazards that may occur in hot tubs and spas include entrapment, electrocution, and spinal injuries from slips, falls, or diving.

A qualified lifeguard should supervise spas and hot tubs at all times they are in use. Due to the relaxing effects of the warm water, patrons using spas and hot tubs can fall asleep, slide under the water, and drown.

The Consumer Product Safety Commission (CPSC; see appendix A) recommends that spa water be no hotter than 104 degrees Fahrenheit. Antivortex drain covers and emergency shutoff switches that can be reached from the tub are also important safety features. Antivortex drain

Facility patrons soak in a hot tub.

covers reduce the risk of entrapment if the user comes in contact with the drain. The antivortex drain cover is curved and breaks up the drain suction by dispersing the force of water entering the drain. Because the force of water entering the drain is dissipated, a "vortex" or whirlpool can't form. Drowning by entrapment is not an uncommon occurrence in hot tubs without these devices. Drowning can occur when the force of the drain is so strong that it holds the swimmer's body part against the drain, preventing the swimmer from getting to the surface to breathe. This is more common among bathers with long hair, which is more easily sucked into the drain.

Keep in mind the following safety tips and procedures for hot tubs:

- Warn your patrons that pregnant women should not use hot tubs due to the risk of birth defects.
- Do not permit diving into hot tubs or spas.
- Do not permit children under the age of 12 to use hot tubs. Their small bodies cannot regulate the high temperatures associated with hot tubs. They may become easily overheated and dehydrated.
- Warn your patrons that people with a history of heart disease or respiratory problems should not use hot tubs.
- Do not permit patrons to consume alcohol while in the spa or hot tub, or immediately before entering. The effects of the alcohol and warm water can relax the swimmers to the point that they may fall asleep and drown. They may also become seriously dehydrated.
- Make sure that patrons taking prescription medication are warned of the increased risk of drowsiness in hot tubs and also of the unknown effect of warm water on their medications.
- Do not allow portable radios, televisions, or other electrical devices in the area due to the risk of electrocution.
- Ensure that hot tubs and spas are supervised at all times to guard against the risk of drowning.
- Do not permit patrons to submerge in the hot tub or spa; their hair may become entrapped in the drain, and they may drown.
- Install antivortex drain devices to reduce the risk of drowning.

- Warn your patrons that people with a history of heart disease, stroke, or high blood pressure should not use hot tubs due to the risk of illness-related maladies.
- Ensure that all plugs surrounding spas and hot tubs have ground fault circuit interrupters. This reduces the risk of electrocution. Areas immediately around hot tubs should have deck drains to reduce standing water and should have nonskid surfaces to reduce slips and falls.
- Limit hot tub use to a maximum of 15 minutes per session to guard against dehydration and overheating (Bennett, 1985).

Spa and Hot Tub Maintenance

- Hot tubs and spas consume disinfectants, such as chlorine and bromine, at a very rapid rate due to their high temperature. You should maintain free disinfectant residual at a minimum of 2.0 PPM.
- Water chemistry for spas should be checked each hour.
- Spas and hot tubs should be drained and cleaned each day if possible. Refill the hot tub with clean water and rebalance the chemicals. This will reduce the buildup of total dissolved solids and particulate matter. It will also keep the tub basin clean and disinfected. Overall, it will reduce the risk of disease transmission.
- Cartridge filters are recommended as the best filter type for use in spas and hot tubs. Sand filters are not recommended because the warm water can turn the sand into a claylike substance.

ENERGY CONSERVATION

Energy conservation should be a high priority in your aquatic management plan. By reducing energy costs, you create a more stable financial environment for your facility and assist in preserving programs, services, and jobs at your facility. This section discusses energy conservation measures related to heating and cooling, water, lighting, and filtration.

Heating and Cooling

Before you can determine how to improve your heating and cooling methods at your facility, you need two pieces of information. You must first decide what temperature you want your pool and nonpool areas to operate at. You must also determine how long it takes for these areas to heat up and cool down from environmental conditions to the desired temperature. Once you know these facts, you can begin to implement some energy-saving plans. Here are some energy-saving tips:

- Cover and lock your thermostat controls so that they cannot be adjusted by unauthorized users.
- Time your thermostat in office spaces to turn on 1 hour before staff members arrive at work and to turn off 1/2 hour after they leave. This will save money by reducing energy consumption when the facility is not in use. If the facility is in an extreme cold climate and there is the risk of freezing pipes or other damage, you should not allow a total shutdown of heat to any space.
- Adjust your vents to maximize the flow of heated and cooled air.
- Keep your HVAC system clean. This increases efficiency.
- Insulate your building to ensure that it retains heated and cooled air.
- Use outside air to cool the building.
- Set exhaust fans on sensors to run only when needed.

Water Conservation

Water is often seen as an inexhaustible, cheap resource and not considered in terms of conservation. However, the resultant cost of lost water can be high because lost water is often heated and chemically treated. Steps that can be taken to reduce water loss include the following:

- Find and repair leaks in plumbing and pool face piping.
- Install low-flow flush toilets or adjust existing toilets to conserve water.
- Install efficiency showerheads.
- Use a pool cover to reduce water loss (for inside or outside pools); this saves money not only on water but also on heating and chemicals.
- Sweep or blow off lawn clippings from walkways rather than using a hose.

- If your facility has dishwashers or laundry equipment, run this equipment only with full loads.
- Fill swimming pools only to the point of overflow into the gutter and not to the point of overflow on deck.
- Educate all staff members regarding water conservation efforts and encourage them to assist with the program.

Lighting Conservation

There are several steps that you can take to reduce the misuse or overuse of lighting in your facility. Lighting conservation can save hundreds of dollars a month on lighting expenses. Steps that you can take to reduce lighting costs include the following:

- Use energy-efficient lamps and bulbs. Fluorescent bulbs are much more efficient than the more widely used incandescent bulbs.
- Regularly dust and clean lamps. Dirty light sources give off less usable light.
- Use natural lighting whenever possible. This can be effected in the design stage if you are building a new facility. If not, try to position work spaces to take advantage of available light. Open blinds and curtains to allow natural light into offices. Keep windows clean to maximize natural lighting effect.
- Ensure that lights are turned off in work spaces that are closed or not in use for long periods. This is particularly important for offices that are closed for the day.
- Replace burned-out lightbulbs promptly. This maximizes light output from the sources you have available.

Filtration Conservation

The major conservation issue associated with the operation of filters is water. If sand and gravel filters are not operated properly, you'll waste water, heat, and chemicals because you'll need to backwash the filters too frequently. For DE filters, you can also waste significant amounts of money through too frequent replacement of DE. Here are some steps you can take to conserve filter resources and expenses:

- Monitor your sand and gravel filters, and backwash when pressure differential exceeds

5 PSI on influent and effluent gauges. More often is unneeded and wastes water.

- Monitor discharged water while backwashing. As soon as discharged water is clear, stop backwashing (your filters are clean). If you backwash after water becomes clear, you're wasting water.

- Practice interrupt filtration with DE vacuum filters. This drains the water out of the "box," allowing the DE to flake off when dry. After the DE has fallen off the screens, keep the outflow valve closed but allow water to flow back into the filter. The DE will recoat the screens, with the newer, cleaner DE on top, which can trap more dirt, and the older saturated DE on the bottom. This extends the filter run and saves you money.

Diatomaceous earth filters require periodic replacement of the filter media to remain effective. However, replacing the media too often is both expensive and wasteful. Be sure to explore methods to extend filter runs, such as interrupt filtration, in order to reduce the need to replace filter media as frequently.

KEY POINT *Energy conservation is not only good for the environment, but it is also a way that your facility can save money. Perform an audit of your facility to determine ways you can reduce energy expenditure.*

WINTERIZING OUTDOOR SWIMMING POOLS

At the close of the operating season for outdoor pools, you must properly prepare for the onset of winter. If you don't, serious damage can be done to the pumps, filters, and other operating systems. This can be very costly in reopening the pool the following season and can reduce the life of your pool. Here are some steps that you can take to winterize your pool:

- Remove the drain plug on filters and allow them to empty completely.
- Disconnect the pump and allow it to drain.
- Disconnect and drain the heater.
- Place all plugs and covers in the skimmer basket so that they are not lost.

- Drain all pipes of water.
- Seal pipe openings to prevent anything unwanted from getting inside.
- Drain the pool and post "Pool Drained" signs around the perimeter.
- Remove starting blocks, ladders, and diving boards and store them in a protected environment, preferably one that is climate controlled.
- Remove lane ropes and floats and store them.
- Remove telephones, cash registers, and other devices to a storage area, preferably one that is climate controlled.
- Place any unused supplies such as first aid supplies or cleaning materials in a storage area for future use.
- Return unused chemical products to the supplier if possible.

RECORD KEEPING

As an administrator, you should believe in the saying "If it isn't on paper, it didn't happen." By this motto, you should keep records of everything. Types of records that have been discussed in this text and that you should maintain in your files include the following:

- Accident reports
- Incident reports
- Lifeguard substitution forms
- Swimming pool or bathing beach permits
- Safety inspections
- Pool chemistry records
- State inspections
- Opening and closing checklists
- Maintenance forms (Van Rossen, 1992)

A well-organized filing system will help you maintain these forms. You should maintain a file cabinet or filing binders for short-term records maintained for a year or less. After a year, records should be removed to a file box and placed in a storeroom. Be sure to mark the contents, including record type and years, on the box in permanent marker so that you can easily identify it as needed. Before you discard any records, you must ensure that they are not needed for any reason. You should retain incident and accident reports for at least 5 years. If the victim involved is a child, you must keep the records for 5 years after the child turns 18.

Many states and counties require that aquatic facilities obtain a permit from the state in order to operate. The procedure for obtaining the permit varies by jurisdiction. Some states require a facility inspection before the permit is issued; some collect a fee, while others do not. When you receive your permit, display it in a prominent place, such as the aquatics office. Keep old permits in case any questions arise regarding whether your facility has been out of regulation with the state.

SUMMARY

Maintaining a safe and clean facility is important to ensuring that your customers find your facility pleasing and want to return regularly. Developing a facility security plan helps to spot and eliminate gaps in your security that thieves and vandals can exploit. Your sanitation plan lays out a standard operating procedure for your staff regarding what cleaning tasks to perform, and when and how to do them; it helps eliminate the guesswork. Chemical and electrical safety plans help to maintain the safety of both your staff and patrons by identifying and eliminating hazards. Facility inventory and energy conservation plans are loss prevention and cost reduction techniques designed to help keep your facility financially viable.

REVIEW QUESTIONS

1. Provide a list of tasks commonly carried out in annual maintenance procedures.
2. What steps can you take to ensure electrical safety at your facility?
3. What function does an antivortex device perform in hot tubs?
4. What are MSDSs? Why are they important and where should they be stored?
5. List the safety rules associated with hot tubs.
6. List the forms associated with record keeping at an aquatic facility.

BIBLIOGRAPHY

Bennett, C. (1985). *Are we really in hot water?* Self Rescue Symposium, Halifax, NS.

Fawcett, P. (2001, October). Proceed with caution: Operators must ensure safe chemical storage and handling. *Aquatics International, 13*(8), 18.

Gabrielsen, M. (1987). *Swimming pools: A guide to their planning, design and operation* (4th ed.). Champaign, IL: Human Kinetics.

Johnson, R. (1994). *YMCA pool operations manual.* Champaign, IL: Human Kinetics.

United States Department of Transportation. (2000). *North American emergency response guidebook.* Washington, DC: USDOT.

Van Rossen, P. (1992). *Aquatic managers handbook.* Springfield, OR: Aquatic Resources and Programs.

Williams, K. (1999). *Aquatic facility operations manual.* Hoffman Estates, IL: National Recreation and Parks Association.

RESOURCES

Chlorine Safety Council Web site (provides a list of suggested chemical safety practices): www.c3.org/chlorine_knowledge_center/pool_chemicals.html.

Consumer Product Safety Commission Web site (contains important safety information regarding the operation of hot tubs): www.cpsc.gov.

Electrical Safety Foundation Web site (contains valuable information related to workplace electrical safety): www.esfi.org.

Emedco Web site (source for chemical safety equipment and warning signs): www.emedco.com.

Environmental Protection Agency Web site (contains water conservation information): www.epa.gov.

National Fire Protection Association Web site (contains information on fire prevention week, safety education, and other useful tools): www.nfpa.org.

Occupational Safety and Health Administration Web site (contains OSHA guidelines as well as links to OSHA Training Institutes [OTI]): www.osha.gov.

Southern California Edison Web site (contains helpful energy conservation tips): www.sce.com.

Aquatic-Related Agencies

Throughout this text, you will encounter references to a myriad of agencies related to aquatics. Some are regulatory agencies; some are professional membership organizations; others are aquatic certification agencies that provide certification for aquatic professionals. This appendix provides an overview of aquatic-related agencies as well as information regarding how to contact them. As you find references to agencies throughout the text, you can refer to this appendix to help you better understand what that organization does and what resources it has to offer. You will find this information helpful as you are reading this book. Likewise, it will prove to be a good reference for you in the future.

AQUATIC CERTIFICATION AGENCIES

Aquatics is an industry driven by certification. As an aquatic professional, your ability to be competitive and to provide value to your employer is directly related to the certifications you hold. There are many agencies that offer aquatic certifications, and each agency has its individual benefits. Two of the largest and most well-known aquatic certification agencies—the American Red Cross and the YMCA of the USA—are voluntary agencies, meaning no owners or shareholders make any income from fees associated with classes taught or products sold. Other certification agencies, such as Ellis and Associates or the American Lifeguard Association, are for-profit businesses. Some certification agencies focus on one particular aspect of aquatics, such as scuba or open water lifeguard training.

When selecting an agency for training, you should ensure that the program you are taking pro-vides certification that is recognized or accepted by the aquatic facility you want to work for. For example, YMCAs often want their employees to hold YMCA certifications. You should also make sure that the training you receive is appropriate for what you want to do. Although the United States Lifesaving Association standards are excellent for open water, training issued by an agency using USLA standards would not certify you for employment as a pool lifeguard.

Professional Membership Agencies

There are many professional organizations to which an aquatic specialist might purchase membership. Some of these agencies, such as the National Intramural Recreational Sports Association and the National Recreation and Parks Association, are not primarily devoted to aquatics, but they have a special section devoted to those members who do have interest in that area. Other agencies, such as the Aquatic Exercise Association and the National Swimming Pool Foundation, are aquatic-specific organizations devoted to one specialty area in aquatics. Although you can join as many organizations as you want, each charges a fee of various amounts, so it's best to select those agencies that will best serve your needs.

Sport Regulatory and Membership Agencies

The primary purpose of aquatic sport regulatory agencies is to provide structure and rule-making authority for the sport that they regulate. However, aquatic sport coaches, officials, and participants can purchase membership in their governing body.

Benefits of purchasing membership include access to coaches' clinics, professional conferences, and professional publications. You should be aware that in many cases the opportunity for you or your team to participate in meets that are regulated by your sport governing body is dependent on you having a membership in that organization. Additionally, your marketability as a coach is often dictated by the certification you hold from your professional agency.

Regulatory Agencies

Most regulation in aquatics is done by state and county governments and, in some instances, city government. The states and counties use a regulation often referred to as the "bathing code," taken from the antiquated term "bathing" once used instead of swimming. Although the table in this appendix doesn't list each state and its code, appendix B does provide a complete list of contact information for the state agencies that produce the bathing codes.

The Americans With Disabilities Act (ADA) regulates accommodations that aquatic facility managers must provide for persons with special needs. The act is regulated by the U.S. Department of Justice, with various segments being regulated by the Department of Transportation, the Department of Interior, National Parks Service, and so on.

Boating Agencies

Boating is a large specialty area within aquatics. There are a variety of agencies that specialize in boating safety (e.g., the U.S. Coast Guard Auxiliary) or specialize in instruction for individual types of boating, such as sailing or kayaking.

Agency name	Primary aquatics function	Services offered	Contact information
Aquatic or first aid certification agencies			
American Red Cross (ARC)	Aquatic and first aid certification	Certification courses in: • Lifeguard training • Water safety instructor • First aid • CPR • Oxygen administration • Automatic external defibrillation	American Red Cross National Headquarters 431 18th St. NW Washington, DC 20006 202-303-4498 www.redcross.org/services/hss/aquatics
YMCA of the USA (YMCA)	Aquatic certification	Certification courses in: • Lifeguard training • Swimming instruction • Scuba • Water polo coaching • Aquatic facility management • Pool operations	YMCA of the USA 101 Wacker Dr. Chicago, IL 60606 312-977-0031 www.ymca.net/index.jsp
Ellis and Associates (E&A)	Aquatic certification	Certification courses in: • Lifeguard training • Facility audit program Best known for specialization in water park lifeguarding and safety.	Ellis & Associates Corporate Offices 3506 Spruce Park Circle Kingwood, TX 77345 800-742-8720 www.jellis.com

Agency name	Primary aquatics function	Services offered	Contact information
Boy Scouts of America (BSA)	Aquatic certification	Merit badges in: • Lifesaving • Lifeguarding • Swimming • Canoeing • Sailing • First aid	Boy Scouts of America 1325 W. Walnut Hill Lane P.O. Box 152079 Irving, TX 75015-2079 972-580-2406 www.scouting.org
National Association of Underwater Instructors (NAUI)	Scuba certification	Scuba certification: Basic, instructor, and specialty diver courses	NAUI Headquarters P.O. Box 89789 Tampa, FL 33689-0413 813-628-6284 Fax: 813-628-8253 www.nauiww.org
Professional Association of Diving Instructors (PADI)	Scuba certification	Scuba certification: Basic, instructor, and specialty diver courses	Professional Association of Diving Instructors 30151 Tomas St. Rancho Santa Margarita, CA 92688-2125 949-858-7234 Fax: 949-858-7264 www.padi.com/english/default.asp?o=am
National Safety Council (NSC)	National health and safety organization	• First aid/CPR courses • Blood-borne pathogen courses • First responder courses	National Safety Council 1121 Spring Lake Dr. Itasca, IL 60143-3201 630-285-1121 www.nsc.org
American Lifeguard Association (ALA)	Certification agency	Certification courses in: • Lifeguard training • CPR/first aid • Pool operations	American Lifeguard Association 8300 Boone Blvd., 5th Floor Vienna, VA 22182 703-761-6750 www.americanlifeguard.com/index.htm
Lifesaving Society Canada	Certification agency (Canada)	Certification courses in: • Lifeguard training • Aquatic emergency care • Lifesaving	Lifesaving Society Canada National Office 287 McArthur Ave. Ottawa, ON K1L 6P3 613-746-5694 Fax: 613-746-9929 www.lifesaving.ca/ls2/main_en.htm
Starfish Aquatics Institute	Aquatic certification and training	• Lifeguard certification • Consulting services • Aquatic merchandise sales	Starfish Aquatics Institute National Office/Aquatics Center 7240 Sallie Mood Dr. Savannah, GA 31406 912-692-1173 Fax: 912-692-0816 www.starfishaquatics.org

Agency name	Primary aquatics function	Services offered	Contact information
Professional associations			
National Intramural Recreational Sports Association (NIRSA)	Membership agency for recreation professionals (specializes in collegiate recreation)	• National annual conference with some aquatics speakers • Aquatics textbook • Aquatics committee • Aquatics symposium	National Intramural Recreational Sports Association 4185 S.W. Research Way Corvallis, OR 97333-1067 541-766-8211 Fax: 541-766-8284 www.nirsa.org
National Recreation and Park Association (NRPA)	Membership agency for recreation professionals	• National annual conference with some aquatics speakers • Aquatics textbook • Aquatics committee • Aquatic facility manager certification	National Recreation and Park Association 22377 Belmont Ridge Rd. Ashburn, VA 20148-4501 703-858-0784 Fax: 703-858-0794 www.nrpa.org
American Camping Association (ACA)	Membership agency for camping professionals	• Camping-related publications • Job placement service • Camp accreditation	American Camping Association 5000 State Road 67 N. Martinsville, IN 46151 765-342-8456 Fax: 765-342-2065 www.acacamps.org
American Alliance for Health, Physical Education, Recreation and Dance (AAHPERD)	Membership agency for physical education professionals	• National annual conference with some aquatics speakers • Aquatics committee • Position papers on aquatic issues	American Alliance for Health, Physical Education, Recreation and Dance 1900 Association Dr. Reston, VA 20191-1598 703-476-3400 www.aahperd.org
National Water Safety Congress	Membership agency for aquatic professionals	• National conference • Professional publications • Water safety grant program • Water safety journal	National Water Safety Congress Executive Director P.O. Box 1632 Mentor, OH 44061 440-209-9805 www.watersafetycongress.org
United States Lifesaving Association (USLA)	Membership agency for open water lifeguards	• *American Lifeguard Magazine* • Standards for open water lifeguard training • Open water lifeguard competitions	United States Lifesaving Association P.O. Box 366 Huntington Beach, CA 92648 866-FOR-USLA www.usla.org

Agency name	Primary aquatics function	Services offered	Contact information
National Swimming Pool Foundation (NSPF)	Nonprofit foundation whose mission is to foster and support programs of education and research in the swimming pool industry	Pool operator certification course	National Swimming Pool Foundation 224 E. Cheyenne Mountain Blvd. Colorado Springs, CO 80906 719-540-9119 www.nspf.org
Aquatic Exercise Association (AEA)	Professional resource and certification agency for aquatic exercise	• Certification courses/ workshops • Conferences	Aquatic Exercise Association 3439 Technology Dr., Ste. 6 Nokomis, FL 34275-3627 941-486-8600 http://aeawave.com
Divers Alert Network (DAN)	Professional membership organization and medical assistance organization for scuba divers	• Divers' insurance • Professional texts • Professional magazine • Certification courses	Divers Alert Network The Peter B. Bennett Center 6 W. Colony Place Durham, NC 27705 919-684-2948 www.diversalertnetwork.org/about
Professional Pool Operators of America (PPOA)	Professional membership agency for swimming pool operators	Magazine	Professional Pool Operators of America P.O. Box 164 Newcastle, CA 95658 916-663-1265 www.ppoa.org
U.S. Water Fitness Association (USWFA)	Professional membership agency for water exercise instructors	• Certification courses • Conferences • Texts and videos	U.S. Water Fitness Association P.O. Box 243279 Boynton Beach, FL 33424-3279 561-732-9908 www.uswfa.com/index.html
Aquatic Fitness Professionals Association	Professional membership agency for water exercise instructors	Certification courses	Aquatic Fitness Professionals Association 1601 Great Western Dr. Longmont, CO 80501 800-484-9666 Code 5939 www.aquacert.org
Sport regulatory/membership agencies			
American Swimming Coaches Association (ASCA)	Membership agency for swimming coaches	• Certification courses • Coaches conferences • Professional texts and videos	American Swimming Coaches Association National Office 2101 N. Andrews Ave. #107 Ft. Lauderdale, FL 33311 800-356-2722 www.swimmingcoach.org

Agency name	Primary aquatics function	Services offered	Contact information
Sport regulatory/membership agencies			
USA Diving	Membership and regulatory organization for competitive springboard and platform divers	• Coaching courses • Professional publications • Sanctioned meets	United States Diving Inc. 201 S. Capitol Ave., Ste. 430 Indianapolis, IN 46225 317-237-5252 www.usdiving.org
USA Swimming	Membership and regulatory organization for competitive swimmers	• Swimmers clinics • Professional resources • Swim officials certification • Sanctioned meets	USA Swimming One Olympic Plaza Colorado Springs, CO 80909 719-866-4578 www.usswim.org/index.shtml
United States Synchronized Swimming	Membership and regulatory organization for synchronized swimmers	• Coaches clinics • Camps • Judges training • Professional texts/manuals • Sanctioned meets	United States Synchronized Swimming 201 S. Capitol Ave., Ste. 901 Indianapolis, IN 46225 317-237-5700 www.usasynchro.org
USA Water Polo	Membership and regulatory organization for water polo	• Coaches clinics • Referee clinics • Professional texts • Sanctioned matches	USA Water Polo 1685 W. Uintah Colorado Springs, CO 80904-2921 719-634-0699 www.usawaterpolo.com
U.S. Masters Swimming (USMS)	Membership and regulatory organization for adult competitive swimmers	• Coaches clinics • Professional publications • Sanctioned meets	U.S. Masters Swimming National Office P.O. Box 185 Londonderry, NH 03053-0185 603-537-0203 www.usms.org
Regulatory and government agencies			
National Sanitation Foundation (NSF)	A nonprofit, nongovernmental organization specializing in standards development, product certification, education, and risk management for public health and safety	Pool and spa equipment certification program	National Sanitation Foundation 789 Dixboro Rd. P.O. Box 130140 Ann Arbor, MI 48113-0140 734-769-8010 Fax: 734-769-0109 www.nsf.org
State agencies	State government: Bathing code regulation	Bathing code regulation	See appendix B.

Agency name	Primary aquatics function	Services offered	Contact information
U.S. Department of Justice	Federal government agency that regulates the Americans With Disabilities Act	Code regulation	U.S. Department of Justice 950 Pennsylvania Ave. NW Washington, DC 20530-0001 800-514-0301 www.ada.gov
Occupational Safety and Health Administration (OSHA)	A federal regulatory administration under the Department of Labor	Code regulation related to blood-borne pathogens and hazard communication standards	Occupational Safety and Health Administration 200 Constitution Ave. NW Washington, DC 20210 800-321-OSHA www.osha.gov
Centers for Disease Control and Prevention (CDC)	A federal health regulatory administration under the Department of Health and Human Services	• Information related to aquatic health and safety • Statistics related to drowning and other aquatic accidents	Centers for Disease Control and Prevention 1600 Clifton Rd. Atlanta, GA 30333 404-639-3311 www.cdc.gov
National Response Center (NRC)	A federal agency responsible for receiving reports of spilled or released hazardous materials, such as swimming pool chlorine	Reporting service only	National Response Center c/o United States Coast Guard (G-OPF), Rm. 2611 2100 2nd St. SW Washington, DC 20593-0001 800-424-8802 www.nrc.uscg.mil/nrchp.html
Consumer Product Safety Commission (CPSC)	Injury data associated with specific products, such as swimming pools, hot tubs, and diving boards	Injury data	Mailing address: U.S. Consumer Product Safety Commission Washington, DC 20207-0001 Street address: 4330 East-West Highway Bethesda, Maryland 20814-4408 301-504-6816 www.cpsc.gov
Environmental Protection Agency (EPA)	A federal agency charged with regulation of air, soil, and water quality	Guidelines related to water quality at bathing beaches	Environmental Protection Agency Ariel Rios Building 1200 Pennsylvania Ave. NW Washington, DC 20460 202-272-0167 www.epa.gov

Agency name	Primary aquatics function	Services offered	Contact information
Regulatory and government agencies			
U.S. Army Corps of Engineers	A federal agency that owns and regulates federal recreational water resources	Water safety educational program for teachers	U.S. Army Corps of Engineers 441 G. St., NW Washington, DC 20314 202-761-0008 http://watersafety.usace.army.mil
Boating agencies			
U.S. Power Squadron (USPS)	A nonprofit educational organization dedicated to making boating safer and more enjoyable by teaching classes in seamanship, navigation, and related subjects	• Boating education courses • Professional publications	U.S. Power Squadron 1504 Blue Ridge Rd. Raleigh, NC 27607 919-821-0281 www.usps.org/newpublic1/guesthome.htm
U.S. Coast Guard Auxiliary (USCGAUX)	Auxiliarists assist the Coast Guard in non-law-enforcement programs such as public education, vessel safety checks, safety patrols, search and rescue, maritime security, and environmental protection	• Boating safety courses • Seamanship manuals	U.S. Coast Guard Auxiliary 2100 Second St. SW Washington, DC 20593 877-875-6296 www.cgaux.org
National Safe Boating Council (NSBC)	An agency whose mission is to reduce accidents and enhance the boating experience	• Boating safety instructor certification courses • Instructional/safety materials • Boating safety grants • Professional meetings	National Safe Boating Council P.O. Box 509 Bristow, VA 20136 703-361-4294 www.safeboatingcouncil.org/index.htm
U.S. Sailing Association	Sailing advocacy, training, and regulatory organization	• Instructional materials • Learn to sail programs • Magazines and journals	U.S. Sailing Association P.O. Box 1260 15 Maritime Dr. Portsmouth, RI 02871-0907 401-683-0800 Fax: 401-683-0840 www.ussailing.org

Agency name	Primary aquatics function	Services offered	Contact information
Agencies that offer aquatic training			
Lifesaving Resources Inc.	Aquatic training and consulting business	• Training seminars • Sales of aquatic equipment and texts	Lifesaving Resources Inc. P.O. Box 905 Harrisville, NH 03450 603-827-4139 www.lifesaving.com
Dive Rescue International	Professional membership agency	• Scuba rescue conferences • Scuba rescue courses • Sales of scuba rescue equipment	Dive Rescue International 201 N. Link Lane Fort Collins, CO 80524-2712 970-482-0887 Toll free: 800-248-3483 www.diverescueintl.com/descriptions.html
Aquatic Consulting Services	Aquatic consulting agency	• Aquatic training • Consulting services	Aquatic Consulting Services 4909 Orchard Ave. #4 San Diego, CA 92107 619-224-3100 www.alisonosinski.com/index.htm
Professional Aquatic Consultants International	Aquatic consulting agency	• Aquatic training • Consulting services	Professional Aquatic Consultants International 6 Grove Park Court Taylors, SC 29687 864-322-9390 www.aquaticweb.com
Aquatic Safety Research Group, LLC	Aquatic consulting agency	• Aquatic training • Consulting services	Aquatic Safety Research Group, LLC 1632 Glenwood Circle State College, PA 16803 814-234-0313 http://aquaticsafetygroup.com/biographies.html
New England Aquatics Network Inc.	Nonprofit aquatics membership association	• Aquatic training • Conferences	New England Aquatics Network Inc. P.O. Box 25 Boston, MA 02130 www.neaquanet.com
International agencies			
International Life Saving Federation (ILS)	Membership, educational, and sport organization for lifesaving	• Lifesaving competitions • Lifesaving library • Symposiums	International Lifesaving Federation Gemeenteplain 26 3010 Leuven Belgium 32.16.35.35.00 Fax: 32.16.35.01.02 http://lifesaving.dsnsports.com

Agency name	Primary aquatics function	Services offered	Contact information
International agencies			
Confédération Mondiale des Activités Subaquatiques (CMAS)	International technical and promotional agency for scuba	• Publications • Research	Confédération Mondiale des Activités Subaquatiques Viale Tiziano, 74 00196 Roma, Italia 39 / 06 / 36 85 84 80 Fax: + 39 / 06 / 32 11 05 95 www.cmas2000.org/main2.asp
Federation International de Natation (FINA)	International regulatory body for all competitive aquatic sports: swimming, diving, water polo, synchronized swimming	• Rule promotion • Magazines • Professional texts	Federation International de Natation Av. de l' Avant-Poste 4 1005 Lausanne Switzerland Country & City Codes: 41-21 310 4710 www.fina.org
The Royal Life Saving Society—Commonwealth	Affiliation agency for national lifesaving federations	• Lifesaving competition • Information sharing between member agencies	The Royal Life Saving Society—Commonwealth River House-High St. Broom Warwickshire Commonwealth RLSS (44) (1789) 773994 Fax: (44) (1789) 773995

State Bathing Code Contact List

APPENDIX

Alabama

Alabama Department of Environmental
  Management
P.O. Box 301463
1400 Coliseum Blvd.
Montgomery, AL 36110
Phone: 334-271-7700
www.adem.state.al.us

Alaska

Juneau Office, ADEC
410 Willoughby Ave., Ste. 303
Juneau, AK 99801-1795
Phone: 907-465-5010
Fax: 907-465-5097
www.state.ak.us/dec/eh/fss/public/pools.htm

Arizona

Department of Environmental Quality
Water Quality Division
1110 W. Washington St.
Phoenix, AZ 85007-2952
Phone: 602-771-2303
Fax: 602-771-4528
www.azsos.com/public_services/Title_18/18-05.htm

Arkansas

Arkansas Department of Health
Division of Environmental Health
4815 W. Markham
Little Rock, AR 72205-3867
Phone: 501-661-2623
Fax: 501-661-2032
www.healthyarkansas.com/services/services_eh2_
  all.html

California

California Department of Health Services
P.O. Box 942732
Sacramento, CA 94234-7320
Phone: 916-323-6111
www.leginfo.ca.gov/cgi-bin/displaycode?section=
  hsc&group=116001-117000&file=116025-116068

Colorado

Department of Public Health & Environment
Water Quality Control Division
4300 Cherry Creek Dr. South
Denver, CO 80222-1530
Phone: 303-692-3500
www.state.co.us/gov_dir/oed/industry/
  IndDetail.cfm?id=75

Connecticut

Connecticut Department of Public Health
410 Capitol Ave.
P.O. Box 340308
Hartford, CT 06134-0308
Phone: 860-509-8000
www.dph.state.ct.us/phc/browse.asp

Delaware

Division of Public Health
Health Protection Systems
417 Federal St.
Dover, DE 19901
Phone: 302-744-4546
Fax: 302-739-3839

District of Columbia

District of Columbia Department of Health
John A. Wilson Bldg.
1350 Pennsylvania Ave. NW
Washington, DC 20004
Phone: 202-535-2180
http://dchealth.dc.gov/index.asp

Florida

Florida Department of Health
4052 Bald Cypress Way
Bin A-04
Tallahassee, FL 32399-1705
Phone: 850-245-4004
www.doh.state.fl.us/environment/swim/64e-9.pdf

Georgia

Georgia Department of Human Resources
Constituent Services
2 Peachtree St. Northwest, Ste. 29-213
Atlanta, GA 30303
Phone: 404-657-2700
www.legis.state.ga.us/legis/1997_98/fulltext/
    sb438.htm

Hawaii

Hawaii State Department of Health
1250 Punchbowl St.
Honolulu, HI 96813
Phone: 808-586-4400
www.state.hi.us/doh/rules/11-10.pdf

Idaho

Idaho Department of Health & Welfare
450 W. State St.
Boise, ID 83720-0036
Phone: 208-334-5500
http://www2.state.id.us/adm/adminrules/rules/
    idapa16/0214.pdf

Illinois

Illinois Department of Public Health
535 W. Jefferson St.
Springfield, IL 62761
Phone: 217-782-4977
Fax: 217-782-3987
www.idph.state.il.us/commission/jcar/
    admincode1077/07700820sections.html

Indiana

State Department of Health
2 N. Meridian St.
Indianapolis, IN 46204
Phone: 317-233-1325
www.in.gov/isdh/regsvcs/saneng/laws_rules/
    410_iac_6-2._1.htm#A

Iowa

Department of Public Health
Lucas State Office Bldg.
321 E. 12th St.
Des Moines, IA 50307-0075
Phone: 515-281-4529
www.legis.state.ia.us/Rules/2002/iac/641iac/64115/
    64115.pdf

Kansas

Kansas Department of Health and Environment
400 S.W. 8th St., Ste. 206
Topeka, KS 66612
Phone: 785-296-1500
www.kdhe.state.ks.us

Kentucky

Department for Public Health
Environmental Management Branch
275 E. Main St.
Frankfort, KY 40621
Phone: 502-564-4856
http://publichealth.state.ky.us/env-public_
    swimming_.htm

Louisiana

Louisiana Department of Health
1201 Capitol Access Rd.
P.O. Box 629
Baton Rouge, LA 70821-0629
Phone: 225-342-9500
Fax: 225-342-5568
www.dhh.state.la.us

Maine

Department of Human Services
Bureau of Health
11 State House Station
Key Plaza
286 Water St.
Augusta, ME 04333
Phone: 207-287-8016
ftp://ftp.state.me.us/pub/sos/cec/rcn/apa/10/144/
    144c202.doc

Maryland

Department of Health and Mental Hygiene
Division of Community Services
6 St. Paul St., Ste. 1301
Baltimore, MD 21202-1608
Phone: 410-767-8417
Fax: 410-333-8926
www.cha.state.md.us/ofpchs/comm_srv/pools.html

Massachusetts

Department of Public Health
Division of Community Sanitation
305 South St., 1st Floor
Jamaica Plain, MA 02130
Phone: 617-983-6761
Fax: 617-983-6770
www.state.ma.us/dph/dcs/dcs.htm

Michigan

Michigan Department of Environmental Quality
Constitution Hall
525 W. Allegan St.
P.O. Box 30473
Lansing, MI 48909-7973
Phone: 517-373-7917
www.michigan.gov/deq/0,1607,7-135-3313_3686_
    3732- - -,00.html
www.michigan.gov/deq

Minnesota

Minnesota Department of Public Health
Division of Environmental Health
P.O. Box 64975
St. Paul, MN 55164-0975
Phone: 651-215-5800
www.health.state.mn.us/divs/eh/pools/index.html

Mississippi

Mississippi State Department of Health
P.O. Box 1700
Jackson, MS 39215-1700
Phone: 601-576-7400
www.msdh.state.ms.us/msdhsite/index.cfm/
11,144,95,32,pdf/sanitationswim%2EPDF

Missouri

Missouri Department of Health and Senior Services
P.O. Box 570
Jefferson City, MO 65102
Phone: 573-751-6041
www.health.state.mo.us

Montana

Department of Public Health and Human Services
1400 Broadway
P.O. Box 202951
Cogswell Bldg.
Helena, MT 59620-2951
Phone: 406-444-4540
www.dphhs.state.mt.us/hpsd/Food-consumer/pdf/
swimming_pools_spas_rules.pdf

Nebraska

Nebraska State Department of Health
301 Centennial Mall South
P.O. Box 95007
Lincoln, NE 68509
Phone: 402-471-2541
www.hhs.state.ne.us/crl/rcs/pool/pool.htm

Nevada

Nevada State Health Division
505 E. King St.
Rm. 201
Carson City, NV 89701
Phone: 775-684-4200
Fax: 775-684-4211
www.leg.state.nv.us/NAC/NAC-444.html

New Hampshire

New Hampshire Department of Environmental
Services
6 Hazen Dr.
P.O. Box 95
Concord, NH 03302-0095
Phone: 603-271-3503
www.des.state.nh.us/pools/env1100.pdf

New Jersey

Department of Health and Senior Services
P.O. Box 369
Trenton, NJ 08625-0369
Phone: 609-292-5605
www.state.nj.us/health/eoh/phss/recbathing.pdf

New Mexico

New Mexico Environment Department
P.O. Box 26110
1190 St. Francis Dr., N4050
Santa Fe, NM 87502-0110
Phone: 800-219-6157 or 505-827-2855
www.nmenv.state.nm.us/NMED_regs/csb/
Pool%20Reg-Final%20Draft.doc

New York

New York State Department of Health
Corning Tower #503
Albany, NY 12237
Phone: 518-474-2160
www.health.state.ny.us/nysdoh/phforum/
nycrr10.htm

North Carolina

Division of Environmental Health
1630 Mail Service Center
Raleigh, NC 27699-1630
Phone: 919-733-2870
www.deh.enr.state.nc.us/ehs/25.htm

North Dakota

North Dakota Department of Health
600 E. Boulevard Ave.
Bismarck, ND 58505-0200
Phone: 701-328-3272
www.state.nd.us/lr//information/acdata/html/
..%5cpdf%5c33-29-01.pdf

Ohio

Ohio Department of Health
Swimming Pools, Spas & Special Use Pools (Public)
246 N. High St.
P.O. Box 118
Columbus, OH 43216-0118
Phone: 614-466-1390
www.odh.state.oh.us/ODHPrograms/Swim/
swim1.htm

Oklahoma

Oklahoma State Department of Health
1000 N.E. 10th St.
Oklahoma City, OK 73117
Phone: 405-271-5600
www.health.state.ok.us/program/cpd/320.pdf

Oregon

Department of Human Services
Health Division
500 Summer St. Northeast, E25
Salem, OR 97301-1098
Phone: 503-945-5944
Fax: 503-378-2897
http://landru.leg.state.or.us/ors/448.html

Pennsylvania

Pennsylvania Department of Health
P.O. Box 90
Health and Welfare Bldg.
Harrisburg, PA 17108
Phone: 877-PA-HEALTH
www.dsf.health.state.pa.us

Rhode Island

Office of Environmental Health Risk Assessment
3 Capitol Hill
Rm. 201
Providence, RI 02908-5097
Phone: 401-222-3424
Fax: 401-222-6953
www.health.ri.gov/environment/risk/index.php

South Carolina

Department of Health and Environmental Control
2600 Bull St.
Columbia, SC 29201
Phone: 803-898-3432
www.scdhec.com/water/html/reg.html#rw

South Dakota

Department of Environment and Natural Resources
Joe Foss Bldg.
523 E. Capitol
Pierre, SD 57501
Phone: 605-773-3151
Fax: 605-773-6035
www.state.sd.us/denr/DES/Drinking/swimming.htm

Tennessee

Tennessee Department of Health
425 Fifth Ave. North
Cordell Hull Bldg., 3rd Floor
Nashville, TN 37247
Phone: 615-741-3111
E-mail: TM.health@state.tn.us
www.state.tn.us/health
www.state.tn.us/sos/rules/1200/1200-23/
    1200-23-05.pdf

Texas

Texas Department of Health
General Sanitation Division
1100 W. 49th St.
Austin, TX 78756-3199
Phone: 888-963-7111
Fax: 512-458-7111
www.tdh.state.tx.us/beh/gs/pools.htm

Utah

Utah Department of Health
P.O. Box 141010
Salt Lake City, UT 84114
Phone: 801-538-6101
www.code-co.com/utah/admin/2000/r392302.htm

Vermont

Vermont Department of Health
108 Cherry St.
P.O. Box 70
Burlington, VT 05402-0070
Phone: 802-863-7200
www.healthyvermonters.info/cph/officers/
    recwater.shtml

Virginia

Virginia Department of Health
Main Street Station
1500 E. Main St.
Richmond, VA 23219
Phone: 804-864-7470
www.vdh.state.va.us/oehs/food/regs/swimpool.htm
www.vdh.state.va.us

Washington

Environmental Health Division
701 E. Main St.
Battle Ground, WA 98604
Phone: 360-687-7126
Fax: 360-687-6794
www.swwhd.wa.gov/envirohlth/recreational_
    health.htm

West Virginia

West Virginia Bureau for Public Health
Rm. 702
350 Capitol St.
Charleston, WV 25301-3712
Phone: 304-558-2971
Fax: 304-558-1035
www.wvsos.com/csr/verify.asp?TitleSeries=64-16

Wisconsin

Department of Health and Family Services
1 W. Wilson St.
Madison, WI 53702
Phone: 608-266-1865
www.legis.state.wi.us/rsb/code/hfs/hfs110.html

Wyoming

Wyoming Department of Agriculture
Consumer Health Services
2219 Carey Ave.
Cheyenne, WY 82002-0100
Phone: 307-777-7321
Fax: 307-777-6593
E-mail: wda@state.wy.us
http://legisweb.state.wy.us/2002/bills/hb0117.pdf

Aquatic and Safety Equipment Sources

Adolph Kiefer and Associates

1700 Kiefer Dr.
Zion, IL 60099
800-323-4071
www.kiefer.com

Aquatic Technology Inc.

26 Duane Dr.
Liberty, ME 04949
800-446-6416
www.poolsigns.com

Filtrex Inc.

450 Hamburg Tpke.
Wayne, NJ 07474
973-595-0400
Fax: 973-595-6506

Galls Inc. (first aid/EMS supplies)

2680 Palumbo Dr.
P.O. Box 54308
Lexington, KY 40555-4308
866-290-3385
www.galls.com

Laeredal Medical

167 Myers Corners Rd.
P.O. Box 1840
Wappingers Falls, NY 12590
845-297-7770
www.laerdal.com

The Lifeguard Store

1016 E. Grove St.
Bloomington, IL 61701
800-846-7052
www.thelifeguardstore.com

Lifesaving Resources Inc.

P.O. Box 905
Harrisville, NH 03450
603-827-4139
www.lifesaving.com

Lincoln Commercial Pool Equipment

2051 Commerce Ave.
Concord, CA 94520
800-223-5450
www.lincolnaquatics.com

Marine Rescue Products Inc.

P.O. Box 3484
Newport, RI 02840
800-341-9500
www.marine-rescue.com

Medtronic Physio-Control (AEDs)

11811 Willows Rd. Northeast
P.O. Box 97006
Redmond, WA 98073-9706
800-442-1142 or 425-867-4000
www.medtronic-ers.com

MrFlag.com (flags)

34 Buckingham Palace Rd., Ste. 753
Belgravia
London SW1W 0RH
United Kingdom
(+44) 845 061 3914
www.mrflag.com/home.asp

Neptune-Benson Inc. (filters)

One Bridal Ave.
West Warwick, RI 02893
401-821-2200 or 800-832-8002
Fax: 401-821-7129
www.neptunebenson.com

Paddock Pool Equipment Company Inc.

P.O. Box 11676
555 Paddock Pkwy.
Rock Hill, SC 29730
803-324-1111
www.paddockpool.com/default2.asp

Paragon Aquatics

1351 Route 55
LaGrangeville, NY 12540
845-452-5500
Fax: 845-452-5426
www.paragonaquatics.com

Poseidon Technologies

200 Galleria Pkway., Ste. 790
Atlanta, GA 30339-5975
866-342-0980
www.poseidon-tech.com/us/index.html

Recreation Supply Company

P.O. Box 2757
Bismarck, ND 58502
800-437-8072
www.recsupply.com

Recreonics Inc.

4200 Schmitt Ave.
Louisville, KY 40213
800-428-3254
www.recreonics.com

Spectrum Pool Products

7100 Spectrum Lane
Missoula, MT 59802
800-776-5309
www.spectrumproducts.com

Sprint Aquatics

P.O. Box 3840
San Luis Obispo, CA 93403
805-541-5330
www.sprintaquatics.com

Stearns Inc. (PFDs)

1100 Stearns Dr.
Sauk Rapids, MN 56379
320-252-1642 or 800-328-3208
Fax: 320-252-4425
www.stearnsinc.com

Suspended Aquatic Mentor Inc.

517 Wyoming Ave.
Millburn, NJ 07041
888-376-3335
Fax: 973-376-1213
www.aquamentor.com

Water Safety Products Inc.

128 Tomahawk Dr.
Indian Harbour Beach, FL 32937
800-987-7238
www.watersafetyproductsinc.com

WMS Aquatic Specialists

Catalog Department
P.O. Box 398
Ellensburg, WA 98926
800-426-9460
www.wmsaquatics.com

Athletics Forms

D

APPENDIX

Patron Survey

Patron gender: ☐ Male ☐ Female

Patron age: ☐ 15-20 ☐ 21-30 ☐ 31-40 ☐ 41-50 ☐ 51+

Date of survey: _____

1. What programs do you currently participate in? (check all that apply)

   ☐ Lap swim
   ☐ Swimming lessons
   ☐ Water exercise
   ☐ Scuba
   ☐ Swim team
   ☐ Lifeguard training
   ☐ Synchronized swimming lessons or team
   ☐ Water polo club

2. My favorite aquatic program is _____.

3. How would you rate the quality of the aquatic programs you participate in?

   ☐ Poor
   ☐ Fair
   ☐ Good
   ☐ Excellent

4. What programs would you like to see offered?

   ☐ Lap swim
   ☐ Swimming lessons
   ☐ Water exercise
   ☐ Scuba
   ☐ Swim team
   ☐ Lifeguard training
   ☐ Synchronized swimming lessons or team
   ☐ Water polo club
   ☐ Other: _____

5. What are the best times and days for you to participate in programs? _____

   _____

6. Do you have any comments about our aquatic programs? _____

   _____

   _____

From *Aquatic Facility Management* by Paul Fawcett, 2005, Champaign, IL: Human Kinetics.

New Aquatic Program Worksheet

New program under consideration: _____

Anticipated enrollment in new program: _____   Projected fees for new program: _____

(see Program Revenue Evaluation Worksheet)

How many weeks will this program be offered? _____

Desired day/time to offer this program: _____

Is the facility available at that time? ☐ Yes   ☐ No

Can this program share the facility with other programs? ☐ Yes   ☐ No

Program Facility Requirements

Required minimum water depth: _____   Required maximum water depth: _____

Required pool length: _____   Required pool width: _____

Required water temperature: _____ Does our facility meet these requirements? ☐ Yes   ☐ No

Explain: _____

Customers for proposed program: _____

Have customers been surveyed regarding their interest in this program? ☐ Yes   ☐ No

If so, explain results: _____

_____

New Program Equipment Requirements

Item	We possess it (Y/N)	If no, cost of purchase/rental
_____	_____	_____
_____	_____	_____
_____	_____	_____
_____	_____	_____
_____	_____	_____

Total cost of new program equipment: _____

Staff Positions Required for This Program

_____   Number: _____

_____   Number: _____

_____   Number: _____

_____   Number: _____

Are special staff qualifications necessary for this program? ☐ Yes   ☐ No

If yes, list: _____

Do we have a staff member currently qualified to offer this program? ☐ Yes   ☐ No

If yes, who? _____ If no, other options: _____

New program will be adopted: ☐ Yes   ☐ No

The following limitations or conditions will apply to this program: _____

Signature of aquatic director: _____

From *Aquatic Facility Management* by Paul Fawcett, 2005, Champaign, IL: Human Kinetics.

Program Revenue Evaluation Worksheet

Program being evaluated: _____ Session: _____

Number of hours this program operated: _____ (year/month)

Part A. Expenses

Wages: Include instructors, lifeguards on duty, and program directors directly involved.

Staff member	Hourly wage ×	Hours worked =	Total
_____	_____ ×	_____ =	_____
_____	_____ ×	_____ =	_____
_____	_____ ×	_____ =	_____
_____	_____ ×	_____ =	_____
_____	_____ ×	_____ =	_____

Total hourly wages of staff for this program: _____

Utilities: Determine cost on an hourly basis.

Lights _____

Heat _____

Water _____

Total utility cost/hr. _____ × _____ program hours = _____ Total utility cost

Chemicals: Determine cost on an hourly basis (monthly cost = hours per month × hours program runs).

Chlorine/bromine _____

Soda ash _____

Muriatic acid _____

Total chemical cost/hr. _____ × _____ program hours = _____ Total chemical cost

Advertising: Include cost for this program only.

Radio spots _____

Newspaper ads _____

Television ads _____

Flyers _____

Total advertising cost _____

Totals:

Wages _____

Utilities _____

Chemicals _____

Advertising _____

Total expenses: _____

Part B. Revenues

Registration fee (amount) _____ × _____ number of students = _____ Fee revenue

Donations _____

Fund-raising _____

Total revenue: _____

Part C. Computations

Total expenses _____ − _____ total revenue = _____ Profit (or loss)

From *Aquatic Facility Management* by Paul Fawcett, 2005, Champaign, IL: Human Kinetics.

Swimming Instructor Evaluation Form

Instructor: _____ Evaluator: _____

Date evaluated: _____ Course/level being taught: _____

Circle the appropriate response.

   1. Instructor began class on time.   Yes   No

     Comments: _____

   2. Instructor was prepared for class.   Yes   No

     Comments: _____

   3. Instructor was dressed properly for this class.   Yes   No

     Comments: _____

   4. Instructor called students by name.   Yes   No

     Comments: _____

   5. Instructor showed enthusiasm about teaching.   Yes   No

     Comments: _____

   6. Instructor appeared interested in students.   Yes   No

     Comments: _____

   7. Lesson was well organized.   Yes   No

     Comments: _____

   8. Instructor followed facility safety rules.   Yes   No

     Comments: _____

   9. Instructor made good use of class time.   Yes   No

     Comments: _____

  10. Instructor maintained class discipline.   Yes   No

     Comments: _____

From *Aquatic Facility Management* by Paul Fawcett, 2005, Champaign, IL: Human Kinetics.

Participant Aquatic Program Evaluation Form

Program participated in:_____

Session: _____ (dates)

Please take a moment to comment on your experience in the aquatic program that you (or your child) participated in. Circle the answer that best indicates your feelings. Your answers will remain anonymous, unless you would like a response. If you desire a response, please include your name on the bottom of this form.

1. The overall quality of the program was

   Poor   Fair   Good   Excellent

2. The time of day of the program was

   Too early   Too late   Just right   Suggested time: _____

3. The day of the week of the program was

   Convenient   Not convenient   Suggested day: _____

4. The number of classes per session was

   Too few   Too many   Just right   Suggested number: _____

5. The number of students in the class was

   Too few   Too many   Just right   Suggested number: _____

6. Rate your (or your child's) instructor for the program:

   Poor   Fair   Good   Excellent

7. Rate the cleanliness of our aquatic facility:

   Poor   Fair   Good   Excellent

Please comment on any of the previous questions or any other issues related to the program or facility:_____

_____

Are there any other aquatic programs that you would like to see offered?_____

_____

Name and address (if you would like a response): _____

_____

From *Aquatic Facility Management* by Paul Fawcett, 2005, Champaign, IL: Human Kinetics.

Staff Aquatic Program Evaluation Form

Please take time to offer suggestions and comments about the program you teach. Your answers can positively affect you and your fellow staff. Please offer useful and constructive feedback. Your answers are confidential.

Name of the program you teach: _____

How many years have you taught this program? _____

Do you enjoy teaching this program? ☐ Yes   ☐ No

Why or why not?_____

_____

How would you describe the length of your class periods?

     Too long   Too short   Just right

If you think your class periods should be longer or shorter, explain why and suggest an appropriate

length: _____

_____

_____

Are the instructor-to-student ratios correct for this class? ☐ Yes   ☐ No

If no, please suggest another ratio and justify your answer:_____

_____

What new equipment do you think is needed for this program?

_____

_____

_____

_____

Justify your need for the new equipment:_____

_____

What new policies do you think are needed for this program?

_____

_____

Explain why you think these new policies are needed:_____

_____

Rate your overall impression of the program in which you teach:

     Poor   Fair   Good   Excellent

Please take time to offer any general suggestions that you think would make this program better:

_____

_____

Persons With Disabilities
Program Volunteer Questionnaire

Name: _____ Address: _____

Phone number: _____ Date of birth: _____

Please check any of the following certificates that you currently hold:

☐ Lifeguard training ☐ Lifeguard instructor

☐ CPR ☐ EMT

☐ First aid ☐ Special populations instructor

☐ Water safety instructor ☐ CPR instructor

Please describe any experience you have working with persons with disabilities: _____

_____

_____

_____

_____

Why do you want to work with persons with disabilities? _____

_____

_____

_____

_____

How did you hear about our program? _____

_____

If you are a student, please fill in the following:

School: _____ Year in school: _____

Major: _____ Course requiring this experience: _____

Instructor: _____ Will you require verification of participation? _____

From *Aquatic Facility Management* by Paul Fawcett, 2005, Champaign, IL: Human Kinetics.

Registration Form

Participant name(s): _____ Age:_____

_____ Age:_____

_____ Age:_____

_____ Age:_____

Parent or guardian name (if participant is under 18):_____

Address: _____

_____

_____

Telephone number: (home) _____ (work) _____

Classes registering for:_____ Days_____ Time_____

_____ Days_____ Time_____

_____ Days_____ Time_____

_____ Days_____ Time_____

Fees paid: _____

Discounts, scholarships, fee waivers: _____

Please list any special needs or medical considerations our staff should be aware of: _____

_____

_____

These entries made by staff

Date registration taken: _____ Staff member: _____

-- Tear below this line --

This is to confirm that you are registered for the following classes.

Name: _____ Class: _____ Start date: _____

Class days:_____ Class time: _____ Class location: _____

Name: _____ Class: _____ Start date: _____

Class days:_____ Class time: _____ Class location: _____

Name: _____ Class: _____ Start date: _____

Class days:_____ Class time: _____ Class location: _____

Name: _____ Class: _____ Start date: _____

Class days:_____ Class time: _____ Class location: _____

Please keep this form as a reminder of the programs you are registered for.

From *Aquatic Facility Management* by Paul Fawcett, 2005, Champaign, IL: Human Kinetics.

Student Progress Report

Student name: _____

Class: _____ Class day and time: _____

Instructor: _____ Report date: _____

New skills the student learned this session:

_____ _____ _____

_____ _____ _____

_____ _____ _____

_____ _____ _____

Skills this student needs to work on:

_____ _____ _____

_____ _____ _____

_____ _____ _____

_____ _____ _____

Instructor's comments:_____

_____

_____

_____

This student should register for _____ class next session.

If you have questions, please contact _____.

Thanks for being in class! I really enjoyed having you!

From *Aquatic Facility Management* by Paul Fawcett, 2005, Champaign, IL: Human Kinetics.

Facility Rental Form and Agreement

Name of group or organization:_____

Name of group contact person: _____

Group mailing address: _____

Contact person telephone number(s):_____

Dates of desired rental:_____ Times of desired rental: _____

Areas to be rented (check all that apply):

□ Entire pool   Cost/hr. _____ × _____ Hours

□ Shallow end only   Cost/hr. _____ × _____ Hours

□ Deep end only   Cost/hr. _____ × _____ Hours

□ Classroom   Cost/hr. _____ × _____ Hours

□ Multipurpose room   Cost/hr. _____ × _____ Hours

□ Gymnasium   Cost/hr. _____ × _____ Hours

□ Kitchen   Cost/hr. _____ × _____ Hours

Estimated cost for facility space:_____ Number of participants/guests attending: _____

Number of chaperones/leaders attending*: _____

Estimated age range of the group attending: _____

Do you require storage of any refrigerated food? □ Yes   □ No

Please describe the purpose for renting the facility and briefly describe any activities that you will conduct:_____

_____

Please describe any special setup or equipment you will need for your event: _____

_____

Will you require parking? □ Yes   □ No   If yes, please give estimated number of vehicles: _____

Will you require parking for any buses? □ Yes   □ No

Estimated Staff Requirements and Costs

Lifeguards: _____ × _____$/hr. × _____ total hr. = _____

Supervisors: _____ × _____$/hr. × _____ total hr. = _____

ID checkers: _____ × _____$/hr. × _____ total hr. = _____

Custodians: _____ × _____$/hr. × _____ total hr. = _____

Security: _____ × _____$/hr. × _____ total hr. = _____

Estimated total staff costs: _____

Total staff costs _____ + _____ total facility rental costs = _____ estimated total fee**

Agreement

By signing this agreement, the renting group and its leaders, agents, and participants agree to abide by all facility use policies specified by the renter. The renting group further agrees to pay all charges associated with their use of the facility, including damages they may have caused whether accidental or intentional, and cleaning costs as a result of use. The renter reserves the right to eject the rental group or any of its individual members from the premises at any time for breach of the rental agreement, illegal activity, or damages caused to the facility.

Signature: _____ Date:_____

* Suggested chaperone-to-guest ratio is 1:7 for elementary age swimmers, higher for older, more competent swimmers.

** This fee is an estimate only and may increase if the estimated number of hours is exceeded or if more staff is required.

From *Aquatic Facility Management* by Paul Fawcett, 2005, Champaign, IL: Human Kinetics.

Program Marketing Planning and Cost Estimation Sheet

Program title:_____

Program dates: _____

Program times: _____

Program location: _____

Registration dates: _____

Registration times: _____

Registration location: _____

Registration fees: _____

Discounts available: _____

Marketing methods (check all planned):

☐ Brochure   Amount _____   Cost _____

☐ Flyer   Amount _____   Cost _____

☐ Poster   Amount _____   Cost _____

☐ Web site   Cost _____

☐ TV ads   Amount _____   Cost _____

☐ Newspaper ads   Amount _____   Cost _____

☐ Radio ads   Amount _____   Cost _____

☐ Direct mail   Amount _____   Cost _____

☐ Bulletin board   Amount _____   Cost _____

Total cost for advertising this program: _____ Is it within budget?_____

Have all facts regarding this program been verified as correct? _____

Projected distribution dates for advertising: _____

Have you allowed sufficient time between distribution and registration for materials to reach their target audience? _____

News Release Worksheet

Name of facility offering program: _____

Program or event title: _____

Program or event dates: _____

Program or event location: _____

Program or event cost: _____   Program or event age group: _____

Program or event registration dates:_____

Program or event registration times:_____

Program or event registration location: _____

Program contact person:_____

Program contact telephone number: _____

Text of news release: _____

_____

_____

_____

_____

_____

_____

_____

Date due at news source: _____

Facility contact and phone number for questions about this news release: _____

_____

From *Aquatic Facility Management* by Paul Fawcett, 2005, Champaign, IL: Human Kinetics.

Marquee Request Form

Group, program, or club requesting marquee usage: _____

Group contact person: _____

Group contact phone number: _____

Dates of program or event: _____

Dates of desired marquee posting: _____

Please place your message in the blocks below. Each block represents a letter, character, number, or space. Do not go over the allotted blocks or your message will be modified or not posted.

After completing this form, please submit to _____.

Forms should be submitted a minimum of 1 week before the desired posting date.

Submission of this form is not a guarantee of marquee posting.

Daily Checklist

Facility: _____

Did the facility open on time today? ☐ Yes   ☐ No   If not, how late and why? _____

_____

Lifeguards:

Are lifeguards in place and in proper position? ☐ Yes   ☐ No

Are all lifeguards in proper uniform, including whistle and rescue equipment? ☐ Yes   ☐ No

Are all lifeguards attentive and actively scanning? ☐ Yes   ☐ No

Locker rooms and rest rooms:

Are floors clean and free of trash? ☐ Yes   ☐ No

Have trash cans been recently emptied? ☐ Yes   ☐ No

Are sinks and commodes clean and disinfected? ☐ Yes   ☐ No

Are paper products and soap fully stocked? ☐ Yes   ☐ No

Are lockers and fixtures all functional and in working order? ☐ Yes   ☐ No

Are all lights currently functioning? ☐ Yes   ☐ No

Swimming pool:

Are decks clean and disinfected? ☐ Yes   ☐ No

Are all lights currently functioning? ☐ Yes   ☐ No

Are lane ropes/safety lines in place as needed? ☐ Yes   ☐ No

Are pool hours posted at the entrance to the pool and on the pool deck? ☐ Yes   ☐ No

Have trash cans been recently emptied? ☐ Yes   ☐ No

Is pool equipment stored neatly and available for use as needed? ☐ Yes   ☐ No

Are facility rules displayed prominently on the pool deck? ☐ Yes   ☐ No

Lobby, lounges, and waiting rooms:

Are floors clean? ☐ Yes   ☐ No

Have counters and tables been recently disinfected? ☐ Yes   ☐ No

Have trash cans been recently emptied? ☐ Yes   ☐ No

Are all lights currently functioning? ☐ Yes   ☐ No

Are bulletin boards clean, attractive, and current? ☐ Yes   ☐ No

Is promotional material available? ☐ Yes   ☐ No

Is promotional material neatly stacked and current? ☐ Yes   ☐ No

Is the public phone functional and clean, and does it have a phone book? ☐ Yes   ☐ No

Exterior of building:

Is grass freshly cut? (summer) ☐ Yes   ☐ No

Are walkways clear of snow and ice? (winter) ☐ Yes   ☐ No

Are grounds and parking lots free of trash? ☐ Yes   ☐ No

Are exterior signs and marquees current? ☐ Yes   ☐ No

Program and administrative staff:

Are all staff members in uniform, including name tags? ☐ Yes   ☐ No

Are all staff members at their appropriate post and duties? ☐ Yes   ☐ No

Are all staff members portraying the image you want your facility to be known for? ☐ Yes   ☐ No

From *Aquatic Facility Management* by Paul Fawcett, 2005, Champaign, IL: Human Kinetics.

Customer Comment Card

Comment type: □ Cleanliness   □ Repair   □ Staff issue   □ Other

Date: _____ Time: _____

Location: _____

Your comments: _____

_____

_____

Have you verbally reported this to any of our staff members? _____

If you would like a follow-up contact from us, please include your name and phone number below. (You are not required to do so.)

Name: _____ Phone number:_____

Thank you! Your comments are important to us!

_____ Office use below line _____

Date repair or cleaning complete: _____

Date follow-up contact made with customer: _____

From *Aquatic Facility Management* by Paul Fawcett, 2005, Champaign, IL: Human Kinetics.

Budget Spreadsheet

Facility name:_____

Fiscal year: _____ Fiscal officer: _____

Account number	Account name	Initial allocation	Current balance

From *Aquatic Facility Management* by Paul Fawcett, 2005, Champaign, IL: Human Kinetics.

Payroll Sheet

Employee name: _____ Facility:_____

Position: _____ Pay period:_____

Date	Time in	Time out	Duty	Staff initial	Supervisor initial

Payroll sheets are due the last day of the pay period. Please submit to the aquatic director's mailbox. By signing this form, you are certifying that you have worked and recorded the above hours in accordance with company policy.

Employee signature: _____ Date: _____

Reviewed by supervisor: _____ Date: _____

From *Aquatic Facility Management* by Paul Fawcett, 2005, Champaign, IL: Human Kinetics.

Purchase Tracking Sheet

Account name:_____   Account number: _____

Account manager: _____   Fiscal year: _____

Item	Date requested	Date received	Description/ supply source	Method of payment	Cost	Staff requesting

From *Aquatic Facility Management* by Paul Fawcett, 2005, Champaign, IL: Human Kinetics.

Pool Operator Preemployment Knowledge Test

1. What is the ideal pH range for swimming pools?

    a. 6.2 to 7.2
    b. 7.2 to 8.2
    c. 7.4 to 7.6
    d. 7.6 to 7.9

2. Swimming pool water pH is raised with the addition of

    a. muriatic acid
    b. soda ash
    c. cyanuratic acid
    d. potassium hypochlorite

3. Sand and gravel filters should be backwashed when the PSI differential between influent and effluent gauges is more than

    a. 5 PSI
    b. 10 PSI
    c. 15 PSI
    d. 20 PSI

4. The form of chlorine with the highest percentage of chlorine is

    a. sodium hypochlorite
    b. calcium hypochlorite
    c. lithium hypochlorite
    d. elemental chlorine

5. The minimum acceptable amount of free chlorine in swimming pools required by most state codes is

    a. 0.5 PPM
    b. 1.0 PPM
    c. 2.0 PPM
    d. 3.0 PPM

6. How often should chlorine and pH be tested at outdoor swimming pools?

    a. daily
    b. twice per day
    c. six times per day
    d. hourly

7. The acceptable range for swimming pool water on the langlier saturation index is

    a. +3 through –3
    b. +2 through –2
    c. +0.3 through –0.3
    d. Zero

8. You should vacuum swimming pools

    a. once daily
    b. twice daily
    c. every other hour
    d. every hour

9. When swimming pool water reaches _____ PPM of total dissolved solids, the pool should be drained and refilled.

    a. 1,000
    b. 2,000
    c. 3,000
    d. 4,000

10. Which of the following personal protective equipment devices should be worn while working with chlorine gas?

    a. scuba
    b. canister gas mask
    c. SCBA
    d. bail out bottle

11. The state law that regulates swimming pools is called

    a. the state swimming pool code
    b. the state sanitation code
    c. the state bathing code
    d. none of the above

From *Aquatic Facility Management* by Paul Fawcett, 2005, Champaign, IL: Human Kinetics.

Pool Operator Preemployment Knowledge Test
Answer Key

1. c

2. b

3. a

4. d

5. b

6. d

7. c

8. a

9. b

10. c

11. c

Administrative Test Questions

Complete the following questions in paragraph or point form and submit it 2 weeks prior to your interview date. Failure to complete this will disqualify you from consideration.

1. One of your lifeguards has failed to show up for his scheduled shift because he overslept. Write a memo to this staff member.

2. In one or two paragraphs, outline your philosophy for delegating responsibility to your staff members.

3. Your swimming pool has just sprung an unexpected leak, and you have lost 10,000 gallons. Your maintenance team tells you it will be several days at best before you will be operational again. You have a major swim meet scheduled at your pool during that period. Outline your actions in this case.

4. Outline your philosophy of swimming pool management.

5. Develop a brief outline for a 3-month period of in-service training for your staff.

6. Fully describe a new or innovative aquatic program that you have managed, developed, or taught.

7. One of the outdoor summer pools that you are responsible for has been experiencing increasingly poor relations between the patrons and the staff. The patrons accuse the staff of racism, and the staff feels threatened by some of the patrons and is accusing them of intimidation. Things are coming to a boiling point. Outline your actions.

8. The skydiving club approaches you and wants to use your pool for water-landing training. Will you permit this? What precautions would you take? They want to bring their own lifeguard instead of paying one of your staff. Will you permit this?

9. Develop and describe a philosophy of merit-based promotion for lifeguards.

10. Outline your philosophy for financial management in aquatics.

From *Aquatic Facility Management* by Paul Fawcett, 2005, Champaign, IL: Human Kinetics.

Employee Evaluation Form

Employee name: _____ Employee position: _____

Years of service for employee:_____ Evaluation period: _____

Date evaluation completed:_____ Date of last evaluation:_____

Evaluator name and title: _____

Reason for evaluation: ☐ Probationary ☐ Semiannual ☐ Annual ☐ Special

Rate the employee on each of the categories below. Circle the number that best represents the employee's performance.

1. Work habits: Arrives for work on time; quality of work; and quantity of work.

1	2	3	4	5	Not observed
Poor	Fair	Satisfactory	Good	Excellent	

   Comments: _____

2. Customer service: How this employee responds to customer needs and desires; quality of his or her interaction with patrons; ability to resolve patron problems.

1	2	3	4	5	Not observed
Poor	Fair	Satisfactory	Good	Excellent	

   Comments: _____

3. Maturity: Ability to accept correction; appropriate conduct in the workplace; able to take appropriate level of responsibility.

1	2	3	4	5	Not observed
Poor	Fair	Satisfactory	Good	Excellent	

   Comments: _____

4. Leadership: Ability to direct others; ability to work without direct supervision.

1	2	3	4	5	Not observed
Poor	Fair	Satisfactory	Good	Excellent	

   Comments: _____

5. Technical expertise: The competence this employee displays in the performance of his or her specialty duties.

1	2	3	4	5	Not observed
Poor	Fair	Satisfactory	Good	Excellent	

   Comments: _____

6. Judgment: Decision-making ability; reaction under pressure.

1	2	3	4	5	Not observed
Poor	Fair	Satisfactory	Good	Excellent	

   Comments: _____

(continued)

From *Aquatic Facility Management* by Paul Fawcett, 2005, Champaign, IL: Human Kinetics.

7. Personal interaction: Relationships with customers, coworkers, subordinates, and superiors.

1	2	3	4	5	Not observed
Poor	Fair	Satisfactory	Good	Excellent	

Comments: _____

8. Professional appearance: Wears appropriate uniform; exhibits appropriate personal grooming.

1	2	3	4	5	Not observed
Poor	Fair	Satisfactory	Good	Excellent	

Comments: _____

9. Creativity: Ability to develop new innovations and ideas.

1	2	3	4	5	Not observed
Poor	Fair	Satisfactory	Good	Excellent	

Comments: _____

10. Professionalism: Maintenance of personal skills and knowledge; the esteem that coworkers feel for the employee; integrity.

1	2	3	4	5	Not observed
Poor	Fair	Satisfactory	Good	Excellent	

Comments: _____

Signature of employee: _____ Date: _____

Signature of evaluator: _____ Date: _____

Date received in human resources office: _____

Employee comments: _____

_____

_____

From *Aquatic Facility Management* by Paul Fawcett, 2005, Champaign, IL: Human Kinetics.

Employee Conduct Form

Name of employee: _____

Name of supervisor: _____

Employee position: _____ Date action occurred: _____

Time action occurred: _____ Action reported by: _____

The action involved the following conduct by the employee:

    ☐ Tardy   ☐ Absent from work   ☐ Poor performance

    ☐ Excellent performance   ☐ Beyond the call of duty   ☐ Other

Explanation: _____

_____

_____

_____

Date of employee meeting: _____

Supervisor signature: _____ Date: _____

Employee signature: _____ Date: _____

From *Aquatic Facility Management* by Paul Fawcett, 2005, Champaign, IL: Human Kinetics.

Staff Substitute Card

_____ agrees to substitute for _____ for the following shift: day _____ month _____ year _____ shift (hours) _____ .

I agree that by signing this substitution card I am responsible for this shift. If I am unable to attend this shift, I must get my own substitute and cannot "give it back" to the originator. If I fail to show up for this shift, I understand that I will receive a disciplinary write-up.

Signature: _____ (substituting staff member)

From _Aquatic Facility Management_ by Paul Fawcett, 2005, Champaign, IL: Human Kinetics.

In-Service Training Log

Date of in-service training:_____ Time:_____

Facility: _____

Topics covered: _____

_____

_____

_____

New policies: _____

_____

_____

_____

New equipment purchases made: _____

_____

_____

Shifts made available at meeting (see head lifeguard if you can take any): _____

_____

_____

Staff attending:

_____   _____   _____

_____   _____   _____

_____   _____   _____

_____   _____   _____

Excused staff absences:

_____   _____   _____

_____   _____   _____

Unexcused staff absences (staff with unexcused absences must see aquatic director):

_____   _____   _____

_____   _____   _____

Trainers:

_____   _____   _____

Date of next in-service training session: _____

Makeup session date for staff who missed the session: _____

From *Aquatic Facility Management* by Paul Fawcett, 2005, Champaign, IL: Human Kinetics.

In-Service Scenario Evaluation Sheet

Team name: _____

Team members:

_____   _____   _____

_____   _____   _____

Evaluator: _____   Date:_____

Scenario(s): _____

1. Speed with which the team recognized the emergency or event.

1	2	3	4	5
Poor	Fair	Satisfactory	Good	Excellent

    Comments: _____

2. Speed with which the team responded to the emergency or event.

1	2	3	4	5
Poor	Fair	Satisfactory	Good	Excellent

    Comments: _____

3. Quality of teamwork exhibited during the emergency or event.

1	2	3	4	5
Poor	Fair	Satisfactory	Good	Excellent

    Comments: _____

4. Appropriateness of response to the emergency or event.

1	2	3	4	5
Poor	Fair	Satisfactory	Good	Excellent

    Comments: _____

5. Skill or technical proficiency.

1	2	3	4	5
Poor	Fair	Satisfactory	Good	Excellent

    Comments: _____

6. Did supervision of the pool lapse at any time during the scenarios?

1	2	3	4	5
Entire time	Repeatedly	Occasionally	Briefly	Never

    Comments: _____

(continued)

From *Aquatic Facility Management* by Paul Fawcett, 2005, Champaign, IL: Human Kinetics.

7. Quality of communication among team members.

1	2	3	4	5	Not observed
Poor	Fair	Satisfactory	Good	Excellent	

Comments: _____

8. Appropriate use of equipment (backboards, pocket masks, AED, manual suction device, supplemental oxygen).

1	2	3	4	5	Not observed
Poor	Fair	Satisfactory	Good	Excellent	

Comments: _____

Total score: _____

Evaluator's overall comments: _____

_____

_____

_____

Audit Evaluation Sheet

Staff member name: _____

Auditor's name: _____

Date audited: _____ Time: _____

Facility: _____ Employee's hire date: _____

Date of last CPR certification: _____

Date of last lifeguard certification: _____

Number of patrons in area during audit: _____

Description of scenario audited: _____

_____

1. Time to recognize scenario from victim start: _____

2. Communication with other lifeguards.

1	2	3	4	5
Poor	Fair	Satisfactory	Good	Excellent

Comments: _____

3. Skill or technical proficiency.

1	2	3	4	5
Poor	Fair	Satisfactory	Good	Excellent

Comments: _____

4. Ability to cope with stress and pressure.

1	2	3	4	5
Poor	Fair	Satisfactory	Good	Excellent

Comments: _____

5. Professionalism exhibited by the staff member during the audit.

1	2	3	4	5
Poor	Fair	Satisfactory	Good	Excellent

Comments: _____

6. Staff member's ability to answer follow-up questions.

1	2	3	4	5
Poor	Fair	Satisfactory	Good	Excellent

Comments: _____

Final assessment: ☐ Pass ☐ Fail

Remedial actions recommended: _____

_____

Auditor signature: _____

Staff member signature: _____

From *Aquatic Facility Management* by Paul Fawcett, 2005, Champaign, IL: Human Kinetics.

Attraction Inspection Form

Facility name:_____ Name of attraction: _____

Date of inspection: _____ Name of inspector:_____

Mark each of the following with S for satisfactory or U for unsatisfactory.

    Steps leading to attraction   _____

    Railings into attraction   _____

    Bolts   _____

    Seams   _____

    Rule boards   _____

    Lighting   _____

    Stability of structure   _____

    Platform   _____

    Nonskid surfaces   _____

    Water flow   _____

    Support beams   _____

    Flume (slide tube)   _____

    Water depth in catch pool   _____

For any items marked U, please describe further: _____

_____

_____

Was this problem reported to management? _____

Was this problem reported to maintenance? _____

Has this attraction been rendered unusable? _____

Have you roped off and placed a sign on this attraction? _____

Has anyone been injured on this attraction?_____

If yes to injury, be sure to fill out an accident report.

From *Aquatic Facility Management* by Paul Fawcett, 2005, Champaign, IL: Human Kinetics.

Lifeguard Competition Volunteer Application

Name: _____

Telephone number: _____ E-mail address: _____

Postal address: _____

Volunteer position you are applying for (please check any you would consider):

Event coordinator   _____

CPR judge   _____

First aid judge   _____

Lifeguard situation judge   _____

Spinal injury rescue judge   _____

Tauplin relay judge   _____

Beach flags judge   _____

Iron guard judge   _____

Run-swim-run judge   _____

Rescue tow relay judge   _____

Timer   _____

Marshal   _____

Runner   _____

Please check any of the following certifications you currently hold:

Lifeguard training   _____   Agency: _____

Lifeguard instructor _____   Agency: _____

CPR instructor   _____   Agency: _____

First aid instructor _____   Agency: _____

Swimming instructor   _____   Agency: _____

Small craft instructor _____   Agency: _____

EMT   _____   Agency: _____

Please describe any previous experience you have with lifeguard competitions or competition officiating: _____

_____

_____

Office use:

Volunteer assigned: _____

From *Aquatic Facility Management* by Paul Fawcett, 2005, Champaign, IL: Human Kinetics.

Lifeguard Competition Volunteer Assignment Letter

_____ (name), you have been assigned as a _____ (position) at the upcoming lifeguard competition. Please report to _____ (location) at _____ (time) to receive your assignment. Please dress appropriately for the weather and be sure to bring sunscreen and insect repellent. Although water will be available, you are encouraged to bring a water bottle.

Signed,

_____

Competition Director

From _Aquatic Facility Management_ by Paul Fawcett, 2005, Champaign, IL: Human Kinetics.

Volunteer Thank-You Letter

Dear _____:

Thank you for your participation as an official in our recent lifeguard competition. Your volunteerism and professionalism are a tribute to your dedication as a professional. Without the assistance of professionals like you, we would be unable to offer important development opportunities such as this competition. Again, please accept my thanks for your service.

Signed,

_____

Competition Director

From *Aquatic Facility Management* by Paul Fawcett, 2005, Champaign, IL: Human Kinetics.

Competition Registration Form

Team name: _____

Facility that team is representing: _____

Team contact name: _____

Team contact telephone number: _____

Team contact postal address: _____

Team contact e-mail address: _____

Team members:

    #1 _____ (captain)   Male ____   Female ____   Shirt size: ____

    #2 _____   Male ____   Female ____   Shirt size: ____

    #3 _____   Male ____   Female ____   Shirt size: ____

    #4 _____   Male ____   Female ____   Shirt size: ____

Competitors are reminded that judging for this competition will be according to _____ _____ (agency) standards, regardless of the certification held by team members. All rule interpretation is the responsibility of the head official.

By signing this form, you agree to abide by competition rules and to compete in a manner that displays good sporting behavior. Rule violations or inappropriate conduct will result in expulsion from the competition without refund of entry fees.

Signed by team captain on behalf of team:_____ Date: _____

------------------------------------- Tear above and keep this section -------------------------------------

Team registration and packet pickup will begin at _____ (time) at _____ _____ (location).

A mandatory captains meeting will take place at _____ (time) at _____ _____(location).

Teams are reminded to bring sunscreen, sunglasses, and towels. Dress appropriately for the weather. Because you may be in "lockup" for a period awaiting situational events, you may bring personal items such as books or music. All team members are responsible for their own property.

(Include a map to your facility with this registration form.)

From *Aquatic Facility Management* by Paul Fawcett, 2005, Champaign, IL: Human Kinetics.

Facility Safety Checklist

Facility name:_____ Date:_____

Name of staff member completing report:_____

Mark each blank as S for satisfactory or U for unsatisfactory.

Facility security

Doors in good repair _____

Locks in good repair _____

Windows secure and unbroken _____

Lifeguard stands

Firmly anchored to ground _____

Steps in good repair _____

No sharp edges _____

Seat in good repair _____

Diving boards

Standards firmly anchored and
free from cracks _____

Restraining bolts firmly anchored _____

Diving board free from cracks;
nonslip surface intact _____

Ladder steps intact, firmly anchored,
and nonslip _____

Ladder rails intact and firmly anchored _____

Set over minimum depth of 12 feet
of water _____

Pool not a hopper bottom _____

Free from sharp edges _____

Slides

Firmly anchored to pool deck _____

Ladder steps intact, firmly anchored,
and nonslip _____

Handles intact and firmly anchored _____

Flume free from cracks and gaps _____

Water continuously runs through slide _____

Slide set in deep water to prevent
neck injury _____

Free from sharp edges _____

Starting blocks

Anchored firmly to deck _____

Structurally sound _____

Steps intact, firmly anchored,
and nonslip _____

Nonslip surface on top of block intact _____

Free from sharp edges _____

Use instruction sticker visible _____

Pool ladders

Rails firmly anchored to pool deck _____

Steps intact, firmly anchored,
and nonslip _____

Free from sharp edges _____

Deck

Free of standing water _____

Free of debris _____

Drains clear and functional _____

Lighting/Electrical

Adequate lights in place for operation
of facility _____

No exposed wires _____

All plugs covered _____

Corrective actions taken for any items marked unsatisfactory: _____

_____

_____

_____

Date problems reported to management: _____

Date problem fixed: _____

From *Aquatic Facility Management* by Paul Fawcett, 2005, Champaign, IL: Human Kinetics.

Statement of Understanding

I understand that there are inherent and unpreventable risks associated with aquatic activity. Although this facility does all in its power to reduce or eliminate hazards, some risk cannot be eliminated. By signing this statement, I agree to abide by all safety rules set by the facility, and I understand that by violating any safety rules I assume all associated risk and that I may be immediately ejected from the facility without refund for said rule violation. I further understand that I agree to bring to the attention of the management or staff any condition that I, or my minor dependents, may have that may endanger myself or others while in the facility. Knowingly failing to do so may result in my totally assuming any liability arising from injuries due to that condition.

Potential risks associated with aquatic activities include but are not limited to the following:

- Head, neck, and back injuries due to diving in shallow water. (Diving in shallow water is expressly forbidden in this facility, except by competitive swimmers under the instruction of a coach.)
- Death by drowning caused by entering deep water without the ability to swim.
- Injury to arms, legs, or head caused by hard contact with the pool wall.

I hereby state that I have read, understand, and agree to abide by the above statement.

Name (printed): _____

Name (signature): _____

Witness: _____

Date: _____

Although you may elect not to sign this form, you will not be admitted to the facility.

Parents or guardians may sign on behalf of minors.

From *Aquatic Facility Management* by Paul Fawcett, 2005, Champaign, IL: Human Kinetics.

Bomb Threat Checklist

Facility name: _____

Name of staff member taking report: _____

Time and date of report: _____

Text of call: _____

_____

_____

If possible, ask the following questions:

Where is the bomb? _____

What does the bomb look like? _____

When will it go off? _____

How many bombs are there? _____

What is your name? _____

Why are you making this threat? _____

Description of caller's voice (check all that apply):

Male	_____
Female	_____
Loud	_____
Soft	_____
Nervous	_____
Angry	_____
Sad	_____
Excited	_____
Happy	_____
Laughing	_____
Raspy	_____
Accent	_____ Type _____

Background noise (check all that apply):

Cars	_____
Planes	_____
Other voices	_____
Wind	_____
Water	_____
Television	_____
Sport event	_____
Music	_____

Other amplifying information: _____

_____

_____

Report call immediately to supervisor on duty and management.

From *Aquatic Facility Management* by Paul Fawcett, 2005, Champaign, IL: Human Kinetics.

Emergency Phone Script

Hello, my name is _____ (your name). I am a lifeguard at _____ (your facility name and address). My telephone number is _____ (your telephone number). We have _____ (state type of emergency). We have _____ (number) victims. We are requesting ambulance/police/fire assistance (state what you need). The victims' condition is _____ (state condition of victims). A staff member will meet you at _____ (state location). Please repeat back to me everything I have just stated. What is your ETA?

* Do not hang up until the dispatcher tells you to.

From *Aquatic Facility Management* by Paul Fawcett, 2005, Champaign, IL: Human Kinetics.

Emergency Phone List

Local police_____ Emergency and nonemergency telephone number

State police_____ Emergency and nonemergency telephone number

Fire department _____ Emergency number

EMS_____ Emergency number

Animal control_____

Power company_____

Gas company _____

Poison control center_____

Child and family services_____

National Weather Service _____ Local office

Coast Guard _____ Local search and rescue (coastal beaches)

Facility manager _____

Facility attorney _____

Local radio stations _____ Weather cancellation line

Pool chemical supplier_____

HAZMAT team _____

From *Aquatic Facility Management* by Paul Fawcett, 2005, Champaign, IL: Human Kinetics.

Accident Report Form

Victim's name: _____   Date of accident: _____

Victim's address: Address 1: _____   Time of accident: _____

Address 2: _____

City: _____   State: _____   Zip: _____

Victim's phone number: _____   Victim's age: _____

Facility in which accident occurred: _____

Location in facility where accident occurred: _____

Type of injury (check all that apply):

☐ Cut   ☐ Bruise   ☐ Fracture   ☐ Sprain/strain

☐ Dislocation   ☐ Burn   ☐ Poisoning   ☐ Amputation

☐ Puncture wound   ☐ Near drowning   ☐ Heart attack   ☐ Stroke

☐ Diabetic emergency   ☐ Respiratory emergency ☐ Sudden illness   ☐ Fainting

☐ Other _____

Location on the body of the injury: _____

Describe the injury: _____

_____

_____

Describe the activity the victim was doing when the injury occurred: _____

_____

_____

Describe the treatment given to the victim: _____

_____

_____

Was the victim referred to advanced medical care?   ☐ Yes   ☐ No

If so, what and where? _____

Trip/case number: _____

Staff on duty at the time of the accident:

1. _____   2. _____

3. _____   4. _____

Witness to the accident:

Name: _____   Address: _____   Phone: _____

Name: _____   Address: _____   Phone: _____

Name of staff member preparing the report: _____

Position: _____

Date report was prepared: _____

Forward this form to the aquatic director when completed.

From *Aquatic Facility Management* by Paul Fawcett, 2005, Champaign, IL: Human Kinetics.

Incident Report Form

Involved party #1:

Name: _____   Date of incident: _____

Address 1: _____   Time of incident: _____

Address 2: _____

City: _____   State: _____   Zip: _____

Phone number: _____   Age: _____

Involved party #2:

Name: _____

Address 1: _____

Address 2: _____

City: _____   State: _____   Zip: _____

Phone number: _____   Age: _____

Facility in which incident occurred: _____

Location in facility where incident occurred: _____

Nature of incident: _____

Describe incident: _____

_____

_____

Describe response to the incident: _____

_____

_____

_____

Were police called?   ☐ Yes   ☐ No

Case/trip number: _____

Amplifying information: _____

Staff on duty at the time of the incident:

     1. _____   2. _____

     3. _____   4. _____

Witness to the incident:

Name: _____   Address: _____   Phone: _____

Name: _____   Address: _____   Phone: _____

Name of staff member preparing the report: _____

Position: _____

Date report was prepared: _____

Forward this form to the aquatic director when completed.

From *Aquatic Facility Management* by Paul Fawcett, 2005, Champaign, IL: Human Kinetics.

Filter Inspection Form

Facility being inspected: _____

Date of inspection: _____ Type of filter: _____

Filter age: _____ Date of last inspection: _____

Inspector: _____

Sand and Gravel Filters

Tank type (circle):   Carbon steel   Stainless steel   Fiberglass

Date of last media replacement:_____

Frequency of backwash: _____

Mark each blank as S for satisfactory or U for unsatisfactory.

Clarity of water immediately after backwash: _____

    Tank stand stability: _____

    Tank gauge functionality: _____

    Tank integrity (leaks):   _____

    Presence of rust on tanks: _____

Vacuum Diatomaceous Earth Filters

Frequency of addition of DE:_____

Clarity of water maintained: _____

    Structural integrity of tank container: _____

    Condition of filter screen covers: _____

    Condition of filter screens: _____

    Condition of valves: _____

Regenerative Diatomaceous Earth Filters

Clarity of water maintained: _____

    Structural integrity of tank container: _____

    Condition of media cords: _____

    Condition of valves: _____

From *Aquatic Facility Management* by Paul Fawcett, 2005, Champaign, IL: Human Kinetics.

Monthly Water Chemistry Report

Facility: _____ Month: _____

Day	pH reading	Chlorine reading	Temperature: deep/shallow	Makeup water added (Y/N)	Notes
1					
2					
3					
4					
5					
6					
7					
8					
9					
10					
11					
12					
13					
14					
15					
16					
17					
18					
19					
20					
21					
22					
23					
24					
25					
26					
27					
28					
29					
30					
31					

Date submitted to the state: _____

Pool operator submitting report: _____

From *Aquatic Facility Management* by Paul Fawcett, 2005, Champaign, IL: Human Kinetics.

Langlier Saturation Index Worksheet

Facility: _____ Date of chemical test:_____

Name of staff member conducting test: _____

Temperature factor (degrees F)	Calcium hardness factor	Total alkalinity factor
32 = 0.0	5 = 0.3	5 = 0.7
37 = 0.1	25 = 1.0	25 = 1.4
46 = 0.2	50 = 1.3	50 = 1.7
53 = 0.3	75 = 1.5	75 = 1.9
60 = 0.4	100 = 1.6	100 = 2.0
66 = 0.5	150 = 1.8	150 = 2.2
76 = 0.6	200 = 1.9	200 = 2.3
84 = 0.7	300 = 2.1	300 = 2.5
94 = 0.8	400 = 2.2	400 = 2.6
105 = 0.9	800 = 2.5	800 = 2.9
128 = 1.0	1,000 = 2.6	1,000 = 3.0

pH _____ + TF_____ + HF _____ + AF _____ − 12.1 = langlier saturation index

1. Using your pool test kit and thermometer, take readings for temperature, calcium hardness, and alkalinity.

2. Compare your readings with the scales above. Select the appropriate number by rounding to the nearest higher or lower number on the scale.

3. Place your factors from the chart above in the formula; add factors together and subtract 12.1. Your answer is the saturation index.

From *Aquatic Facility Management* by Paul Fawcett, 2005, Champaign, IL: Human Kinetics.

Opening and Closing Checklist

Facility name:_____ Date: _____

Name of staff member opening:_____

Name of staff member closing: _____

Mark each blank as S for satisfactory or U for unsatisfactory.

   For any U entries, you must state what the problem is in the comments area at the bottom of this form. Use this checklist at the opening and closing of the facility each day. Report any immediate problems to your supervisor.

Security	*Opening*	*Closing*
Doors (lock at close of shift)	_____	_____
Windows (closed and locked)	_____	_____
Deck (clean)	_____	_____
Fence	_____	_____
Lights (turn off at end of shift)	_____	_____
Equipment secured (closing only)	_____	_____
Equipment		
First aid kit (fully stocked)	_____	_____
Backboard	_____	_____
Flashlights (working)	_____	_____
Bag-valve mask	_____	_____
Rescue tubes	_____	_____
Ring buoys	_____	_____
Throw bags	_____	_____
All equipment stacked neatly	_____	_____
Administration		
Cash drop made (closing only)	_____	_____
Change fund in opening cash drawer (opening only)	_____	_____
Accident report filed (closing only)	_____	_____

Comments: _____

_____

_____

_____

Opening staff: _____

Closing staff: _____

Date: _____

From *Aquatic Facility Management* by Paul Fawcett, 2005, Champaign, IL: Human Kinetics.

Daily Cleaning Checklist

Facility name:_____ Date: _____

Name of staff member: _____

The following items are to be completed each night after the close of business. Please initial after each item to signify it has been done.

Pool area

Hose deck _____   Brush standing water into deck drains _____

Empty trash cans _____   Collect loose items and store properly _____

Put in automatic vacuum _____   Test pool water and record readings _____

Add chemicals as needed _____   Hang rescue equipment in proper place _____

Add makeup water to the pool as needed _____

Pool office

Vacuum/sweep office floor _____   File reports properly _____

Take items to lost and found _____   Empty trash cans _____

Clean countertops _____

Rest rooms and locker rooms

Clean commodes with 5% bleach solution _____   Empty trash cans _____

Clean sinks with nonabrasive cleanser _____   Clean mirrors _____

Disinfect floors with 5% bleach solution _____   Restock soap _____

Restock paper products _____   Remove loose trash _____

Disinfect countertops _____   Clean floor drains _____

Brush standing water into deck drains _____   Deodorize area _____

Spray trash cans with disinfectant spray _____

Common areas (hallways/lobby/lounges)

Empty trash cans _____   Sweep/wet mop floors _____

Remove loose trash _____   Disinfect countertops _____

Remove scuff marks from floor _____   Water plants _____

Problems or maintenance and cleaning issues encountered: _____

_____

_____

Supplies needed:_____

_____

Staff member signature: _____ Date:_____

Submit this form to the maintenance supervisor at the end of your shift.

From *Aquatic Facility Management* by Paul Fawcett, 2005, Champaign, IL: Human Kinetics.

Weekly Cleaning Checklist

Facility name:_____ Date: _____

Name of staff member: _____

The following cleaning and maintenance items are to be completed each week. Please initial after each item to signify it has been done.

Pool area

Scrub stainless steel surfaces on starting blocks, ladders, and diving boards (steel wool or a scratch pad should remove calcium and rust) _____

Scrub starting block surfaces and diving boards with a 5% bleach solution and a stiff bristle brush _____

Wash windows _____

Disinfect door handles _____

Clean and reorganize pool storage areas _____

Note burned-out lights and report to maintenance supervisor _____

Locker rooms

Dust locker tops _____

Wipe down lockers _____

Scrub showerheads _____

Clean benches _____

Wipe down doors _____

Note burned-out lights and report to maintenance supervisor _____

Common areas

Wash windows _____

Wipe down doors _____

Disinfect furniture _____

Wipe down vending machines _____

Wash walls as needed _____

Remove area rugs to vacuum or wash underneath as appropriate _____

Clean area rugs as appropriate (wash or vacuum) _____

Wax floors _____

Note burned-out lights and report to maintenance supervisor _____

From *Aquatic Facility Management* by Paul Fawcett, 2005, Champaign, IL: Human Kinetics.

Exterior Facility Maintenance Checklist

Facility name: _____ Date of inspection: _____

Name of inspector: _____

Mark each blank as S for satisfactory or U for unsatisfactory.

Parking lot

Free of debris and garbage _____

Painted parking lines clearly visible _____

Lot free of potholes _____

Handicapped accessible spots clearly labeled _____

Traffic control signs (stop signs, crosswalk) in place _____

Parking lot lights functional _____

Lawns

Free of debris and garbage _____

Shrubs properly trimmed _____

Grass recently cut _____

No danger from falling limbs or trees _____

Tree beds have adequate new mulch _____

Flower beds weeded _____

Lawns edged _____

Walkways

Free of debris and garbage _____

Walkway lights functional _____

Paths in good repair _____

Free of obstruction by tree limbs, signs, and so on _____

Free from snow and ice (in season and climate) _____

Fences

Posts securely anchored to ground _____

No major gaps or holes _____

Fence material in good repair _____

Gates closed and locked as required _____

Corrective action taken for any unsatisfactory marks made above: _____

_____

_____

_____

From *Aquatic Facility Management* by Paul Fawcett, 2005, Champaign, IL: Human Kinetics.

Chemical Storage Area Inspection Form

Facility name:_____ Date of inspection:_____

Name of inspector: _____

Mark each blank as S for satisfactory or U for unsatisfactory.

Door

Door has a secure lock   _____

Door is in good repair   _____

An "Authorized Personnel Only" sign is on door   _____

Door is locked when a staff member is not inside   _____

Key or combination control limited to appropriate staff _____

Chemical storage

Chemicals stored in their original containers   _____

All chemicals properly labeled   _____

Chemicals in bags or metal containers stored on pallets _____

Chemical barrels stored with lids on and locked   _____

Different chemicals not stored on top of each other   _____

All chemicals have date of purchase written on labels   _____

Expired chemicals are disposed of according to
manufacturer instructions   _____

Petroleum products not stored in chemical areas   _____

Facility

Storage area is adequately ventilated   _____

Storage area has a vent fan running 24/7   _____

Storage area is well lit   _____

Walkway in storage area is clear of obstructions   _____

Floors are clean   _____

Walls are secure and prevent unauthorized entry   _____

Safety

Material safety data sheets are available   _____

Eye protection is available   _____

Eye wash station is available   _____

Protective clothing is available   _____

Emergency shower is available   _____

First aid procedures for chemical exposure are posted   _____

Self-contained breathing apparatus is available   _____

Plan of action for items marked unsatisfactory: _____

_____

From *Aquatic Facility Management* by Paul Fawcett, 2005, Champaign, IL: Human Kinetics.

Electrical Safety Checklist

Name of facility: _____ Date of inspection:_____

Name of inspector: _____

Mark each blank as S for satisfactory or U for unsatisfactory.

Electrical outlets in pool area, locker rooms, rest rooms,
and filter and storage areas are GFCI.   _____

Electrical outlets in pool area and locker rooms have spring-loaded covers. _____

Electrical outlets are secure and in good repair.   _____

Circuit breaker panels are locked when not in use.   _____

All breakers in breaker panels are labeled.   _____

Electrical cords are not tucked under rugs.   _____

Electrical cords are not frayed or worn.   _____

Extension cords in traffic areas are taped down.   _____

Extension cords are stored and secured when not in use.   _____

Electrical outlets in child care areas are covered with safety plugs.   _____

Light sockets are never left without bulbs.   _____

List corrective actions for any items marked unsatisfactory: _____

_____

_____

Date reported to maintenance: _____

Date problem fixed: _____

From *Aquatic Facility Management* by Paul Fawcett, 2005, Champaign, IL: Human Kinetics.

Glossary of Aquatic Terms

abandonment—Beginning treatment on a victim and then stopping treatment, not at the victim's request, before the victim is able to care for himself or before turning care over to another rescuer.

active victim—A struggling near drowning victim. This victim is characterized by arms flailing uselessly at sides, little or ineffective leg movement, wide eyes, and little or no sound. This victim is incapable of helping herself and will drown if not rescued. Drowning for this victim may take as few as 20 seconds and no longer than a few minutes.

alkalinity—A combination of materials such as carbonates, bicarbonates, and hydroxides present in water.

Americans With Disabilities Act (ADA)—A U.S. federal law requiring equal access to facilities and services for persons with special needs.

anaphylaxis—A severe form of shock brought on by an allergic reaction. Also called *anaphylactic shock*.

anoxia—Total lack of oxygen in the circulating blood.

aquatics—Activities that take place in, on, or under the water.

automatic external defibrillator (AED)—A device that uses a controlled electric shock to restart the heart.

backboard—A 6-foot by 1.5-foot (182.9 by 45.7-centimeter) board used to secure victims of spinal injury.

backwash—The act of running water backward through sand and gravel filters to remove dirt, debris, and grime.

bag-valve mask (BVM)—A manual device used for assisting a nonbreathing victim. A resuscitation mask is fitted over the victim's mouth and nose, and a bag is attached by means of a valve. Each time the bag is squeezed, air is forced into the victim's lungs. It requires two persons to operate.

bathing code—A law, regulation, or code enforced by the state, county, or city designed to regulate the operation of a swimming pool.

buddy board—A board used at open water facilities, usually camps, to maintain accountability for swimmers. Swimmers and boaters check themselves in and out by means of tags hung on the board.

buddy system—A safety measure, normally used at waterfronts, whereby all swimmers are required to have a partner. Partners are responsible for each other.

calcium hardness—A measure of the calcium content in swimming pool water.

calcium hypochlorite—A dry granular form of chlorine used in swimming pool disinfection. Normally 45 percent chlorine by weight.

certified—In possession of a certificate from a recognized agency attesting that on a given date the holder could perform a specified set of skills.

consent—Permission, expressed or implied, given to treat an injured victim.

CPR—Cardiopulmonary resuscitation. External heart massage used to restart the heart.

cryptosporidium—A diarrheal disease caused by a microscopic parasite. It is passed in the stool of an infected person. Known as *crypto* for short.

diatomaceous earth—A white form of earth comprised of the fossilized remains of microscopic prehistoric sea creatures. Used in filter systems as a medium for filtration of pool water.

distressed swimmer—A swimmer in need of assistance to reach safety due to fatigue, injury, illness, or any other reason. At this stage, the victim is still able to support himself at the surface of the water in some manner, if not make forward progress toward safety. If not assisted, this victim will become an active or passive victim.

drive time—A marketing term used to refer to the weekday morning and evening rush hour or commute periods when commuters are normally in their cars and more likely to have the radio on.

drowning—Suffocation due to total immersion in liquid (usually water).

dry drowning—The form of drowning in which the victim drowns immersed in water, but there is no water in the lungs. The victim's vocal cords are closed off early in the drowning process due to the introduction of a small amount of water.

duty—A legal obligation owed someone.

elemental chlorine—Gaseous chlorine used for swimming pool disinfection. Normally 99.9 percent chlorine.

EMT—Emergency medical technician. A prehospital-care emergency medicine certification.

face piping—Visible water recirculation lines.

giardia—A diarrheal illness, the parasite is passed in the stool of an infected person or animal. Giardia has become recognized as one of the most common causes of waterborne disease (drinking and recreational) in humans in the United States.

GPM—Gallons per minute. The rate of flow of water through a pool's filter system.

grand mal—Translated from French it means literally "big sickness." A form of epilepsy characterized by violent physical seizures in which the victim shakes and loses control of her muscles.

ground fault circuit interrupter (GFCI)—A device used to shut off electricity to outlets in the event of water entering the plug.

heat exhaustion—A form of physical distress characterized by cool, pale, and clammy skin; feelings of nausea; vomiting; and weakness.

heatstroke—A progression of heat illness more serious than heat exhaustion and characterized by red, dry, and hot skin. Victim may be unconscious or incoherent if conscious. Victim will die if not treated rapidly.

hemiplegia—Paralysis of one half of the body, the right or left side.

hemoconcentration—Thickening of the blood brought about by the introduction of salt into the blood through saltwater drowning.

hemodilution—Thinning of the blood brought about by the introduction of excess water into the blood through freshwater drowning.

hydantonin bromine—The form of bromine used to disinfect swimming pools. Normally packaged as a brown stick that feeds into the water by erosion.

ingestion—Taking in a substance by mouth, such as eating.

in loco parentis—A Latin term meaning "in the place of the parent."

in-service training—A planned, systematic, regularly scheduled program of training that lifeguards and other aquatic staff undertake at their aquatic facility of employment to maintain skills and fitness, improve knowledge, and become familiar with the unique characteristics of the facility they work at.

kickboard—A foam flotation board approximately 19 inches (48.3 centimeters) long and 11.5 inches (29.2 centimeters) wide. The kickboard is most commonly used as an aid by lap and competitive swimmers to strengthen the kick by allowing flotation of the upper body so that the swimmer can swim using only the legs.

langlier saturation index—A formula combining temperature, pH, alkalinity, and calcium hardness to determine the corrosiveness of pool water.

laryngospasm—A closing off of the lungs by the vocal cords due to the introduction of water into the upper airway. Causes cessation of airflow to the lungs and leads to dry drowning.

lifeguard—Anyone currently certified by a nationally recognized agency in lifeguard training, CPR, and first aid.

material safety data sheet (MSDS)—A form containing product and safety information related to chemicals.

medevac—Medical evacuation, normally by air (most commonly helicopter).

minors—Persons under the age of 18.

muriatic acid—A form of acid fed into swimming pool water to lower the pH of the water.

mushroom—A play structure set in a children's swim area that has a dome shape at the top and flows water off the sides to create a cascade effect.

nagleria—A germ that is found throughout the world. Nagleria is found in warm, stagnant bodies of water and can cause severe illness. Nagleria enters the body through the nose when you are swimming underwater or diving into water.

near drowning—An active drowning victim who has been rescued before death occurs.

negligence of commission—Carrying out an activity that resulted in an injury or harm occurring.

negligence of omission—Failure to carry out a task that would have prevented a harm from occurring.

oxidation-reduction potential (ORP)—A measurement of water's ability to oxidize or burn off contaminants.

passive victim—A near drowning victim who is displaying no movement. Victim may be floating, often face-down at or near the surface. Victim may be conscious or unconscious. Passive victims may result from heart attack, epileptic seizure, head injury, drunkenness, drug overdose, or active victims who have been overcome. If not rapidly rescued, this victim will cease breathing and pulse and will die within minutes.

pathogen—Agent for causing disease.

petit mal—Translated from French it means "little sickness." A form of epilepsy characterized by brief periods of staring off into space or a blank look on the victim's face.

pH—Potens hydrogen. A measure of the amount of hydrogen ions in the water.

phenol red—A chemical reagent used to test the pH of pool water.

pocket mask—A device used by rescue personnel, such as lifeguards and EMTs, to create a barrier between the rescuer and the victim when performing rescue breathing to minimize the risk of disease transmission.

pool operator—A swimming pool employee who is responsible for the chemical control and filtration of swimming pool water.

PSI—Pounds per square inch. A measure of pressure. In aquatics, it is most commonly associated with filter influent and effluent pressure.

recreational water illness (RWI)—Any one of a number of bacterial or parasitic infections that can be contracted from a swimming pool.

rescue board—Also known as a "paddle board." A surfboardlike item used by lifeguards at open water beaches to effect rescues over long distances.

rescue breathing—Using your own expired air to inflate the lungs and provide artificial respiration for someone not breathing.

rescue can—A rescue device constructed of hard plastic (in a torpedolike shape). Normally red in color and ranging from 28 to 33 inches (71.1 to 83.8 centimeters) in length with 10 feet (3 meters) of attached tow line and a black nylon shoulder strap. This device is most commonly used at open water facilities due to its excellent flotation qualities. It is not commonly used at pools and water parks due to its hardness.

rescue tube—A rescue device made of foam, approximately 5 feet (152.4 centimeters) long and 1 foot (30.5 centimeters) wide, used to assist drowning victims.

restraining bolts—The attachments that fasten the diving board to the standard on which the diving board rests.

safety stop—A safety measure where all swimmers in a pool stop activity on a given signal so that the pool or waterfront bottom can be checked and the safety of all swimmers can be determined.

scanning—The lifeguards' act of methodically visually sweeping their area of responsibility searching for victims in distress.

scuba—Self-contained underwater breathing apparatus. Using artificial air supply for underwater exploration and sport.

secondary drowning—A type of drowning that occurs after a near drowning case when the victim has been safely removed from the water. Secondary drowning occurs due to the presence of water in the lungs causing suffocation and death of the victim from water in the alveoli of the lungs. Secondary drowning can occur up to 48 hours after the victim has been rescued from a near drowning situation.

seizure—Involuntary, ineffective, and uncoordinated twitching of muscles brought on by illness or injury.

self-contained breathing apparatus (SCBA)—A device used on land to effect rescue in low oxygen environments.

semaphore—A form of communication using flags to represent each letter of the alphabet.

sentry light—A light left constantly on. Often found at swimming pools.

sight glass—A view port attached to face piping that allows viewing of water during backwash to determine its progress.

sodium carbonate—Commonly known as "soda ash," a substance used to raise the pH of swimming pool water.

sodium hypochlorite—A liquid form of chlorine used in swimming pool disinfection. Normally 10 to 16 percent chlorine by weight.

solenoid switch—Part of a magnetic lock that interrupts the current needed to magnetically keep a door locked and allows people to enter the door.

special populations—A term referring to individuals who have mental or physical impairments.

standard of care—Not a legal requirement codified in law, but a level of care that the public can expect due to guidelines set out by agencies in the profession, such as the YMCA, American Red Cross, and United States Lifesaving Association.

surface dive—One of a series of head- or foot-first motions undertaken in the water for the purpose of reaching the bottom.

synchro—Short for synchronized swimming, an aquatic sport mainly undertaken by women that requires movements set to music to be performed uniformly by all participants.

Tarzan swing—A thick rope set to hang over a swimming area for swimmers to swing or hang from.

tauplin—An open water lifeguard competition event involving timed running and rowing over a measured distance.

total dissolved solids (TDS)—A measure of all items dissolved into pool water, such as lotion, shampoo, deodorant, and so forth.

tot dock—A platformlike device used in aquatics that is placed in the pool to provide a temporarily shallower area so that children may play or be taught without being over their heads in water.

transfer of risk—A legal strategy of avoiding risk by shifting responsibility for risk from the facility to patrons, contractors, suppliers, or any other party.

turbid—Cloudy or murky. In aquatics, it most commonly refers to water quality.

ventricular fibrillation—Ineffective and uncoordinated twitching of the heart muscle.

vital signs absent (VSA)—Term used to refer to someone who is not breathing and has no pulse.

wet drowning—The form of death by drowning in which water has entered the victim's lungs.

zip line—A water attraction consisting of ropes arranged horizontally over a pool and set at a down angle. The rider grasps a handle that is attached to the line by wheels. When the rider picks up his feet, gravity carries him rapidly at a downward angle toward the pool.

zone coverage—A method of dividing a swimming area into segments for easier supervision by lifeguards.

Index

Note: Page numbers followed by an italicized *f* or *t* refer to the figure or table on that page, respectively.

About the Author

Paul A. Fawcett, MA, a lieutenant in the United States Coast Guard, led the development of and implemented the first aquatics majors program in the United States. Frequently published in aquatic journals and magazines, Fawcett received the Alex Haley Award in 2004 for writing on U.S. Coast Guard–related topics. He has more than 10 years' experience in the field of aquatics with a variety of organizations, including YMCAs, summer camps, community aquatics programs, college recreation programs, and college physical education programs. He holds numerous instructor and instructor trainer certifications, including American Red Cross water safety instructor, lifeguard instructor, and CPR and first aid instructor. Fawcett is also the former chair of the Aquatics Committee of the National Intramural-Recreational Sports Association.

*You'll find
other outstanding
aquatics resources at*

www.HumanKinetics.com

In the U.S. call

1-800-747-4457

Australia.. 08 8277 1555
Canada 1-800-465-7301
Europe... +44 (0) 113 255 5665
New Zealand...................................... 0064 9 448 1207

HUMAN KINETICS
The Information Leader in Physical Activity
P.O. Box 5076 • Champaign, IL 61825-5076 USA